MUSSOLINI'S INTELLECTUALS

MUSSOLINI'S INTELLECTUALS

FASCIST SOCIAL AND
POLITICAL THOUGHT

A. James Gregor

PRINCETON UNIVERSITY PRESS   PRINCETON AND OXFORD

Library of Congress Cataloging-in-Publication Data

Gregor, A. James (Anthony James), 1929–
Mussolini's intellectuals : fascist social and political thought /
A. James Gregor.
p.   cm.
Includes bibliographical references and index.
ISBN: 0-691-12009-9 (acid-free paper)
1. Fascism—Italy—History—20th century. 2. Intellectuals—Italy—
History—20th century. 3. Intellectuals—Italy—Political activity—History—
20th century. 4. Italy—Intellectual life—20th century. 5. Italy—Politics and
government—20th century. I. Title.
DG571.G734 2005
320.53′3′094509042—dc22   2004049133

British Library Cataloging-in-Publication Data is available

Contents

Preface   ix

Acknowledgments   xi

Chapter One
Some Issues in the Intellectual History of Fascism   1

Chapter Two
The Historic Background and Enrico Corradini   18

Chapter Three
Alfredo Rocco and the Elements of Fascist Doctrine   38

Chapter Four
Sergio Panunzio: From Revolutionary to National Syndicalism   61

Chapter Five
Idealism, Ugo Spirito, and the Outlines of Fascist Doctrine   85

Chapter Six
Ugo Spirito and the Rationale of the Corporative State   111

Chapter Seven
Sergio Panunzio and the Maturing of Fascist Doctrine   140

Chapter Eight
Camillo Pellizzi, Carlo Costamagna, and the Final Issues   165

Chapter Nine
Doctrinal Interlude: The Initiatic Racism of Julius Evola   191

Chapter Ten
Doctrinal Continuity and the Fascist Social Republic   222

Chapter Eleven
Conclusions   246

Index   263

Preface

THIS BOOK appears after almost four decades of study, conferences, discussion, and publication. Over those years, students of "fascism,"[1] as a subject of inquiry, have seen its "essence" change, in the judgments of scholars, from a movement of the "extreme right" into one that was neither of the "right" nor the "left."[2] We are now told that "Fascist ideology represented a synthesis of organic nationalism with the antimaterialist revision of Marxism."[3]

From a political revolution entirely without any pretense of a rational belief system, we are now told, by those best informed, that "fascism's ability to appeal to important intellectuals . . . underlines that it cannot be dismissed as . . . irrational. . . . [In] truth, fascism was an ideology just like the others."[4] Moreover, it has been acknowledged that "Fascism was possible only if based on genuine belief."[5]

In effect, the study of Italian Fascism has delivered itself of significantly altered assessments over the past decades. Where, at one time, Fascism was simply dismissed as a phenomenon understood to be without intellectual substance, a right-wing excrescence that invoked violence and war, it is now more and more regularly understood to be a movement, and a regime, predicated on a reasonably well articulated belief system that engaged the rational commitment of many.

For all that, there remains a residue of opinion that continues to deny Fascism the same reasoned beliefs that everyone readily grants to the political movements and regimes of Joseph Stalin or Mao Zedong. We are still told, for example, that unlike Stalinism and Maoism, "Fascism had few true believers who could also write articles and books."[6] Strange.

One of the principal purposes of the present work is to attempt to challenge such notions. Fascist intellectuals wrote and published as many arti-

---

[1] Generally the lowercase "fascism" refers to a class of movements or regimes. The term "Fascism," capitalized, refers to Mussolini's political movement and regime.

[2] "Fascism did not belong to the extreme Left, yet defining it as part of the extreme Right is not very illuminating either. In many respects, fascism was not conservative at all in inspiration." Walter Laqueur, *Fascism: Past, Present, Future* (New York: Oxford University Press, 1999), p. 13.

[3] Zeev Sternhell, *The Birth of Fascist Ideology: From Cultural Rebellion to Political Revolution* (Princeton: Princeton University Press, 1994), p. 6.

[4] Roger Eatwell, *Fascism: A History* (New York: Penguin Books, 1997), pp. xix–xx, 4.

[5] Laqueur, *Fascism*, p. 27.

[6] Ibid., p. 97.

cles and books as apologists for any comparable system. Their quality varied with each author, just as was, and is, the case with comparable systems. It would be hard to convincingly argue that the intellectual yield of authors in the former Soviet Union or Maoist China was superior in any way to that produced by Fascist intellectuals. The expository account, before the reader, is evidence in support of that contention.

In that context, there is a discussion made available in the present exposition that has struck several prepublication readers as anomalous. Considerable space in the text is devoted to the eccentric and "suprarational" vagaries of Julius Evola. The reason is that there are some specialists who seem to think that Evola was a "major" Fascist intellectual, and that he provided the rationale for "Ur-fascism"—the belief system that animated Fascism and all the forms of "neofascism" with which scholarship now occupies itself.[7] The discussion provided below, devoted to the thought of Evola, is intended to serve as its counterargument. I consider the space devoted to the exercise well spent. Conceiving Evola's thought as "fascist" has led many scholars astray in their efforts to understand what they imagine to be contemporary "neofascism."[8] Moreover, Evola's notions do document the impact of National Socialist thought on the coherence and fundamental rationality of Fascist doctrine.

This book is essentially the conclusion of an argument I first advanced a long time ago.[9] Long resisted by my peers, the central claim—that Fascism was, in fact, animated by a credible and coherent belief system—has now been generally accepted by those best informed. Acknowledging that, I believe that the retrospective study of Italian Fascism—and the inquiry into what passes, in our immediate present, as "neofascism"—can only prosper.

Alongside all the volumes devoted to the lucubrations of Soviet, Chinese, East German, North Korean, and Albanian intellectuals in support of their respective Marxist-Leninist dictatorships, there is space for this one. It argues that Fascist intellectuals, in support of their dictatorship, produced works no less competent. Even if this proves true, however, I should make it clear at the outset that I do not view either Marxism or Fascism as particularly plausible, and I certainly do not recommend that we embrace either. I simply recommend that we understand them.

---

[7] See Umberto Eco, "Pointing a Finger at the Fascists," *Guardian*, 19 August 1995, p. 27.

[8] See the discussion of neofascism in Eatwell, *Fascism: A History*; and Roger Griffin, *The Nature of Fascism* (London: Routledge, 1991).

[9] A. James Gregor, *The Ideology of Fascism: The Rationale of Totalitarianism* (New York: Free Press, 1969).

_____ *Acknowledgments* _____

THE DEBT AN author owes to those who have directly or indirectly assisted in the production of almost any work is incalculable. In the case of the present volume, the debt is particularly great.

This book is the product of a lifetime's preoccupation, study, and reflection. In the course of the journey, I enjoyed the counsel, the insights, and the experience of those who have experienced more, lived more, and studied the subject more intensely than I. Many years ago, Giuseppe Prezzolini spent several afternoons with me. He spoke of times long past—and led me to some small comprehension of what Italy was like at the beginning of the twentieth century for those who actually lived it. There was Ugo Spirito and his lovely wife, who spent more time with me than I had any reason to expect. We spoke of corporativism and economic programming. In the time he allowed me, Ing. Giovanni Volpe and I spoke of his father, Gioacchino Volpe, a prominent figure in Fascist intellectual circles. And there was Julius Evola, surrounded by his acolytes, who allowed me an interview although convinced that I was an agent of some foreign intelligence service—and Giovanni Perona, "Gamma," who served in the armed forces of the final days. Lastly, there was Rachele and Vittorio Mussolini, who spoke to me of long ago things painfully remembered.

All these persons allowed me to share some of their remembrances of time past. All of them now gone, I would like to here record my indebtedness to them for their kindnesses and their patience—to allow a stranger to rummage through their lives.

To accomplished academics like Zeev Sternhell, Stanley Payne, Ludovico Incisa di Camerana, and Domenico Settembrini, I owe more than I can say—certainly more than I can ever repay. To the University of California, Berkeley, I am grateful for having provided me with a stimulating intellectual home for more than three decades—and for allowing me contact with some of the finest students in the world. To my wife, Maria Hsia Chang, I owe all manner of good things, not the least of which is the brood of "Little Ones" that have pleasured my life.

I am especially grateful to Ian Malcolm of Princeton University Press for his patience and absolute professionalism. Other than all that, I am grateful beyond measure to all the institutions in which, and all the professors with whom, I learned my trade. This book is but a small token of appreciation for all I owe.

A. James Gregor
Berkeley
Winter 2004

MUSSOLINI'S INTELLECTUALS

CHAPTER ONE

Some Issues in the Intellectual History of Fascism

For about three-quarters of a century, almost all academic discussion concerning Mussolini's Fascism[1] has tended to imagine the movement it animated, and the regime it informed, as entirely lacking a reasoned rationale. It early became commonplace to attribute to Fascism a unique irrationality, accompanied by a ready recourse to violence. Fascism, it has been argued, was full of emotion, but entirely empty of cognitive content. Fascists were, and are, understood to have renounced all rational discourse, in order to "glorify the non-rational." Their ideology, movement, revolution, and behavior were made distinctive by the appeal to two, and only two, "absolutes": "violence and war."[2]

Before the advent of the Second World War, some analysts had gone so far as to insist that "fascism" was the product of "orgasm anxiety," a sexual dysfunction that found release only in "mystic intoxication," homicidal hostility, and the complete suppression of rational thought.[3] Marxists and fellow travelers argued that since Fascism was "the violent attempt of decaying capitalism to defeat the proletarian revolution and forcibly arrest the growing contradictions of its whole development," it could not support itself with a sustained rationale. Its conceptions were "empty and hollow," finding expession in "deceitful terminology" consciously designed to conceal the "realities of class-rule and class-exploitation."[4]

For many, "Fascism [was] essentially a political weapon adopted by the ruling class . . . that takes root in the minds of millions . . . [appealing] to certain uncritical and infantile impulses which, in a people debarred from a rational, healthy existence . . . tend to dominate their mental lives." Fascism, in general, constituted a "flight from reason," advancing "the

---

[1] When the term "fascism" is employed in lowercase, it refers to a presumptive, inclusive, generic fascism. When the term is capitalized, it refers to the movement, revolution, and regime associated with Benito Mussolini.

[2] Mark Neocleous, *Fascism* (Minneapolis: University of Minnesota Press, 1997), pp. x, 13, 14, 17.

[3] Wilhelm Reich, *The Mass Psychology of Fascism* (1933; reprint, New York: Orgone Institute, 1946), pp. 110–11.

[4] R. Palme Dutt, *Fascism and Social Revolution* (1934; reprint, San Francisco: Proletarian Publishers, 1974), pp. 198–99.

claims of mysticism and intuition in opposition . . . to reason . . . and glorifying the irrational."[5]

While there were some serious treatments of Fascist thought that made their appearance between the two world wars,[6] all objectivity dissolved in the alembic of the Second. By the time of the Second World War, Fascism had simply merged into Hitler's National Socialism—and discussants spoke of "nazi-fascism" as though the two were indissolubly one.[7]

Generic fascism was the enemy of "Western ideals," of the "Enlightenment tradition," as well as of the sociopolitical and philosophical aspirations of the French Revolution. It was the unregenerate agent of evil, driven by an irrational mysticism, and committed to mayhem and gross inhumanity. By the end of the 1990s, there were those who could insist that "fascism shuffles together every myth and lie that the rotten history of capitalism has ever produced like a pack of greasy cards and then deals them out." As with Angelo Tasca, such a notion is advanced in support of a contention that the only use Fascism, like Mussolini, had "of ideas was to dispense with ideas."[8]

By the end of the twentieth century, there was a conviction that a generic fascism existed that included a curious collection of radically diverse political phenomena that ranged from General Augusto Pinochet's coup in Chile, the French Front National, Jorg Haider's Austrian Freedom Party, Vladimir Zhirinovsky's Russian Liberal Democratic Party, Italy's Alleanza nazionale, to the terroristic lunacy of Timothy McVeigh and Muslim fundamentalists.[9] "Fascism" had become, largely, a meaningless term of abuse.

What remained constant over seven decades was the incorrigible conviction that "paradigmatic Fascism," the Fascism of Mussolini, was "based on myths, intuition, instinct . . . and the irrational, rather than on a closely argued system based on a detailed analysis of historical, political and economic trends."[10] Given such a characterization, Italian Fascism has been considered the anti-intellectual source for all the "right wing" political movements of the past century. In fact, some commentators have held that all contemporary right-wing movements find their origin in a single "Ur-fascism"—an identifiable *fons et origo malorum*. While Fas-

---

[5] R. Osborn, *The Psychology of Reaction* (London: Victor Gollancz, 1938), pp. 5, 238, 239.

[6] The best of these included that of Herbert W. Schneider, *Making the Fascist State* (New York: Oxford University Press, 1928).

[7] See, for example, Eduardo Haro Tecglen, *Fascismo: Genesis y desarrollo* (Madrid: CVS Ediciones, 1975).

[8] Dave Renton, *Fascism: Theory and Practice* (London: Pluto Press, 1999), pp. 27–28.

[9] See ibid., chap. 1; and Walter Laqueur, *Fascism: Past, Present, Future* (New York: Oxford University Press, 1996), pts. 2 and 3.

[10] Laqueur, *Fascism*, p. 96.

cism, in and of itself, apparently possessed no identifiable ideological sub-stance—being little more than a collage of contradictory ideas —it has been argued that whatever ideas *are* to be found, they are shared by every right-wing political impulse. Given that Fascism had no content, it seems that what is shared is the tendency to irrationality and violence. It is not clear how helpful such a classificatory strategy might be in any effort to undertake a responsible history of ideas.

Generic fascism, it would seem, shares a common, if irrational, sub-stance with the entire political right wing. That substance, devoid of meaning, finds its origin in the nonthought of Mussolini's apologists. It is argued that the nonideology of fascism is linearly related to all the "extremist" thought of contemporary Europe and North America. We are told that if we would discuss contemporary extremist thought, we must "denotatively define" the range of our inquiry—and definition be made in terms of its "ideology"—and, finally, that "the extreme right's ideology is provided by fascism."[11]

Fascist studies, it would seem, as an intellectual, historic, and social science discipline, has collapsed into a clinical study of an omnibus, psy-chopathic "right-wing extremism." "By extreme right" is meant "that political/ideological space where fascism is the key reference"—with fas-cism being little more than a "pathological form of social and political energy."[12] As a consequence, the study of Italian Fascism is treated as the antechamber to the scrutiny of contemporary right-wing political psycho-pathology—to include any and all groups, movements or regimes that have been identified by anyone as "fascist," any time during the twentieth, and now the twenty-first, centuries—as well as any that might somehow be associated with one or another form of irrationalism and criminal vio-lence. Under such circumstances, fascism studies, as a discipline, ex-panded into a circle of inquiries that now includes soccer thugs, skinhead fanatics, graveyard vandals, anti-Semites, racists, and terrorists of all and whatever sort.[13] Some have suggested that "in the West," one might profitably study Ronald Reagan Republicans as well.[14]

---

[11] Piero Ignazi, "The Extreme Right in Europe: A Survey," in Peter H. Merkl and Leonard Weinberg, eds., *The Revival of Right-Wing Extremism in the Nineties* (London: Frank Cass, 1997), p. 48.

[12] Ibid., p. 49; Roger Griffin, *The Nature of Fascism* (London: Routledge, 1991), p. xii.

[13] Renton, *Fascism: Theory and Practice*, pp. 8–9. See the intricate and fascinating treat-ment of all these "fascist" individuals and groups by Kevin Coogan, *Dreamer of the Day: Francis Parker Yockey and the Postwar Fascist International* (Brooklyn, N.Y.: Auto-nomedia, 1997).

[14] See the discussion in Leonard Weinberg, "Conclusions," in Merkl and Weinberg, eds., *The Revival of Right-Wing Extremism in the Nineties*, pp. 278–79.

The "extreme right" is essentially and irremediably irrational and criminal—because Fascism was uniquely irrational and criminal.[15] The connection advanced is an *empirical* one. To be convincing, it would have to be shown that Fascists in general, and Fascist intellectuals in particular, were possessed of nothing that might pass as right reason or moral purpose—and that somehow the contemporary "right-wing extremists" share that unfortunate disability.

Given the prevailing clutch of opinions, one might easily anticipate the outcome. With the absence of any discriminating list of traits—other than irrationality and bestiality—one might well have predicted that it would be impossible for research to distinguish fascists from simple lunatics and ordinary footpads. Today, in common usage, the word "fascist" does little more than "conjure up visions of nihilistic violence, war and *Götterdämmerung*," together with a "world of . . . uniforms and discipline, of bondage and sadomasochism."[16]

The term hardly has any cognitive reference at all. By and large, the term "fascism" has only pejorative uses. It is employed to disparage and defame.

None of that should puzzle laypersons. It is a heritage of usage made commonplace during the Second World War. In the course of that war, the term "fascist" was employed to refer indiscriminately to both Mussolini's Fascism and Hitler's National Socialism—irrespective of the fact that serious National Socialist theoreticians rarely, if ever, referred to their belief system, their movement, or their regime as "fascist." Similarly, Fascist intellectuals never identified their ideology or their political system as "National Socialist." The notion of a generic fascism that encompassed Italian Fascism, German National Socialism, Spanish Falangism, Portugese National Syndicalism, the Hungarian Arrow Cross, and the Romanian Legion of the Archangel Michael, among an indeterminate number of others, was largely an artifact of the war. Rarely, if ever, was a serious comparative study undertaken that might provide the grounds for identification. As a result, membership of all or any of those political movements in the class of "fascisms" has been a matter of contention ever since.[17]

---

[15] See Griffin, *The Nature of Fascism*, p. 18.

[16] Roger Eatwell, *Fascism: A History* (New York: Penguin, 1997), p. xix.

[17] Renzo De Felice, perhaps the most knowledgeable scholar in the field of fascism studies, had rejected the notion of a class of regimes that might be identified as "fascist." See Renzo De Felice, *Interpretations of Fascism* (Cambridge: Harvard University Press, 1977), pp. 10–11, 180; and *Fascism: An Informal Introduction to Its Theory and Practice* (New Brunswick, N.J.: Transaction, 1976), pp. 92–96. Zeev Sternhell has argued that "Fascism can in no way be identified with Nazism." Sternhell, with Mario Sznajder and Maia Asheri, *The Birth of Fascist Ideology* (Princeton: Princeton University Press, 1994), p. 4.

In our own time, any individual or group of individuals that might in some sense, or some measure, be identified as "extremely irrational,"[18] "antidemocratic," "racist," or "nationalist," is identified as "neofascist," "parafascist," "quasi-fascist," or "cryptofascist." "Fascism" has devolved into a conceptual term whose grasp far exceeds its reach—almost entirely devoid of any ability to offer empirical distinctions that might serve any cognitive purpose. Entirely devoid of meaning, the term is used arbitrarily, generally with little empirical reference to any historical, social, or political reality.

Because the notion that Fascism might have had ideological convictions, or a rational program for its revolution and the regime it fostered and sustained, is dismissed, explanations for its rise and success are sought in individual and collective psychopathology or "historic circumstances."[19] A variety of these efforts have been made. None have been notably successful. One of the more common has been to associate fascism with "an ideology generated by modern industrial capitalism."[20]

It is not at all clear what that can be taken to mean. Fascism would appear to have an ideology—however internally contradictory and meaningless. It is confidently asserted that fascist ideology, however meaningless, is apparently the specific product of "modern industrial capitalism."

The putative causal association is difficult to interpret. It could not possibly mean that Italian Fascism arose in an environment of *modern* industrial capitalism. Informed Marxists have long since recognized that Fascism arose and prevailed on the Italian peninsula in what was, without question, a transitional and only marginalized industrial environment. There was very little that was modern about the Italian economy at the time of the First World War. In 1924, Antonio Gramsci—usually identified as among the more astute of analysts—spoke of the political successes of Fascism as following, in part, from the fact that "capitalism [in Italy] was only weakly developed."[21]

Perhaps the reference to "modern capitalism" can be taken to mean *any* capitalism at all. Since capitalism is a modern product, the insistence that fascist ideology is the product of modern capitalism may simply mean that the ideology of fascism appears only in a capitalist environment. If that is

---

[18] Griffin, *The Nature of Fascism*, p. 18.

[19] See the discussion in A. James Gregor, *Interpretations of Fascism* (New Brunswick, N.J.: Transaction, 1997).

[20] Neocleous, *Fascism*, p. xi.

[21] Antonio Gramsci, "Fascismo e forze borghesi tradizionali," in *Sul fascismo* (Rome: Riuniti, 1973), p. 217.

what is intended, it is not very helpful. Some forms of "fascism" (however conceived) have evidently appeared in noncapitalist environments.[22]

More than that, for some commentators, any ideology, doctrine, or intellectual rationale for fascism would have to be, on its face, irrational and contradictory. For Marxist intellectuals, any individual or movement that failed to anticipate the imminent collapse of capitalism and the advent of the proletarian revolution was deemed irrational, incapable of the most elementary rationality. For a Marxist like Gramsci, any ideology other than Marxism could only be contradictory and irrational. Italian Fascism, as a non-Marxism, simply could not have a coherent ideology. Any intellectuals who sought to provide its vindication could only be bereft of reason and morality.

Whether the product of senescent, established, or emergent capitalism, Fascism was apparently not capable of formulating a consistent belief system—because, for Gramsci (as was the case for all Marxists), Fascism itself was a "contradictory" movement representing a middle-class attempt to avoid "proletarianization" in a capitalist environment. Marx had always contended that industrial capitalism would inevitably generate concentrations of enterprise at the cost of small and medium industry. As a predictable consequence, more and more members of the "middle class" would be jettisoned into the proletariat.

According to Gramsci, however weakly developed capitalism may have been in post–World War One Italy, Mussolini was nonetheless "fatally driven to assist in [its] historic development."[23] In Gramsci's judgment, it seemed transparent that Fascism could not represent the efforts of the middle class to resist proletarianization and at the same time assist capitalism in its historic development. Fascism could not do both without "contradiction."

Why such a course should inescapeably prove "contradictory" is explicable only if one assumes that the development of capitalism must necessarily "proletarianize" the middle classes. One could not pursue a course of industrialization without sacrificing the middle classes. Marx, after all, had insisted that industrialization would inevitably reduce the class inventory of modern society to but two: the proletariat and *grand capital*. As capitalist plant became increasingly large, complex, and costly, the larger, more complex, and costly would swallow the smaller, simpler, and less capital intensive. Fewer and fewer middle-class capitalists would survive

---

[22] See the discussions in Alexander Yanov, *The Russian New Right: Right-Wing Ideologies in the Contemporary USSR* (Berkeley: Institute of International Studies, 1978); and A. James Gregor, *Phoenix: Fascism in Our Time* (New Brunswick, N.J.: Transaction, 1999), chap. 7.

[23] Gramsci, "Tra realtà e arbitrio," in *Socialismo e fascismo: L'ordine nuovo, 1921–1922* (Turin: Einaudi, 1967), p. 302.

the winnowing. Over time and with greater and greater frequency, members of the lesser bourgeoisie would become proletarians. According to Marx, the *petite bourgeoisie* was a class destined for extinction in a social environment analogous to the biological struggle for survival—in which the "weaker" were destined for extinction as the "fittest" survive.

According to the thesis, Fascism was driven to support capitalist industrial development—even though that development would destroy the middle classes, the very recruitment base of the movement. Given those convictions, Marxists could only imagine that Fascist normative and doctrinal appeals would have to be "contradictory"—devoid of real significance. That conviction could only be predicated on the "scientific" truth that as industrial capitalism advances, the *petite bourgeoisie* would necessarily suffer gradual extinction. And yet, *petite bourgeois* elements persist in all, including the most advanced, capitalist societies. Those elements may assume different functions, and take on different properties, but they survive and prosper, no matter what the stage of industrialization. The notion that one could not consistently represent the middle classes and at the same time advocate rapid industrial development seems to be empirically disconfirmed.

It would seem that, in an informal discipline like intellectual history, rather than accepting the postulate that a given "theory of history" is true, thereby rendering it "necessary" that Fascist ideology *must* be contradictory and empty of substance, one might first apply oneself to a detailed inspection of that ideology, to judge it on its own merit. The alternative would appear to be nothing other than a dedicated search for self-serving "contradictions." As will be suggested, it is not at all self-evident that Mussolini's pursuit of industrialization inescapably involved contradictions—or that such contradictions surfaced in Fascist doctrine.[24]

All that notwithstanding, some contemporary analysts insist that Mussolini's Fascism, like all fascism, was and is a product of industrial capitalism, whether emergent, mature, or senescent. As such, according to such appraisals, it will always be irrational and contradictory because it casts itself athwart the tide of history—the imminent and inevitable anticapitalist proletarian revolution.[25] Again, in order to defend such notions, one would have to defend all its associated, but interred, premises. One would have to assume that history had one and only one course—culminating in the "ineluctable" revolution of the proletariat. There is little objective evidence to support any of that.

These are the kinds of curiosities to be found in considerable abundance throughout the literature devoted to the study of the intellectual substance

---

[24] See the discussion in Gramsci, "Il fascismo e la sua politica," in *Sul fascismo*, p. 304.
[25] See the discussion in Neocleous, *Fascism*.

of Mussolini's Fascism. The result has been an inability of historians and political scientists to deal, in some significant measure, with the intellectual history not only of Fascism, but with the history of the twentieth century as well—and whatever influence that history might have on the political life of the twenty-first.

The identification of fascism with the exclusive interests of capitalism, the petite bourgeoisie, together with a rage against Enlightenment values and the political fancies of the French Revolution—to see Fascism the paladin of the world's machine and market economy, to make of Fascism the foundation of modern evil—seems to satisfy a deep and abiding psychological hunger among many in our postmodern circumstances, but assists us very little in the effort to understand either the twentieth century or our own troubled times. There is the evident necessity, among some analysts, to identify fascism, however understood, not with any syndrome of ideas, but with late capitalism, ultranationalism, racism, antifeminism, and every antidemocratic impulse—simple violence, bourgeois perversity, and irremediable irrationality. As a consequence, many commentators choose to see "fascism" as a right-wing excrescence, exclusively as a "recurrent feature of capitalism"—a "form of counterrevolution acting in the interests of capital." Burdened with all these moral and intellectual disabilities, Fascism could only be inspired by an evil and "very contradictory ideology" in the service of what has been frequently identified as a capitalistic "open dictatorship of high finance."[26]

Of course, it was not always so. Prior to the Second World War, while non-Marxists, in general, deplored Fascism,[27] there were American intellectuals who were not prepared to identify Fascism with either capitalism or incarnate evil. There were even those prepared to acknowledge that Mussolini's movement and regime was, in fact, possessed of a reasonably well articulated and coherent belief system.[28]

All of that dramatically changed with the coming of the Second World War. It served the purposes of that conflict to dismiss Fascist ideology as not only evil, but as internally inconsistent and fundamentally irrational

---

[26] Renton, *Fascism: Theory and Practice*, pp. 3, 16–17, 25. To all that, Renzo De Felice, perhaps the best informed historian of Fascism, states simply, "It is unthinkable that Italy's great economic forces wanted to bring fascism to power." De Felice, *Fascism: An Informal Introduction to Its Theory and Practice*, p. 63.

[27] See the account in John P. Diggins, *Mussolini and Fascism: The View from America* (Princeton: Princeton University Press, 1972), chap. 17.

[28] For example, Schneider, *Making the Fascist State*; Paul Einzig, *The Economic Foundations of Fascism* (London: Macmillan and Co., 1933); and William G. Welk, *Fascist Economic Policy: An Analysis of Italy's Economic Experiment* (Cambridge: Harvard University Press, 1938). Welk speaks of Fascist ideology as a "curious mixture of Nationalism and Socialist doctrine" (p. 11)—and of the "philosophy upon which the new Fascist state was to be based" as "set forth in detail" (p. 20)—but he nowhere speaks of its "irrationality."

as well. Left-wing notions, already abundant in the intellectual atmosphere, were quickly pressed into service—to become fixtures for years thereafter.

Only decades after the passions of the most destructive war in human history had abated did some academics, once more, find "a coherent body of thought" among Fascist thinkers.[29] Thus, in 1994, Zeev Sternhell affirmed that "the intellectual content of fascism had the same importance in the growth and development of the movement as it had in liberalism or later in Marxism."[30] In effect, some scholars were prepared to grant that the intellectual folk wisdom that held that Fascism was innocent of doctrinal coherence was less than simply unconvincing—it was in error.

Some have sought to provide a justification for the conviction that fascism was irrational, and devoid of ideological sophistication, by pointing out that there were "radical differences" between Fascism's revolutionary tenets "and the realities to which it [gave] rise."[31] The argument is not at all persuasive, for if the marked discrepancies between antecedent ideological affirmations and the realities that emerge after successful revolution were enough to identify a political creed as "irrational," one of the first to so qualify would be the Marxism of revolutionary Bolshevism.

V. I. Lenin anticipated the "withering away" of the state to be among the first consequences of successful revolution. That would entail the advent of anarchistic government, peace, "workers' emancipation," and "voluntary centralism."[32] The fact is that everything of the subsequent reality of the Soviet Union belied all that. Almost everything about post-revolutionary Russia stood in stark and emphatic contrast to the specific theoretical anticipations that had carried the Bolsheviks to the October Revolution. The differences, in fact, were more emphatic than anything to be found in the comparison of Fascist thought and Fascist practice. If the discrepancies between doctrinal formulations and the reality that emerges out of revolution were a measure of "irrationality" or the potential for violence, then Lenin's Bolshevism was perhaps the most irrational and violence-prone doctrine of the twentieth century.

Actually, the conviction that Mussolini's Fascism had no ideology to speak of—or that whatever tenets it entertained were irrational and contradictory—is the product of a complex series of conjectures that arose out of the political circumstances of the first quarter of the twentieth cen-

---

The thought of Fascist intellectuals is presented with accuracy and academic detachment in chap. 2.

[29] Eatwell, *Fascism*, p. xix.

[30] Sternhell, *The Birth of Fascist Ideology*, p. 4.

[31] See Griffin, *The Nature of Fascism*, p. 18.

[32] V. I. Lenin, *The State and Revolution* in *Selected Works* (Moscow: Foreign Languages Press, 1950–51), vol. 2, p. 251.

juncture that Clara Zetkin affirmed that Mussolini's success was not the simple consequence of military victory; it was "an ideological and political victory over the working class movement"[40]

That did not mean, in the least, that Fascism employed an ideology that enjoyed superiority over that of Marxism. What it meant was that Marxists had not employed inherited "theory" to best advantage. Prior to its victory, Marxists had not understood the "essence" of Fascism. Once understood, there was an aggressive effort among members of the Third International to formulate a convincing account of Italian Fascism to better counteract its toxin. Unfortunately, there was never to be any consistency among the Marxist assessments. Marxist theoreticians settled on only one consistency: Fascism was deemed counterrevolutionary, opposed to the course of history. So disposed, Fascism had to be, necessarily, irrational—and, as irrational, contradictory.

Other than that, Marxists were to characterize Fascism in any number of overlapping, and sometimes mutually exclusive, fashion. At first it was seen as a rural, agrarian reaction, in the service of those possessed of extensive landholdings. Then it was understood to be enlisted in the service of the urban middle classes. Then it was envisaged the creature of industrialists. Then it was conceived the instrument of finance capitalists. Some even attempted to portray Fascism as the tool of all such interests in all their complexity.[41]

By the mid-1930s, most of the proffered Marxist interpretations of Fascism had become standardized under the weight of Stalinist orthodoxy.[42] Fascism was the creature and the tool of "finance capitalism," struggling to survive during the end-days of the final crisis of capitalism.[43] As capitalism sank into its inevitable and irreversible decline, Fascism was compelled to ratchet down the nation's productive processes in the effort to sustain monopoly price levels. Finance capitalists, the owners of the means of production, demanded that Fascism limit production, curtail technological innovation and systematically destroy inventory. What was attempted was an artificially reduced, stabilized but profitable rate of con-

---

[40] Clara Zetkin, "Der Kampf gegen den Faschismus," in Ernst Nolte, ed., *Theorien ueber den Faschismus* (Berlin: Kiepenheuer and Witsch, 1967), p. 99.

[41] See the discussion in Gregor, *Interpretations of Fascism*, chap. 5; and *The Faces of Janus: Marxism and Fascism in the Twentieth Century* (New Haven: Yale University Press, 2000), chap. 2.

[42] See the comments in the "Introduction" to David Beetham, ed., *Marxists in Face of Fascism: Writings by Marxists on Fascism from the Inter-war Years* (Manchester: Manchester University Press, 1983), particularly p. 1.

[43] Georgi Dimitroff, "The United Front against War and Fascism," *Report to the Seventh World Congress of the Communist International, 1935* (New York: Gamma Publishing Co., n.d.), p. 7, passim.

sumption. Completely cartelized or monopolized production was distributed in fixed quantitites calculated to maximize profit.[44]

The maximization of profit would be pursued at the cost of technological proficiency and productivity. That would necessarily impair the efficiency and survival potential of Fascist military capabilities. Fascism was seen as an institutional irrationality, driving Italy into international conflict through irredentist demands while, at the same time, reducing the technological and industrial output of Italy's economic system to preindustrial levels—thus crippling any military potentialities the nation might have developed. Under Fascism, Italy would be reduced to a "lower technical and economic level" as a consequence of the constraints imposed by productive relations—property and distributive modalities—that had become obsolete.[45] Torn by the contradictions dictated by the "laws of history," Fascism could only compel the economy of the Italian peninsula to spiral down into economic senescence. Whatever the consequences, Mussolini had no alternative but to drive the nation into catastrophic wartime destruction. Fascism was animated exclusively by political, economic, and military irrationality and an irrepressible impulse to collective violence. All of these notions easily fed into the passions of the Second World War.

For all that, there was to be no closure for those who sought a credible interpretation of Fascism, and its ideological expressions, in whatever form. During the quarter century that followed the Second World War, both Soviet and Chinese Communist Marxists began to reinterpret their understanding of Mussolini's Fascism, international capitalism, and the history of the twentieth century. Very soon the notion that Fascism was the inevitable product of capitalism in its final crisis was abandoned— and the conviction that capitalism would inevitably collapse because of its "internal contradictions" was similarly foresworn.

The economic growth rate in the post–World War Two West clearly discredited the belief that capitalism had been, or was, suffering its terminal crisis. Industrial capitalism had clearly entered an ascending trajectory of growth. It followed that the Fascism of the interwar years could hardly have been the product of a moribund capitalism.

By the mid-1960s, Soviet Marxists argued that Fascism was only one political form that contemporary capitalism might assume. More than that, they granted that Fascism was neither a creature nor a tool of finance capital. Nor was it a function of the ownership of property. Fascism, we were told, exercised power over Italy independent of whoever owned the

[44] R. Palme Dutt, *Fascism and Social Revolution* (New York: International Publishers, 1934), pp. 225–26.

[45] Ibid., pp. 103, 206–8.

means of production.[46] More than that, rather than supervising the productive and technological retrogression of Italian industry, Fascism administered its growth. By the beginning of the 1970s, we were told that rather than undermining productive output, "fascism really represented a development of capitalist forces of production. . . . It represented industrial development, technological innovation and an increase in the productivity of labor." We were informed that after the First World War, Fascist Italy's "industrial recovery . . . was the strongest in capitalist Europe" and after the Great Depression, its recovery "was quite spectacular."[47]

At about the same time, other Marxists informed us that after the First World War, Fascism emerged as "the *only* political form adequate to the new phase of capitalist development." Fascism was "an objectively progressive, anti-capitalist, and . . . antiproletarian movement . . . that fulfilled an historical function. . . ." It was argued that Italian Fascism provided the conditions for a period of extensive growth on the peninsula that had only begun at the turn of the twentieth century. It was held that in the retrograde conditions of the economically underdeveloped peninsula, the notion of a socialist revolution was entirely counterproductive. Associated as it was with "trade union demands," the account continued, socialism "hindered capitalist accumulation, prevented the modernization of the economic structure of the country, and completely ruined the petty bourgeois strata without offering them any opportunity. . . . Italian Fascism remained the only progressive solution."[48]

The most familiar claims had characterized Fascist thought as contradictory and incoherent—as a simple pastiche of themes, without any intrinsic meaning. Given the transformations that had proceeded over time, all of that was critically reviewed. Non-Marxists began to speak of Fascist thought as "fascinating," as having elaborated myths "far more powerful and psychologically astute than that provided either by its liberal or socialist rivals."[49] At about the same time, others affirmed that Fascism's political ideology, "taken as a whole, represented a coherent, logical and well-structured totality."[50] In 1997, others spoke of a "coherent body of thought" that lay behind the reigning stereotype of Fascist doctrinal irra-

---

[46] See the discussion and the source citations in Gregor, *The Faces of Janus*, chap. 3.

[47] Nicos Poulantzas, *Fascism and Dictatorship* (London: NLB, 1974), pp. 98–99.

[48] Mihaly Vajda, "The Rise of Fascism in Italy and Germany," *Telos* no. 12 (Summer 1972), pp. 6, 9–10, 11, 12; see also Vajda, *Fascisme et mouvement de masse* (Paris: Le sycomore, 1979), pp. 73–78, 121–24.

[49] See J. T. Schnapp, "18BL: Fascist Mass Spectacle," *Representations*, no. 43 (1993), pp. 90, 92–93.

[50] Sternhell, *The Birth of Fascist Ideology*, p. 8.

tionality.[51] Still others spoke vaguely of fascism's ideology as "relatively original, coherent and homogeneous."[52] There was a tendency among more serious scholars to reevaluate the omnibus judgments about Fascist doctrine that had influenced "committed" scholars.

The "revisionism" that resulted was not uniformly welcomed. With the changes that were becoming more and more apparent in the field of fascism studies during the 1990s, some warned that they presaged a cynical and manipulative attack against decency and democracy.[53] Some scholars attempted to reconstruct a framework that might still capture the full malevolence that had been attributed to Fascism by making Fascism the direct ancestor of an inclusive ideological "right." That the right was irremediably evil remained prominent in the institutional memory of many intellectuals. By the early 1990s, as a consequence, there was a tendency among some thinkers in the advanced industrial countries to retreat to the antifascist formulations of the interwar years. There could be nothing "progressive" about fascism. It was not to be seen as discharging any "historic function." More than all that, its ideology was to be understood once again as devoid of reason, as fundamentally irrational, and as remorselessly homicidal.

In those years, a wave of new publications appeared, particularly in the anglophone countries, that sought to deliver a convincing interpretation of fascism that might still accommodate the notions so prevalent during the times of committed scholarship. There seemed to have been a genuine revulsion among some scholars to the thought that Mussolini's Fascism might be considered as having been "underpinned by a genuine intellectual base."[54]

It is in that parlous state that the study of Mussolini's Fascism and the assessment of contemporary "extremism" finds itself. It is evident that many scholars concern themselves with the instances of senseless violence that trouble Europe and North America in the twenty-first century—terrorist attacks on innocents, murder at soccer matches, vandalism of houses of worship, attacks on immigrants, together with a host of other atrocities. To identify these criminal acts as "fascist" is neither informative nor does it advance the cause of their suppression. Beyond that, the entire notion that graveyard vandals and race-baiters are fascists does nothing to reduce the confusion that has traditionally attended the study of Italian Fascism.

---

[51] Eatwell, *Fascism*, p. xix.

[52] Griffin, *The Nature of Fascism*, p. xii.

[53] R.J.B. Bosworth, *The Italian Dictatorship: Problems and Perspectives in the Interpretation of Mussolini and Fascism* (London: Arnold, 1998), pp. 231–38.

[54] See the response by Bosworth, ibid., p. 23.

Among the desperate efforts made to find the irrationality and malevolence that typifies contemporary mayhem in a Fascist source, some have seized on the work of Julius Evola.[55] Elevated to the stature of "the philosopher of Fascism," Evola has been identified as one of the principal sources of "right-wing extremism."

The fact is that whatever the case might be with respect to Evola's connections with contemporary extremism, there are virtually no grounds for identifying him as a spokesman for Fascist doctrine. Such an identification has become possible only because Fascism as an historic reality has receded further and further into the mists of stereotypy and political science fiction. An entire quarter century of Italian history has taken on the banal qualities of a poor morality play. Fascism no longer appears as an historical reality, but becomes a waking horror, without substance and without an intellectual history.

In fact, Italian Fascism has very little, if anything, to do with either Julius Evola or modern extremism of whatever sort. Those today identified as "neofascists," "cryptofascists," and "parafascists" are, most frequently, not fascists at all, but persons suffering clinical afflictions.

There are a great many reasons why one could not expect to find Fascists among the marginal persons of the postindustrial Western communities. The problems that concerned the revolutionary intellectuals of the Italian peninsula at the advent of the twentieth century are no longer issues for their successors. In order to understand something of all that, one would have to be familiar with the evolving ideology of historic Fascism.

To begin to understand the ideology of Fascism—with whatever rationality and coherence it possessed—one would have to acquire some familiarity with its emerging substance as it traversed the entire course of its historic parabola. That would require familiarizing oneself with a substantial body of primary doctrinal literature: that of Italian nationalism, idealism, and syndicalism. Only by doing something like that—something that has only rarely been done—might one begin to understand how Fascist thought enjoyed the measure of coherence and intelligibility that it has been typically denied.

More than that, one would be required to provide a catalog of central themes to be found in the earliest formulations of Mussolini's Fascism. Such a roster of political, economic, and social intentions would afford a convenient and responsible guide to the dynamic evolution that governed Fascism's complex rationale.

All of that is available in the best of the doctrinal literature produced by some of Italy's most gifted intellectuals after the termination of the

---

[55] See, for example, the treatment of Evola in Griffin, *The Nature of Fascism*, pp. 47, 51, 69, 147, 152, 169, 172; Eatwell, *Fascism*, pp. 253–55, 263, 270, 313–14, 319, 321, 341.

First World War. The fact is that much of Fascism's rationale, as Zeev Sternhell has persuasively argued, had been "fully elaborated even before the movement came to power."[56] Internationally celebrated scholars such as Giovanni Gentile, a philosophic nationalist and idealist, and Roberto Michels, a revolutionary syndicalist, had both contributed to its initial articulation and were to influence its subsequent development.

Given the intellectual gifts of those who contributed to its articulation, it would be hard, for example, to find the simple advocacy of violence and war in the ideology of historic Fascism. Whatever rationale for violence one does find in the doctrinal statements of the best of Fascist thinkers is no more immoral than similar vindications found in the works of Marxists and revolutionaries in general.[57] Much the same might be said of the "irrationality" of Fascist thought. That more "contradictions" are to be found in Fascist ideology than any other is a claim that defies any kind of confirmation. Vaguenesses and ambiguities are found everywhere in the most sophisticated ideological argument. That granted, locating *formal* contradictions in those arguments becomes, for all intents and purposes, logically impossible.

Radiating outward, Fascist doctrine influenced, and was influenced by, such major intellectuals as Henri De Man. Growing out of the Marxism of Georges Sorel and the positivism of Vilfredo Pareto, Fascism, as a set of ideas, was to dominate the European world of ideas for almost three decades. In effect, to understand something important about the twentieth century is to understand something of the thought of half a dozen Italian intellectuals who produced the public rationale of Fascism between the time of its first appearance and its extinction in 1945.

However Fascism is judged by history, the movement, the revolution, and the regime itself had, at their disposal, as talented and moral a cadre of intellectuals as any found in the ranks of revolutionary Marxism or traditional liberalism. Those thinkers who fabricated the ideology of Fascism were gifted intellectuals—whose works were as interesting and as persuasive as any found in the libraries of contemporary revolution. To trace the development of their ideas is a responsibility of contemporary political theorists and intellectual historians.

---

[56] Sternhell, *The Birth of Fascist Ideology*, p. 229.

[57] See, for example, Sergio Panunzio, *Diritto, forza, e violenza: Lineamenti di una teoria della violenza* (Bologna: Licinio Cappelli, 1921), where we find an account of a "theory of violence." I have provided a brief account of some of Panunzio's ideas in A. James Gregor, "Some Thoughts on State and Rebel Terror," in David C. Rapoport and Yonah Alexander, eds., *The Rationalization of Terrorism* (Frederick, Md.: Aletheia Books, 1982), pp. 56–66. In this context, one must compare Leon Trotsky's *Terrorism and Communism* (Ann Arbor: University of Michigan Press, 1961).

CHAPTER TWO

The Historic Background and Enrico Corradini

ONE OF THE presumed distinctions between the left- and right-wing revolutions in the twentieth century has persisted almost to the present. Left-wing revolutions were intuitively anticapitalist; right-wing revolutions were not—certainly not in the same fashion. More than that, right-wing revolutions were purportedly "supported," "underwritten," "directed," and "organized" by "capitalism."[1] Fascism, we have been told as late as 1997, is "implicit in the nature of modernity and capitalism. . . ."[2]

The argument, fully articulated as early as the middle years of the 1930s,[3] identified fascism as a reactive product of industrial capitalism. The economic depression of the 1930s convinced many that industrial capitalism could no longer realize a rate of profit that might sustain the system. The consequence, the argument proceeded, was the desperate search by "finance capitalists" for "reactionary" political instrumentalities that could effectively resist the inevitable and irreversible catastrophic collapse of the system. Fascism, according to the argument, provided precisely that instrumentality. All of which implied that one would expect fascism to make its appearance exclusively in mature and nonviable industrial economies. Today, given what we know, none of that is, in the least, likely.[4]

Not only has capitalism not entered into its final crisis anywhere in the world, but Fascism was first successful in marginally industrialized Italy—in a nation that had only begun its industrial development. Italian industrial capitalism was hardly at the end of its life cycle. It was at little more

---

[1] There were various characterizations of how "capitalism" was related to "fascism": sometimes it was seen as a simple support, sometimes as direct control. Sometimes fascist dictators were "lackies" and subordinates of "finance capialists," and sometimes they were simply "gangsters" who dominated the environment through the indirect connivance of the capitalists. For a more ample discussion, and specific references to the publications involved in making the case for Italian Fascism as a "tool" of "finance capitalism," see A. James Gregor, *Interpretations of Fascism* (New Brunswick, N.J.: Transaction, 1997), chap. 5.

[2] Mark Neocleous, *Fascism* (Minneapolis: University of Minnesota Press, 1997), p. xi.

[3] While variants of the argument appeared as early as the advent of Fascism to power in Italy, the full, classic expressions are found in Daniel Guerin, *Fascism and Big Business* (New York: Pioneer, 1939); and Rajani Palme Dutt, *Fascism and Social Revolution* (New York: International Press, 1934).

[4] See the discussion in François Furet, *The Passing of an Illusion: The Idea of Communism in the Twentieth Century* (Chicago: University of Chicago Press, 1999), chaps. 6 and 7.

than its commencement. Moreover, subsequent movements elsewhere in Europe that have been characterized as fascist proved to "have been most successful in mobilizing the lower classes in *underdeveloped . . .* countries." Where a variant of fascism—Adolf Hitler's National Socialism— arose in an industrialized economy, "most large-scale business and industrial enterprise . . . did not support the Nazis before their seizure of power, and indeed looked upon them as potential radicals."[5] The fact is that fascism, in all its variants, had a relationship with industrial capitalism largely misunderstood by theoreticians. "Modernity"—if it is understood primarily as industrialization and technological development—was critical to fascism as a revolutionary goal.

In Fascist Italy, economic modernization, industrialization, and technological development were critical to its political enterprise from the very origins of Mussolini's movement.[6] As a consequence, there were intellectuals, supported by antitraditionalists and Futurists, who sought technological proficiency and economic expansion—formulating programs characterized by "unconditional adherence to logic and reason."[7] Their reasonings may have been impaired and the programs flawed, but it is clear that their rationale was as competent as any. Fascism was animated by a search for rational programs and functional strategies. The exortative enjoinments Fascism employed to mobilize mass energies, to extract resources, or to ensure popular support were instrumental to the technological modernization and industrialization of Italy—in the effort to create a nation that would assume the economic, political, and military responsibilities of a major power in the modern world. As a consequence, Fascism was, as will be argued, goal directed and functionally rational.

The principal leaders of Italian Fascism were heretical Marxists precisely in the sense that their experience had taught them that traditional Marxism offered little guidance in the tortured reality of the first decades of the twentieth century. Mussolini, an acknowledged Marxist thinker, had been both the intellectual and political leader of the Italian Socialist Party prior to the First World War—and collected around himself some of Italian Marxism's most competent theoreticians.[8] They were the thinkers who early recognized that *advanced industrial economies* were the exclusive subject of classical Marxist analyses—economies in which the

---

[5] George L. Mosse, *The Fascist Revolution: Toward a General Theory of Fascism* (New York: Howard Fertig, 1999), p. 22 (emphasis supplied); see Walter Laqueur, *Fascism: Past, Present, Future* (New York: Oxford, 1996), pp. 19, 47–50, 89.

[6] See the discussion in A. James Gregor, *Italian Fascism and Developmental Dictatorship* (Princeton: Princeton University Press, 1979), chaps. 4 and 5.

[7] Mosse, *Fascist Revolution*, p. 143.

[8] See A. James Gregor, *Young Mussolini and the Intellectual Origins of Fascism* (Berkeley and Los Angeles: University of California Press, 1979).

concentration and centralization of capital, together with its "high organic composition,"[9] generated crises that irreversibly reduced their rate of profit, their viability, and led to "inevitable proletarian revolution."

They were the thinkers who early understood that revolution in the retarded economic environments in which they found themselves required something other than a "proletarian revolution" and a program to more equitably redistribute the welfare benefits of industrial capitalism. Retrograde industrial development in the twentieth century carried with it consequences that had overwhelming technological and productive, rather than distributive, implications for all sectors of society.

At the turn of the twentieth century, industrial capitalism in Italy had only begun its sustained growth. At that time, Italy was a marginally industrialized nation. It took its place among the most economically and industrially laggard communities of Europe— a fact that rendered Italy a polity of little consequence among the international powers.[10] In those circumstances, it was very unlikely that "industrial capitalism" would be in a position to "generate," foster, or sustain so complex a movement as Fascism either as an ideology or a revolution. There were precious few "magnates of industry" or "finance capitalists" with the power and wherewithal who might create and employ Fascism as a tool to dominate the national economy.

The entire notion that Fascism was a product of late-industrial or finance capitalism has shown itself to be so improbable that there are few serious contemporary scholars who entertain it any longer. Italian Fascism was neither the creature nor the tool of "capitalism"—industrial, financial, or agrarian.[11]

The Italy that saw the rise of the first Fascism hosted a retrograde industrial capitalism—hardly the agency that possessed the resources or was infilled with the systemic urgencies that would lead to the creation, sustenance, and organization of a dynamic mass movement capable of controlling a nation for a quarter of a century. At the time of Fascism's rise, Italy was largely agrarian, with the bulk of its labor force involved in

---

[9] See the account in A. James Gregor, *The Fascist Persuasion in Radical Politics* (Princeton: Princeton University Press, 1974), chaps. 2 and 3.

[10] See the account in Bruno Caizzi, *Storia dell'industria Italiana* (Turin: UTET, 1965), pt. 2, chaps. 2, 3, and 4. See the account of the "Primitivism of the Italian Industrial Environment" at the end of the nineteenth and commencement of the twentieth centuries. Rodolfo Morandi, *Storia della grande industria in Italia* (Turin: Einaudi, 1966), pt. 2.

[11] Renzo De Felice has reviewed all the available evidence and has dismissed the notion as unsupported. Other than his multivolume biography of Mussolini in Italian, there are English texts available that summarize his findings; see Renzo De Felice, *Interpretations of Fascism* (Cambridge: Harvard University Press, 1977); and *Fascism: An Informal Introduction to Its Theory and Practice* (New Brunswick, N.J.: Transaction, 1976), particularly pp. 62–63.

agricultural pursuits.[12] Like Russia at the time of the Bolshevik revolution, the Fascist revolution came to power in Italy just after the nation had traversed an initial period of preliminary economic and minimal industrial growth, immediately followed by the social and political crises of the First World War.

In both environments, the revolutionaries received financial and political support from whatever economic, and financial leaders were available in their respective communities.[13] Bolsheviks no more solicited funds nor recruited exclusively from the proletariat than Fascism did from capitalists. In both environments, monied elements contributed to their respective enterprise, and the revolutionaries in both Russia and Italy enjoyed the intellectual and political support of a significant number of important thinkers of all classes. In both instances, some of those same thinkers were to supply the rationale for the revolution and subsequent regime developments.

For Fascist intellectuals, even before the March on Rome that brought Mussolini to power in Italy in 1922, in the retarded economic and industrial development in which they found themselves, Marxism, in whatever variant, was totally irrelevant. Fascist theoreticians provided an alternative.

That Fascism provided a political, economic, and revolutionary strategy for a less-developed nation grew out of the intellectual and political environment Fascists inherited from a long history. The proposed alternative assumed specific form almost immediately upon Fascism's accession to power in Italy. It was the evolutionary product of a long development of Italian socialism and nationalism—political convictions that were to pass almost unaltered into the regime rationale of Fascism.[14]

The rationale offered by Fascism grew out of a protracted history of political and national development on the Italian peninsula. Until the nineteenth century Italy was not a nation; it was a congeries of principalities, city-states, and geographic enclaves more often than not invaded, and ruled over, by foreigners. As early as 1513, Niccolò Machiavelli had called for the creation of a united community on the peninsula. He exhorted the people of the broken nation to "deliver Italy from foreign powers." He held that Italy, as a nation, had been reduced to slavery. He went on to argue that perhaps it was inevitable, given the nature of the world, that such humilia-

---

[12] See the discussions in the collection edited by Alberto Caracciolo, ed., *La formazione dell'Italia industriale* (Rome: Laterza, 1977).

[13] See the account in Marcello Lucini, *Chi finanziò la rivoluzione d'ottobre?* (Rome: Editrice Italiana, 1967).

[14] See Alexander J. DeGrand, *The Italian Nationalist Association and the Rise of Fascism in Italy* (Lincoln: University of Nebraska Press, 1978), pp. 48–49; Nazareno Mezzetti, *Alfredo Rocco nel dottrina e nel diritto della rivoluzione fascista* (Rome: Pinciana, 1930), pp. 42–43.

tion was necessary in order to foster rebirth—to awaken the interests and kindle the energy of so demeaned a people. Italy, he averred, had been reduced to so miserable a condition that Italians were "greater slaves than the Israelites, more oppressed than the Persians, and still more dispersed than the Athenians. . . . In a word, [Italians were] without laws and without chiefs, pillaged, torn to pieces, and enslaved by foreign powers."[15]

The theme of Italian inferiority, exploitation, and humiliation is a recurrent feature of Italian literature throughout the years between Machiavelli and the turn of the twentieth century. After 1530, it was said, "Venice endures, but does not live; Florence lives, but does not create; Rome governs, but does not reign; Naples reigns, but does not govern; Turin both reigns and governs, but only obscurely."[16] In 1614, Alessandro Tassoni sought to reprove Italians for enduring the pretense of others—to continue to allow themselves to be "downtrodden by the arrogance and conceit of foreign peoples."[17]

Characteristic of these circumstances is the reaction that inevitably follows. Cognizant of the wretched state of the peninsula, Giambattista Vico offered Italians heart. At the onset of the eighteenth century, Vico claimed to have divined, through his "new science," that peoples and nations went through "natural" cycles. After the glories of its youth in antiquity, he maintained, Italy had fallen into senescence and decay. The old Italy had died. A new Italy, his "science" proclaimed, was destined for rebirth and resurgence. He anticipated a nation freed of foreign intervention, "master of itself, great among the great nations of Europe, . . . conscious of its dignity, proud of its glory, . . . capable of the most splendid arts and original science. . . ."[18] His was a full expression of *reactive nationalism*—a cry of redemptive desire made by a people, once proud, shorn of self-esteem and collective purpose.

For all the expectations aroused by Vico's message, at the end of the same century, Vittorio Alfieri could still speak of Italy as that "August Matron," who for so long had been the "principal seat of all human wisdom and values," and who yet found herself, in his own time, "disarmed, divided, despised [and] enslaved."[19] With the advent of the nineteenth

---

[15] Niccolo Machiavelli, *The History of Florence and The Prince* (London: George Bell and Sons, 1891), p. 484 (chap. 26 of *The Prince*).

[16] Alfredo Oriani, *La lotta politica in Italia: Origini della lotta attuale 476/1887* (Rocca San Casciano: Cappelli, 1956), p. 106.

[17] Alessandro Tassoni, "Filippiche contro gli spagnuoli," *Prose politiche e morali* (Bari: Laterza, 1930), pp. 341–42.

[18] Giovanni Gentile, *Giambattista Vico* (Florence: Sansoni, 1936), p. 5; see Gentile, *Studi Vichiani* (Florence: Felice le Monnier, 1927).

[19] As cited in Ronald S. Cunsolo, *Italian Nationalism* (Malabar, Fl.: Robert E. Krieger, 1990), p. 184.

century, entire strata of the Italian political and intellectual elite were astir with the reactive nationalist demands of unification and regeneration.

If anything, the reactive nationalist sentiments of many had become still more exacerbated. Vincenzo Gioberti spoke of the "primacy" of Italy, of the superiority of Italians in almost every endeavor. His book on the moral and civil primacy of Italians (*Del primato morale e civile degli italiani*) of 1843, however hyperbolic, gave expression to the desire for the restoration of the nation's lost grandeur. The mere literary statement, however, was of little consolation to those who longed for the restoration of Italy's one-time glory. At almost the same time, Giacomo Leopardi lamented the "pitiful condition" of the nation, divested of glory, "sad and abandoned," still so disheartened that she was compelled to "conceal her face" from the world.[20]

With the coming of the nineteenth century, Europe embarked on a protracted period of political instability. The French Revolution and the Napoleonic period had unleashed forces no longer to be contained. *Nationalism*, everywhere, became the inspiration for sustained revolutionary efforts on the part of communities that aspired to nationhood, or which, like Italy, sought not only political reunification, but national resurgence as well.

Italy's Risorgimento, its effort at reunification and rebirth, made the name of Giuseppe Mazzini familiar to Western thought— however uninterested Westerners might have been in developments on the Italian peninsula. Mazzini spoke, with passion, of an Italian rebirth. He spoke of a reunited Italy that would represent a redemptive "Third Rome," to bring a new message of civilization and morality to a world that had become increasingly materialistic and devoid of purpose. He spoke of the "great memories" of a past that would inspire a new Italy to a "new mission." He called for an anti-individualistic unity of all Italians at home and a new development of civilization, inspired by Italy, abroad—the "vast ambition of a nation, intoxicated by its independence of the foreigner, [and] founded by its own strength."

That strength of the anticipated new Italy would be mobilized by a "government that [would] be the *mind* of a nation, the people its *arm*, and the educated and free individual its prophet of *future progress*. The first will point out the path that leads to the *ideal*, its national *idea*, which . . . is the only thing that makes a nation." For Mazzini, the nation was to be "something more than an aggregation of individuals born to produce and consume corn, the foundations of its life are, fraternity of faith, consciousness of a common *ideal*, and the association of all faculties to work in harmony and with success towards that ideal . . . [with] *duty* the

---

[20] Giacomo Leopardi, *Opere* (Milan: Communità, 1937), 1, pp. 137–38.

sole standard of life [and] self-sacrifice . . . the only pure virtue, holy and mighty in power, the noblest jewel that crowns and hallows the human soul. . . . People and government must proceed united, like thought and action in individuals, towards the accomplishment of [their] mission." Mazzini sought the nation's *redemptive renewal* in what he identified as a "National Italian Revolution."[21]

Similar themes recur in the literature of Italy's Risorgimento —often in different combinations and with different emphases. There were those who, after the founding of the Kingdom in March 1861 and the establishment of Rome as its capital in October 1870, devoted themselves to sustaining and fostering the strength of the new state; others were to attempt to serve the needs and wants of the new nation's working classes. The first were identified as of the right and the others as of the left. There were those who sought the complete separation of the state and the Roman Catholic Church—while others sought their collaboration in the creation of a strong and independent nation.

By the end of the nineteenth century, with the first impressive developments by Italy's liberal government that signaled the beginnings of a national industrial base, there were those Italians who sought infant industry protection through tariff and nontariff means. Others appealed to the injunctions of Adam Smith on "free trade" in order to foster the anticipated industrial development. To that purpose, some sought state intervention; others rejected it. In 1892–93, in what could only be the premature response to the first appearance of medium-sized industry on the peninsula, the first organized socialist elements appeared, inspired by the Marxism of France and Germany. During that year, the Italian Socialist party was founded. For Italian Marxism, socialism sought not national ideals, but social revolution. The revolution it sought had nothing to do with the creation of a "Third Rome," but with worldwide "proletarian revolution."

With the expansion of suffrage, the opposing political forces in Italy, marshaled in a variety of relatively small organizations, influenced an indecisive government inextricably caught up in internal conflict. In a Europe alive with energy—the explosive expansion of British, French, and Belgian imperialism, together with the rapid industrialization of Germany—a newly reunited Italy continued to languish in manifest political, cultural, industrial, military, and imperial inferiority.[22]

---

[21] Giuseppe Mazzini, "To the Italians: The Program of the 'Roma del popolo,' (1871)," in *The Duties of Man and Other Essays* (New York: E. P. Dutton, 1907), pp. 222, 224, 228, 229, 231–32, 234, 238, 240.

[22] See the comments in Oriani, *La lotta politica in Italia*, bk. 9, chapter 3.

It was in that atmosphere of failed political purpose that a modern Italian nationalism began to take shape. Rather than a single Italian nationalism, there were at that time "many nationalisms," each distinctive in its own fashion.[23] Some expressions had been precipitated by Italy's defeat in Ethiopia in 1896—its first real venture into colonialism. Others were the product of the humiliation produced by the awareness that millions of Italians had been forced by poverty to emigrate to other lands in the search for survival—there to serve foreign masters. Some were influenced by the "cultural imperialism" that had Italians submissively adopt foreign customs and mannerisms—which, in turn, generated that entire lack of moral cohesion without which Italians slipped into servility and bondage to others.

Some time within the first decade of the twentieth century, all its differences notwithstanding, Italian nationalism began to assume a specific configuration. Without question, one of those who were to mold emergent Italian nationalism was Enrico Corradini—born on 20 July 1865 in the town of Samminiatello di Montelupo near Florence. While still a student, Corradini embarked on a career as a writer—the author of a number of works more literary than political—but by 1902, he was giving expression to an uncertain, if passionate, nationalism that still lacked doctrinal coherence.[24]

In 1903, Corradini founded *Il Regno*, a journal that only briefly endured—characterized by major disagreements among the authors contributing to its pages. It was a journal that, in its own words, was more or less devoted to the moral regeneration of a new nation afflicted with all the disabilities of decadence: anarchism and antinomianism, narcissism and servility. Italy suffered venality and incompetence—suffused with a "putrid decrepitude"—manifest not only in the behaviors of a socialism that would destroy the nation through class conflict, but also in the behaviors of the "Italian bourgeoisie" that while it "ruled and governed," was apparently prepared to "bring to earth all the high values of humankind and the nation."[25]

In that same year, Giuseppe Prezzolini and Giovanni Papini, who had collaborated with Corradini in the founding of *Il Regno*, founded *Leonardo*, a political journal welcomed by Corradini as another voice devoted to "restoring to Italy its consciousness as a great nation"—a consciousness necessary not only for the "prosperity and dignity of the

---

[23] See Gioacchino Volpe, *Italia moderna 1910/1914* (Florence: Sansoni, 1973), pp. 274–313.

[24] See the relatively extensive discussion of Corradini's literary works in Giacomo Pavoni, *Enrico Corradini nella vita nazionale e nel giornalismo* (Rome: Pinciana, n.d.).

[25] Ibid., pp. 36 and 37.

fatherland, but for that of the working class as well."[26] These were generic themes—supported at that time by notables such as Benedetto Croce—that were to remain central to Italian nationalism as it matured in the conferences and through the journals so abundant throughout the first two decades of the twentieth century.

Commencing in December 1908, Prezzolini edited *La Voce*, a journal of ideas that sought to bring together various groups and individuals committed to "the renewal of Italy, . . . to the creation of a new environment of truth, of sincerity, and of realism—to study the problems of the new generation."[27] In the discussions, conferences, polemics, and exchanges that followed, Italian nationalism began to take on the character of a political movement.

It had already become evident that nationalists of all varieties sought the rapid economic development of the peninsula.[28] That was the necessary condition for Italy's resumption of its proper place in the community of nations. In a discourse delivered in 1904, and subsequently elaborated upon, Papini identified three stages in the evolution of Italian nationalism: the first, from Dante to Leopardi was almost exclusively poetic; the second, from Gioberti to Mazzini was philosophical; and the third—that which had begun with the then-new century—was economic.[29]

What the new nationalism—the nationalism of rapid industrial development—required was a transformation of the psychology of Italians. No longer were Italians to be talkers, the spinners of phrases. They were to become *serious*, passionately devoted to *performance*. They were to develop a proper sense of time—like the industrial English and the industrializing Germans. To the exclusion of fine phrases that have as their referent a vague and misty humanism, Italians were to recognize in the nation that organic reality in which all interests, material and moral, were rooted. For Papini, neither the "proletariat" nor the "bourgeoisie" represented self-sufficient entities that could survive or prosper without the other. The working classes and the entrepreneurial bourgeoisie were all united in the concrete actuality of the historic nation—for which they must be prepared to sacrifice immediate for more substantial, more enduring, more profound, and more ethical future benefits.

---

[26] As cited in Piero Buscaroli, "Introduction," in Giovanni Papini and Giuseppe Prezzolini, *Vecchio e nuovo nazionalismo* (1914; reprint, Rome: Volpe, 1967), p. 2.

[27] Giuseppe Prezzolini, *L'Italiano inutile* (Florence: Vallecchi, 1964), p. 155.

[28] Corradini had spoken of the necessity of industrializing the peninsula in his novels; see the discussion in Pavoni, *Enrico Corradini*, pp. 76–77.

[29] Giovanni Papini, "L'Italia rinasce," in Papini and Prezzolini, *Vecchio e nuovo nazionalismo*, pp. 125–31; see the account in Paola Maria Arcari, *Le elaborazioni della dottrina politica nazionale fra l'unità e l'intervento (1870–1914)* (Florence: Marzocco, 1934–39), vol. 1, chap. 2.

Because the tasks faced by the new nation would be so onerous and demanding, they required a committed and heroic minority prepared to assume responsibility. Papini reminded his audience that everything known concerning the political life of humankind indicated that everywhere and throughout time, minorities have effectively ruled. Gaetano Mosca and Vilfredo Pareto had made the case. For all the grand words of democratic theory, only aristocracies, of one sort or another, govern communities. The distinction is not between democratic and aristocratic rule; it is between the rule of incompetents and brigands and an *epistemocracy*—rule by those who are informed and competent.

In a resurgent Italy, Papini argued, it would be an aristocracy that would address the problems of forced emigration by its citizens. In such an Italy, it would be a leadership that understood that the nation lacked both domestic capital and essential raw materials for industrial development. Whatever the natural obstacles, however, that leadership would create a government that would accelerate the creation of an industrial base adequate to support the geographic, cultural, economic, and political expansion of a regenerate nation.[30]

These were the essentials of the new Italian nationalism that began to take shape between the turn of the new century and 1913. It was a doctrinal nationalism that gradually emerged primarily, but not exclusively, out of the thought of Enrico Corradini. As early as 1902, he had given expression to the sociological premises that he understood to be the intellectual foundations of his nationalism. He had argued that all the studies of animal and human behavior supported the empirical claim that virtually all communities composed of sentient creatures are structured by a sentiment of in-group amity and out-group enmity—and that wherever it was found that a community was no longer informed by such sentiments, that community was decadent—veritably moribund. Any community that had lost its sense of unity, that was riven by internal conflict, Corradini maintained, was threatened with extinction. As a consequence, he was prepared to argue that the Marxist insistence on "class struggle" within communities heralded not liberating revolution, but threatened such communities with dissolution. Corradini understood domestic class struggle as symptomatic of imminent extinction.[31]

Corradini argued that everything we know of group dynamics indicated that the sense of community that sustained the nation was a product of geography, of enduring interaction over time, and an abiding sense of

---

[30] See Papini, "Un programma nazionalista," in Papini and Prezzolini, *Vecchio e nuovo nazionalismo*, pp. 1–36.

[31] Enrico Corradini, "Le opinioni degli uomini e i fatti dell'uomo," *Discorsi politici (1902–1923)* (Florence: Vallecchi, 1923, hereafter *DP*), pp. 24–25.

similarity—in language, art, politics, and collective enterprise—sustained through sympathy, mimicry, and instruction. A nation was an association of "similars" united in a consciousness of a collective mission.[32] It was "the maximum unity of the maximum number of similars," at any given historic period, pursuing a collective goal that promised the fulfillment of deeply felt communal needs.

Such a community of similars was vital as long as it was animated by a sense of mission, a "faith and an obedience . . . to a task to complete, to a destiny as yet uncertain."[33] This was as true for tribes, clans, federations, city-states, and empires as it was for modern nations.[34] The nationalism of Italy at the beginning of the twentieth century, Corradini argued, was an expression of that universal faith and that general psychological disposition to obey, to sacrifice, and to commit oneself to the fulfillment of a collective mission that was a function of the individual's involvement in an historic "community of destiny."[35]

It was obvious that the unity implied in such convictions would make both the pure "proletarianism" and the class struggle advocated by Italian Marxists, at that time, manifestly dysfunctional in terms of the nation's future. Given those assessments, Corradini, by 1909, felt compelled to address the complex and emotional issue of the role that any form of socialism might play in the nationalist resurgence of Italy. Socialism, with the advent of mass politics, had become a critical issue.

In December 1909,[36] Corradini outlined the elements of a kind of Italian syndicalism that he conceived might be fully compatible with the nationalism for which he had become spokesman. As distinct from the reformist socialism of the Italian Socialist Party, Corradini occupied himself with the antitraditional revolutionary socialism of Italian syndicalism—as it articulated itself under the influence of French revolutionaries. Many features of Italian syndicalism attracted Corradini. First of all, syndicalism gave expression to the exacerbated moralism of Georges Sorel.[37]

Corradini early found himself opposed to the "positivism" that had settled down on Italian thought by the turn of the century. That positivism

[32] See the discussion in Corradini, *L'unità e la potenza delle nazioni* (Florence: Valecchi, 1922), pp. 61–62.

[33] Corradini, "La vita nazionale," in *DP*, pp. 36–40.

[34] See the discussion in Corradini, *L'ombra della vita* (Naples: Ricciardi, 1908), pp. 281, 285–87.

[35] Corradini, "Le nazioni proletarie e il nazionalismo," in *DP*, pp. 113–18.

[36] Corradini, "Sindacalismo, nazionalismo, imperialismo," in *DP*, pp. 53–69.

[37] See Emile Pouget, *Les Bases du Syndicalisme* (Paris: L'Emancipatrice, n.d.); Arturo Labriola, "Le Syndicalisme et le Socialisme en Italie," in *Syndicalisme et Socialisme* (Paris: Marcel Rivière, 1908); Emile Pouget, *Le Syndicat* (Paris: L'Emancipatrice, n.d.); Georges Guy-Grand, *La Philosophie Syndicaliste* (Paris: Grasset, 1911); Louis Levine, *Syndicalism in France* (New York: Columbia University, 1914).

was a form of *scientism* that conceived *all* issues subject to scientific resolution.[38] What the positivists considered "metaphysics"—moral inquiry,
theology, any speculation on philosophical "meaning"—was dismissed as
simple nonsense. Religion was disparaged as the preoccupation of old
women—and philosophical speculation was considered nothing more
than reflections on empty concerns.[39]

Corradini saw the "traditional" Marxism of the orthodox socialists—
with its economic determinism and its "dialectical materialism"—as representative of the then-prevalent and objectionable scientism. For orthodox Marxists, moral concerns and philosophical principles were simply
derivatives of the "earthy" economic base of contemporary society. They
allowed little space for the influence of moral or intellectual factors.

Corradini, like the syndicalists of his time, was convinced that moral
sentiments and philosophical convictions animated the vast majority of
political actors—and served a critical function in the progression of historic events. To attempt to reduce those sentiments and convictions to the
derivative effect of economic determinants was to misunderstand the very
nature of human beings as well as history itself. Corradini held that
human beings are disposed to give themselves over to causes that make
their lives worthwhile—causes that found expression in what Sorel identified as "myths."[40]

"Myths," for Corradini and the syndicalists, were not untruths. They
were broad anticipations of a chosen future—a vision for which human
beings were prepared to sacrifice, for which they were prepared to labor,
and for which, if necessary, they were prepared to die.[41] They were understood to be critical motivating elements in the mobilization of "masses,"
a mobilization necessary for the realization of political purpose.

It was within that conception of political reality that both nationalists
and syndicalists devoted their intellectual energies in assessing the character of the psychology of crowds: how assemblies were mobilized and how
their belief systems were influenced. Within the first decade of the twentieth century, both nationalists and syndicalists sought to understand the
psychology of associated life.

Revolutionary syndicalists like A. O. Olivetti and Paolo Orano both
published substantial works on the psychology of crowds during the first

---

[38] See, for example, E. Troilo, *Idee e ideali del positivismo* (Rome: Voghera, 1909).

[39] See the discussion in A. James Gregor, *Giovanni Gentile: Philosopher of Fascism* (New
Brunswick, N.J.: Transaction Press, 2001), chaps. 1 and 2.

[40] See the discussion in Corradini, *L'unità e la potenza delle nazioni* (Florence: Vallecchi,
1922), pp. 37–40.

[41] For a more ample account of the role of "myth" and the mobilization of "masses," see
A. James Gregor, *The Ideology of Fascism: The Rationale of Totalitarianism* (New York:
Free Press, 1969), pp. 46–71.

years of the century. They undertook inquiries into the nature of the psychology of life lived in common, and how collective psychology might be influenced by *meneurs*—leaders.[42] Scipio Sighele, one of the intellectual leaders of the nationalists at that time, had similarly produced substantial works devoted to the same issues.[43]

Both syndicalists and nationalists recognized that collective psychology informed political behavior. Both sought to understand the processes involved. Traditional Marxism had not provided an account of how revolutions proceeded—how masses were moved to revolutionary enterprise. Marxism had not spoken of the role of leaders in the mobilization of masses. It did not address itself to the role of "great men," the "heroes" of history—and what factors entered into their program of historic change.

Conversely, syndicalists and nationalists sought to engineer revolution by invoking the sentiments of humans living in association. Both acknowledged that the task involved understanding problems that animated humans as group animals. What both syndicalists and nationalists sought to understand was the nature and the scope of influence excercized by suggestion and imitation among similars living a life in common—what externalities influenced political actors. They tried to appreciate the role of those externalities, the regularities governing the psychology of masses, and the educative role of "heroes" in history. They understood the processes as falling somewhere between the conceptions of Herbert Spencer and Ralph Waldo Emerson.[44]

In effect, there were many intellectual affinities that reduced the political distance between the nationalists and the revolutionary syndicalists at the turn of the twentieth century. Corradini argued that everything indicated that the distance between the right and the left could be negotiated. Their affinities were clear.

It was within that context, by 1910,[45] that Corradini was prepared to applaud the antidemocratic and antiparliamentarian predispositions of the radical Marxist syndicalists. Like the syndicalists, Corradini saw parliamentarianism as an institution designed to frustrate the accomplishment of great tasks—to corrupt the political consciousness of masses. In parliamentary systems, he argued, parties and factions served parochial interests, and used the representative body of the nation as an arena in which they negotiated their tawdry compromises. Within parliamentary

[42] See, for example, A. O. Olivetti, "Il problema della folla," *Nuova Antologia* 38, no. 761 (1 September 1903), pp. 281–91; and Paolo Orano, *La psicologia sociale* (Bari: Laterza, 1902).

[43] See Scipio Sighele, *La delinquenza settaria* (Milan: Treves, 1897), *Le scienze sociale* (Milan: Vallardi, 1903); and *L'Intelligenza della folla* (Turin: Bocca, 1903).

[44] Sighele, *L'intelligenza della folla*, chap. 4, para. 4.

[45] Corradini, "Principi di nazionalismo," in *DP*, pp. 91–102.

arrangements, none sought to serve the general interests; and none committed themselves to a vision of the nation that would see Italy once again a great power, a founder of a new civilization.

Syndicalists similarly opposed parliamentarianism with all its venality and narrow interests.[46] They sought a revolutionary resolution of the problems that beset their times. Like nationalists, the revolutionary syndicalists understood the nature of politics and the mobilization of masses in terms of the psychology of associated human life. They understood that any historic mission assumed by a collectivity of human beings would have to be supported by an infrangible integrity. The mission of the syndicalists was to discharge the tasks of the "revolution" to which they had committed themselves. The mission of the nationalists was to realize the redemption and rebirth of the historic and millennial Italian nation.

Both movements conceived themselves seeking the fullness of equity and justice. They understood that only through a proletarian or a national revolution might that equity and justice be attained. Revolutionary syndicalists understood that the syndicates, as "communities of destiny," incorporated in themselves that unity of similars essential to the fulfillment of a collective mission—just as nationalists identified the political nation-state as the requisite revolutionary association. What syndicalists failed to appreciate, Corradini argued, was the reality of the function of the *nation* in the contemporary world.[47]

While a firm sense of the unity of similars—the union of laborers in modern industry—was the foundation of what the syndicalists conceived as their community, Corradini argued that such a collective, in isolation, could neither prosper nor survive in the contemporary world. Corradini argued that as long as there were nations, workers would constitute only a functional part of an historic and organic whole.[48] Any *class*, in isolation, could not survive in the contemporary world.

In the world at the beginning of the twentieth century, Corradini maintained, only *nations* could serve as international actors. The world, almost all nationalists argued, was an arena of Darwinian struggle for survival. If Italian workers expected to survive and prosper in such a world, they required entrepreneurs, functionaries, merchants, financiers, intellectuals, educators, and state officials.[49] Once syndicalists understood that, Cor-

---

[46] See the comments by A. O. Olivetti, "Il sindacalismo: Socialismo e sindacalismo," in *Battaglie sindacaliste: Dal sindacalismo al fascismo*, a typescript collection of Olivetti's writings of the period provided by the Olivetti family. The selection is found in the first volume, dated 6 March 1906.

[47] See the entire discussion in Corradini, *L'Ombra della vita*, pp. 285–87.

[48] Corradini, "Le nuove dottrine nazionali e il rinnovamento spirituale," in *DP*, pp. 200, 203.

[49] Corradini, "Nazionalismo e socialismo," in *DP*, pp. 214–15, 218–19, 220.

radini concluded, they could only become advocates and practitioners of a *national syndicalism*—a revolutionary syndicalism that nationalists could wholeheartedly support.

Like most "new" nationalists, and revolutionary syndicalists, Corradini anticipated the emergence of a revolutionary elite in Italy—an aristocracy of commitment and competence—that would shepherd the nation from its status as an international inferior to that of a "great power." The revolutionary syndicalists, like the nationalists, sought just such an elite in their own search for proletarian justice.

Corradini maintained that the syndicalists fully understood the character of intact and vital communities. They understood that only the bonding of similars, united in a mission against opponents, might assure success in external conflict. Syndicalists, like nationalists, appreciated the fact that vital communities were invariably led by effective elites—an aristocracy of purpose—capable of transforming the psychology of masses.[50] More than that, syndicalists, like nationalists, sought justice in a world in which injustice was all but universal.

The political aristocracy anticipated by the syndicalists was an aristocracy that would lead the working-class movement to victory against a complacent and ineffectual ruling class—an effete ruling class no longer possessed of the qualities of leadership. Corradini argued that the syndicalists were essentially correct in their assessment of the Italian political scene.

Italy required an elite of strength, competence, and courage. Such an elite was not to be found among the orthodox Marxists of the Italian Socialist party. It was not to be found among the established Italian middle class. What was required was a new political class, an elite that would assume control of the peninsula through a "rotation of elites." Such a rotation, anticipated by Vilfredo Pareto, would bring forward a small minority of persons committed to the creation of a new Italy—a class that understood accelerated productivity, antidemocratic strength in political leadership, and an aggressive pursuit of the nation's interests. It would be the aristocracy of an emergent Italy. It would be an aristocracy of heroic demeanor, cognizant of the fact that Italy's late development would require sacrifice, discipline, and enterprise of almost preternatural character.[51]

Given such a conception of the environment in which both syndicalists and nationalists were obliged to operate, syndicalists had no more sympathy for parliamentary compromise and incompetence than had the nationalists. Both sought elites that would accomplish great things, without compromise and without negotiation, committed to goals that would shape the modern world. Syndicalists sought revolution by Italy's workers

---

[50] See the discussion in Corradini, *Il volere d'Italia* (Naples: Perrella, 1911), pp. 161–65.
[51] Corradini, "Le nazioni proletarie e il nazionalismo," in *DP*, pp. 113–18.

in the service of world proletarian revolution. Corradini sought a revolution by all Italians in the service of Italy as a "proletarian nation."[52]

Corradini argued that "proletarianism" had some singular merits in the Italian environment. He reminded the domestic leaders of the proletariat that for a quarter of a century Italian workers had been forced to leave their homeland to work in lands more prosperous—"capitalist" lands. Emigrant Italian workers throughout the advanced industrial nations were compelled to submit to the overlordship of foreign capitalists in order to simply survive.[53]

Corradini suggested that the distinctions that the syndicalists recognized within Italy were much more emphatic outside of Italy. If domestic capitalists were seen as oppressors, they were of negligible consequence compared to the world dominance of the capitalists of the advanced industrial nations. The advanced capitalist nations maintained an abiding and exacting control over an impoverished "proletarian" Italy. Even if a proletarian class revolution overthrew Italy's impoverished bourgeoisie, Italy itself would remain a proletarian nation subject to the dominance of foreign "plutocracies."

Corradini anticipated that thinking syndicalists would inevitably recognize the reality of the modern world. Syndicalism, with its call to discipline, sacrifice, and heroism, could only eventually become a *national* syndicalism and become a collateral support for revolutionary nationalism. Corradini, as early as 1909–11, anticipated an ultimate coming together of both revolutionary movements.

Given these notions, Corradini went further. He suggested that the entire conception of "class warfare," advocated by revolutionary syndicalists, had an appropriate referent in the modern world—not a counterproductive warfare between elements of the same nation—but a warfare of "proletarian nations" against the "plutocracies."[54] Corradini argued that emergent nations, those characterized by delayed industrial development—proletarian nations—found themselves victims of those nations that had already acceded to the level of advanced industrialization—plutocratic nations. Those nations suffering delayed industrial development found themselves subject to the impostures of those more advanced.

Corradini maintained that all the trade and financial infrastructure of the modern world was controlled by the plutocracies. The result was the threat of perpetual inferiority for those proletarian nations that were late

---

[52] Corradini, *Il volere d'Italia*, pp. 205–7.

[53] See the discussion in Corradini's *La patria lontana* (Milan: Treves, 1910); and the commentary in Pavoni, *Enrico Corradini nella vita nazionale e nel giornalismo*, pp. 47–66.

[54] Pavoni, *Enrico Corradini*, pp. 93, 100, "Le nazioni proletarie e il nazionalism," in *DP*, pp. 104–18; and "Nazionalismo e democrazia," in *DP*, p. 161.

in achieving industrial development.[55] Almost from the very commencement of his political activity, Corradini had insisted on the distinction between "proletarian" and "plutocratic" nations.[56]

Corradini contended that, given those conditions, the less developed nations were condemned to a threat of perpetual dependency on the plutocracies.[57] England would forever command the seas and the financial markets—and France would dominate the Continent with its culture and its armed forces. Italy, capital and resource deficient,[58] would subsist on the sufferance of wealthy nations. It would remain forever an economic and cultural colony of its "superiors." "Rich nations" would forever dominate "proletarian Italy."

For Corradini, success in the international class war he anticipated required a readiness to sacrifice on the part of Italians—part of the world's proletariat—a readiness to commit themselves to disciplined struggle against their oppressors. Italians must be prepared, he argued, to assume the qualities of a "soldier-producer"—a readiness to die for their commitments and an equal readiness to undertake protracted sacrificial labor in order to fashion the material base for the resurgent nation.[59]

By 1910, Italian nationalism had organized itself in the Associazione nationalista italiano (ANI), an association of like-minded intellectuals who saw Italy's salvation in rapid industrial and economic development—a development that would insulate it from the exactions of the plutocracies: economic exploitation, cultural "imperialism," and military subordination.[60] A "revitalized" entrepreneurial class was understood as necessary to provide the antecedent essential to a nation in the process of rebirth.

The argument was that the industrial development of Italy was the "historic task" of the nation's entrepreneurial middle class—a class that had, throughout the years of the Risorgimento, failed its mission. For the nationalists, a reawakening of the sense of responsibility among the bourgeoisie was essential to the fulfillment of the tasks of Italy's Risorgimento. Together with a political aristocracy conscious of the regenerative tasks that faced the nation, Italy required an industrial middle class capable of discharging the economic responsibilities of the new age.[61] As preconditions, those responsibilities would necessitate the intregration of all pro-

---

[55] See Corradini, "Nazionalismo e socialismo," in *DP*, pp. 217, 218, 222, 227.

[56] See Pavoni, *Enrico Corradini*, pp. 110–11.

[57] Corradini, "Le nazioni proletarie e il nazionalism," in *DP*, p. 109.

[58] Corradini, *L'Ora di Tripoli* (Milan: Treves, 1911), pp. 239–41.

[59] Corradini, "La morale della guerra," in *DP*, pp. 141–42, 149.

[60] Arcari, *Le elaborazioni della dottrina politica nazionale*, vol. 2, pp. 404–77.

[61] See the entire discussion in Vincenzo Amoruso, *Il sindacalismo di Enrico Corradini* (Palermo: Società Editrice Orazio Fiorenza, 1929), pp. 99–140.

ductive elements in a juridical national union in which workers' organizations would be provided legal recognition on a par with the organizations of entrepreneurs. Labor disputes would be resolved—to the exclusion of work stoppages—through arbitration that would recognize the ultimate unity of interests between labor and capital enterprise.

What Corradini alluded to was a sort of "corporativism" in which the productive elements of modern society would be politically organized under the aegis of the state. The goal was the restoration of Italy to the ranks of the "great powers." That could be accomplished only by uniting the energies of the nation's working classes and its entrepreneurs together with the authority of the state.

By 1910, Italian nationalism had taken on almost all the characteristics that would follow it into Fascism. Mario Viana had founded the journal *Tricolore*, in Turin, a publication that advocated the fusion of revolutionary syndicalism and nationalism. Paolo Orano had assumed the responsibilities of editing the journal *La Lupa*[62] and sought the union of syndicalism and nationalism in some form of national syndicalism.

The first nationalist congress opened in Florence on 4 December 1910. While Scipio Sighele was chosen president, in retrospect it is clear that Corradini dominated the proceedings. It was he who argued that the only revolutionary movements in retrograde Italy were the nationalists and the revolutionary syndicalists. Syndicalists like A. O. Olivetti, Orano, and Massimo Rocca acknowledged the affinities shared by the two movements, a fact that heralded their ultimate union.

In 1911, Italy entered into protracted political and diplomatic crises. The French, British, and Germans devoted much of their international attention to the Turkish provinces of Tripolitania and Cyrenaica—that together composed the North African territory of Libya. Italy had negotiated an agreement with France, in 1899, that anticipated that those provinces would become regions of Italian interest. Italian immigrants had settled in the region, and Italy sought to protect them. After 1905, it was no longer clear that France would respect Italy's interests in North Africa. In July 1911, when France's accession to control over Morocco was realized, Italy proceeded to move to protect her interests in Tripolitania.

On 30 September 1911, Italy declared war on Turkey. Nationalists quickly supported the enterprise. The nationalist journal, *Idea Nazionale*, advocated war against Turkey in the pursuit of the nation's interests. With the declaration of war, many Italians identified themselves with the undertaking. Patriotic sentiment found mass expression with which socialists and antinationalists were compelled to deal.

---

[62] See Arcari, *Dottrina politica nazionale*, vol. 3, pp. 96–97.

Even before the war against the Ottoman Empire evoked the spontaneous patriotism that made nationalism an issue, a significant number of
revolutionary syndicalists, including Arturo Labriola, A. O. Olivetti, and
Paolo Orano, had begun to identify backward and impoverished Italy
with a "proletarian" struggle against the established "plutocracies" of
Northern Europe. By 1911, Olivetti alluded to those affinities between
revolutionary syndicalism and nationalism in much the same fashion as
had Corradini.

For Olivetti,[63] both syndicalism and nationalism were "modern" and
"intellectually respectable" revolutionary movements, distinguishing
themselves from the "conservatism" of both reform socialism and the
traditional parliamentary politics of the nation. Both were "collectivistic"
in orientation, recognizing that human beings were creatures inextricably
born and shaped in association, animated by the will and leadership of
those sensitive to the historic needs of any given time.

For syndicalists, all that was derivative of the Marxism with which
they had long been familiar and to which they had committed themselves.
Marx had identified the human being as a *Gemeinwesen*, a "collective
being"—and dismissed the liberal notion of the primacy of individuality
as a counterrevolutionary fiction.

In the *Communist Manifesto*, Marx had spoken of the "theoreticians"
of communism as sharing identical interests with the proletariat, but
seeing farther and with greater clarity. They would constitute a professional intellectual leadership essential to the making of revolution.[64] Seiz-
ing on that idea, syndicalists argued that without the decisive intervention
of such an elite, the working masses would lapse back into the indolence
of compromise and the venal bargaining of trade unionism.

In that sense, both syndicalists and nationalists acknowledged the role
of communitarianism, will, decisiveness, and leadership in the politics of
the time. Like the nationalists, syndicalists sought an aristocracy of commitment—an intransigent elite—incapable of "adapting" to the compromises required by the parliamentary politics of electoral democracy or
class relations in bourgeois circumstances.

Because of their recognition of the decisive role of will and leadership,
Olivetti continued, syndicalists, like nationalists, spoke with the language
of Friedrich Nietzsche and Arthur Schopenhauer. They opposed themselves to the vain and unmanly positivism of the turn of the century that

---

[63] The subsequent discussion is taken from A. O. Olivetti, "Sindacalismo e nazionalismo:
Le due realtà del pensiero contemporaneo," in *Pro e contro Tripoli*, reproduced in *Battaglie
sindacalista* (15 February 1911), pp. 60–67.

[64] See the account in A. James Gregor, *A Survey of Marxism: Problems in Philosophy
and the Theory of History* (New York: Random House, 1965), chap. 6.

conceived human life determined by some set of "immutable laws." Syndicalists, like nationalists, were *voluntarists*, given to the inescapable influence of spirit and moral conviction in the affairs of humankind.

Like nationalists, Olivetti reminded his readers, syndicalists were animated by moral convictions that allowed little compromise. Like nationalists, syndicalists sought an antibourgeois, antitraditional remaking of Italy and Italians. They sought to create a nation of "producers" out of an inert and unresponsive population.

Olivetti argued that what distinguished syndicalists from nationalists was the fact that whatever nationalism there had been among Italians was a by-product of the dominance of bourgeois cultural inculcation. He argued that Italian workers had no fundamental interest in the future of the nation-state. Their interests were tied to the future of the international proletarian revolution and all that it implied.

Nonetheless, in the course of the first decade of the twentieth century, some of the leaders of revolutionary syndicalism transferred their loyalties from Marxist internationalism to the revolutionary nationalism of Corradini. Roberto Forges Davanzati and Maurizio Maraviglia, subsequently to become two of the most important political leaders of nationalism, were recruited at that time. Tommaso Monicelli, who saw the emergence of themes shared by syndicalists and nationalists as the grounds for collaboration, became one of the intellectual leaders of Corradini's publication, *Idea Nazionale*.[65]

By 1913, Italian nationalism had matured into a coherent, comprehensive, and revolutionary doctrine for a "proletarian Italy" that sought redemption and rebirth in a world of international competition dominated by hegemonic "plutocratic powers." It was a doctrine shaped by the influence of some of the most important intellectuals of Europe. References to the thought of Vilfredo Pareto, Gaetano Mosca, Gabriel Tarde, Georges Sorel, Gustave Le Bon and Ludwig Gumplowicz dotted its pages. Before the end of the next decade Giovanni Gentile, by that time, one of the most prominent philosophical thinkers in Europe, was numbered among its advocates.[66]

It was in that year that Italian nationalism attracted yet another intellectual who was to influence not only nationalism as a doctrine, but Fascism as a political regime. In that year Professor Alfredo Rocco abandoned Marxist socialism and the politics of Italy's Radical party, to commit himself to nationalism. He brought with him a formidable intellect and a remarkable sense of politics.

---

[65] De Grand, *The Italian Nationalist Association and the Rise of Fascism in Italy*, p. 21.

[66] See the discussion in A. James Gregor, *Phoenix: Fascism in Our Time* (New Brunswick, N.J.: Transaction, 1999), chap. 5; and Gregor, *Giovanni Gentile: Philosopher of Fascism*.

CHAPTER THREE

Alfredo Rocco and the Elements
of Fascist Doctrine

THE NATIONALIST congress held in Florence in December 1910 provided the opportunity for the expression of many of its doctrinal variants. Many factions made their appearance. There were clear uncertainties concerning what the relationship of the movement to the Roman Catholic Church was to be, as well as how the movement's tentative connection with the radicalism of Italian syndicalism was to be understood. Nonetheless, by the end of the congress a doctrinal statement was put together by Luigi Valli in which a given set of "principles of nationalism" received expression.[1]

In providing his account, Valli followed the directive insights of Enrico Corradini. He correspondingly distinguished Italian nationalism from the *sentiment* of generic Italian patriotism—by defining the former as a substantive *doctrine* committing its followers to a set of relatively specific political behaviors.[2] First and foremost, it was maintained, nationalists were sociologically *collectivists*—seeing the survival and destiny of individuals fundamentally governed by their multifaceted involvement in community. Nationalists were to argue that in the contemporary world, that privileged community in which individuals found security and succor was the nation.

In terms of the social theory of nationalism, its advocates were neither exclusively "primordialists" nor "instrumentalists."[3] They neither held nationalist sentiment to be simply primordial, nor did they conceive it to be learned behavior or the consequence of psychological manipulation by elites.

---

[1] See the ample discussion in Paola Maria Arcari, *Le elaborazioni della dottrina politica nazionale fra l'unità e l'intervento (1870–1914)* (Florence: Marzocco, 1934–39), vol. 2, pp. 606–48.

[2] The following account follows the text in Luigi Valli, "Che cosa è e che cosa vuole il nazionalismo," in Francesco Perfetti, ed., *Il nazionalismo italiano* (Rome: Il Borghese, 1969), pp. 37–58.

[3] Concerning the "primordialist" and "instrumentalist" schools of thought as interpretative strategies in explaining nationalism, see Crawford Young, "The Temple of Ethnicity," *World Politics* 35, no. 4 (July 1983), pp. 652–62.

As has been suggested, Corradini held that collectivist sentiment among human beings was the product of a psychological predisposition that was itself a function of a "primordialist" evolutionary selection. Corradini argued that throughout evolutionary history, individuals inclined to identify with an intact community enjoyed greater survival potential than those who lived solitary lives exposed to the threat of all. The consequence was that human beings, early in evolutionary history, were preselected to identify with an association of similars—to find comfort in their presence and discomfort in their absence.

Such innate dispositions, the argument continued, found expression in a variety of fashions—influenced by surrounding external conditions and given instrumental specificity by *meneurs*—those capable of articulating emotional and reasoned arguments supporting the identification of the individual with one or another specific "community of destiny." Nationalists thus argued that the disposition to identify with a community could find expression in a variety of forms.

Nationalists, as has been suggested, recognized the same psychological dispositions among the revolutionary syndicalists of their time—those who argued for the identification of individuals with their *class* associations. The sense of group identity could, under appropriate circumstances, be transferred to an alternative community. Nationalists were prepared to recognize in the syndicalist advocacy of identification with their cohorts in labor a legitimate expression of psychological collectivism. Nationalists were ready to admit that under a different set of historic circumstances, those same individuals might identify with their tribe, confederation, city-state, or political league.[4]

Given all that, Valli maintained that because of the historic, economic, political, and military realities of the twentieth century, the *nation* was the only agency that could successfully harbor, protect, and foster the well-being of individuals and groups of individuals. In an international environment of constant competition—economic, military, and demographic—the nation, as the privileged community, must be forever prepared to struggle for survival, security, and place.

Success in that struggle required several necessary conditions: (1) an effective material base—an extensive and intensively developed industrial foundation; that, to survive and expand, required (2) state support

---

[4] There are a variety of expressions of very similar analyses among contemporary thinkers; see particularly Arthur Keith, *A New Theory of Human Evolution* (New York: Philosophical Library, 1949); John A. Armstrong, *National before Nationalism* (Chapel Hill: University of North Carolina Press, 1982); Anthony D. Smith, *The Ethnic Origins of Nations* (Oxford: Balckwell, 1986); in this context see Alfredo Rocco's comments in "L'ora del nazionalismo," in *Scritti e discorsi politici* (Milan: Giuffre, 1938. Hereafter cited as *SDP*), 2, pp. 507–8.

through tariff protection for infant industries and subventions for the development of a merchant fleet capable of assuring the expansion of domestic industry through the acquisition of foreign market share. That would begin to provide the wherewithal for (3) a competent and effective military that would allow for (4) the power projection capabilities of a strong, goal-directed, and integral state that, mobilizing all the forces of the nation, would navigate the perils of an extremely dangerous international environment. The state would be "integral" in the sense that all the vital elements of the nation, without prejudice, would be therein seamlessly incorporated.

In such an environment, one would have to be forever prepared for conflict. Such conflict might reveal itself in economic, cultural, or military competition. The nation must be prepared to enter the lists, struggle and prevail in each and every contest. In that respect, Italian nationalists held that their newly reunited nation was fundamentally ill-prepared for survival in the twentieth century.

Italians, it was argued, suffered a flawed national consciousness. The nation was "weak and inert."[5] The schools, where it might be expected that citizens were to be trained in civil and military discipline, were "agnostic"— disinclined toward any expression of healthy nationalism. At the same time, one-sixth of the nation had been forced to emigrate, leaving the homeland in order to simply survive. At the same time, socialists of a variety of persuasions proceeded to alienate perhaps as many nationals in the vain pursuit of a utopian antinational "international proletarian revolution."

Between the first and second congress of the Italian Nationalist Association—1910 and 1912—the ideology of Italian nationalism significantly matured. After the declaration of war against the Ottoman Turks in 1911, the nation had indifferently, if with some success, pursued war in North Africa. Whatever the success, nationalist theoreticians, in general, were dissatisfied. There was a demand that the nation be more assertive, that the military be made more effective, that Italy pursue its material and "spiritual" interests with more determination.

At the same time, between 1910 and 1912, Italian nationalism fractured on the issue of its relationship with the Catholic Church, and that of the role of "democracy" in the expanding movement. Valli himself and Scipio Sighele both insisted that the movement invest itself in some form of "democracy." For all that, those nationalists who imagined that democracy might be a constituent of an effective nationalism soon found themselves isolated in the ranks. Between 1912 and the nationalist congress in Milan in 1914, both Valli and Sighele, together with hundreds of others, absented themselves from the increasingly antidemocratic, imperialistic

---

[5] Valli, "Che cosa è e che cosa vuole il nazionalismo," p. 46.

Corradinian majority of the Nationalist Association.[6] For the Corradini-ans, democracy had demonstrated its inefficacy in dealing both with economic competition and armed conflict. Italian parliamentary democracy identified itself with economic liberalism—a commitment to free markets and international competition that only served to demonstrate the manifest disabilities that attended the nation's attempt to compete with better-established and more-advanced industrial nations. More than that, political democracy had shown its tendential socialist bias by supporting domestic welfare programs at the expense of the nation's productivity. The discriminatory distribution of material benefits tended to undermine the collective effort calculated to accumulate the capital necessary for production. More than that, political democracy's individualistic bias prejudiced the integral unity of the nation.

Nationalists argued that *distributionistic* domestic policies weakened the capital accumulation and *productivistic* essentials of a sound economic policy. For a nation that was resource and capital poor, "equitable distribution," the distribution of material benefits to those who would employ them for simple consumption, reduced the availability of resources for production. It signaled a failure to accumulate resources that would sustain and foster the development of essential infrastructure.

Political democracy had shown itself incapable of pursuing all the potential delivered to Italy as a new nation after the victory in Tripoli. With its "populist," individualistic, and distributionistic politics, it had domestically undermined capital and resource accumulation, essential to the resolution of the nation's critical developmental problems. For the Corradinians, Italian nationalism was to be antiparliamentarian, antidemocratic, collectivistic, and expansionist—with "expansionism" predicated on rapid capital accumulation and industrial growth. Only in such fashion might Italy support and enhance its ability to acquire increasing external market shares, exercize cultural influence, as well as fuel irredentist and colonialist territorial expansion.

By 1913, the Italian Nationalist Association enlisted Professor Alfredo Rocco into its ranks. Born in Naples on the ninth of September 1875—by the time he joined the Association, Rocco was a scholar recognized for his expertise in commercial and financial law. At twenty-four, he served as professor at Urbino and Macerata—ultimately, at thirty-eight, to serve as professor of commercial law at the University of Padua, to be recognized as a scholar of considerable reputation.[7]

---

[6] Ronald S. Cunsolo, *Italian Nationalism: From Its Origins to World War II* (Malabar, Fl.: Robert E. Krieger, 1990), p. 111.

[7] Nazareno Mezzetti, *Alfredo Rocco nella dottrina e nel diritto della rivoluzione fascista* (Rome: Pinciana, 1930), p. 35.

As a very young man, Rocco had flirted with traditional Italian social-ism—and had briefly enlisted in the Italian Radical party.[8] Immediately before the nationalist congress in Rome in 1914, he enscribed himself a member of the Nationalist Association.[9] He was to give explicit expression to Italian nationalism in the form of a theory of the state—that, in its time and in modified form, was to inform Mussolini's Fascism.[10]

By the time of his entry into the ranks of Italian nationalism, Rocco had not only accepted the essentials of the Corradinian view of the contemporary world; he had given full articulation to a program of national economic regeneration. It was based on a conviction that late industrial development in the modern world was necessarily beset by critical and disabling difficulties.

Rocco argued that because Italy had reunified late, and had begun its industrial development equally late, it faced special infirmities.[11] Unlike other European nations, Italy had commenced its process of growth after Great Britain, France, and Germany had established themselves as expansive, "imperialist" powers. Although only recently united, Germany had begun its industrial growth early in the nineteenth century.

Not only had Italy united itself as a sovereign nation late; it possessed little in the way of material or capital resources to sustain development. It had embarked on indigenous industrial development only late in the nineteenth century. By the time of the first decade of the twentieth century, its per capita productivity was less than one-fifth that of Great Britain.

As a consequence of its disabilities, Rocco argued, Italy was being systematically plundered by the advanced industrial "plutocracies." English, French, and German investment, by repatriating profit from loans and investments, was depleting the peninsula of its capital resources. Furthermore, the established economies were luring Italian labor to service their needs. Outmigration was bleeding a developing Italy of its labor. Together with all that, the advanced industrial powers were undermining the native culture of the peninsula. Foreign cultural influences were everywhere, and more often than not, more sought after by a passive population than those that were indigenous.

---

[8] See the account in Paolo Ungari, *Alfredo Rocco e l'ideologia giuridica del fascismo* (Brescia: Morcelliana, 1963), pp. 29, n. 15; and Mezzetti, *Alfredo Rocco*, p. 42.

[9] At the end of December 1913, Corradini specifically referred to Rocco's adherence to nationalism. Corradini, "Liberali e nazionalisti," in *Discorsi politici (1902–1923)* (Florence: Vallecchi, 1923), p. 188.

[10] See Alexander J. De Grand, *The Italian Nationalist Association and the Rise of Fascism in Italy* (Lincoln: University of Nebraska Press, 1978), p. 48.

[11] The following account is taken from Alfredo Rocco, "Cause remote e prossime della crisi dei partiti italiani"; "Il problema economico italiano"; and "Economia liberale, economia socialista, ed economia nazionale," in *SDP*, vol. 1, pp. 5–58.

Cultural "imperialism" manifested itself in a variety of pernicious fashions. Rocco argued that because of their relatively unique histories in a struggle against monarchial absolutism, the advanced industrial nations of Europe had committed themselves to a form of exaggerated political individualism. However efficacious that might have been in the struggle against monarchial absolutism in those environments, political individualism, when transferred to late developers like Italy, did them a grievous disservice. Political individualism made an effective defense of a recently reunited political community extremely difficult. Nations that did not enjoy a tradition of political unity suffered in terms of national consciousness when significantly influenced by the culture of emphatic individualism. For Rocco, nations that had undertaken political and economic development late faced very special handicaps.

Burdened by political individualism, those late-developing nations that found themselves in competition with early developers could not mobilize domestic forces to the tasks of solidarity and production. Fragmented by parliamentary factionalism, the uncertainties of government response to clientalistic influences, a "democratic" state could hardly serve the collective interests of the emerging nation.[12]

Individuals who exclusively sought their personal well-being, to the exclusion of all else, were not equipped to defend their community or sacrifice in its enterprise. If the irreducible concerns of the individual were personal happiness and personal advantage, it was difficult to imagine that the individual might be marshaled to the defense of the collectivity in the contest with plutocratic states—or to the arduous labor required by intensive and extensive industrial development.

If the community were required by circumstances to embark on rapid economic and industrial development, it would be difficult to imagine that such a program could enlist each individual's enterprise if personal well-being and welfare were his or her only motivations. Philosophical individualism, and its expansive civil rights, made the process of political and economic growth particularly difficult for late-developing nations.

Almost immediately upon his accession to membership in the Nationalist Association, Rocco brought considerable theoretical depth to its doctrine. Evident in his exposition were the argued insights of Friedrich List, the mid-nineteenth-century German developmental economist.[13] List, an

---

[12] See the discussion in Rocco, "L'insufficienza dello state," *SDP*, vol. 1, pp. 311–15.

[13] See Rocco, "Economia liberale, economia socialista, ed economia nazionale," *SDP*, 1, pp. 40, 47; Mezzetti, *Alfredo Rocco*, p. 28. List exercised notable influence on the ideas that governed the economic development of both Germany and the United States. See the introduction to the English translation of 1916. Friedrich List, *The National System of Political Economy* (New York; Longmans, Green and Co., 1916, a translation of the 1844 German edition).

early contemporary of Karl Marx,[14] had argued, in contradistinction to the prevailing free trade convictions of the time, that any economic policy not predicated on the preeminent collective interests of the nation invariably betrayed that nation's long-term interests in pursuit of the immediate benefits of living individuals. List, in effect, argued against economic liberalism as an initial strategy for late-developing nations.

Rocco, following List, maintained that those nations that had already industrialized could very well allow economic liberalism to dictate national policy. It was a policy almost exclusively calculated to deliver material advantage to individuals, and special interest groups, rather than to support national enterprise. It was not the case that a "hidden hand" integrated the interests of individuals with those of a larger community. An industrially developed economy might function reasonably well under a laissez-faire regime—since it had already achieved the abundance that allowed it to satisfy individual demands. In such an established industrial economy, steadily increasing consumption would provide the escalating effective demand that would supply a steady profit stream for the continuously expanding industrial base.

In a marginally developed system, Rocco argued, a disposition to increase general consumption would deplete potential capital resources.[15] What a developing system required was not a rising or "more equitable" rate of consumption, but an increasing measure of saving, essential for rapid infrastructural, industrial, and technological development, the necessary condition for the commercial, financial, industrial, agricultural, and military expansion of a new nation prepared to compete with those established plutocracies with which it was forced to contend.

In the twentieth century, newly developing nations were not faced with a landed aristocracy disposed to dissipate profit—extracted from agriculture—in conspicuous consumption. Emerging industrial nations hosted a class of entrepreneurs prepared to reinvest the bulk of their profit in rapidly expanding infant industries. It was characteristic of an emerging capitalist class, Rocco maintained, that its members display a personal frugality that permits the resource accumulation necessary for the construction of an infrastructure necessary for broad-based development.

With those arguments, Rocco reinforced the nationalist opposition to political individualism, economic liberalism, and Marxian socialism. With respect to socialism, he specifically argued that its entire program predicated on the "equitable" distribution of "surplus value"—presumably "extorted" from the proletariat—would inevitably diminish the rate

---

[14] See Roman Szporluk, *Communism and Nationalism: Karl Marx versus Friedrich List* (New York: Oxford University Press, 1988).

[15] See Rocco, "Il problema economico italiano," in *SDP*, vol. 1, pp. 14–15.

of capital accumulation essential to rapid economic and industrial growth of developmental latecomers. Since domestic commodity production could hardly be well established in such circumstances, any "equitable" distribution of purchasing power would predictably see capital dissipated in the purchase of foreign goods.

At the very center of Rocco's account were all the elements of what had already found expression in List's "theory of the productive forces" (*Theorie der produktiven Kräfte*).[16] List had argued that the fate of nations was substantially influenced, if not determined, by the development of its productive forces—and that development was contingent on those factors rehearsed by Rocco.

Young nations, List had further argued, were significantly disadvantaged in the international competition with those already established. Established nations had every reason to foster "cosmopolitan," or free trade, orientations. Access to market supplements and investment opportunities outside the metropolitan nation were critical to the rising profit levels necessary to sustain the expanded reproductive cycles of advanced industry. "Free trade" and "free markets" served an instrumental purpose in an economic system predicated on the already accomplished extensive and intensive development of productive forces.

For less-developed nations, List admonished, it was necessary to generate, foster, and sustain the "courage to believe in a grand national future and with such a faith to march forward with irrepressible national spirit." With the strength born of that courage and that faith, less-developed nations were required to bring together all the spiritual and material assets required to provide the preconditions and fashion the infrastructure necessary for rapid industrial development and economic growth.[17] Should they be unable to mobilize those energies required for such tasks, the denizens of less-developed, agrarian nations were condemned to simple agricultural pursuits, "dullness of mind, awkwardness of body, obstinate adherence to old notions, customs, methods and processes, want of culture, of prosperity, and of liberty." Such people were condemned to poverty and powerlessness. "Who had not learned," List went on, ". . . how greatly the existence, the independence, and the strength of the nation depends on its possession of a manufacturing power of its own, developed in all its branches."[18] Because of their parlous circumstances in the mod-

---

[16] See the entire discussion in Hartfrid Voss's introduction to Friedrich List, *Kräfte und Mächte: Grundsätze-Lehren-Gedanken* (Munich: Wilhelm Langewiesche-Brandt, 1942), with particular reference to p. 23 for the identification of List's ideas as a "theory of productive forces."

[17] Voss, in List, *Kräfte und Mächte*, pp. 10–13.

[18] Friedrich List, *The National System of Political Economy* (London: Longmans, Green, 1916), pp. 159, 320.

ern world of reasonably well developed industrial competitors, less-developed nations were compelled to create a strong, centralized government capable of marshaling all the community's material and spiritual forces if it were to accomplish the rapid development of its infrastructure, its agriculture, and its industries.

In his discussion of the economic and political development of Italy, for example, List rehearsed a catalog of conditions necessary to husband that community through the phases of "slavery and serfdom, of barbarism and superstition, of national disunity and of caste privileges" to national unity, the acknowledgment that collective interests might enjoy precedence over those of the individual, until there was a clear onset of development. In the process, List anticipated periods of antiliberal authoritarianism of indeterminate duration. Those periods would provide the stability, the integrity, and the order, the security of property and the inculcation of institutional efficiencies essential to rapid economic growth and industrial expansion.[19]

List's "theory of the productive forces" clearly conceived *productivity* to be at the center of human history. Those nations that had achieved a level of industrial development capable of providing them power projection capabilities were nations that exercised superior political and cultural influence over those less developed. Given their greater productive capability, their influence radiated outward to overwhelm and invest those regions as yet less developed. Until less-developed nations matured to the point where they could effectively compete with those more industrially developed, they were destined to play only tangential roles in the drama of human history.

List's conception of the dynamics of human history shared some critical similarities with that of traditional Marxism. Karl Marx entertained a notion of the role of "productive forces" in the course of human development. The central conviction of historical materialism was that human history proceeded on the energy supplied by the growth of productive forces. When a community's "material productive forces" found themselves throttled by confining "productive relations," revolution ensued—freeing the productive forces to recommence an increased tempo of output.

When productivity expanded, communities projected their power over lesser-developed regions. List, Marx, and Engels had all noted what was a self-evident phenomenon in an environment characterized by the industrial revolution. England's inroads into Africa and Asia were the substance of the diplomatic, military, and colonial history of the nineteenth century. For Marx and Engels such a process was simply part of the "logic of history." For List, they constituted a political program.

[19] Ibid., pp. 266–68.

All found the methods of penetration by the advanced industrial powers objectionable, but all recognized that such incursions "served the ends of progress." Marx reflected on the fact that while the British exploited India and China for their own purposes, they also served the ultimate ends of progress. He maintained that the British "had a double mission in India: one destructive and the other regenerating—the annihilation of old Asiatic society, and laying the material foundation of Western society in Asia."[20] Driven by their search for profit, the British would advance "civilization." Marx insisted that British imperialism had precipitated "social revolution" in Asia; imperialism "was the unconscious tool of history."[21] The consequence could only be massive incentives for the rapid economic and industrial development of the subcontinent.

Engels gave expression to the same concepts in his treatment of French imperialism in North Africa. Commenting on the Bedouin resistence to French rule, Engels maintained that it "was very fortunate that the Arabian chief had been taken" by the French. "The conquest of Algeria," Engels insisted, was "important and fortunate . . . for the progress of civilization. . . . After all," he continued, "the modern bourgeois, with civilization, industry, order, and at least relative enlightenment following him, is preferable to the feudal lord or to the marauding robber, with the barbarian state of society to which they belong."[22]

Engels expressed the same convictions in discussing the seizure of "Mexican lands" by the "energetic Yankees." Engels argued, in the U.S.-Mexican conflict of 1848, that the "energetic Yankees" had "increased the medium of circulation, . . . concentrated in a few years a heavy population and an extensive trade on the most suitable part of the Pacific Coast, . . . built great cities, . . . opened up steamship lines. . . . Because of this the 'independence' of a few Spanish Californians and Texans may be injured, but what do they count compared to such world historic events? . . . When it is a question of the existence, of the free development of all the resources of great nations, then . . . sentimentalities . . . will decide nothing." It is a matter of "trade, industry and profitable methods of agriculture, . . . [the] level of social development of the individual peoples, . . . [the] influence of the more highly developed nation on the undeveloped one."

The expansion of an industrially advanced nation into underdeveloped regions marked a specific stage in the process of international economic and manufacturing growth. Like List, Engels understood progress in his-

---

[20] Karl Marx, "The Future Results of British Rule in India," in Shlomo Avineri, *Karl Marx on Colonialism and Modernization* (Garden City, N.Y.: Doubleday, 1968), p. 125.

[21] Marx, "The British Rule in India," ibid., pp. 88, 89.

[22] Engels, "French Rule in Algeria," ibid., p. 44.

tory to be a function of the expansion of the more highly developed industrial nations binding together "tiny, crippled, powerless little nations . . . in a great empire, and thereby [to enable] them to take part in an historical role which, if left to themselves, would [remain] entirely foreign to them! . . . Without force and without an iron ruthlessness, nothing is accomplished in history."[23] The entire sequence was "natural" and "inexorable."

Whether Marx and Engels developed these insights from the earlier perusal of the works of List remains uncertain—and is unimportant for the purposes of this exposition. What is clear is that the notions entertained are the same as those found in the account provided by List before either Marx or Engels published their major works after 1848.

For List, levels of productivity influence the ability of nations to extend their economic, political, cultural, and military influence over less-developed territories. That process brought "progress" and "civilization" in its wake. In his national developmental conceptions and those of historical materialism, all that was the consequence of the development of the "forces of production."

To find the same collection of convictions in the essays written by Corradini and Rocco is unexceptional. They understood history to move with the tempo supplied by the dynamics of production. The more-productive nations extend their influence over those less productive, to stimulate in them a cycle of economic growth and maturation. Imperialist powers, "blindly responding to the natural order of things . . . make their 'altruistic contribution' to the collective good of humankind."[24] For Corradini, economic "imperialism is space converted into wealth through labor" and a fundamental part of the processes involved in the evolution of humankind.[25] "Young nations," to participate in those world historical processes, were required to discipline themselves to the use of available human and material resources to sustain the rapid growth rates requisite to compete effectively in an adversarial international environment.[26]

Rocco's introduction of the thought of List into the deliberations of the Nationalist Association accelerated the formulation of doctrine that was to pass almost without alteration into the mature ideology of Fascism. By 1916, with Italy at war, Corradini gave fulsome shape to nationalism's own "theory" of imperialism, international development, as well as an attendant "theory" of productive forces.

---

[23] Engels, "Democratic Panslavism," in P. W. Blackstock and B. F. Hoselitz, eds., *The Russian Menace to Europe* (Glencoe: Free Press, 1952), pp. 71, 74, 75, 76.

[24] Corradini, "La marcia dei produttori," in *La marcia dei produttori*, pp. 187–88.

[25] Ibid., p. 189.

[26] Ibid., pp. 197–98.

In 1916, Corradini drew a picture of the modern world at the center of which were *productive forces* as determinants.[27] Like List and Rocco, Corradini argued that the dynamic energy of the world as we knew it was to be found in *productivity*. Those communities capable of superior productivity expanded—commercially, economically, culturally, politically, and militarily. Their expansion permitted them to both inform and fashion the world around them. Out of tribes and confederations, city-states and principalities of the past, modern nations and empires were to grow, to cross-fertilize each other in a process into which the new Italy found itself thrust. If Italy was to shape, rather than be shaped, in the process, it would have to undertake industrial expansion and economic growth at an accelerated pace.

The implications of the nationalist "theory of the productive forces" were evident in the writings that appeared in the publications of the Nationalist Association. Economic growth and industrial development, it was argued, assured the accumulation of assets that would benefit all classes and sectors of the nation. It would demonstrate the pointlessness of "class warfare." The demand for increased productivity would place a premium on ability and competence—and would commensurately reward both. Increasing abundance would enhance the life circumstances of all and allow for the education and skill training of the least qualified members of modern society—resulting in a constant infusion of new talents into the ranks of prevailing functional elites. That would enrich the "productive aristocracy" of the nation to the benefit of all.

In the course of its development, the new nation would generate new elites and new aristocracies—in a circulation of elites and aristocracies that would ensure a continuous reaffirmation of talent and competence. Class warfare would reveal itself as dysfunctional, fundamentally counterproductive, and irremediably reactionary.

By the advent of the First World War, both Rocco and Corradini argued that Italy's involvement made all that increasingly obvious. If the nation were to survive the war that had become worldwide, and historic in implication, it required a measure of technical proficiency and industrial productivity that would assure a flow of armaments and weapon platforms capable of surviving and prevailing against the products of advanced German industry.[28] The extant "liberal," "parliamentary" state that governed the nation at war had shown itself to be wanting in a variety of ways. It failed to effectively organize military production. It failed to ensure the

---

[27] The following is taken from the account in Corradini, "La marcia dei produttori," pp. 182–99.

[28] See the section entitled "Artiglieria e munizionamento," in Rocco, *SDP*, vol. 1, pp. 417–58.

necessary raw materials to sustain lines of production. It failed to mobilize the population to war. It failed to inspire through instruction or example. And it allowed those who would undermine the war effort to continue their subversions in both parliament and the state bureaucracy.[29]

By the time the Great War was drawing to its close, the intellectuals of the Nationalist Association had drawn together all the lines of argument here rehearsed. Implicit in that complex doctrinal argument was the acknowledgment that the classical Marxist argument concerning the role of the productive forces in social development carried with it the entailment that a specifically *proletarian* revolution made theoretical sense only in advanced industrial environments. Only in such circumstances would the "vast majority" of the working masses be urban-based "proletarians" capable of assuming the governance of advanced industrial systems. Only in such circumstances might socialism inherit the abundance necessary to make "equitable distribution" feasible without economically disabling the community. With the socialization of the fully mature "means of production," and the distribution of its commodities, an advanced industrial system might conceivably survive and prosper. Only where industrial capitalism had matured, concentrated itself in vast conglomerates, in environments dominated by a "vast majority" of proletarians, might traditional socialism recommend itself. Rocco, Corradini, and the nationalists argued that the case was entirely different with late-developing nations.

In a community only then commencing its economic and industrial growth, traditional socialism was almost entirely without merit. Italy, as a nation oppressed by the more advanced industrial powers at the turn of the twentieth century, did not require proletarian revolution. What it required was rapid industrial and economic development.[30] What it required on the part of its citizens was a recognition that the welfare of all, in the long term, depended on the heroic sacrifice of individuals—intense individual labor and self-sacrificial commitment—in the short term.

Rocco argued that redistribution at the beginning of Italy's industrial development would net individuals but a small fraction of the benefits that a dedicated policy of broad-based industrialization would ultimately provide.[31] He maintained that a program of heroic sacrifice and self-re-

---

[29] See Rocco, "L'insufficienza dello stato" and "La sesta arma: La propaganda"; and "Il dovere del governo e quello degli industriali," in *SDP*, vol. 1, pp. 311–14, 365–68, 439–44; Corradini, "La nuova forza dello stato"; and "La funzione morale degli uomini politici," in *La marcia dei produttori*, pp. 44–54, 63–69.

[30] See the discussion in Corradini, "Il nazionalismo e i sindacati," in *DP*, p. 421; Rocco, "Il programma politico dell'Associazione nazionalista," in *SDP*, vol. 2, p. 477; Rocco "Replica agli oratori," in *SDP*, vol. 1, pp. 482, 483; "Il programma nazionalista," in *SDP*, vol. 1, pp. 494, 502.

[31] Rocco, "Il problema economico italiano," *SDP*, 1, pp. 18–19.

straint on the part of labor would allow the rapid accumulation of capital necessary for the maintenance, fostering, and sustenance of domestic industry[32]—which would ultimately redound to the benefit of all.

At the same time, Rocco argued that the working classes of the new nation could not be alienated if the nation were to succeed in its development. He early maintained that the corporate interests of the working classes would be defended by any nationalist and developmental government—however authoritarian—in order to ensure that the whole would enjoy the level of collective integrity necessary for rapid economic expansion.

To discharge its tasks, Rocco argued, the state in emerging Italy must assume onerous responsibilities. It must seek not only to bring together all constituents of the nation in an "organic and integral" unity; it must labor to foster and maintain that unity.

For Rocco, like all the nationalists that had survived the winnowing of nationalist ranks after 1911, the state in emerging Italy was to be absolutely sovereign. It could no longer remain passive, responsive to initiatives emanating from parochial interests. The argument was that as long as the state remained unresponsive to its historic tasks, it would remain hostage to the interests of ephemeral groups and parochial concerns that found expression in a parliamentary system that was neither representative nor functional.

What emergent Italy required, Rocco contended, was a strong state, animated by its own sovereign interests—capable of subordinating fractional and transient preoccupations to those both long term and primary. What is interesting for the purposes of exposition is the fact that, by 1914, some of the most notable revolutionary syndicalists, some of whom had long given evidence of their antistate convictions, had begun to acknowledge the historical importance of the state in the circumstances in which Italy found itself.

As the threat of war clouded Europe's horizon during the summer of 1914, Panfilo Gentile reminded Italy's revolutionary syndicalists that the unreflecting rejection of the state that typified the movement in the past required reassessment.[33] He argued that the state might serve the community even after the threat of war had passed. He insisted that whatever transpired during, and after, the war that had settled down on Europe, the fact was that the state could very well be a critical agency—even after the anticipated "socialist revolution." Gentile argued that given the diverse interests that would have to be accommodated in any complex industrial community, the state, "ejected through the door [by the socialist revolution] would reenter through the window." Evolving contemporary circumstances made it clear that any revolutionary arrangements required "an authority, a force, superior to the parts, that would discipline and coordinate all constituents to fully respect and discharge commitments made."

Even antistate syndicalists began to reconsider their unreflecting rejection of the political state. Obviously precipitated by the realities of a war that involved everyone in a fateful enterprise, revolutionary syndicalists seemed prepared to transfer such insights to a postwar Italy that would face all the burdens of readjustment, growth, and international competition.

By the commencement of the First World War, syndicalists argued that while class-based syndicates might very well serve the corporate interests of industrial labor, there was the evident need for some overarching national agency that could coordinate interests and negotiate differences. It was suggested that syndicalists who had learned their antistatism from the half-century-old analyses of Karl Marx and Friedrich Engels might do well to reconsider the unanticipated circumstances that governed the modern world.

Revolutionary syndicalists like A. O. Olivetti, witnessing the disintegration of "socialist internationalism" under the pressure of events during the summer and fall of 1914, made the case that some conception of a "national socialism" should not be summarily dismissed.[34] Given the new reality, syndicalists must be prepared to acknowledge the influence of national sentiment on the overt political loyalties of Italy's working classes.[35] Olivetti recognized that the nation, presumably exorcised by traditional Marxism, still retained a critical hold on many.[36] He alluded to the increasingly evident emergence of a new conception of society and revolution—one that was both idealist and aristocratic, regenerative and transformative, voluntaristic and heroic. Olivetti spoke of the first outlines of a new society that appeared to be emerging—one no longer hostage to "mummified doctrines," materialist or hedonistic. The new society would be one of *producers*.[37]

---

[34] With the founding of the Fascio rivoluzionario d'azione, Olivetti spoke of the role of *nationality* as a factor in the unfolding of events. See A. O. Olivetti, "Manifesto del Fascio rivoluzionario d'azione," and "Ricominciando . . . ," *Pagine libere*, 10 October 1914, reprinted in *Battaglie sindacaliste: Dal sindacalismo al fascismo* (typescript provided by the Olivetti family), 2, pp. 86–93.

[35] Olivetti, "Salutatemi i pacifisti," *Pagine libere* 10 October 1914, pp. 94–96.

[36] Olivetti, "La grande contraddizione," *Pagine libere* 30 (November 1914), reprinted in *Battaglie sindacalista*, pp. 105–9.

[37] Olivetti, "Ricominciando . . . ," in *Battaglie sindacalista*, pp. 89–93.

More than that, Olivetti, long antistatist in principle, suggested that all features of inherited doctrines required review. International war had revealed how much the sentiment of nationality influenced the masses of Europe. That suggested a role for a superior agency that might mediate the differences between the constituent elements of the national community. The state might serve as that agency, representing general *national interests* as distinct from those that were parochial.[38] He went on to suggest that the state might defend the general interests as distinct from any class functions it might perform. The possibility that the state, long abjured by syndicalists, might serve trans-class functions signaled a fundamental, and hitherto unexpected, doctrinal change for Italy's revolutionary left.[39]

It quickly became clear that the crisis that had overwhelmed Europe at the end of the summer of 1914 had precipitated massive changes in the ideological orientation of some of the most radical of Italy's revolutionaries. The most significant changes took place in the thought of Benito Mussolini, political and intellectual leader of Italian socialism. As early as the end of 1913, when the clear signs of the emerging crisis became clear, Mussolini gave evidence of a kind of doctrinal restlessness.

At that time, Mussolini was prepared to acknowledge that events had overtaken theoretical Marxism. As editor of his own journal, *Utopia*, Mussolini sought serious theoretical review of the commitments made by revolutionary socialists.[40] He published a series of articles that signaled a major revision of traditional socialist postures. He spoke, without equivocation, of an anticipated "revolutionary revision of socialism."[41] He spoke, for example, of the failure of philosophical positivism that traditional Marxists had made their own. He held that contemporary science had shown that human concerns were far too complicated to be resolved, without remainder, into some set of deterministic propositions without appeal to human will and commitment.

It was within that context that Mussolini published Giovanni Baldazzi's article on the heroism, audacity, idealism, and sacrifice of revolutionaries like August Blanqui. The review of such elements in revolutionary activity was to serve as clear counsel to Italian socialists.[42] Mussolini

---

[38] Olivetti, "Postilla a 'Socialismo e guerra sono termini antitetici?' Ancora per la neutralità di Arnoldo Norlenghi," *Pagine libere*, in *Battaglie Sindacalista*, pp. 113.

[39] Olivetti, "Noi e lo stato," *Pagine libere* (15 November 1914), in *Battaglie Sindacalista*, pp. 99–104.

[40] Mussolini maintained that as editor of *Utopia* he could speak in the "first person," expressing his own views, and not as spokesman for the institutional Socialist Party. See Mussolini, "Impresa disperata," *Utopia* 2, no. 1 (15 January 1914), p. 1.

[41] Mussolini, "Al largo!" *Utopia* 1, no. 1 (22 November 1913), p. 2.

[42] Giovanni Baldazzi, "Augusto Blanqui," *Utopia* 1, no. 1 (22 November 1913), pp. 18–25.

published the article by Gerolamo Lazzei, who spoke unashamedly of the "profoundly national" work of socialists.[43] It was clear that Lazzei saw no contradiction in a revolutionary commitment to both the nation as well as to socialism. The fact that Mussolini chose to afford Lazzei space in his journal was a matter of no small consequence.

In his journal, Mussolini published the article by Valentino Piccoli—an exposition of the ideas of Henri Bergson and Georges Sorel—that argued against the determinism and materialism of the socialism of the mid-nineteenth century. The article also alluded to the renovative influence of the ideas of Giovanni Gentile—a nationalist—on the new ideas of an emerging modern revolutionary socialism.[44] Angelo Tasca examined the ideas of Giuseppe Lombardo-Radice, a follower of Gentile, that alluded to the role of sentiment, will, passion, faith, and commitment in human action. He spoke of the sentiment of nationality as one with which the working classes might well identify.[45]

All of this constituted growing evidence of the emerging affinities between nationalism, revolutionary syndicalism, philosophical idealism, and Italian socialism that had begun even before the war in Tripoli. Intimations of a form of statism, nationalism, antiparliamentarianism, together with an increasing emphasis on industrial production, began to surface in the most radical syndicalist and socialist journals. The early intellectual beliefs assumed by syndicalists like Paolo Orano—the elitism, nationalism, productivism, and tentative statism of A. O. Olivetti—together with the transformative innovations of Mussolinian socialism after 1914[46]—began to take on more and more of the doctrinal features of Corradinian and Roccian nationalism.

The period between the war in Tripoli and the outbreak of the First World War marked the increasing articulation of Corradinian and Roccian Italian nationalism. At the same time, there is clear evidence of a transformation of the political thought of Mussolini —and many syndicalist and socialist "Mussoliniani"—away from that of an orthodox, if revolutionary, Marxism, to an heretical, equally revolutionary, *national* socialism. By the end of September 1914, Mussolini spoke of the "death of the traditional socialist international" and the first intimations of a new, dynamic, and revolutionary national socialism.[47]

---

[43] Gerolamo Lazzeri, "Italiani e slavi a Trieste," *Utopia* 2, no. 2 (30 January 1914), p. 53.

[44] See the entire discussion in Valentino Piccoli, "Bergson e Sorel," *Utopia* 2, nos. 3–4 (15–28 February 1914), pp. 94–100.

[45] Angelo Tasca, "I socialisti e la scuola," *Utopia* 2, nos. 3–4 (15–28 February 1914), pp. 101–11.

[46] See A. James Gregor, *Young Mussolini and the Intellectual Origins of Fascism* (Berkeley and Los Angeles: University of California Press, 1979).

[47] "L'homme qui cherche" (pen name of Mussolini), "Note di guerra," *Utopia* 2, nos. 11–12 (15 August–1 September 1914), pp. 305–10.

In his journal, Mussolini gave prominence to an article by Mario Missiroli[48]—at the time, a Gentilean nationalist—that spoke of the necessity of developing an industrial base for Italy. As a new nation, Missiroli argued, Italy required a broad industrial base to support the capabilities that would be essential if the nation were to face the political, economic, and military challenges of the time. Missiroli spoke of the collateral necessity of a strong state, if Italy were to develop, compete, and survive in international competition with the advanced industrial powers.

In order to assure the degree of discipline and commitment necessary for the complex process he anticipated, Missiroli spoke of a total moral and political *identification* of the individual with the state and the nation. Not only would such an identification foster the developmental, regenerative, and renovative process, but would serve as the necessary condition of individual self-realization. He alluded to the philosophy of personal fulfillment to which Giovanni Gentile, a nationalist and statist, had already given expression.[49]

Missiroli spoke of such a "modern state," profoundly "idealist" and "spiritual," as the unexpected fulfillment of the promise of classical Marxism. Missiroli, in 1914, in the pages of Mussolini's *Utopia*, provided the intimations of a revolutionary national socialism—infilled with the properties of a mature nationalism and an antimaterialist, neo-Hegelian idealism.[50]

The circumstances surrounding the Italian war in Tripoli and the advent of the First World War had transformed the political environment on the Italian peninsula. The nationalists had anticipated much of what was, and would be, transpiring. Initially, revolutionary syndicalists had not.

Certainly, revolutionary syndicalists were philosophic and sociological collectivists. Like the nationalists, they were intrinsically opposed to political individualism and the representative system it supported. They had early committed themselves to the role of heroic minorities in the resolution of the revolutionary problems of their time—and they fully acknowledged the role of moral purpose and ideal commitment to the mobilization of revolutionaries. Revolutionary syndicalists initially imagined that class identification was a privileged identification. As a consequence, they originally dismissed the nation, the military, and all their attendant traditions as simply "oppressive" and "counterrevolutionary."

---

[48] Mario Missiroli, "L'Italia e la Triplice," *Utopia* 2, nos. 11–12 (15 August–1 September 1914), pp. 343–48. See Mussolini's comments on the piece on p. 343.

[49] By the time of the publication of Missiroli's essay, Gentile had already outlined his political philosophy. See the discussion in A. James Gregor, *Giovanni Gentile: Philosopher of Fascism* (New Brunswick, N.J.: Transaction, 2001).

[50] Missiroli, "L'Italia e la Triplice," pp. 343–48.

Political nationalists, for their part, expected that the reality of the world at the beginning of the twentieth century, involved as it was in the relentless competition of the less-developed "new" nations against those already established, would rapidly convince revolutionary syndicalists that their interests would compel the "working classes" to identify with their "proletarian nation" rather than with some fictive "promethean, international class." In fact, the intellectuals of the Italian Nationalist Association anticipated that revolutionary syndicalism, given the prevailing realities, would rapidly transform itself into a recognizable form of *national syndicalism* that would prove compatible with the emerging doctrine of revolutionary nationalism. In fact, by 1915, by the time of Italy's entrance into the First World War, syndicalism had already taken on some of the properties of a revolutionary nationalism. The reality of the national sentiment that mobilized the revolutionary syndicalists and socialists of France and Germany around the standards of the nation discounted the "internationalism" and "classism" of traditional Marxist revolutionary thought.

At the same time, most of the syndicalist intellectuals recognized that Italy was industrially retrograde. As a necessary consequence, all the prognostications of classical Marxists were entirely unconvincing. There could be no proletarian revolution in Italy. The proletarians of the peninsula, even in terms of Marxist orthodoxy, were necessarily "immature." Marxist revolution was perhaps on the agenda of a mature industrial economy—but there was scant prospect of a proletarian revolution in essentially agrarian Italy. Where an economy was "immature," the proletariat must necessarily be similarly "immature."

In those circumstances, revolutionaries were charged with entirely unanticipated responsibilities. They were compelled to discharge "bourgeois" historic tasks: to advocate and collaborate in the industrialization of the economically underdeveloped national territory. In effect, reality dictated that revolutionary syndicalists be prepared to assume historic responsibilities Marxism had not foreseen. They charged themselves with the responsibility of bringing Italy, as a new nation, into the industrialized twentieth century.

It was Filippo Corridoni, one of the most radical revolutionary syndicalists, who clearly articulated the changing obligations of revolutionaries.[51] Corridoni reminded the Marxist revolutionaries of Italy that impoverished Italy was still in the "swaddling clothes" of industrial capitalism, and, by implication, innocent of the conditions necessary for proletarian revolution. An ineffectual bourgeoisie, failing to industrialize the nation,

---

[51] See the biography of Ivon de Begnac, *L'Arcangelo sindacalista (Filippo Corridoni)* (Verona: Mondadori, 1943).

left the peninsula adrift, to face the depredations of foreign imperialisms.[52] An "immature" proletariat was ill-equipped to assume meaningful responsibilities in a retrograde economic environment.

Corridoni reminded revolutionaries that Italy languished in "essentially precapitalist" economic conditions—and, as a result, proletarian revolution was simply not on the historic agenda. What serious revolutionaries were required to undertake, Corridoni asserted, was support for the rapid industrialization of Italy as a "late developing nation."[53] He anticipated that Italy's historic responsibility was the rapid economic development of its backward peninsula until it could directly and effectively compete with those nations that had already developed and possessed the military and economic capabilities that made them "great powers."[54]

By the time of his death in the First World War, leading an attack on the Austro-Hungarian enemy from the trenches of Frasche, Corridoni had put together an unmistakable form of *national* syndicalism that shared affinities with revolutionary nationalism. Corridoni, like the nationalists, had made the "material productive forces" central to his analysis—and had drawn conclusions similar to those entertained by Corradini and Rocco. At least one variant of Italian syndicalism had transformed itself into a qualified analogue of the revolutionary nationalism of the Italian Nationalist Association.

This was the intellectual environment in which Alfredo Rocco produced the series of essays that shaped nationalist thought into a coherent, comprehensive, and explicit doctrine—one that he identified as both "organic" in character and "spiritual" in substance. He duly spoke of the articulation of principles from which doctrinal injunctions might be derived.[55] It was a doctrine with which many revolutionary syndicalists were prepared to identify—whatever their qualification.

In effect, by the time of the First World War, nationalism had matured into a fulsome ideology from which an inclusive and practical political doctrine might be forthcoming that could attract the most radical of Italy's leftist revolutionaries. Rocco, like Corradini, had anticipated the rapid approximation of revolutionary syndicalism to the developmental nationalism that constituted the core of the doctrine of the Italian Nationalist Association. History was to prove them to be fundamentally correct. Thereafter, nationalism was to represent itself with an explicit political

---

[52] See Filippo Corridoni, *Sindacalismo e repubblica* (1915; reprint Milan: SAREP, 1945), pp. 19, 20, 23, 25–27, 34, 37–38, 48.

[53] See ibid., pp. 32, 70–71, 80–82, 92.

[54] See Corridoni's comments in "Testamento," in Tullio Masotti, *Corridoni* (Milan: Canaro, 1932), pp. 253–57.

[55] See Rocco, "Il programma politico dell'Associazione Nazionalista," in *SDP*, vol. 2, p. 476.

character. It was to be manifestly developmental, antidemocratic, antiparliamentarian, and statist. It was to be a doctrine that would attract leftist
as well as rightist intellectuals. In historic fact, what was transpiring was
a "synthesis between extreme Right and Left, which lay at the basis of
Fascism."[56]

As early as 1913 and 1914, Rocco, like the revolutionary syndicalists,
had identified political and representative democracy with a form of debil-
itating individualism that made any collective, enduring, and demanding
national enterprise all but impossible. Rocco, like the revolutionary syndicalists, held that any commitment to protracted sacrifice—to heroic self-
abnegation—required something more than the individualistic hedonism
that informed the liberal democracy of then contemporary Italy. If Italy
was to rapidly industrialize, in order to assume its rightful place among
the major powers, it would have to abandon political democracy, economic liberalism, and distributionistic socialism. By the advent of the First
World War, revolutionary syndicalists like Paolo Orano, A. O. Olivetti,
and Filippo Corridoni were professing convictions all but indistinguishable from those of the intellectuals of the Italian Nationalist Association.

The distinctions that remained between the doctrinal postures of the
increasingly nationalist syndicalists and the nationalists of the Italian Nationalist Association turned on (1) the character of the state, (2) the role
of the military in the development of the nation, (3) the nature of the
relationship between the new revolutionary state and the constituents of
the nation, and finally, (4) the developmental strategy of the forthcoming
revolution.

Even before the successful conclusion of the First World War, the intellectuals of the Italian Nationalist Association, unlike those of the revolutionary syndicalist organizations, sought the creation of a "strong" state,
more authoritarian than liberal, enjoying a measure of sovereignty not
anticipated by the most heretical of syndicalists. Nationalists anticipated
a recalibration of the relations between the Roman Catholic Church and
the sovereign state. Since the Church had resisted the secular reintegration
of Italy as a nation in defense of its own corporate interests, the initial
nationalist position was tendentially anticlerical. After the war in Libya,
however, a segment of political Catholicism had broken away from the
traditionalism of the Catholic past and had opened itself to the political
suasions of the nationalists. As a nationalist, Rocco argued that the "integral" regeneration of the nation—the marshaling of all elements of the
population in the mission to restore the grandeur of Italy—required a
proper political concern for the all-but-universal Roman Catholic reli-

[56] De Grand, *The Italian Nationalist Association and the Rise of Fascism in Italy*, p. 60.

gious commitment of Italians.[57] Revolutionary nationalism would be obliged to accommodate representatives of the Church as it would be obliged to accommodate the representatives of what had been the antinationalist revolutionary proletariat.

Already by the time of the elections of 1913, an alliance of nationalists and political Roman Catholics had brought some success to the antiliberal and antisocialist policies of the Nationalist Association. Rocco had engineered gains for nationalism in the Veneto, and a regional federation was formed. It was to go on to publish its own newspaper, *Il Dovere nazionale.* At the same time, in accordance with the policy implications of its evolving doctrine, ties were forged with some industrial associations, attracted by the nationalist program of rapid industrial and technological development of the peninsula. Among the most important of the industrial notables supporting the developmental program of the Italian Nationalist Association were Alberto Maria Bombrini, director of the Cogne Mining Company, and Dante Ferraris, vice president of Fiat and president of Turin's Industrial League. The growing relationship represented a convergence of interests between the nationalists, who advocated a rapid acceleration of Italy's industrial and technological economic development, and industrialists, whose interests such a policy might serve.[58] Thus, at the same time that Italy's nationalists were fabricating a substantive relationship with the nation's revolutionary syndicalists, they were establishing connections with the Roman Church and the peninsula's industrialists—in the pursuit of a functional union of all within the integument of the sovereign state.

It was during this period that nationalists formulated the first intimations of a future "corporative state," a political arrangement in which organized Church, labor, and industrial interests would be accorded juridical recognition—in order to create a legal environment in which all would collaborate in a national enterprise committed to the creation of a "Greater Italy" —involving the rapid and intensive industrialization of the peninsula.[59] Rocco maintained that the modern period had introduced the necessity of an organization of corporate interests—all those aggregated and articulate interests to be involved in the development of the nation.

Rocco argued that after the turn of the century, labor had organized itself in syndicates—just as the Church had so organized itself by the time of the nation's reunification. By the advent of the First World War, entre-

---

[57] See Rocco, "Che cosa è il nazionalismo e che cosa vogliono i nazionalisti," in *SDP,* vol. 1, pp. 80–81.

[58] See De Grand, *The Italian Nationalist Association and the Rise of Fascism in Italy,* p. 52.

[59] See Corradini, "Il nazionalismo e i sindacati," in *DP,* pp. 423–24; Rocco, "Replica agli oratori," in *SDP,* vol. 2, p. 484.

preneurs had similarly organized themselves in parallel organizations. The empirical fact of such organization was demonstrable. The question was how might an emerging nation deal with such an insistent, and potentially conflict laden, reality.

In order to embark upon its developmental program, Rocco contended that a strong state would have to organize all syndical, church, academic, educational, political, labor, and entrepreneurial associations within its compass. The rationale rested on the conviction that "democratic" and "liberal" states dissipated their sovereign energy in episodic responses to clientelistic demands—something the developmental "integralist" state could not.

Between 1914 and 1919, Rocco clearly anticipated the creation of a revolutionary "corporate state" that would enlist all constituent corporate bodies of the nation in the service of the "massive productive enterprise" that was the necessary condition for the realization of Italy's regeneration. Only in that fashion could the incompetent and flaccid state of Italy's forelorn past be displaced in order to realize the instauration of a strong, centralizing, integrative corporative body.[60]

Rocco had given expression to a doctrinal conviction that a revolutionary state would emerge from an Italian victory at the conclusion of the First World War. The war, he argued, had taught the nation a significant lesson. Its victory in that war argued for Italy's intrinsic capacity to achieve the status of a major European power. Rocco insisted that what victorious Italy required was a political and constitutional revolution that would discard the liberal and representative parliament. Such revolution would put together a strong, irreducibly sovereign state, which would shepherd Italy into the modern age.

The prospect of achieving such an end turned on the union of nationalism with revolutionary national syndicalism. By 1918, the potential for accomplishing such a union was manifest. It is only necessary to trace the evolution of syndicalist thought, prior to that time, in the work of one of its most accomplished theoreticians to appreciate that.

---

[60] In his commentary on Rocco's views, Nazareno Mezzetti argued that Rocco's doctrine was a consequence of his subscription to Fascism. That clearly was not the case. Rocco had given voice to his views on the corporate state long before there was a Fascism. He had, in fact, anticipated Fascism. See the discussion in Mezzetti, *Alfredo Rocco*, pp. 95–119.

CHAPTER FOUR

Sergio Panunzio: From Revolutionary
to National Syndicalism

THROUGH THE decade prior to the First World War, and the war's culmination in 1918, the Italian political scene featured doctrinal changes among Marxists that were to gradually allow a union of developmental nationalism and revolutionary syndicalism. To trace the doctrinal developments during that period is essential to understanding how their ultimate union was to infuse Fascism with distinctive ideological character. At each stage in the process, differences were clearly discernible—sometimes obscuring the maturing synthesis. Nationalist theoreticians, nonetheless, had early anticipated just such an outcome—and the informal logic governing the development is relatively easy to reconstruct.

By the first years of the twentieth century, socialism in Italy had bifurcated, for all intents and purposes, into two main currents: reformist and revisionist. Influenced by ideological developments in Germany, the majority of Italian socialists had early opted for a form of Marxism that conceived the Italian Socialist Party a partner in a democratic and liberal political enterprise that could be mobilized, through electoral victories, to the advantage of the working class.

Why that should be so would require a complicated answer that would tax the patience of readers and exceed the scope of this account. It is interesting, however, that Eduard Bernstein, one of the principal intellectual heirs of classical Marxism, had undertaken to revise the inherited formulations of Karl Marx and Friedrich Engels to "better accord" with the evident facts of the turn of the century.[1] The capitalist industrial system had not collapsed; there was no credible evidence of a secular decline in the overall rate of profit in capitalist undertakings; society had not been reduced to two hostile camps—bourgeois and proletarian—with the proletarians constituting the "vast majority" of the population; there had not been a concentration of capital in the hands of an exiguous minority to the exclusion of small and medium enterprises; and, finally, the German Social Democratic party had enjoyed considerable success in its competi-

---

[1] See Eduard Bernstein, *Die Voraussetzungen des Sozialismus und die Aufgaben der Sozialdemokratie* available in English in abbreviated form as *Evolutionary Socialism* (New York: Schocken, 1961).

tion with its "bourgeois" political competitors.[2] German socialism had every reason to become reformist.

The result, in the judgment of some revolutionaries, was a German Social Democracy that was "indecisive, prudent, legalitarian, and parliamentarian—postures that could only prolong the existence of the established system and obstruct the emergence of youthful forces."[3] More and more European intellectuals found reformist, legalitarian, and parliamentary socialism increasingly unattractive.

Partially as a consequence of the influence of German Social Democracy, Italian socialism itself became increasingly reformist, choosing a path of systemic reform through accommodation with the prevailing political system.[4] Italian reformists became increasingly preoccupied with "facts," and political tactics. Unlike their German counterparts, however, they were far less interested in the architecture of theory. Animated by the prevailing epistemological positivism of the period, intellectuals like Napoleone Colajanni interpreted the inherited Marxism in terms of the prevailing evolutionary natural and social sciences of the end of the nineteenth century. Many revolutionary intellectuals, Paolo Orano, Alfredo Niceforo, and Sergio Panunzio among them, came under the sway of philosophical positivists like Roberto Ardigò[5]—who succeeded in significantly influencing the ideological reflections of the period.

Positivism saw traditional Marxism in terms of lawlike social regularities—regularities very much like those that governed the physical universe. However "dialectical" those laws might be in the eyes of Marxists, they were sublimely "objective" and independent of human influence.[6] Regularities were to be observed and confirmed in overt social behaviors. There were objective patterns in the complexities of history—in the collective behaviors of classes—that Karl Marx had outlined in his works.

---

[2] See Georges Sorel's account in *Les polémiques pour l'interprétation du Marxisme: Bernstein et Kautsky* (Paris: Giard et E. Briere, 1900), pp. 31–34 and the comments of Enrico Leone, *Il sindacalismo*, 2nd ed. (1906; Milan: Sandron), pp. 33–35, 63.

[3] Roberto Michels, "Le syndicalisme et le socialisme en Allegmagne," in *Syndicalisme et socialisme* (Paris: Marcel Rivière, 1908), p. 27.

[4] Filippo Turati, *Il Partito socialista italiano e le sue pretese tendenze* (Milan: "Critica sociale," 1902), pp. 9–10.

[5] See the account in Giovanni Marchesini, *Roberto Ardigò: L'uomo e l'umanista* (Florence: Felice Le Monnier, 1922).

[6] See Paolo Orano, *La logica della sociologia* (Rome: Pensiero nuovo, 1898); and *La società-organismo ed il materialismo storico* (Rome: Pensiero nuovo, 1898). In the preface of his *Il precursore Italiano di Carlo Marx* (Rome: Enrico Voghera, 1899), p. v, Giacomo Barzellotti identifies Orano's work as representative of "positivistic methods." Orano saw "positivism" finding its completion in the "materialist interpretation of history." Pp. 3–11, 167–68, 205.

Given such convictions, Marxist theoreticans like Filippo Turati oriented Italian socialism toward strategies compatible with the "laws" revealed in the work of the "Masters." Society proceeded toward a predictable socialism with an "automaticity and an irresistibility" made manifest in an "organic development of things."[7] Socialists were admonished to pursue "immediate" and "practical" political endeavors that would parallel a sequence of events governed by historic "laws." Moreover, conformity to those laws confined socialist options to what were perceived as prevailing political realities. Friedrich Engels himself had written—at about the time of his death—that "for forty years, Marx and I have consistently repeated that a democratic republic was the only political form in which the struggle between the working class and the capitalist class can first universalize itself, to subsequently achieve its goal with the decisive victory of the proletariat."[8] It appeared that the die had been cast.

What seemed central to such convictions was the commitment to competitive political activities within the context of a parliamentary system. The corollary to such a commitment was the notion that whatever the resistance of its class enemies during and at the conclusion of such a protracted political process, the proletariat would inevitably be triumphant. That was the predictable terminus of the lawlike, if "dialectical," processes outlined by Marx in his works—and insisted upon by Engels. Until the bourgeois class makes its inevitable recourse to violence, the working class would proceed toward its goal, employing political means, with the assurance that electoral success and legislative reform were necessary stages in the imprescriptible and lawlike process. Engels had asserted that "counter-revolutionary violence might retard [the success of the proletariat] for a few years—but, in the end, that could only render the triumph of the working class more complete."[9]

On the Italian peninsula, socialism was to pursue its goals through the liberal and broadly democratic institutions of post-Risorgimento Italy. Socialism was conceived a kind of lay Mazzinianism—without God, without the abiding sense of mission, without the symbols, and without the nationalism. Armed revolution was subordinated to the status of a reactive response by the working class to initiatives undertaken by the ruling bourgeoisie.

At about the same time, in both France and Italy, there developed a reaction to what was seen to be essentially a commitment to meliorism

---

[7] W. Kolb, "Zur Frage des Generalstreiks," *Sozialistische Monatshefte*, 1904, p. 209, cited in Arturo Labriola, *Riforme e revoluzione sociale*, 3rd ed. (1904; Naples: Partenopea, 1914), p. 3.

[8] As cited, Roberto Michels, *Storia critica del movimento socialista italiano* (Florence: "La voce," 1926), p. 114.

[9] Engels, as cited in Michels, *Storia critica*, p. 115.

and reformism among European socialists. French and Italian anarchists and intellectual dissidents insisted that the truest Marxian ideals were not reformist, but fundamentally *revolutionary*, as well as irrepressibly *antistatist* and *libertarian*—all betrayed by institutional socialism.

In 1898, Georges Sorel published his *L'Avenir socialiste des syndicats* in which he argued that reformism, with its inextricable involvement in parliamentary democracy, dissipated the moral energy and neglected the developing technical skill and productive enterprise of the rising proletariat—to produce a movement that was neither revolutionary nor effective.[10] He proposed that the working class, organized in autonomous and voluntary associations, undertake the revolution anticipated by Karl Marx—without the interference of intellectuals or the dysfunctional commitment to politics.[11]

The *Avenir socialiste des syndicats* was quickly followed by a series of works devoted to the appearance of what Sorel called the "new school."[12] Sorel's volume *Reflections on Violence*, which appeared in Italy in 1906 (although parts had been published as early as 1901), exercised enormous impact on Italian Marxists of sundry persuasions.[13]

By his own admission, Sorel was not given to systematic exposition. His writings, he lamented, like those of J. J. Rousseau, lacked "harmony, order and that connection of the parts which constitutes a unity."[14] As a consequence, many revolutionary Marxists came away from them with different understandings of their claims and attendant implications. That notwithstanding, the central message of Sorel's work was eminently clear. He recommended an abandonment of "party socialism" and advocated a return to "pure proletarianism"—an exclusive organization of workers themselves. The "pure workers' organizations" would arise spontaneously in modern industry—without the intervention of "intellectuals"— more disposed as they were to detached rumination than action.[15]

For Sorel, intellectuals were responsible for the deflection of proletarian energies. Intellectuals made recourse to intermediary institutions that stood between the organized working class and their bourgeois enemies.

---

[10] Georges Sorel, *L'Avenir socialiste des syndicats* (Paris: Librairie de l'art social, 1898), pp. 26–31; and "Mes raisons du syndicalisme," in *Matériaux d'une théorie du prolétariat* (Paris: Marcel Riviére, 1909), translated into Italian to appear in *Divenire sociale* in 1910 with the title "Confessioni: Come divenni sindacalista."

[11] See the account given by Arturo Labriola, *Riforme e rivoluzione sociale* (1904; reprint, Naples: Società editrice Partenopea, 1914), pp. 1–16.

[12] Georges Sorel, *Reflections on Violence* (London: Collier-Macmillan, 1950, translation of the 1906 edition with attachments), p. 137.

[13] See Enzo Santarelli, *La revisione del Marxismo in Italia: Studi di critica storica* (Milan: Feltrinelli, 1977), pp. 80–92; Michels, *Storia critica*, chap. 8.

[14] See "Letter to Daniel Halevy," in the introduction to Sorel, *Reflections*, p. 32.

[15] Sorel, *Reflections*, pp. 50–52, 117.

It was they who—between the proletariat and the bourgeoisie—interposed the "state," fell back upon the sentiment of generic "patriotism," and invoked the military to suppress the righteous violence of the oppressed. Within this context, Sorel was intransigently opposed to the state and all its collateral appurtenances.[16]

What was immediately transparent was the fact that Sorel was more concerned with revolutionary behavior than he was with Marxist "science." He sought to more adequately account for what moved revolutionaries to action, what made human beings courageous in the face of challenge and heroic when exposed to mortal danger. He sought to understand what made human beings virtuous and selfless in a world that every day gave more and more evidence of moral decay.

In response to that imperative, Sorel isolated those elements in human behavior that appeared to sustain and inform individual and collective heroism, sacrifice, and commitment. He identified those elements with what he chose to call "myths," figures of speech that, within themselves, captured the essence of an imaginary future sought for with an irrepressible passion.[17] Such evocative images of an anticipated future overcome the sterilities of intellectualism—born of an absence of passion and a lack of vitality.[18] They create the ideal tension that inspires in the individual, and in the group, the readiness to sacrifice in heroic selflessness in the service of a higher good. Myths are generative of a salvific, renovating, and uplifting "new" ethics.[19]

Myths, for Sorel, were characteristically born in battle. Throughout history, war and its surrogate in revolution were the occasions out of which myths arose, to shape human beings, and the civilizations they, in turn, shaped. Democracy, compromise, and negotiation deflected the promise and damped the ideal tension productive of myth—and the virtues that were its direct consequence.

For Sorel, the fact that Marx's prediction that contemporary society would increasingly divide itself into two, and no more than two, mutually hostile classes was falsified by time, could be offset by the readiness of the proletariat to remain intransigent, opposing its nonproletarian opponents with absolute determination. The many groups in contemporary society would thereby be reduced to two—divided on the field of battle—to restore the integrity of the original Marxist vision of socialist revolution.[20] However much in error Marx might be in terms of his pretended predic-

[16] Ibid., pp. 48, 129, 133, 134, 138, 210.
[17] Ibid., pp. 48, 50–53, 57, 117, 140, 143–45, 147.
[18] Ibid., pp. 50–53, 117.
[19] Ibid., pp. 276–77.
[20] Ibid., pp. 150, 154, 179.

tions, the readiness of the proletariat to commit itself to combat in order to realize its liberating vision of the future would restore vitality to Marx's revolutionary anticipations. Out of the crucible of class combat would emerge the "sublimely heroic" worker, warrior, and producer of the anticipated syndicalist future.[21]

This was the ideological environment into which Sergio Panunzio, as little more than a youth, found himself thrust. Panunzio—who, ultimately, was to serve as the "semiofficial theoretician of the Fascist regime"[22]—was born in Molfetta, in Southern Italy, on 20 September 1886, and was active in socialist circles probably as early as 1901—and certainly no later than 1903. In that year, his first articles appeared in the *Avanguardia socialista*, a revolutionary journal founded by Arturo Labriola, one of the major intellectual leaders of the rapidly emerging syndicalist movement in Italy.[23]

The substantive core of Panunzio's earliest publications clearly reflected Sorelian concepts. In his graduate thesis, *Una nuova aristocrazia sociale: I sindacati*, for the Faculty of Jurisprudence at the University of Naples, Panunzio argued that select workers among those organized into syndicates (which at that time counted as members no more than 10 or 11 percent of the peninsula's workers)[24] constituted a "new aristocracy."[25] Among the members of the syndicates, an elite emerged to distinguish themselves by their abilities and their virtues, superior to their confreres in the self-affirming struggle against their oppressors. They were the select of their community, around whom the general proletariat, with sacrifice and selfless heroism, would accede to revolutionary power in Italy.[26]

Panunzio accepted all the essentials of revolutionary syndicalism: the "myth" of the general strike that would inspire the revolutionary working class to heroic enterprise; the insistence on direct action against class enemies; the explicit and intransigent opposition to the "bourgeois state" with its seductive appeal to patriotic sentiment and militarism.[27] There is

[21] Ibid., p. 269.

[22] Susanna de Angelis, "Sergio Panunzio: Rivoluzione e/o stato dei sindacati," *Storia contemporanea* 11, no. 6 (December 1980), p. 969.

[23] Francesco Perfetti, "Introduction," to Sergio Panunzio, *Il fondamento giuridico del fascismo* (Rome: Bonacci, 1987), pp. 9–10, 12; see Labriola, *Riforme e rivoluzione sociale*.

[24] See the discussion concerning the gradual industrialization of backward Italy during this period in Michels, *Storia critica*, pp. 223–25, 233–35, and the estimate of organized workers on pp. 326–27.

[25] See the account in Giuseppe Prezzolini, *La teoria sindacalista* (Naples: Perrella, 1909), pp. 95, 181, 191.

[26] See the discussion in Panunzio, *La persistenza del diritto* (Pescara: Abruzzese, 1910), pp. 277–78.

[27] See Panunzio, *Sindacalismo e Medio Evo (Politica contemporanea)* (Naples: Partenopea, 1911), pp. 117–18, 128; and *Persistenza del diritto*, p. 253.

no doubt that, at that time, Panunzio considered himself an orthodox and thoroughly committed revolutionary Marxist.[28] Nonetheless, there was evident, even in his earliest essays, a uniqueness of perspective, a subtlety of analysis, that, in retrospect, suggested something of his future intellectual and political evolution.

At no time were Panunzio's reflections confined exclusively to the inherited doctrinal literature of Karl Marx or Friedrich Engels. In his systematic study of revolutionary dynamics, he read widely in the available non-Marxist social science literature of the period. His pages were dotted with references, among others, to Vilfredo Pareto, Gaetano Mosca, Lester Ward, Friedrich Ratzel, Gabriel Tarde, Herbert Spencer, Werner Sombart, Alfred Marshall, and Gustav Ratzenhofer. For our purposes, one name recurs with perhaps more frequency than the rest: that of Ludwig Gumplowicz. In one of his first essays, Panunzio refered specifically to Gumplowicz's *Die sociologische Staatsidee*.[29] Thereafter, at least until the advent of the First World War, references to Gumplowicz appear in almost everything Panunzio wrote.

In the writings of Gumplowicz we find a rich conceptualization of social dynamics far more intricate and discriminating than anything immediately available in the Marx-Engels corpus. While Marx and Engels speak of history as the history of *class* conflict, Gumplowicz offers a textured account of history composed of a complex interaction of social *elements*—hordes, tribes, clans, sects, ethnic communities, city-states, classes, nations, and sundry "syngenetic" groups—spontaneous associations formed by a natural solidarity, each configured by group-building influences—kinship, shared interests, common territory, collective purpose, and a hostility to outgroups—all interacting to produce the fabric of events.[30]

It is evident that Panunzio found Gumplowicz's account persuasive. In his "Socialismo, sindacalismo e sociologia" of 1907, Panunzio speaks of history as being made up of the "eternal struggle" of "groups"—and (unlike Marx) not exclusively of "classes"—attributing the conception to Gumplowicz.[31] Nonetheless, Panunzio argues that in the modern period, *class* has become *real*—taking precedence over any other collectivity—because predicated on critical and irreducible life-sustaining and life-essential common interests. Out of the struggle for the very necessities of

---

[28] Panunzio reported that he was "firmly convinced of historical materialism." *Persistenza del diritto*, p. 214; see de Angelis, "Sergio Panunzio," p. 969.

[29] Panunzio, "Socialismo, sindacalismo e sociologia," p. 170 n. 3, and pp. 231–32 n. 2.

[30] The first major work outlining his conceptual framework was Ludwig Gumplowicz, *Der Rassenkampf: Sociologische Untersuchungen* (Innsbruck: Wagner'schen Universität Buchhandlung, 1883).

[31] Panunzio, "Socialismo, sindacalismo e sociologia," p. 170; and *La persistenza del diritto*, p. 195.

life, the working class, and the individuals of which it is composed, develop a clear sense of "vital interests," of collective concerns, in what is spoken of as "an instinct of self-affirmation."[32]

In formulating his views in such a fashion, Panunzio was following the lead of Sorel. Sorel spoke of the proletariat sharing the dispositions of the tribes of antiquity, consecrated as it was to the ends of an association of limited membership bound together by in-group amity and out-group enmity.[33] The class struggle, for Sorel, Gumplowicz, and Panunzio, was simply one form of universal group struggle that has forever typified human history.[34]

In his discussion of the formation of class consciousness, Panunzio employs all the central concepts of Gumplowicz.[35] Aggregates of human beings, become—for both Gumplowicz and Panunzio—self-conscious and self-regarding communities through cooperation reinforced by competition and conflict—through unconscious conformity to group suggestion, mimetism, repetitive interaction, positive and negative reinforcement, and social suasion.[36]

All of this served as a self-conscious supplement to traditional Marxism—innocent as Marxism was of any notion of the psychology of class formation. Sorel had made Panunzio sensitive to the shortcomings of traditional Marxism as social science, and Panunzio was aware that there was an intuitive sense of the incompatibility of Marxist economism and the social science findings of the first decade of the twentieth century. Panunzio spoke, in fact, of *two* theories, that of Marx's historical materialism and that of then contemporary social psychology—arguing that they were ultimately compatible and together delivered a more persuasive account of social processes than either could alone.[37]

Panunzio was familiar with the reservations articulated by Sorel concerning the "scientific" status of much of traditional Marxism. Sorel maintained that most of the explanations advanced by the founders of Marxism were, at their best, explanation sketches, laced together with trope and metaphor, given substance by virtue of empty truisms accompanied by broad and unconfirmed generalizations.[38] There is little doubt that Panun-

[32] See Panunzio, *Sindacalismo e Medio Evo*, pp. 118–19; and "Socialismo, sindacalismo e sociologia," p. 237.

[33] See the comments by Edward Shils in his introduction to Sorel, *Reflections on Violence*, pp. 17–18.

[34] See, for example, Panunzio, *La persistenza del diritto*, pp. 261, 274.

[35] See the account in Gumplowicz, *Die sociologische Staatsidee*, pp. 205–19.

[36] See Panunzio. *Il socialismo giuridico* (Genoa: Libreria moderna, 1907), pp. 59–60. Panunzio specifically cites Gumplowicz as his source; see p. 60 n. 1.

[37] Panunzio, *Socialismo giuridico*, pp. 215–16.

[38] "[In the Marxist texts] the relations . . . between the different orders of the ideological superstructure and economics as [its base] can only be expressed by means of figurative

zio was fully aware of these reservations. Initially, he seemed disposed to imagine them resolved by the works of others—Roberto Ardigò, Achille Loria, and Antonio Labriola among them[39]—but it remained clear that Sorel persisted in his reservations and continued to view the Marxism of the nineteenth century not as science, but as a form of evocative epic.[40]

Panunzio's first major work spoke somewhat cavalierly of the relationship of law to any given society's economic base. He dismissed any notion of law as the unique product of "solidarist sentiment" or "transcendental ideas." In his *Il socialismo giuridico*, Panunzio maintained that the "foundation of revolutionary socialism is economic, and that the ethical and juridical changes contemplated by that revolution are a result of economic change. Law is materialistically conceived not as self-standing, but as a 'superstructure,' an 'epiphenomenon,' that has its roots in the *economic substructure.*"[41] He made regular appeal to Gumplowicz's *identification* of *force* as the source and origin of *law*,[42] going on to assert that "positive law . . . is the infernal instrument with which the *dominant classes* seek to maintain their privileges, legalizing their crimes against those classes they dominate"—notions he equated with those of Marx's "materialist conception of history."[43]

If the law of the anticipated socialist society was to be "solidarist," based on collectively oriented ethical and humane convictions, Panunzio maintained, it could only be a *reflection* of antecedent revolutionary changes in the economic base. Law was an "immediate reflex" of the "economic base," while the social psychology of any given period was its "secondary reflex."[44]

The account of law and society Panunzio delivered at twenty-one was singularly simple and uncomplicated. He conceived the revolutionary future the direct product of changes in the economic base of society. As the industrial economy deepens and expands, drawing workers together in vast conglomerates, intensifying the exploitation without which capitalism cannot survive in circumstances of a declining rate of profit, labor is

---

speech. These figures of speech abound in the writings of Marx—making evident that none of them is really satisfactory. If the relationship [between the ideological superstructure and the economic base] was *direct and determinant*, one could characterize it with a specific terminology, doing without metaphors." Sorel, *Saggi di critica del Marxismo* (Milan: Sandron, 1903), p. 191.

[39] Panunzio, *Socialismo giuridico*, pp. 193–94.

[40] See Sorel's introduction to the French edition of Arturo Labriola, *Studio su Marx* (Naples: Morano, 1926), appendix, pp. 269–87.

[41] Panunazio, *Il socialismo giuridico*, p. 17.

[42] Ibid., p. 195; in this regard, see Gumplowicz, *Die sociologische Staatsidee*, pp. 139–41.

[43] Panunzio, *Il socialismo giuridico*, pp. 199, 201.

[44] Ibid., pp. 211–13, 216–17.

compelled to organize itself in voluntary associations that constitute the first intimations of the future socialist society.

In fact, Sorel had delivered himself of a much more complicated picture of the relationship of law and social change. Among the essays with which Panunzio was clearly familiar was one entitled "The Juridical Ideas of Marxism."[45]

In that essay, Sorel argued that Marx's account of the relationship between law and social change was much more sophisticated than most Marxists were prepared to recognize. There were clearly instances, in Marx's account of British factory legislation and the administration of British law, in which the role of ideological—that is to say, moral and ethical, convictions—directly influenced social change. Marx, Sorel argued, did not enter into the particulars of these instances because he "always felt embarrassed when he found it necessary to deal with ideological movements." In the case of the British legislation of 1867 with which Marx occupied himself, what was clear was that an "enormous transformation in law" had been an evident response to ideological pressures. However little workers might have directly benefited from the law—disadvantaged as they were in an environment of "bourgeois dominance"—ideological considerations had, nonetheless, influenced the laws governing Great Britain.[46] The relationship of law, force, governance and the economy was much more complicated than the twenty-one-year-old Panunzio had suggested in his *Il socialismo giuridico*.

What is clear is that Panunzio proceeded to develop a much more sophisticated conception of the relationship of law and society in works that were to follow. In 1910, Panunzio published his *La persistenza del diritto* in which he argued that law was intrinsic to society—and would persist beyond the anticipated universal proletarian revolution. "I have always been convinced," he informed his readers, "of the *social necessity* of law . . . and have so maintained against those anarchists who see the fulfillment of human liberty only in opposition to the positive ordinances of law."[47]

In his *Il socialismo giuridico* he had made general reference to the persistence of both *law* and *authority* in society, insisting upon the distinction between his syndicalist convictions and those of anarchists.[48] In *La persistenza del diritto* he developed those themes in a fashion that prefigured his subsequent intellectual development.

---

[45] Sorel, *Saggi di critica del Marxismo*, pp. 189–23.

[46] Ibid., pp. 210–11.

[47] Panunzio, *La persistenza del diritto*, p. x.

[48] Panunzio, *Il socialismo giuridico*, p. 230 n. 2, where he argued that the new positive law that would emerge from the syndicalist system would be governed by the same authority as that of bourgeois law.

In that latter work, Panunzio argued that law was intrinsic and necessary to human society, essential to human liberty, requiring for its actua-
tion the power of command—authority. The text was devoted to an account of how law and authority arise and function in a community.
Panunzio argued that the disposition to obey social norms, characterized
as a *natural* feature of social life, was a constant feature of associated life.
The willed regularities of collective behavior, when governed by public
sanctions, constitute the substance of law. Obedience to law, he argued,
was not simply or characteristically coerced; it arises out of the very circumstances of social life.[49] The authority that sustains law, Panunzio proceeded, is not *external* to the willed behaviors of individuals, but is *intrinsic* to them and to the human condition.

Panunzio identified both law and authority as among the most exalted
products of the social spirit of humankind.[50] He devoted a substantial
part of his text to the provision of an *empirical* account of what philosophers of law dealt with in a priori fashion. Law, for Panunzio, grew out
of the custom and usage that typifies the conduct of human beings living
in "organic" association—that is to say, living together in functional rela-
tionships typified by families in which there is a division of labor designed
to sustain the viability and unity of the association as well as produce
offspring equipped to carry the community into the future. Such associations, for Panunzio, are "organic," not the simple arbitrary products of
a thoughtless "authority."

Obedience to law, and respect for the authority that sustains it, Panunzio argued, finds its origin in the natural human trait of making positive
response to suggestion from primary group members, imitating the behavior of peers and superiors, and being responsive to affirmations of value
common to the community. The very nature of in-group amity renders
the individual susceptible to social influences that govern not only behaviors, but a sense of appropriate conduct, and helps generate the moral
and ethical convictions that sustain all of that.[51]

Such group behaviors, obedience to law and respect for authority,
strengthen the community in circumstances of threat. They enhance survival in a dangerous environment, ensuring the continuity of the community and its members. Departures from those behaviors threaten that survival. When a community is sound, the functional behavior of its members
is spontaneous and uncoerced. It is only when the community is stressed,
in a state of real or potential disaggregation, that coercive authority must

[49] Panunzio, *La persistenza del diritto*, pp. x–xi, xxi.
[50] Ibid., p. xii.
[51] Ibid., pp. 18–28.

be invoked in order to preserve what used to be its organic integration. Authority then becomes peremptory and absolute.[52]

Panunzio argued that the modern state, the class-based state analyzed by Marx, was a state intrinsically afflicted by those critical tensions attendant on the effort to bind together opposing *classes* that were animated by fundamentally antithetical interests. Such a state can elicit group-sustaining conformity only through the imposition of arbitrary and inflexible authority. The modern state, for Panunzio, was an *unnatural* aggregate, composed of a disparate collection of entities artificially put together and identified as a "people."[53]

As indicated, Panunzio had early identified human society as composed of *groups*, sociological entities manifest in a variety of empirical forms, some *real* and some *artificial*. In *La persistenza del diritto*, he held that the modern state, the "bourgeois" nation, and the "people" who made up its citizenry were "artificial"[54]—held together with arbitrary power sustained by security and military formations.[55] Panunzio, like all of his contemporary syndicalists, was antistate and antimilitary. For him, the only immediately real sociologically significant groups were the economic syndicates, the organized industrial workers of his time.

Panunzio held that the industrial syndicates were voluntary associations that reflected the true and abiding interests of their members. Unlike the political state, the syndicates were *homogeneous* in their composition, reflecting the homogeneity of the interests of their members.

In those circumstances, the conduct of individual members reflected the shared interests and the group sympathy natural to organic, functional communities. The behavior of individuals was uncoerced and spontaneous, unselfish and unreflective. Their conduct was unselfconsciously moral, governed by ethical principles, which might well be only implicit, but which could be identified by observation. Law and authority, in such situations, appeared effortless, rendered apparent only to constrain the conduct of those few suffering personality disorders that left them incapable of normal primary and secondary socialization.

Compared to the effortless law and ethical conduct that characterized the syndicates and their members, Panunzio maintained that the political state of his time gave every evidence of senescence, disintegrating into its constituents. The political democracy and representative parliamentarianism jerry built by the bourgeoisie could no longer hold the prevailing state structure together. The rising revolutionary proletariat could no

---

[52] See, for example, the discussion ibid., pp. 67, 71–72, 84–85.
[53] Ibid., pp. 34, 192–94.
[54] Ibid., pp. 193–94, 197, 254.
[55] See ibid., p. 204.

longer be contained in the old, unresponsive system. The general strike, the principal weapon available to organized labor, could bring down the entire shabby structure of modern society. At the same time, the syndicates, possessed of their own autonomous law and authority, would federate into agencies "harmoniously" incorporating all the lesser syndical entities into a superior "organic" body that would represent a "perfect and distinct incarnation of authority."[56]

To the complaint of critics that he had only "transformed" rather than abolished the state, Panunzio responded that what syndicalism anticipated was a form of social order that no longer featured the properties of that "artificial" political agency identified as the "bourgeois state." Syndicalists sought governance through autonomous, decentralized, law-engendering, real communities, rather than the artificially contrived political state. The syndicalist community would be a form of institutionalized, *corporative* self-governance—a "Social Republic of Labor." The federated syndicalist community would extend its authority over a defined territory and would represent the specifically *political* interests of the combined constituent syndicates. It would represent the interdependent will of the more ample and more general corporative interests of the confederated syndicates.[57]

Panunzio viewed all this as a modern conception of social and political organization predicated on the new learning of social psychology. He suggested that political communities composed of functional entities, each vested with a kind of initial political autonomy, would remain interdependent—and would represent a more inclusive, more diversified collective *will* that would find itself embodied in a single, larger, federated sovereignty.[58]

Such a law-governed and spontaneously authoritarian syndicalist-corporativist sovereignty would be the product of violent revolution—like all fundamental changes in law and authority in human history. Old systems of law and authority, once they were no longer capable of fostering and sustaining the prevailing order, were overthrown by a more functional and energetic alternative. The content of law and authority change, but their forms remain the same.

Thus, while Panunzio recognized that law and authority are given different content as a consequence of the threat or employment of violence, law and authority are neither intrinsically the products of, nor imposed by, violence. By 1910, Panunzio had moved a considerable distance from the position he had earlier assumed. Law was no longer spoken of as

---

[56] Ibid., pp. 206, 212.
[57] Ibid., pp. 199–201, 203, 207–17.
[58] Ibid., p. 199.

essentially the product of violence; it was seen as the natural product of custom, usage, and mimetism among the members of an organic community united in a common destiny. Authority was portrayed as the source of legitimation. It warrants the exercise of sanction that, in turn, makes law of mimetism, custom, and usage.[59] Authority itself has a rationale to which legitimacy ultimately makes appeal.

By 1911, Panunzio had articulated a conception of syndicalism that conceived it a new revolutionary movement, animated by pedagogical responsibilities and moral imperatives, almost religious in character, that would mobilize masses in the heroic service of a vast and complex mission that would transform the world of the twentieth century.[60] It was a movement, led by self-selected elites, that anticipated a political and territorially defined regime, based on vital economic interests, characterized by law, and governed by an authority to which an integral and organic union of persons would voluntarily submit.

In all of this, the young Panunzio recognized that his intellectual work had only commenced. He recognized that he was little schooled in the philosophy of law and had restricted himself largely to law and authority as empirical realities with which revolutionaries were compelled to deal. In 1912, on the other hand, he began to undertake more systematic study of his subject matter. He assumed professional obligations with the teaching of pedagogy at the Royal Normal Schools at Casale Monferrato and Ferrara and law at the Universities of Naples and Bologna.

Panunzio's *Il diritto e l'autorità*, which appeared in 1912, marked a significant change in the nature and character of his thought. In that work, he clearly separated himself from the prevailing positivism so evident in his first publications. In his introduction, Panunzio confessed that the then prevailing positivism, the scientism, of the turn of the century, so seductive to so many, had been grievously misleading. Positivism's dismissal of philosophical inquiry as empty metaphyics had led many thinkers to neglect the serious philosophical study of the subjects that engaged them.[61] For Panunzio, the study of law and authority had suffered.

In seeking to remedy the circumstances, Panunzio appealed to a roster of *idealist* philosophers, ranging from Rousseau to Kant through Hegel. In *Il diritto e l'autorità*, Panunzio recognized that any specifically sociological account of the origins and nature of law and authority[62] was to be

---

[59] See the discussion ibid., pp. 257–61.

[60] See Panunzio, *Sindacalismo e Medio Evo*, p. 107; and *La persistenza del diritto*, p. 259.

[61] Panunzio, *Il diritto e l'autorità: Contributo alla concezione filosofica del diritto* (Turin: UTET, 1912), pp. vii–vii.

[62] See the account in Gumplowicz, *Die sociologische Staatsidee*, pp. 127–32; and *Outlines of Sociology* (New York: Paine-Whitman, 1963), pp. 260–80.

considered, at best, a preliminary effort at understanding. In order to actually achieve comprehensive understanding, any such study would have to be subordinate to a careful, a priori conceptual analysis without which it would remain "blind." Conceptual analysis, "thought about thought," Panunzio held, must necessarily precede the serious study of law and authority. It had become clear that Panunzio was no longer content with any suggestion that law, justice, and authority were simply "reflections" of an economic "base," or contrivences to "serve the interests of the stronger."[63]

For Panunzio, in the study of law and society, of revolution and the state, *thought* would have to precede *experience*. One could not simply inspect the past and cobble together a collection of convictions about the *essence* of law, rights, revolution and authority. Only through the possession of *ideas* might one recognize the *facts* out of which defensible views might, in principle, be formulated. In any serious study, the relationship of ideas to facts is reciprocal. Cognitive *form* is necessary to provide a vehicle for empirical *content*, but content can, and does, render form comprehensible.[64]

By 1912, Panunzio was clearly under the intellectual influence of Benedetto Croce, at that time the principal spokesman for Italian neo-Hegelianism. Allusions to Croce had been made as early as Panunzio's first published works, but most of the references were general in nature. In *Il diritto e l'autorità* there was no doubt that much of Panunzio's analysis was Crocean in inspiration.

What had happened was a confluence of Kantian and neo-Hegelian insights that produced a volume that argued that law was a specifically *utilitarian* concern, an expression of Kant's *practical* reason, that carried with it, in its administration, *authority*.[65] Panunzio argued that the very nature of human beings implied society, society implied law, and law implied authority. As the very existence of community implied a sustaining economy, it also implied law as a functional and calculated necessity. And law implied authority.

For Panunzio, several things were demonstrably true: (1) the very idea of humanity implies community; (2) law is *logically* anterior to community;[66] (3) and law implies authority—a "preponderant, superindividual, and informing will."[67] What did not follow, Panunzio argued at that time, was that the *state*, alone, was the respository of law and authority.

---

[63] See Gumplowicz's comment in *Outlines of Sociology*, p. 265.
[64] Panunzio, *Il diritto e l'autorità*, pp. xv–xvi, xvii, xxii.
[65] Ibid., pp. 7–14.
[66] Ibid., pp. 83–84.
[67] Ibid., pp. 196 and 197–98 n. 2.

He argued that any association of human beings—united in interest and destiny—employed law and authority to sustain itself. It was clear that he was arguing that autonomous workers' associations, syndicates, might be fully capable of invoking and administering law without the superintendence of the state. In his *Sindacalismo e Medio Evo*, written about the same time as *Il diritto e l'autorità*, almost his entire account was devoted to the nature of law, and its sustaining authority, that governed syndical and corporative behavior in medieval Italy.[68]

The argument, derivative of philosophical idealism, was that law and authority *preceded* the political state, and would survive it. The state was only one of the possible and contingent agencies of law and authority. Thus, while law and authority were *immanent* and essential to collective life, the "modern bourgeois state" was not. Any functional community was fully capable, under appropriate historic circumstances, of exercising judicial power through the law and invoking the authority always implicit in associated life. Throughout time, Panunzio reminded his audience, law and authority were found manifest in clan, village, polis, communal and corporate entities.[69]

The argument was very clear. Workers voluntarily associated themselves in industrial unions. They governed themselves by laws of their own making. For Panunzio those voluntary associations, composed of intelligent and committed proletarian members—a new "social aristocracy"—would produce the "new, free, strong and beautiful" creators of a new morality—the denizens of the revolutionary future.[70]

For all intents and purposes, Panunzio concluded this period in his intellectual and political development with *Lo stato di diritto*, a systematic study of the German concept *Rechtsstaat*—the "law-governed state" or the "state of laws." That work was devoted to an account of the "juridical state," the state devoted to the maintenance and protection of individual freedom.

By that time, Panunzio identified his interests in law with the philosophy of Kant—who conceived human beings exclusively as *ends* and never *means*. Panunzio argued that the modern era had been born in the French Revolution and that European law had emerged from that doctrinal and historic experience intent upon the defense of individual political and civil rights. It was Kant who provided that defense with its philosophical rationale.[71]

---

[68] Panunzio, *Sindacalismo e Medio Evo*.
[69] Panunzio, *Il diritto e l'autorità*, pp. 215–17.
[70] Panunzio, "Socialismo, sindacalismo e sociologia," pp. 234, 236, 238.
[71] Panunzio, *Lo stato di diritto* (Ferrara: Taddei, 1921, but written in 1913–14. See p. vii.).

Panunzio argued that true socialism descended through the revolutionary thought of J. J. Rousseau and Kant—embodied in Rousseau's social contract convictions and Kant's *Rechtsstaat*, with its defense of the rights of individuals. For Panunzio, revolutionary socialism could only find expression in freedom for all, in a society in which all had property, and in which the authority that animated law was a reflection of the will of all.

In that socialism, the bourgeois state, as such, had no place. The purpose of revoluton was "the violent overthrow of the prevailing superstructure of the state and its law" that was the contemporary world's inheritance from the past. The consequence would be the instauration of a syndicalist society in which governance would be through the law and authority of an "overarching confederational agency" imbued with the "eternal and immortal principles of idealism and natural law."[72]

The First World War interrupted Panunzio's philosophical and political development. He had already, by the time of Italy's war in Tripoli in 1911–12, shown some signs of disaffection from traditional socialism's implacable internationalism.[73] With the advent of the European war, all of Italy's socialists found themselves overwhelmed by the prospect that the nation might be drawn into international conflict.

At that time Italy was, by treaty, allied with Germany and Austria-Hungary. Most of its irredentist, economic, sentimental, and military interests argued, however, for alignment with Great Britain, France, and Russia. The official Socialist party insisted on absolute neutrality. The proletariat was not to be employed in a "capitalists' war."

It became evident almost immediately that socialists of a variety of persuasions would not be content with the injunction to maintain neutrality in a conflict that promised to shape the future for the major powers of the continent. Revolutionary syndicalists were among the first to break ranks with the official socialist position. Panunzio was among them. By December 1914, Panunzio was among the founders of a *fascio interventionista* (an association for intervention in the conflict) in Ferrara.[74] Immediately upon the outbreak of war, Panunzio had submitted an article, "Il socialismo e la guerra," to *Utopia*, a journal edited by Benito Mussolini, devoted to recounting the compelling reasons why Italy must enter the conflict on the side of the Allied powers.

In his argument, Panunzio reminded Mussolini and his readers that "revolutionaries had forever been committed to fight for . . . the [socialist]

---

[72] Panunzio, "Il socialismo, la filosofia del diritto e lo stato," in *Rivista giuridica del socialismo*, 1914, pp. 81, 84.

[73] Francesco Perfetti, "Introduction" in Sergio Panunzio, *Il fondamento giuridico del fascismo* (Rome: Bonacci, 1987), p. 38.

[74] See Paul Corner, *Fascism in Ferrara, 1915–1925* (London: Oxford University Press, 1975), pp. 24–25.

idea to the exclusion of every materialistic and egoistic motive." The defeat of Germany and Austria-Hungary in war would open a future in
which socialism would triumph. If socialists truly opposed the "feudal
militarism" of Germany on the grounds of socialist principles, then Italy's
entrance into the war was morally obligatory.[75]

In the course of his account, while he did not himself invoke the issue
of nationality or national interest to support his case, Panunzio noted that
the war had provided *absolute* evidence that the "principle of nationality"
had united the peoples of France and Germany each into an integral unity.[76]
It was in the totally unanticipated patriotic response of millions to the
demands made by war that Panunzio first saw the outlines of what would
constitute the mobilizing myth of his revolution. In May 1915, in the days
immediately following Italy's commitment to war against Germany and
Austria-Hungary, Panunzio addressed himself, without hesitation and with
consuming sentiment, to the call of the "nation"—the "fatherland."

In his judgment, he had witnessed a united people rise up and overwhelm
the obstructionism of an increasingly dysfunctional parliament. He insisted
that he had witnessed a united nation commit itself to the test of mortal
conflict through the "direct action" about which syndicalism had long spoken.[77] He expected that the evolving conflict would tax Italians in a fashion
unknown in any "class struggle." Italians would emerge from the "hurri-
cane of death and fire" as "new men," the "warrior-producers" anticipated
by the early syndicalist vision of Georges Sorel. Italians, forged in war,
would emerge as a *Fascio nazionale*, a dedicated "national union." The
aristocracy of warrior-producers that would survive the Great War would
marshal all nationalists of the peninsula to meet the demands of a revolutionary mission that was taking on increasingly clear form.

As an interventionist, Panunzio anticipated that a new nation would
emerge from the war that would unite all classes, factions, and regions
within its confines to the service of a mission that would be of historic
consequence. The new nation that would emerge from the war would be
informed by "a strong, austere and rigorous moral character—a character
that was the glory of those first heroic times of disciplined socialism."[78]
All of the courage, commitment, and selflessness syndicalists had seen
in the laboring masses of Italy, throughout the long struggle against the
unresponsive and callous state, had been reborn in the combat veterans

---

[75] Panunzio, "Il socialismo e la guerra," *Utopia* 2, nos. 11–12 (15 August–15 September
1914), p. 324.

[76] Ibid.

[77] Panunzio, "La monarchia nazionale," *Popolo d'Italia*, 24 June 1915, reprinted in *Stato
nazionale e sindacati* (Milan: "Imperia," 1924), pp. 13–21.

[78] "Educazione politica," and "Una forza," in *Stato nazionale e sindacati*, pp. 28, 34,
35, 36.

who had survived the holocaust along the Isonzo, the Carso, and the Piave.

By the end of the war, Panunzio saw in the Great War the moral and political equivalent of the syndicalist "general strike." It was a conflict that had exposed all the frailties of the prevailing arrangements. The Italian parliament and the Italian state both lacked efficacy and coherence. The entire structure of society, composed of independent associations, professional leagues, and voluntary groups, failed to have representation in, or identify themselves with, the larger community. All the arguments Panunzio had formulated concerning the union of syndicalist and corporate bodies in a superintendent confederation were reinvoked. Only with that new invocation, the *nation* was identified as the foundation of a union of functional components—and the *revolutionary state*, unlike the state of the bourgeoisie, was seen as that agency endowed with the authority necessary for the administration of law as collective will.[79]

The nation was recognized as one of those critical communities early identified by Gumplowicz as agents of history. Panunzio had originally discounted the nation because he counted it an artificial collection of communities, each with its own interests. By the end of the Great War he was prepared to acknowledge that Italians, the body of a "nation," were unmistakably animated by a "living and vital national sentiment" that superseded narrower and more parochial interests. "The war had proved beyond question," in his judgment, "that an Italian worker and an Italian entrepreneur shared a greater sense of affinity . . . than was possible between an Italian and German worker."[80] Shared territory and a shared history—in which entire nations, animated by common culture and common aspirations, reacted to the offenses, the exactions, and the pretenses of others—made nationality an active principle in modern history.

By 1918, the nation had become a core concept of Panunzio's evolving "national syndicalism." In the emerging circumstances of post–World War One Italy, Panunzio saw all organized interests finding representation in a revolutionary syndicalist-corporativist state—a state "indisputeably superior to the parochial interests of classes, sects, categories, and all particular interests." It would be a state that would bring together, in an inclusive unity, all the factors necessary to render the nation "an organic, concrete, and historic" reality.[81]

Panunzio clearly recognized that all this had been implicit in his first theoretical writings. He recognized that the historical vehicle—the exclu-

---

[79] The following discussion is taken from Panunzio, "Il sindacalismo nazionale," which was written in November 1918 and was published in Panunzio, *La lega delle nazioni* (Ferrara: Taddei, 1920) and republished in *Stato nazionale e sindacati*, pp. 92–105.

[80] "Il sindacalismo nazionale," p. 100.

[81] Ibid., p. 105.

sively economic and proletarian syndicates—that he had chosen to represent the revolutionary future in 1907 simply could not serve. All the assessments he had worked through in the years between that time and the war were perfectly valid—it was their referent that was wrong. It was not the proletarian *syndicate* that was the agency of the future revolution—it was the "young and proletarian *nation.*"[82]

Panunzio was never to renounce those works produced between 1907 and 1915. He was simply to transfer the assessments that were made in them to the political, social, and economic environment of the Italy newly emerged from First World War. After 1918, Panunzio recognized the nation as the Sorelian "myth" he had first sought in the revolutionary "proletarian general strike." That sense of "mission"—so important to Sorel and all the syndicalists he inspired—Panunzio found in the revolutionary challenge of making "proletarian Italy" a great nation. The men of valor and purpose who were to have led the syndicalist revolution Panunzio found in those who emerged from the war as the heroes of the trenches. They were to constitute the elite that would energize masses through example and invocation. By 1919, Panunzio conceived the producer-warriors marshaled around the guidons of the first Fascism to have been the "new men" envisioned by revolutionary proletarian syndicalism before the Great War.

Panunzio expected the nationalists of Italy to join the ranks of national syndicalism. They had early recognized the affinities shared by both antidemocratic, antiparlimentarian, nationalist, developmental, and revolutionary movements.[83] Because of the productionistic intentions of nationalism, the leaders of nationalism expected to recruit among workers. Panunzio anticipated those workers would be from the syndicalist organizations already active. By 1918, Panunzio correctly anticipated the formal fusion between the political nationalist and the national syndicalist movements that, in fact, took place in 1923 in the course of Fascism's entrenchment as a regime.

By 1918, a year before the founding of Fascism, national syndicalism had matured as a doctrine. At the very commencement of the European war in 1914, A. O. Olivetti, one of syndicalism's foremost theoreticians, pointed to an evident reality: socialism, as an international revolutionary association, had disintegrated under the pressure of nationalism. By 1915, almost every socialist organization in Europe had opted to support its respective nation in the conflict.[84] By May 1918, Olivetti spoke, without theoretical embarrassment, of the "nation as the permanent patrimony of his-

---

[82] Panunzio, "Il sindacalismo nazionale II," *Stato nazionale e sindacati*, p. 108.

[83] Ibid., p. 109.

[84] A. O. Olivetti, "Parole chiare: La grande contradizione," *Pagine libere*, 30 November 1914, in *Battaglie sindacaliste*, pp. 105–9.

tory" for which masses were prepared to sacrifice their lives, their health, and their property. More than that, the nation was a functional association designed to produce the goods that would not only sustain its population, but underwrite its future in a threatening international environment.[85]

In November 1918, Mussolini himself identified national syndicalism as a doctrine that would unite economic classes behind a program of national growth and development. For the nation to emerge from the Great War as a potential member of the circle of victorious "great powers," it would be necessary to establish a "constructive" regime of "major production . . . a mode of reorganization of economic relations [calculated to generate] maximum return. . . . National syndicalism will make of Italy . . . a greater nation."[86]

Mussolini followed the theoretical developments among the syndicalist revolutionaries of France and Italy. In France, Leon Jouhaux had led a group within the Confederation generale du Travail to accept *production*, and *national orientation*, as revolutionary imperatives for a postwar syndicalism.[87] Mussolini carefully followed the development, and it is of some significance that on the first of August 1918, Mussolini changed the subtitle of his newspaper, *Il popolo d'Italia*, from "A socialist newspaper," to "A paper of combatants and producers," to reflect the national syndicalist conviction that the revolutionary future would belong to the "warrior-producers" early anticipated by the proletarian syndicalism of Georges Sorel.

By that time, Sorel himself had discovered affinities with French nationalism. He had long held that the heroic struggle of human beings in the consecrated and selfless service to the ends of a community bound in committed solidarity constituted the highest moral good. Sorel had originally perceived that committed community of solidarity in the workers' syndicates of the first decade of the twentieth century. By the end of the First World War, the nation appeared a more likely prospect.[88]

In substance, the thought of Panunzio had followed a sequence that was not uncommon among the revolutionaries of the first two decades of the twentieth century. From the initial positivism and scientism that had dominated the thought of those revolutionaries, he progressed through philosophical pragmatism to some form of critical idealism.

---

[85] Olivetti, "Nazione e class," *Battaglie sindacaliste*, pp. 116–18.

[86] Benito Mussolini, "Il sindacalismo nazionale: Per rinascere!" *Opera omnia* (Florence: La fenice, 1953–64), vol. 12, 11–14.

[87] See Francesco Perfetti, *Il sindacalismo fascista: I—Dalle origini alla vigilia dello stato corporativo (1919–1930)* (Rome: Bonacci, 1988), pp. 10–11.

[88] Richard Humphrey, *Georges Sorel: Prophet without Honor* (Cambridge: Harvard University Press, 1951), pp. 20–21.

Sorel had led the way.[89] Never convinced that there were deterministic laws governing the behavior of human beings, he had left latitude for the social and historic influence of "myth," sentiment, commitment to duty, and the abiding sense of moral obligation.[90] By the time he had written *Il concetto della guerra giusta* in 1917, Panunzio had assimilated all the qualifications concerning the "scientific" conviction that there were "laws" governing individual and collective human life. By that time, he spoke of the works of Ludwig Gumplowicz—which he had originally identified as providing "positive social science" confirmation of the economic materialism of Karl Marx—as "ultramaterialistic" and "mechanistic." Panunzio had come to understand that law, morality, ethics and group sentiment were potent factors in the evolution of society. He sought illumination in epistemological and ontological idealism. He spoke of history as a product of the human spirit and saw, in the best of Marx, the intimations of a "philosophic, idealistic, and humanistic" conception of individual and social life.[91]

In 1914, Panunzio had largely given himself over to a form of Kantianism, an emphasis on individualism, and a philosophy of law as an application of Kant's practical ethics to life and society. He had, by then, been introduced to neo-Hegelianism in the works of Benedetto Croce and had accepted many of its analyses. By 1917, Panunzio spoke of justice as a product of human activity. Law was not something fixed and finished to be discovered; it was something that emerged from a process that was inherent in the human condition. "Justice," Panunzio argued, " . . . like truth, was something that was in and with humankind," not something external. Justice, truth, and history were all products of "the incessant and irrepressible human spirit—divine because human." All these were products of the human spirit, the result of what he identified as "*autoctisi*," the "immanent self-development of the the human being," a concept central to the idealist philosophy of Giovanni Gentile.[92]

While there were approximations of Gentile's idealism in the work of Panunzio, it is clear, at the time of the conclusion of the First World War,

---

[89] See Pierre Andreu, *Sorel: Il nostro maestro* (Rome: Volpe, 1966), chap. 6.

[90] Georgi Plekhanov raised objection to such qualifications in the works of Italian syndicalists. He persisted in the conviction that Marx and Engels had discovered the "laws" of human behavior. See Plekhanov, *Sindicalismo y marxismo* (Mexico, D.F.: Grijalbo, 1968. Translated from the Russian edition of 1920).

[91] See the discussion in Panunzio, *Il concetto della guerra giusta* (Campobasso: Giolitti e figlio, 1917), pp. 69–71, n. 2 in its entirety.

[92] Panunzio, *Il concetto della guerra giusta*, p. 67. Panunzio, on this occasion, chose to speak of his conception of justice as predicated on Gentilean inspiration, and as "immanent juridical idealism" citing the "beautiful pages" on the subject to be found in Gentile's *Sommario di pedagogia*. See pp. 67–68, n. 1 in its entirety.

that the main arguments, critical to his analyses, were Kantian, individual-istic, and libertarian in character. While he continued to cite the work of Gentile,[93] he made eminently clear his commitment to the "natural law"[94] basis of his conception of the state, law, and society—a notion, because *transcendent* to, rather than *immanent* in, human consciousness, differed from that of Gentile's *absolute* idealism.

It is evident that Panunzio had not settled his account with modern philosophy by the time of the appearance of the first Fascism. Like many syndicalist thinkers, Panunzio had moved from philosophical positivism to one or another form of idealism.[95] What was not resolved, apparently, was the specific intellectual form that commitment would take.

By the end of the First World War, Panunzio expected Europe, if not the world, to enter into a period of systematic reconstruction after a long revolutionary interlude—a period he anticipated would be under the in-fluence of Gentile's "Actualist" idealism, together with nationalism, so-cialism, and futurism[96]—all movements that would come together to pro-duce Fascism. The period he anticipated would be one of order and solidarity, in which there would be a decided inclination among human beings to "obey and serve, to be free within order and within a system, to not so much search for rights as they would for law."[97]

By the time that the first Fascist squads arose, almost spontaneously, from the violence of the Great War, Panunzio had subscribed to, and in part articulated, the doctrine that was to be national syndicalism—an intrinsic component of the ideology of Fascism. National syndicalism shared evident affinities with the political nationalism of Enrico Corradini and Alfredo Rocco. It had begun to feature some of the species traits of neo-Hegelian idealism. In that latter regard, there remained a persistent tension between the Kantian libertarianism of Panunzio's earlier writings and the universalism and totalitarianism of Gentile's Actualism—a neo-Hegelian and post-Kantian idealism that had already begun, by the time of the formal establishment of Fascism, to inform the movement.

Nationalism, national syndicalism, and Gentile's neo-Hegelianism had begun to come together to produce the ideology of Mussolini's Fascism. It was within those fateful years, between 1919 and 1925, that Fascism

---

[93] See Panunzio *Introduzione alla società delle nazioni* (Ferrara: Taddei e figli, 1920), pp. 22, 30.

[94] Ibid., p. 26.

[95] This was true of Mussolini as well, who began his career as a socialist intellectual with a commitment to the scientism of the beginning of the century to finally settle on an epistemological, and perhaps an ontological, idealism. See Mussolini, "Per la vera pacifi-cazione," in *Opera omnia*, 18, p. 298.

[96] Panunzio, *Introduzione all società delle nazioni*, p. 19.

[97] Ibid., p. 25.

matured into the developmental totalitarianism that was to shape much of the twentieth century. It was the thought of Giovanni Gentile that was to provide many of the ligaments that wove together its ideology. And it was to be Ugo Spirito who was to translate Gentile's thought into the political currency of the period.

CHAPTER FIVE

Idealism, Ugo Spirito, and the Outlines of Fascist Doctrine

YEARS BEFORE the outbreak of the First World War, Giovanni Gentile articulated an interpretation of reality and politics into which prewar nationalism and revolutionary syndicalism were subsequently to merge.[1] By the first years of the 1920s, Gentile's philosophical Actualism became the vehicle of an inclusive national syndicalism that accommodated the thought of Enrico Corradini, Alfredo Rocco, and Sergio Panunzio. By the time the March on Rome brought Fascism to power, both Rocco and Panunzio had identified nationalism and syndicalism as critical constituents of its ideological rationale.[2] As has been indicated, both had gradually come together in the years before the Great War, until there was remarkably little doctrinal distance between them. It was clear that nationalists had early anticipated a coalescence of nationalism and syndicalism—and by the end of the war, the revolutionary syndicalism of A. O. Olivetti, Paolo Orano, and Sergio Panunzio had adopted so many of the essentials of Italian nationalism that their subsequent merger might easily have been anticipated.

Immediately before the Fascist March on Rome in October 1922, Panunzio published his "Stato e sindacati," in which he called for the creation of a "syndicalist state," in which the state, "as idea," would become "absolute"—the "living incarnation of the social idea."[3] By the time of the Fascist revolution, Panunzio identified the first period of syndicalist agitation—from the beginning of the twentieth century until about the time of the Great War—as "revolutionary," and "critical." The subsequent period, which he anticipated would follow the Fascist seizure of power, was conceived "synthetic" and "constructive." After

---

[1] For a fuller account of the work of Gentile and its relationship to Fascism, see A. James Gregor, *Giovanni Gentile: The Philosopher of Fascism* (New Brunswick, N.J.: Transaction, 2001); and *Phoenix: Fascism in Our Time* (New Brunswick, N.J.: Transaction, 1999), chap. 5.

[2] See Alfredo Rocco, "Costituzione e funzioni delle corporazioni," in *La formazione dello stato fascista* (Milan: Giuffre, 1935), p. 1008; and Sergio Panunzio, *Italo Balbo* (Milan: Imperia, 1922), p. 11.

[3] Sergio Panunzio, "Stato e sindacati," *Rivista internazionale di filosofia del diritto* 3 (January–March 1923), p. 9. The article was written in mid-1922; see p. 1 n. 1.

the disintegration of the liberal state, during the initial heroic period of Sorellian revolutionary violence, Panunzio expected the Fascist state to emerge as "absolute," with the plurality of syndicates "living with and for the state."[4]

By 1923, Panunzio traced revolutionary syndicalism from its origins with Georges Sorel through the philosophical insights of Georg W. F. Hegel to the idealism of the Gentileans.[5] Panunzio understood the "syndicalist state" he anticipated to be the constructive response of the nation to the disintegration of the antebellum liberal state.

By the time Fascism came to power, Panunzio argued that revolutionary syndicalism had been transformed by history and circumstance from a defender of anarchism and individualism into an advocate of the social and juridical reconstruction of the anti-individualistic and authoritarian state. It was at that time that Gentile's Actualism gave every appearance of being capable of providing a synthesizing philosophical rationale for emerging Fascism.

The nationalist preoccupation with law and the state, and revolutionary syndicalism's rapid abandonment of the simple materialism and the antistate postures that had sustained it during the first years of the new century, cried out for an inclusive *normative* rationale that would be their common vindication. It soon became evident to more astute observers, Benito Mussolini among them, that Actualism might fulfill that critical function.

By the end of the Great War, Gentile had formulated the principal outlines of a political philosophy that was to provide the union of nationalism and syndicalism with its rationale.[6] By 1918, Gentile spoke of anticipating the postwar emergence of a revolutionary "new state" that would be the expression of the "fully rational and concrete" national will of Italians in their collectivity. In that "revolutionary state," politics and morality, parochial and national interests, would combine in such a fashion that individuals would fully identify themselves with its actions. That new state would be a spiritual reality in which all would find their place. It would be a modern state that would provide labor fulsome standing. It would be a state charged with the accelerated development of an industrially, culturally, and politically retrograde peninsula. Gentile recognized that just such developments would be essential if the newly reunited nation was to escape from the palpably inferior position to which it was assigned by its industrially advanced contemporaries.[7]

[4] Ibid., p. 20.
[5] Ibid., pp. 4, 6, 7.
[6] For a more detailed treatment, see Gregor, *Giovanni Gentile*, chaps. 2–5.
[7] See the discussion in Giovanni Gentile, "Politica e filosofia," *Politica* 1, no. 2 (15 December 1918), pp. 39–54; and Gregor, *Giovanni Gentile*, pp. 25, 35, 46, 52, 65, 84–85.

The new state would find its leaders among those who would sense the needs of their time. Gentile was convinced that, particularly in times of crisis, uniquely gifted individuals were capable of intuiting prevailing political sentiment. Such leaders would be those who would represent their people as heads of state, or leaders of revolutions—manifesting a will not limited to his or her own individuality, but which would encompass the general will of all.[8]

Gentile's was a political concept rooted in the antiindividualism of classical idealism. The concept of politics entertained by Actualism was typical of that tradition. It was eminently inclusive—one in which the empirical, solitary, "abstract," individual, together with classes of individuals, the leadership of the state, and the state itself, constituted, in Gentile's judgment, an integral moral unity—what Gentile chose to consider a collective, if pluriform, "concrete individuality."[9]

That inclusive and collective sense of personhood underlay Gentile's entire conception of politics, law, and the state. By 1916, as a teacher of jurisprudence at the Atheneum in Pisa, Gentile taught that law and morality were, in some comprehensive sense, all one—with abstract distinctions to be made at the point at which the empirical individual found himself or herself confronted by statute law. For Gentile, law—at its very origins—was necessarily and inextricably *moral*—and, by implication, inescapably universal. As statute law, morality took on the features of "externality"—but faced with the responsibility of conforming, or not, to its strictures, the individual is compelled to deal with the intrinsic universality involved in the entire process.[10]

Out of that practical experience, the abstract individual of liberalism was introduced to the concrete, collective reality of the more expansive self of public morality. Morality entails universality—implying a "totalitarian" collectivity.

In effect, Gentile began his analysis with the Kantian distinction between practical and pure reason, between the mundane empirical self and the theoretical "transcendental self," in much the same fashion as had Sergio Panunzio at about the same time.[11] For Gentile, by 1916, all those

[8] Gregor, *Giovanni Gentile*, p. 6.

[9] See Gentile, *L'Atto del pensare come atto puro* (1912; reprint, Florence: Sansoni, 1937), para. 11, pp. 23–24; and "Politica e filosofia," pp. 50–51.

[10] See the discussion in Giovanni Gentile, *I fondamenti della filosofia del diritto*, 3rd ed. (1916; Florence: Sansoni, 1955), pp. 100–1.

[11] At about the same time that Panunzio wrote his *La persistenza del diritto* (Pescara: Abruzzese, 1910), Gentile was writing an introduction to Bertrando Spaventa's *Principii di Etica* (1903), in which the distinction between law, morality, and ethics was still argued within the Hegelian concept of the "practical spirit." See the discussion in Giuseppe Maggiore, "Il problema del diritto nel pensiero di Giovanni Gentile," in *Giovanni Gentile: La vita e il pensiero* (Florence: Sansoni, 1948), 1, pp. 231–44.

distinctions originally introduced by Panunzio in 1907 were identified as "abstract" moments actually immanent in the ultimate concreteness of jurisprudence and ethics—of law and morality.[12] By the end of the First World War, Gentile had, by and large, completed his post-Kantian and radical reformation of the Hegelian dialectic to produce the "Actualism," the "philosophy of pure act," that was to address all the issues of politics, law, ethics, and morality that were to engage Fascism.[13]

By the time the first Fascist "action squads" mobilized in Northern Italy in 1919, nationalism, national syndicalism, and Actualism had begun to come together to provide them their first clear intimations of a nationalist, developmental, revolutionary, and philosophical rationale.[14] At that juncture, Panunzio gave explicit expression to his national syndicalist commitments. Like the Actualists, he spoke of genuine political convictions as a union of thought and action.[15] He clearly held that his convictions, just such a synthesis, inspired his political behaviors. He spoke of an emerging political aristocracy expected to staff a revolutionary state that would, in turn, foster a new and revolutionary collective consciousness. He spoke of the state organizing inarticulate masses into productive "corporations" that would serve as institutionalized agents of the state.[16]

Mussolini succeeded, constitutionally, to rule in October 1922 with the invitation of King Victor Emmanuel to form a new government. With his ascendency, he immediately called upon Giovanni Gentile to serve as his counselor. He identified his new Minister of Education as his "teacher,"[17] and subsequently named him president of the commission charged with the responsibility of suggesting changes to the essentially liberal Albertine Constitution—to better conform to the requirements of the new regime.

---

[12] Gentile, *I fondamenti della filosofia del diritto*, pp. 98–100.

[13] See Gentile, *La riforma della dialettica hegeliana* (Messina: Principato, 1913).

[14] By the time of the rise of Fascism, Mussolini was addressing himself to the role of the "spirit" in the political processes of the peninsula. He clearly identified himself with a form of epistemological and probably ontological idealism. See Benito Mussolini, "Da che parte va il mondo?" and "Per la vera pacificazione," in *Opera omnia* (Florence: Fenice, 1967. Hereafter *Oo*), 18, pp. 70, 298; and "La culla e il resto," together with "Deviazioni," in *Oo*, vol. 17, pp. 90 and 129. Already in 1918, the antidemocratic, antipacifist nationalists of the Associazione nazionalista published the first issue of *Politica* in which they identified the nation with *spirit* and the *state* as its central institution—all calculated to further the industrial, territorial, and diplomatic expansion of the Fatherland (see "Manifesto," *Politica* 1, no. 1 [15 December 1918], pp. 1–17).

[15] Gentile had long since insisted on the immanence of action in thought. See Gentile, "Politica e filosofia," pp. 42, 44, 52–53. Panunzio made regular recourse to such a characterization.

[16] Sergio Panunzio, "Un programma d'azione," *Il Rinnovamento* 1, no. 2 (15 March 1919), pp. 83–89.

[17] Gabriele Turi, *Giovanni Gentile: Una biografia* (Florence: Giunti, 1995), p. 307.

As yet uncertain in power, Fascism was to proceed with the articulation of its formal ideology between 1923 and 1925. It was during that period that Panunzio, already an intimate of Mussolini, formulated the outlines of a revolutionary doctrine that combined elements of the syndicalism with which he had grown, the nationalism of the Associazione nazionalista, and the Actualism of Gentile.

Panunzio spoke of the poverty and humiliation suffered by Italians in modern times, and addressed himself to the critical functions expected of the state if the nation were to enter into the ranks of those already developed—those powers that dominated the peace arrangements that concluded the First World War. He spoke of the union of national syndicalism and nationalism as essential to the creation of just such a state.[18]

By the time of the first formulations of the political program of Fascism, it was manifestly evident that reactive and developmental *nationalism* was at the center of its convictions. Mussolini identified the nation as "the social organization" that "at that historic moment" was "dominant in the world."

The single imperative ideal "to which all else is subordinated," Mussolini maintained, was the maximization of the interests of the nation.[19] Should the evidence indicate that the nation prospered under a monarchy, Fascists were monarchists. Should there be evidence that the monarchy was dysfunctional, Fascists would be republicans.

Governed by the same criteria, neither war nor violence were ends in themselves. They were approved if instrumental to the purposes of the nation and abjured if not.[20] Neither a collectivism nor an individualist economy—an economy govered by state administration or by "free market" initiatives—were, in and of themselves, perceived as essentially Fascist. Their advocacy turned on their ability to enhance those productive capabilities that were critical to national purpose.[21] The arrangements that were considered conducive to those ends were chosen by Fascist theoreticians, at any given time, by what they considered best evidence.

That, once acknowledged, the informal logic of the Fascist position becomes apparent. The nation-state, as the contemporary vehicle of individual and group fulfillment, enjoys priority of commitment. Only in the development and expansion of the nation-state would the individual and constituent classes find their own fulfillment.[22]

---

[18] Sergio Panunzio, *Che cos'è il fascismo* (Milan: Alpes, 1924), pp. 15, 23.

[19] Mussolini, "Programma," in *Oo*, vol. 17), p. 321.

[20] See the comment made by Mussolini concerning war in "Il programma fascista," *Oo*, vol. 17, p. 219.

[21] Mussolini, "Programma e statuti del partito nazionale fascista," *Oo*, vol. 17, p. 338.

[22] Mussolini, "Le linee programmatiche del partito fascista," *Oo* vol. 17, p. 175.

Before the March on Rome, Mussolini insisted that "Fascism sees the nation before all else"—all else being subordinate to its interests.[23] In the formal party program of 1921, it was insisted that while the nation was the dominant form of social organization in the contemporary world, it was by virtue of the state, as the incarnation of the nation, "that individuals and associations of individuals in families, communes and corporate bodies, are enhanced, developed and defended."[24]

By the time Fascism had organized itself into a revolutionary movement, Panunzio had accepted all those tenets. He spoke of an emerging "state syndicalism"—a union of a "powerful state," revolutionary syndicalism, and developmental nationalism. Under the auspices of that state, retrograde Italy would become a powerful nation. The state would stimulate and sustain the development of an industrial base that would render the nation the equal of the major European powers.[25] The nation, so long humbled, would finally carve out its place in the sun.

Gone was the anarchic antistate rhetoric of his youth. Equally absent was the individualistic, libertarian, self-governing syndicalism that gave substance to his thought in the years before the War of Tripoli. Now Panunzio's syndicalism was collectivist—nationalist in content and statist in form and in structure. The state had become the hegemonic center of his political thought. It became the center of his system—its "ethical core." In the new formulation, the state was understood to be "infinitely superior" to all its components.[26]

Panunzio duly identified his political thought as the modern product of an Hegelian "metaphysics of the state."[27] By the time he collected together the essays that made up his *Lo stato fascista* in 1925, Panunzio had almost completed the transit from the positivism of Gumplowicz through the heretical Marxism of Sorel, the vitalism of Bergson, and the critical idealism of Immanuel Kant, to the ultimate identification of Fascism with neo-Hegelianism.

Among the neo-Hegelians who were to shape the ideology of Fascism was Ugo Spirito—one of the most notable students of Giovanni Gentile. Born in 1896, in Arezzo, Southern Italy, Spirito spent most of his youth in the provinces of Caserta and Chieti amid the poverty and backwardness

---

[23] Mussolini, "Fatto compiuto," *Oo*, vol. 17, p. 81. "The nation before all else; the nation above all else," "Il manifesto della nuova direzione del partito nazionale fascista," *Oo* vol. 17, p. 272. Mussolini affirmed that "the nation is that to which all else must be subordinated." "Programma," *Oo* vol. 17, p. 321.

[24] Mussolini, "Programma e statuti del partito nazionale fascista," *Oo* vol. 17, p. 219.

[25] Sergio Panunzio, *Che cos'è il fascismo*, pp. 19, 21, 23–25, 53; Panunzio, *Lo stato fascista* (Bologna: Cappelli, 1925), pp. 36–37, 47, 59, 66–67.

[26] Panunzio, *Lo stato fascista*, pp. 92, 95, 134, 165.

[27] Ibid., pp. 66–67, 71, 80, 85.

that typified the region. In 1914, at eighteen, he began his university studies. He was born, he affirmed later, in a revolutionary epoch—in a period
in which the inherited old order was being rapidly transformed. He reminded his readers that the dramatic changes of the period were accompanied by equally dramatic changes in patterns of thought.

The "scientistic" positivism of the first years of the new century had
very quickly succeeded in overwhelming virtually all philosophical speculation during a time that witnessed the first signs of sustained industrial
growth and development on the peninsula. Caught up in practical concerns, everyone became, in some measure, scientistic, positivistic. He re-
called that Roman Catholic modernists were as much positivists as were
revolutionary Marxists. In that company, Spirito began his intellectual
itinerary as much a positivist as anyone.[28]

Only in 1918, at the University of Rome and under the influence of
Gentile, did Spirito find himself drawn to the "new idealism" that had
gradually come to dominate Italian thought. By that time, Gentile had
already achieved notable status among Italy's philosophical luminaries.
An associate of Benedetto Croce, he had, by the end of the First World
War, distinguished himself in his own right. By 1918, Actualism had all
but fully taken shape.

In 1914, with the outbreak of the First World War, Gentile had become
an "interventionist"—advocating Italy's entry into the conflict against the
Central Powers. He published extensively in the political journals and
nationalist newspapers of the time,[29] and his ideas were well known
among the members of the Associazione nazionalista as well as among
individual revolutionary syndicalists. By the end of the Great War, the
substance of Gentile's philosophical and political thought was available.[30]

After 1918, under Gentile's influence, Spirito covered the distance from
his initial positivism to neo-Hegelianism—in very much the same sequence as had Panunzio and Mussolini—and almost immediately thereafter entered the ranks of Fascist intellectuals.[31] Years later, Spirito averred

---

[28] Ugo Spirito, *Memorie di un incosciente* (Milan: Rusconi, 1977), chap. 1.

[29] Most of Gentile's articles written during the First World War were collected in *Guerra
e fede* (Rome: De Alberti, 1927); and *Dopo la vittoria: Nuovi frammenti politici* (Rome: La
Voce, 1920).

[30] By the end of the First World War, some of Gentile's major works had already been
published. They included *Scuola e filosofia* (Palermo: Sandron, 1908); the two volumes of
Sommario di pedagogia come scienza filosofica (Bari: Laterza, vol. 1 1913, and vol. 2 1914);
I fondamenti della filosofia del diritto (Laterza: Bari, 1924); *Teoria generale dello spirito
come atto puro* (Laterza: Bari, 1924); and *Sistema di logica come teoria del conoscere*, 2
vols. (Pisa: Spoerri, 1917).

[31] By 1923, after Gentile formally entered the *Partito nazionale fascista*, Spirito partici-
pated in Gentile's intellectual and political activities that culminated in his adherence to the
Istituto nazionale fascista di cultura that both Gentile and Mussolini conceived a critical

that by 1922 he had acceded to Fascism via the Actualist thought of Gentile—and had remained an unqualified adherent—for at least a decade thereafter. For Spirito, one could comprehend Fascism's ideal commitments only by understanding something of the "actual" idealism of Giovanni Gentile.[32]

Spirito, as a disciple of Gentilean Actualism, was to serve as one of Fascism's most gifted spokesmen. He was to join the ranks of talented intellectuals, such as Curzio Malaparte,[33] who were to give expression to the complex thought that animated and sustained the "Regime."

Spirito had published his first major philosophical work in 1921, *Il pragmatismo nella filosofia contemporanea*[34]—clearly an expression of Actualist convictions. In that work he dealt with pragmatism as a body of thought, largely the product of *activists, voluntarists,* and *antipositivists* who, in Spirito's judgment, shared meaningful affinities with the thought of Gentile. In that sense, he was reflecting, in part, something essential about Fascism's own intellectual evolution. Fascism early displayed acknowledged affinities with generic pragmatism and Bergsonianism—bodies of thought that moved Fascism from socialist materialism to political, epistemological, and perhaps ontological idealism.

Spirito traced the development of general epistemology from the first suggestions that human activity intrinsically influenced the character of knowing on the part of the perceiving subject to be found in the empiricism of Francis Bacon and John Locke; to the intimations of "subjectivism" and philosophical idealism that progressively developed in the thought of David Hume and George Berkeley; to ultimately identify the role of the knowing subject in the epistemological idealism of Immanuel Kant, F. H. Bradley, and J. H. Green. Spirito, as we shall see, held knowledge to be a product of the intervention of the cognizing self in the process. In his judgment, the pragmatists of his time said nothing less.[35]

For Spirito, pragmatism was a kind of halfway house for modern idealism. Pragmatists, in general, were prepared to grant that human beings, per se, contributed in fundamental fashion to the process of coming to know. In some intelligible sense, "man was the measure of all things,"[36] an elliptical expression of the conviction that there are no "objective"

---

instrument in the formation of the political consciousness of Italians. See Gisella Longo, *"L'Istituto nazionale fascista di cultura": Gli intellettuali tra partito e regime* (Rome: Pellicani, 2000), passim.

[32] See Sergio Zavoli, *Nascita di una dittatura* (Turin: SEI, 1973), pp. 192–98.

[33] For the relevant work of Malaparte, see Curzio Malaparte, *L'Europa vivente e altri saggi politici (1921–1931)* (Florence: Vallecchi, 1961).

[34] Florence: Vallecchi, 1921.

[35] Ibid., chap. 1.

[36] Ibid., p. 15.

truths, if "objective" was understood to mean that human senses, senti-ment, values, judgments, conceptualization, interests, and will had noth-ing to do with its determination. That kind of purported "truth" would be dogmatic—inflexibly affirmed—for which intersubjective certification could not possibly be forthcoming. That sort of "truth" required a com-mitment to a form of abstract *intellectualism*[37] to which Actualism, and Spirito as its spokesman, objected in principle.[38]

By 1923, during the course of the Fascist revolution, Ugo Spirito be-came Gentile's most articulate spokesman in Italy.[39] In his exposition of Gentile's thought, its implications became increasingly apparent. By that time, Italian Fascism had carefully distinguished itself from the social and philosophical materialism of the Leninism[40] that had swept to power in what had been czarist Russia.

Spirito, like all Actualists, objected to any epistemology that conceived the world in dualistic fashion: as a fixed and finished "law-governed na-ture," which human consciousness simply encountered. Spirito, like Gen-tile,[41] was opposed to a "materialism" that imagined that there was an "objective world" outside of human consciousness that awaited discov-ery. The dualism of matter and consciousness that was a by-product of a primitive "commonsensical" epistemology was rejected.

[37] "We can . . . define intellectualism as the conception of a reality which is intended as the opposite, and nothing but the opposite, of mind. If mind has such independent reality confronting it, it can only know it by presupposing it already realized, and therefore by limiting itself to the role of simple spectator." Giovanni Gentile, *Teoria generale dello spirito come atto puro* (Laterza: Bari, 1924), p. 222; see "The classical conception [of philosophy] is *intellectualistic*: it presupposes that thought has before it a reality with which it enters into rapport . . . an antecedent reality . . . which devours it, to remain alone and infinite. [What] results is materialism. Intellectualism can result in nothing else." Gentile, "Politica e filosofia," p. 40.

[38] An "intellectualistic" epistemology is one that conceives "facts" as "absolutely objec-tive"—as passively "observed" by the perceiving subject. See Gentile, "Politica e filosofia," pp. 38–39, and for Spirito's further allusions to "intellectualism," see Ugo Spirito, *Il prag-matismo nella filosofia contemporani* (Florence: Vallechi, 1921), pp. 45, 50–51, 67, 73, 87–88, 106–19, 122, 131–32, 150, 158–59, 168. "A dogma is an affirmation that not only has never been confirmed [proven], but which, by definition, excludes any possible confirma-tion." P. 184. Spirito approved of pragmatism because, in his judgment, it was *anti-intellec-tualist*, pp. 50–51.

[39] Ugo Spirito, "Giovanni Gentile" (written in 1923), *L'Idealismo italiano e i suoi critici* (Florence: Felice le Monnier, 1930), pp. 39–57.

[40] It is manifestly clear that Spirito entertained significant distinctions between the general epistemology, ontology and political philosophy of Karl Marx and that of V. I. Lenin and Josef Stalin—the latter compromised the former through the tactical and strategic necessities of surviving in the modern world. See the discussion in Ugo Spirito, *La filosofia del comu-nismo* (Florence: Sansoni, 1947), particularly pp. 18–20.

[41] See Gentile's comments in Giovanni Gentile, *La riforma dell'educazione: Discorsi ai maestri di Trieste*, 5th ed. (1919; Florence: Sansoni, 1955), chap. 4.

Spirito, like Gentile, rejected the intellectualistic conviction that there could be a "reality," a "nature," antecedent to knowing—a reality that could only be detected through human sensations, sensations that somehow "reflected" the properties of that "external and material" nature. Actualism rejected such notions—and held that, under the conditions envisioned by materialists, any such external reality could only be, like Kant's *noumena*, essentially unknowable. It would constitute a philosophical absurdity.[42] Given that assessment, *all* forms of epistemological and ontological materialism were summarily dismissed as forms of sterile "intellectualism."[43]

Like Gentile, Spirito argued that the act of thinking, spiritual awareness itself, must somehow encompass, within itself, all truth values and moral enjoinments. Like Gentile, the young Spirito was an *absolute* idealist—who began with an elementary awareness out of which thinking (*pensiero pensante*) would "dialectically" generate the categories that would give descriptive and normative form to "reality."[44]

Rejecting the presupposition of ontological realists—who attempt to fashion reality out of a suppositious relationship of individual *subjects* interacting with *external objects*—Spirito characterized "reality" as *pensiero pensate*, as something *thought*, a *product* of collective thinking. In effect, he sought (as did Gentile) to render reality "concrete"—as a form of collective consciousness. For Spirito, the very notion that one might coherently speak of an objective reality independent of collective reasoning was cognitively meaningless. For Actualists, reality could only be a product of the reasoning of a thinking community. The evidence for any reality, whatever, could only be given as part of a shared consciousness—*immanent* in collective consciousness itself. To speak of a reality that was independent of and/or antecedent to such consciousness could only involve ("intellectualistic," i.e., dogmatic) presuppositions that were epistemologically indefensible.

Clearly, the talk of a reality independent of a collective consciousness was recognized as methodologically *useful* for the various empirical sciences. The pragmatists of the period had established that reasonably well. Spirito's point, like that of Gentile, was that whatever intellectual strategy

---

[42] See the discussion in Ugo Spirito, "Giovanni Gentile," *L'Idealismo italiano*, pp. 42–43.

[43] Throughout the history of the Soviet Union, Leninist thinkers attempted to defend the epistemological and ontological materialism of V. I. Lenin. See the discussion in A. James Gregor, *A Survey of Marxism: Problems in Philosophy and the Theory of History* (New York: Random House, 1965), chap. 3. Gentile did not attribute that form of epistemological materialism (or realism) to Marx. See Gentile's discussion in Gentile, "La filosofia della prassi," in *I fondamenti della filosofia del diritto* (Florence: Sansoni, 1955), pp. 205–19.

[44] Spirito, "Giovanni Gentile," pp. 44–45.

might prove *useful* need not be *true* nor philosophically defensible—and might have entirely negative moral implications for human actors.

It was eminently clear to Spirito that all the categories that informed the empirical sciences were ultimately subjective, and inescapably dependent on some kind of analytic process intrinsic to interactive thinking itself—rather than the consequence of individual responses to some reality independent of mind.[45] Human judgment, choices, criteria, and purpose gave substance to scientific description, the assessment of probabilities, the categorization of subject matter, and the complex theoretical constructs of standard inquiry. There could be no "reality" independent of consciousness.

While Spirito recognized the practical purposes of empirical science, he insisted that such "abstract" sciences, once "concretely" considered, however otherwise useful, could no longer serve as a philosophical rationale for determinism and amorality. For Spirito, the sciences were the products of shared reflection— as consciousness or "spirit"—parsed into useful, but ever-changing, dynamic categories. To pretend that science was composed of individually perceived "pictures" of a mind-independent reality was cognitively unintelligible[46] and proved to be morally repugnant. That had become eminently clear with the recognition that "realists" and "materialists" could only speak, counterintuitively, of the reality of the world in terms of a "matter" having no objective properties whatever[47]—as well as being entirely devoid of anything that might be instructive in terms of individual human morality.[48]

The categories that provide descriptive content to the individual sciences constitute the "abstract logic" of ordinary knowing—the "concreteness" of which is to be found in the activity of the "transcendental self," that conscious, collective self that is the communal source not only of comprehensive knowing, but of moral principles as well. Spirito, like Gentile, argued that the criteria employed in the generation of categories, as well as those invoked to establish their truth, are the result of an array of individual human decisions made in the course of *shared* reflection — rendering every human judgment a moral choice. Both Gentile and Spirito argued that the most fundamental human experiences reveal the totalitarian complexity of immediate consciousnesses. Concrete thinking distinguishes itself radically from the "things" that emerge upon reflection. *Immanent* in thinking itself is its complexity, a dialectical complexity that

---

[45] Ibid., pp. 47–48.

[46] Spirito, *Il pragmatismo*, p. 31.

[47] Ibid., p. 64.

[48] See the discussion in Gentile, *Teoria generale dello spirito come atto puro*, chap. 15; and compare Spirito, *Il pragmatismo*, p. 29.

requires other "things" and other "spirits" in order to actively proceed. Those things and other persons are immanent in thinking and essential to morality.

Gentilean idealism conceived the "absolute self" to be the unity out of which all scientific and moral diversity arises.[49] It is the *act* of thinking out of which all particularity emerges. Thinking (*pensiero pensante*) is *collective—universal* in essence. Concrete consciousness, spirituality, per se, knows no limits, no restrictions. It is truly *presuppositionless*— and thus ceases to be the thinking of the *empirical* self of naturalistic psychology. Thinking, in its ultimate reality, involves action that resolves everything into itself—and therefore implies a more profound or collective self than that of the immediate individual. It involves a "profound" self, which recognizes all other thinking selves as at once other—while yet one with itself. Those "other selves," however they are metaphysically or ontologically conceived, provide us the simple and complex empirical "facts" that constitute some of the principal elements of our "concrete" thinking—the thinking of our greater self.[50]

Spirito, as a consequence of this conception of the transcendental or profound self, identified *ethics* as the critical center of Actualism. Without others, there could be no confirmed truths—and without others there would be no ethics or applied morality. Recognizing a community of "other selves" as critical to thinking renders not only truth, but interpersonal morality, central to Actualist thought.[51]

Gentile often referred to other selves as essential to moral maturation, to the *universality* that ethics requires of the initial finite self. "When we look within our own consciousness and consider the value of what we are doing and of what we are saying to ourselves, it is as though innumerable eyes were looking in upon us as judges. . . . We are not a pure theoretical experience. And therefore our world is peopled with other minds, with other persons." In the concrete reality of "dialectical development," the finite, empirical self, in truth and morality, reveals itself as a "transcendental 'we.' "[52]

What appears to be clear in the Actualism of both Spirito and Gentile is a notion that other selves are critical to the actualization (*autoctisi*) of the self. The Actualist concept of the transcendental self provides the

---

[49] See the account in Gentile, *Teoria generale dello spirito come atto pure*, chaps. 17 and 18. Chapter 18 was added to the later editions of the *Teoria generale*. The discussion of the "self-development" of the "transcendental self" is found prominently in Gentile, *Sistema di logica come teoria del conoscere* (Florence: Sansoni, 1942), vol. 2, chap. 5.

[50] See the entire discussion of Spirito, *L'Idealismo italiano e i suoi critici*, pp. 55–57.

[51] Ibid., pp. 54–55.

[52] Gentile, *Teoria generale dello spirito come atto puro*, pp. 32–33, 37.

unmistakable essentials of a social conception of truth and an Actualist political ethics.

Long before the advent of Fascism—as early as the second decade of the twentieth century—Actualism had already argued that the individual self of liberal political thought was "unreal," in some significant senses a fiction. For Gentile and Spirito, the multiplicity of selves, understood by liberalism to be the foundation of politics, was not a common sum, but a transcendental community. Political liberalism mistakingly regarded the empirical selves as "true" selves—and dismissed the communal self, "which alone is the true subject of our experience and therefore the only true self."[53]

The Actualist conception of the communal "true" self, which identified itself with the state as the executive expression of the political community, was to become the normative rationale for Fascist totalitarianism. It was to displace the insistent individualism that characterized political liberalism since its emergence in the seventeenth and eighteenth centuries.

The notion of the Hegelian "more profound self"—in which the "narrow" empirical individual was identified—was incorporated into Fascism's rationale as an identification of the ordinary individual, as political subject, with the inclusive, unitary will of the historic community. It was a philosophical notion that abandoned the libertarian individualism of "bourgeois democracy" for a form of collectivism in which empirical individuals identified with a "larger," more profound self. Within the reflections of Gentilean Actualism, the ordinary individual of political liberalism had become more and more "abstract" and unreal over time, achieving "concreteness" only in the neo-Hegelian analysis of the empirical individual's boundless communion with others in society and the state.

The Actualist identification of the individual of common sense with the political state was to serve as the linchpin of Fascist corporativism and totalitarianism—the economic and political system articulated to unite all citizens in that enterprise committed to the rapid and comprehensive economic development of the retrograde Italian peninsula. In that process, Spirito was to emphasize the functional utility of the moral and pedagogical quality of Actualism, a quality that made of the interaction of persons the occasion of "love and spiritual communion" even when separated by differences. Differences with others were not conceived obstacles to self-articulation or commitments to collective mission.

For Actualists, at the foundation of the empirical self is a more profound self "that knows no plurality."[54] Real and imagined differences can, and must, be overcome if self-development is to proceed and mission re-

---

[53] Ibid., p. 30.
[54] Spirito, *L'Idealismo italiano e i suoi critici*, p. 56; see the discussion in chap. 8.

sponsibilities are to be discharged.[55] Implicit in such formulations is the seamless identification of the individuals of common sense with the revolutionary and developmental will of the totalitarian state.

Actualism argued that human beings achieve the fullness of self through a process of self-actualization—involving exchanges with others and against things in the course of establishing truth and fulfilling responsibilities. In that sense, interaction with others was an essential part of the enterprise. Nationalists and syndicalists themselves had both identified the consuming developmental responsibilities of the revolutionary state with the occasion for truth determination and the self-actualization of individuals.

It was in that context that, as early as 1920, Gentile argued that *labor*, in general, constituted one of those special forms of interactive spiritual activity through which human beings shaped themselves.[56] It was a conviction that was to significantly influence the subsequent work of Ugo Spirito. Out of those convictions, the work of Spirito as a corporativist theorist was to take on form. It demonstrably reduced the doctrinal distance, already diminished, between Actualists, national syndicalists, and the nationalists of the Associazione nazionalista.

By the beginning of 1925, the Fascism that had acceded to power in October 1922 transformed itself into the "Regime" with which historians have identified it ever since. Its animating doctrine became specific insofar as it manifested itself in institutions.

While the program of the Partito nazionale fascista of 1921 anticipated "reducing the state to the essential functions of political and juridical order,"[57] by 1925 Mussolini spoke, without qualification, of the necessity of marshaling all the forces of the nation into the overarching unity of one single state solidarity that represented the collective "totalitarian will" of Fascism.[58] What had transpired in the interim is relatively easy to trace. Actualism had given the substance of its ideas to Mussolini's Fascism. How that had come about is equally transparent.

On 10 June 1924, individual Fascists kidnapped a socialist member of the lower house of the Italian parliament who had been extremely critical of Mussolini, in particular, and of Fascists, in general. Almost immediately, it was feared that he had been murdered. Eight weeks later his body

---

[55] This was the central argument of Gentile's pedagogical writings. See the entire discussion in *La Reforma dell'educazione: Discorsi ai maestri di Trieste* (1920; reprint, Florence: Sansoni, 1955).

[56] Giovanni Gentile, *Discorsi di religione* 3rd ed. (Florence: Sansoni, 1955), p. 26.

[57] "Programma del PNF (1921)," in Renzo De Felice, *Mussolini il fascista: La conquista del potere, 1921–1925)* (Turin: Einaudi, 1966), p. 756.

[58] See Mussolini, "58 Riunione del Gran Consiglio del Fascismo," and "Intransigenza assoluta," in *Oo*, vol. 21, pp. 250–51, 362.

was discovered. There was palpable revulsion on the part of Italians every-where on the peninsula—and the regime descended into immediate crisis. For a time it appeared that Mussolini might be compelled to resign, pre-cipitating the restoration of the "old order."[59]

Only on 3 January 1925 did Mussolini feel secure enough to denounce those who had called, six months before, for his dismissal and the suppres-sion of Fascism. He announced, without equivocation, that Fascism, as a government, and as a party, was in complete and effective control of the nation. Fascism sought to give "the peace, the tranquility and the oppor-tunity to return to labor that the people sought—with love if possible, or with force, if necessary."[60] Thereafter, neither Mussolini nor Fascism spoke of any accommodation with the elements of the former system. The talk, thereafter, was of the totalitarian, corporative, and ethical state— the final collectivist synthesis of nationalism, syndicalism, and Actualism.

It was at that juncture that the Actualism of Spirito took on the special character that was to shape the subsequent history of Fascism. After 1925, it became evident that Mussolini sought to institutionalize the *totalitarian* and *ethical* state anticipated by Giovanni Gentile years before. After 1925, there was to be no further talk of an individualistic "Manchestrian" state—a limited state performing only ancillary functions for the nation.[61]

Mussolini had always been an astute politician. He had been a gifted tactician, a recognized *"tempista,"* one who could calculate probabilities of success in given political circumstances. Throughout the preliminary stages of the revolution, those talents served him well. During that period, he had gathered around himself a collection of representatives of some-times conflicting interests. There were syndicalists preoccupied with the well-being of their organizations; there were industrialists concerned with their individual and collective business interests; there were landowners and tenant farmers, each group pursuing its own real or conceived inter-ests. All these groups were to be drawn into the vortex of events during the years of civil strife and revolutionary activity that preceded Fascism's ascent to power.

In those circumstances, tactical compromise became critical to the strat-egy of success. Even the seizure of power had been a compromise between the Blackshirt squads, the king, his conservative counselors, intellectuals,

---

[59] See the account in De Felice, *Mussolini il fascista, La conquista del potere 1921–1925,* chap. 7.

[60] Mussolini, "Discorso del 3 Gennaio," in *Oo,* vol. 21, p. 240.

[61] In the Fascist party program of 1921, the state was to be "reduced to its essential political and juridical functions" in defense of the "autonomous values of individuals and associated individuals that are expressed in the form of collective persons (families, com-munes, corporations, etc.)." Renzo De Felice, "Programma del PNF (1921)," in *Mussolini il fascista, La conquista del potere, 1921–1925,* p. 756.

and the parliament composed of as many political democrats and liberals as anti-Fascist socialists. What distinguished Mussolini from the politicians who had practiced compromisory strategies since the establishment of the new Italian state in the nineteenth century was his continued investment in a collection of doctrinal commitments that resurfaced in his overt behavior whenever conditions permitted.

To anyone who knew anything about Mussolini, it was clear that there was very little that was conservative, liberal, or politically democratic about his most fundamental convictions. Through all the phases of his political apprenticeship, Mussolini had always been an elitist, as well as a singularly antidemocratic revolutionary. By the beginning of 1925, the liberals, together with the advocates of political democracy, had either fallen away or reinterpreted their convictions in order to render them compatible with those given expression by Mussolini on 3 January 1925.

For a brief period of time during the mobilization of the movement and immediately after his accession to power, Mussolini advocated liberal economic policies—opposing state interference in the productive process. The advocacy of a strong state was central to Fascism's prospective domestic political policy, but together with that advocacy was a general commitment to noninterference by the state in economic matters. In 1921, the Fascist program held that Fascist economic policy was essentially liberal—that "in economic matters, we are liberal."[62]

Such a programmatic position appeared counterintuitive. One would expect a "strong" state to be prepared to intervene in the national economy whenever it chose. Why Mussolini chose such a stance can be reconstructed with a measure of confidence.

At the very core of Fascist beliefs was the certainty that Italy required rapid economic growth and industrial development if it were to survive and prevail in the twentieth century. At the same time, Mussolini became increasingly aware of the massive economic and industrial failures that stalked the Bolshevik revolution. By 1922, the world had witnessed the catastrophic collapse of the Russian economy,[63] a reality that could only influence Mussolini's judgments concerning the efficacy of state intervention in the productive process.[64] He had followed the revolution in Russia with particular application and was convinced that its failures were object lessons for revolutionaries everywhere. That, together with some early influences that recommended "free enterprise" arrangements as instrumental to rapid industrial growth, led Mussolini to maintain that Fas-

---

[62] Mussolini, "Il programma fascista," in *Oo* vol. 17, p. 220.
[63] Mussolini, "Quando il mito tramonta," in *Oo* vol. 17, pp. 323–25.
[64] See, for example, Mussolini, "Il fascismo nel 1921," in *Oo*, vol. 16, pp. 101–3.

cism's developmental program anticipated a decentralized[65] "Manchestrian state" for the peninsula—reducing the state's function to the protection of its citizens through a well-organized and provisioned police force, a military for the defense against foreign aggression, and the formulation of a foreign policy that would serve the national interests.

Divested of its economic functions, the state would serve rapid economic development by maintaining discipline in the nation and order among the factors of production. "The state must maintain all imaginable possible controls," Mussolini maintained, "but it must renounce every form of economic management."[66]

The devastating consequences of the Bolshevik policy of "war communism"—with its state dominance of the economy—reinforced the liberal economic policy suggestions that were commonplace among Italian syndicalists. Before his death in the First World War, for example, Filippo Corridoni, a revolutionary syndicalist and an intimate of Mussolini, had argued that Italy was an underdeveloped nation with an economy still in its "swaddling clothes." If Italy was to discharge its historic and revolutionary functions, he continued, it would have to develop its economy very rapidly to produce a requisite revolutionary proletarian majority, and an economy capable of offsetting the influence of its international "plutocratic" opponents—who saw in less-developed nations their legitimate prey. Less-developed nations that had entered late into the process of industrial and technological development would otherwise remain forever the victims of the advanced industrial powers.[67]

To avoid that doleful prospect, Corridoni advocated an unqualified commitment to liberal and free-trade policies: the protection of infant domestic industries, and a complete withdrawal of state influence in the productive processes of the nation.[68] The rapid economic growth and development would provide those financial and military capabilities that would not only protect the nation from predation, but it would also create the preconditions for its revolutionary renewal.

The realities of the devastation state dominance of the economy had brought to Bolshevik Russia, together with the insights of Italian syndical-

[65] Mussolini, "Il programma fascista," in Oo vol. 17, p. 218.

[66] Mussolini, "Il fascismo nel 1921," in Oo, vol. 16, p. 101.

[67] Filippo Corridoni, Sindacalismo e repubblica (1915; reprint, Rome; Bibliotechina sociale, 1945), pp. 19, 22–23, 25, 32–33, 41, 48–49, 55–56, 82, 110–11. See the account in Ivon De Begnac, L'Arcangelo sindacalista (Filippo Corridoni) (Verona: Mondadori, 1943), chap. 32; and Vito Rastelli, Filippo Corridoni: La figura storica e la dottrina politica (Rome Conquiste d'impero, 1940), chaps. 1–3.

[68] Corridoni, Sindacalismo e repubblica, pp. 57, 75, 80–81, 86, 88, 91–93. For a more substantial discussion of the thought of Corridoni, see Gennaro Malgieri, "Il 'sindacalismo eroico,' di Filippo Corridoni," Rivista di studi corporativi 17, nos. 3–6 (September–December 1987), pp. 607–37.

ists, led Mussolini initially to propose laissez-faire economic policies for a Fascist Italy. That attracted the support from those classical liberal economists who saw only calamity in the intended policies of revolutionary Marxism.

Both Vilfredo Pareto and Maffeo Pantaleoni gravitated into the orbit of Fascism because both, as essentially free-market economists, saw merit in Fascism's opposition to socialism and Marxist economics.[69] Pantaleoni argued that, in his judgment, Mussolini was among the most serious economic "Manchestrians" that had ever served in the Italian parliament.[70] With the advent of Fascism to power, serving with distinction in a commission under the administration of Alberto de'Stefani—organized to reform the nation's tax and financial system—Pantaleoni maintained that Mussolini's anti-Marxist revolutionary intervention in the nation's politics had saved Italy from following Bolshevik Russia into economic chaos.[71]

Pareto's relationship to Fascism was very similar. There is not the slightest doubt that Pareto was an advocate of the free market in the governance of a nation's economy.[72] He opposed "statism," because interventions of the state, he maintained, tended to corrupt, dissipate incentive, reduce competition and bureaucratize enterprise.[73] On the other hand, he considered "economic liberty" uniquely capable of "producing vast increments of wealth."[74] His support of Fascism (which he served as delegate to the League of Nations, and for which he wrote three articles for its theoretical journal, *Gerarchia*)[75] was predicated on the conviction that the movement had saved Italy from a descent into anarchy and counterproductive socialism.[76]

[69] Pareto is counted among the precursors of Fascism by Werner Stark, "In Search of the True Pareto," *British Journal of Sociology* 14 (1963), pp. 103–12; Ellsworth Faris, "An Estimate of Pareto," *American Journal of Sociology* 41 (1936), p. 657; James W. Vander Zanden, "Pareto and Fascism Reconsidered," *American Journal of Economics and Sociology* 19, no. 4 (July 1960), pp. 409–11.

[70] Maffeo Pantaleoni, *Bolshevismo italiano* (Bari: Laterza, 1922), pp. 212–13.

[71] See Alberto de'Stefani, *La restaurazione finanziaria: I risultati 'impossibili' della parsimonia* (Rome; Volpe, 1978), pp. vii–viii xxiii, and xxx.

[72] See Piet Tommissen, "L'Apport de Pareto a la science economique," *Nouvelle ecole* 36 (July 1981), pp. 41–56.

[73] See, for example, Vilfredo Pareto, *Corso di economia politica* (Turin Einaudi, 1949), vol. 2, paras. 682, 837, 998, n. l, and "Lasciate fare, lasciate passare," *Scritti politici* (Turin: UTET, 1974), p. 457. In this context, consult Giovanni Busino's comments in "Introduction to Vilfredo Pareto," *I sistemi socialisti* (Turin: UTET, 1974), p. 29.

[74] Pareto, "Stato etico," in *Scritti politici*, vol. 1, p. 758.

[75] See Paola Maria Arcari, Introduction to *Socialismo e democrazia nel pensiero di Vilfredo Pareto* (Rome: Volpe, 1966), pp. 5–35.

[76] See the discussion in Luigi Montini, *Vilfredo Pareto e il fascismo* (Rome: Volpe, 1974), introduction and chap. 1.

Neither Pareto nor Pantaleoni were Fascists per se. They both saw merit in some of its policies. Equally clear was Pareto's conviction that Fascism would enjoy only a brief tenure. He conceived Mussolini's regime as transitional, ultimately to act as an agent for one of restored individual liberty and for a market-based economy.[77] A strong state would be necessary only to carry the nation through a troubled transit from the postwar period to the subsequent liberal arrangement. Pareto had made evident his suspicions of any proposed intrusive and presumably omnicompetent state.[78]

We know that Mussolini had been influenced by Pareto's thought; he was certainly familiar with his writings. He attended Pareto's lectures in Lausanne—and he reviewed his books for socialist journals. Granted that the scope of Pareto's reflections was so vast and inclusive, it is difficult to identify with any precision those elements that exercised most influence on the youthful Mussolini. Nonetheless, Mussolini welcomed Pareto's support because Fascism's immediate program found confirmation in the views of the "prince of economists."[79]

Acknowledging all that, what is clear is that during the first years of Fascist mobilization, many of those intellectuals that would help shape its ideology remained uncertain as to which developmental strategies most recommended themselves. Alfredo Rocco, for example, while an advocate of a strong state, was initially convinced, nonetheless, that a liberal economic policy "undeniably fostered the maximum utilization of the forces of production."[80] Sergio Panunzio, in 1919, equally committed to the creation of a strong state for the peninsula, similarly conceived liberal economic modalities as most conducive to rapid economic growth and industrial development.

At that time, as a national syndicalist, Panunzio maintained that neither the productive system of the Italian peninsula nor the consciousness of its workers was sufficiently mature to recommend either the abolition of private property or the collective control of production.[81] Unprepared for the

---

[77] See the informed discussion of Piet Tommissen, "Vilfredo Pareto und der italienische Faschismus," in Ernst Forsthoof and Reinhard Hoerstel, eds., *Standorte im Zeitstrom* (n.p.: Athenaeum, 1975), pp. 365–91, particularly pp. 375–79.

[78] "Beginning with state monopolies, one proceeds to the obligatory organization of labor [*sindacati obbligatori*] . . . [then] the collective organization of production . . . the destruction of every individual initiative, the annihilation of every human dignity as well as the reduction of human beings to the level of a herd of rams." Pareto, *Corso di economia politica*, para. 998 n. 1.

[79] Mussolini, "Il pensiero di Mussolini sulla crisi ministeriale," in *Oo*, vol. 18, p. 37 and "All'Università Bocconi," in *Oo*, 21, p. 100.

[80] Alfredo Rocco, "Il principio economico della nazione," *Scriti e discorsi politici* (Milan: Giuffre, 1938), vol. 2, p. 718.

[81] Panunzio, "Un programma d'azione," *Il Rinnovamento* 1, no. 2 (15 March 1919), pp. 83–89; see his comments in *Che cos'è il fascismo*, pp. 24–25.

revolution heralded by Marxism, the revolution in economically retrograde Italy could only support a "revolutionary conservatism," characterized by "a very strong state—a veritable Leviathan"[82]—that would provide disciplined order and stability, coupled with a market-governed economy, within which the industrial production of underdeveloped Italy might flourish.[83] If the "young, proletarian nation" was to both mature and become a major international power capable of protecting itself against foreign plutocracies, it required the discipline of labor and the marshaling of resources, which only a strong and goal-inspired state might provide.[84] As late as 1924, Panunzio held that the state should be strong, but not necessarily deal administratively with the economy. Fascism, he insisted at the time, was essentially a political, and not an economic, doctrine.[85] During Fascism's first years in power, Mussolini recognized the merits of just such contentions. He had witnessed the magnitude of the economic failure of Bolshevism—and its recourse to free-market alternatives in the search for solutions. Lenin's New Economic Policy (NEP), with its unmistakable capitalist features, was pressed into service in the effort to restart the economy of Bolshevik Russia.[86] That strongly suggested that the principles of a free market economy still had some relevance for the contemporary world—as well as for revolutionary Italy.

That capitalism had not yet exhausted its "historic function" was anything but a "reactionary" and venal abandonment of socialism—it was recognition of an evident reality.[87] Mussolini had early, and consistently, maintained that he would pursue any economic policy that promised to maximize, and render more sophisticated, the material productivity of the nation. That was the commitment—it did not entail any allegiance to some specific means for its accomplishment.[88]

In the years immediately following the March on Rome, a liberal economic policy contributed to the rapid stabilization and expansion of the Italian economy. With the suppression of disorder and labor stoppages, the economy commenced a rate of growth that distinguished it among the economies of Europe.

[82] Panunzio, "Per lo stato forte," *Giornale di Roma*, 13 May 1923, reprinted in *Stato nazionale e sindacati* (Milan: Imperia, 1924), pp. 94, 164–67.

[83] See Panunzio, *Che cos'è il fascismo*, pp. 28–29, 68, 72; and *Lo stato fascista*, p. 92, and his discussion concerning modernization and industrialization in "Contro il regionalismo," *Critica sociale* 1, nos. 17–18 (16 September–1 October 1921), reprinted in *Stato nazionale e sindacati*, pp. 85–86.

[84] Panunzio, *Stato nazionale e sindacati*, pp. 108–9.

[85] See Panunzio, *Lo stato fascista*, pp. 134, 159.

[86] See Mussolini's comments in "Dove impera Lenin," in *Oo* vol. 17, p. 78; "Punti fermi," in *Oo* vol. 17, p. 207.

[87] Mussolini, "Segni del tempo," in *Oo* vol. 17, pp. 17–18; and "Tiro a segno," in *Oo* vol. 17, p. 249.

[88] Mussolini, "Discorso di Cremona," in *Oo*, vol. 15, p. 186.

All that notwithstanding, Fascist policy, as its doctrine recommended, was a function of deliberation concerning policies best calculated to further the general interests of the nation. As a consequence—irrespective of its initial presumption in favor of liberal economic strategies—at the end of 1923, the first efforts were made that were to mature into comprehensive land reclamation and infrastructureal development that were to occupy the Fascist government for years as the Bonifica integrale (comprehensive land reclamation) and Il battaglia del grano (the Battle for Grain).

Compehensive land development, with its programs for rural training, land reclamation, road construction, and the provision of low-cost housing, contributed to the drive to increase grain yields. The nation required a well-developed agrarian base for its industrialization in order to avoid capital depletion because of the costs involved in the foreign purchase of comestibles. Together with those considerations there was the conviction that a rural population consistently enjoyed a higher birthrate than urban dwellers. It was a conviction—supported by considerable credible evidence—long entertained by both nationalists and Fascists.

If Italy were to become a "great power," it required a population capable of providing sufficient workers and soldiers to sustain its efforts—and agricultural yields that would support them. An abundant and healthy population was a necessary precondition for greatness.

A considerable amount of social science evidence indicated that the growth of European populations had decelerated with the urbanization attendant on industrial development—a preamble to political, military, and economic eclipse. Italian nationalists had warned their conationals of such prospects even before the Great War.[89] The consequence was that Fascism came to power with the intention of sustaining and stimulating the nation's birthrate with a variety of incentives. Not only was a program of comprehensive rural development undertaken, but in 1925, the Fascist government commenced its program for the "Protection of Motherhood and Infancy"—as collateral support for such ends. Mussolini, long before, had committed himself to just such projects.[90] Corrado Gini had made the case for state intervention in a program of population growth before the First World War and was to subsequently make the full case during the Fascist period.

Such programs made it evident that Fascism's initial liberal economic policies were contingent—not predicated on inflexible principle. Fascism was prepared to involve the state in complex economic activities if that

---

[89] Corrado Gini, who was to serve Fascism as a member of its constitutional reform commission and distinguish himself as an internationally celebrated statistician, published his *I fattori demografici dell'evoluzione delle nazioni* (Turin: Bocca) in 1912. He identified a declining rate of population growth with the general senescence of nations; see pp. 102–7, 135.

[90] See Mussolini, preface to Riccardo Korherr, *Regresso delle nascite: Morte dei popoli* (Rome: Libreria del Littorio, 1928).

intervention was conceived necessary to further one or another primary ideological commitment. Under those circumstances, as time passed, it became more and more difficult to distinguish purely economic matters from those that were political and the proper function of a presumptively Manchestrian administration.

As a consequence, during the first years of the regime, conservatives and revolutionaries, both within and outside the Fascist party, jockeyed for positions and advantage. Under the circumstances, Fascist theoreticians often papered over tensions by maintaining that the revolution was disposed to "conserving" whatever was of value from the past. That seemed to satisfy the class of "fellow travelers" who imagined that Fascism would serve their conservative or liberal interests. They chose to understand Fascism as a transitional regime, destined to restore the antecedent economically and politically liberal order.

With the murder of Matteotti in June 1924, those conservatives and liberals who had collected around Fascism prior to the March on Rome began to fall away. At the same time, there was a sudden erosion of equity values. Apprehension grew among the propertied classes—many withdrew their support—and the opposition press arrayed itself against the government. There were large-scale defections—particularly among the business and financial communities—together with a substantial number from the Fascist syndicates.[91] To add to the mounting difficulties, the formal political opposition "seceded" from parliament in moral outrage— and sought to mobilize the public as well as the Crown against the government. The entire system was threatened.[92]

As the year drew to its close, it became apparent that neither the monarchy nor the military were steadfast in their support of the Fascist government. The hemorrhaging of membership among the Fascist syndicates continued. It became increasingly evident that either Mussolini would have to surrender the government or embark on an alternative that could promise more control over every aspect of domestic politics.[93] Mussolini chose the second alternative.

On 3 January 1925, Mussolini affirmed that Fascism would thereafter control Italy; he made very clear what his intentions were. On 23 January, the Fascist Grand Council announced that all the economic forces of the nation would thereafter be "integrated into the life of the state."[94] Never again would allusion be made to the minimalist "Manchestrian state."

---

[91] For a chronology of events during this period, see Renzo De Felice, *Mussolini il fascista*, *La conquista del potere, 1921–1925*, chap. 7.

[92] See the account ibid., chap. 7, particularly pp. 640, 666, and 677.

[93] See Mussolini, "42a riunion del Gran Consiglio del fascismo," in *Oo*, vol. 21, p. 23.

[94] Mussolini, "58a riunione del Gran Consiglio del fascismo," in *Oo*, vol. 21, p. 325.

On 5 May, Mussolini spoke of the unqualified "subordination of all to the will of a leader" as the strategy calculated to bring glory to the nation.[95] On the twenty-third he insisted that "nothing should be above the state."[96] That June, Mussolini called for "all power to Fascism"—the necessary correlative to its "absolute intransigence"—and its irrepressible "totalitarian will."[97] Fascism would be totalitarian. Political idealism had come into its own.

It had always been transparent to anyone who was minimally informed that Fascism, as Fascism was understood by Mussolini, was ill-disposed toward parliamentary democracy of any sort. Few of those around Mussolini—Futurists, syndicalists, or Actualists, other than some of the traditional nationalists—supported anything that might be reasonably characterized as democratic in any identifiable conservative or liberal sense.

When National Syndicalists or Actualists spoke of the state, it was without any principled commitment to the Manchestrian state of the classical economists. Correspondingly, in the doctrinal literature of the regime, the initial tentative period that extended from October 1922 until January 1925 is generally characterized as preliminary to the actual institutionalization of the revolutionary Fascist state.[98]

Only after Mussolini's definitive address of 3 January 1925 did the features that were to define the Fascist state receive their full articulation and doctrinal defense. After 1925, Fascism became totalitarian. Those who failed to identify with it were deemed to be against it.

More important still, the intellectuals who had always supported the revolution sought, thereafter, to clearly explicate their intentions and shape the emerging system. Among the most important work in that regard was that of Ugo Spirito. By early 1927, both he and Arnaldo Volpicelli agreed to carry Gentile's Actualism into the applied realm of economic relations within the evolving revolutionary community created by the Fascist accession to power in October 1922—and its readiness to clearly define itself without equivocation by the beginning of 1925.

Less than three weeks after his address on 3 January, in which he made his dictatorial and totalitarian intentions unequivocally clear, Mussolini addressed the Grand Council of Fascism and spoke of "fully incorporating and organizing the economic forces of the nation into the life of the state."[99] Four months later, Giovanni Gentile brought the results of the

---

[95] Mussolini, "La donna e il voto," in *Oo*, vol. 21, p. 305.

[96] Mussolini, "Nulla deve essere al disopra dello stato," in *Oo*, vol. 21, p. 325.

[97] Mussolini, "Intransigenza assoluta," in *Oo*, vol. 21, pp. 362–63.

[98] See, for example, the instructive case of Paolo Orano, *Il fascismo: Rivoluzione delle camicie nere e lo stato totalitario* (Rome: Pinciana, 1940), particularly "Stato e partito," pp. 97–126.

[99] Mussolini, "58a Riunione del Gran Consiglio del fascismo," in *Oo*, vol. 21, pp. 250–51.

deliberations of the "Committee of Eighteen" on constitutional revision to that same Grand Council. The issue of the relationship of the workers' and industrialists' organizations to the state increasingly became the focus of attention. On 3 April, 1926, legislation was promulgated that was calculated to empower the Fascist state "to direct the national economy."[100]

The law of 3 April 1926 was preliminary to the formal declaration on 21 April, 1927 of *La Carta del lavoro*, the Fascist Labor Charter,[101] in which Italians were informed that "the nation is an organism having ends, life and capabilities superior to those of the individuals or groups of individuals of which it is composed. It is a moral, political and ethical unity that finds its integral realization in the Fascist state. Work in all its forms . . . is a social duty." Mussolini further informed his audience that "production . . . has one and a single object, the well-being of the individual and the development of national power."[102] Fascism was to answer not only the imperatives of developmental nationalism, but those of Actualism as well.

The Charter spoke of state intervention in the nation's economy whenever "private initiative proved lacking or inadequate, or when the state's political interests" were involved. That intervention could take the form of "control, assistance, or direct management."[103] In effect, the Labor Charter revealed that the Fascist state was prepared to assume the responsibilities of the ultimate arbiter of the nation's economic as well as its political destiny.

In all of this, elements of the nationalism of Corradini and Rocco, as well as the National Syndicalism of Panunzio, are clearly discernable. Italy was to be industrialized and modernized. Both nationalists and syndicalists had early acknowledged those responsibilities.[104] Giovanni Gen-

---

[100] See the account of Giuseppe Bottai in his exposition of the *Carta del lavoro* (Rome: Diritto del lavoro, 1928), p. 33.

[101] An English language version of the *Carta del lavoro* may be found as an appendix to William G. Welk, *Fascist Economic Policy: An Analysis of Italy's Economic Experiment* (Cambridge: Harvard University Press, 1938), pp. 287–92.

[102] "La carta del lavoro 1927," in *Atti fondamentali del fascismo* (Rome: Lara, 1969), p. 7. An English translation is available as an appendix A in Fausto Pitigliani, *The Italian Corporative State* (London: P. S. King and Son, 1933), p. 245.

[103] *Atti fondamental del fascismo*, p. 10.

[104] See Enrico Corradini, "Sindacalismo, nazionalismo, imperialismo," in *Discorsi politici (1902–1923)* (Florence: Vallecchi, 1923), pp. 51–69; and A. O. Olivetti, "Sindacalismo e nazionalismo: Le due realtà del pensiero contemporaneo," *Pagine libere* 15 February 1911, in the typescript collection; *Battaglie sindacaliste: Dal sindacalismo al fascismo*, provided by Olivetti's daughter, Livia Olivetti, pp. 60–64. By 1910, Mario Viana and Paolo Orano had identified the same affinities. Francesco Perfetti, ed., *Il nazionalismo italiano* (Rome: Il Borghese, 1969), p. 25.By 1920, Giovanni Gentile had associated Actualism with the nationalism of Enrico Corradini and had intimated a connection with some form of syndicalism. Spirito identified himself with the emerging synthesis that was to become the ideology of Fascism by the end of the decade.

tile, in turn, had identified Actualism with the dynamic self-fulfillment of individuals by identifying them with their historic community. In substance, Actualism was to serve as the rationale that lay behind the synthesis of nationalism and syndicalism that fully emerged after 1925. By 1927, it was Spirito who was to emphasize Actualism's convictions concerning the identification of the individual's ultimate interests with Fascism's evolving developmental syndicalism and corporativism.

In that year, Ugo Spirito, together with Volpicelli, himself an Actualist, assumed the editorship of the journal *Nuovi studi di diritto, economica e politica,* devoted to law, economics, and politics. In its pages, Spirito and Volpicelli sought to address the issues of syndicalism, the economic restructuring of Italian industry, and revolutionary social politics. In *Nuovi studi,* Spirito was prepared to argue against the economic, antistate liberalism that had survived the Fascist March on Rome in 1922—and which had sought thereafter to influence the policies of the regime until the political crisis of 1924 and 1925.

By the end of the decade of the 1920s, Spirito had begun to apply Actualist principles to the study of developmental economics that more and more systematically occupied Fascist intellectuals. In 1930, Spirito published his *La critica dell'economia liberale,* and in August 1931 received acknowledgment from Mussolini, who had read the volume and applauded its contents.[105] Spirito's *I fondamenti dell'economia corporativa*[106] followed in 1932 and then it was followed, almost immediately, by *Capitalismo e corporativismo,*[107] an amplified account of his communication before the Second Congress of Syndicalist and Corporativist Studies held in Ferrara in May 1932.

In the decade between the Fascist March on Rome and the Second Congress of Syndicalist and Corporativist Studies, syndicalism had completed its transition from the antistate, antinationalist, antimilitary, anarchic, libertarian, and exclusively workingmen's doctrine into one supporting organizations composed of both workingmen and entrepreneurs serving essentially as agents of the developmental Fascist state. As early as October 1925, about two months before the political crisis that followed the murder of Matteotti was resolved in his affirmation of control, Mussolini spoke of Fascist syndicalism as a system that celebrated the "obedience in silence of disciplined labor"—and insisted upon labor's "discharge of duties before the exercise of rights."[108]

---

[105] Ugo Spirito, *Memorie di un incosciente,* pp. 173–74.
[106] Ugo Spirito, *La critica dell'economia liberale* (Milan: Treves, 1930); and *I fondamenti dell'economia corporativa* (Milan: Treves, 1932).
[107] Ugo Spirito, *Capitalismo e corporativismo* (Florence: Sansoni, 1933).
[108] Mussolini, "Sindacalismo fascista," in *Oo,* vol. 21, pp. 414, 415.

On 6 March 1926, Mussolini outlined the argument for the emerging totalitarian and corporativist state. He spoke of an Italy that had been humiliated and resigned to its inferiority—and then he spoke, correspondingly, of the "enormous tasks" that confronted the state that sought to restore the nation to its proper place in the international community. He spoke of a system in which "everything would be within the state, nothing outside the state, and, above all, nothing against the state. Today," he continued, "we come to control the forces of industry, all the forces of finance, and all the forces of labor."[109]

Mussolini spoke of the "rigid, . . . felt, substantial, and profoundly moral discipline" that informed a state "that controlled all of the nation's forces." He went on to indicate that only when there was control over all "political, moral and economic forces, one would realize the fullness of the Fascist corporate state"[110]—the industrialization of the peninsula and the fulfillment of the more profound self identified by Actualism.

There was more in Mussolini's pronouncements concerning the Fascist state than was to be found in the statism of antebellum nationalism. And there was demonstrably more than one might find in the statism of National Syndicalism. By 1927, Mussolini had abandoned whatever reservations concerning the state he had entertained when the Fascist party program spoke of the creation and defense of a Manchestrian state for an Italy, newly emerged from the Great War, compelled to compete with the advanced industrial "plutocracies" for a proper "place in the sun."

There was more than nationalism or National Syndicalism in the Fascism that followed the crisis of 1925. There was the clear anticipation of the Gentilean collectivist, totalitarian state. It was left to Ugo Spirito to draw out the implications of what totalitarianism meant to a nation required to contend with the demands of rapid industrialization in an environment dominated by the most advanced industrial communities. It became the task of Actualists, Ugo Spirito first among them, to formulate a comprehensive and compelling rationale that might subtend not only the Carta del lavoro, but the totalitarian, corporativist, institutions to which it would give rise in the years that were to follow.

---

[109] Mussolini, "La legge sindacale," in *Oo*, vol. 22, p. 91.
[110] Mussolini, "Se avanzo, seguitemi, se indietreggio, uccidetemi; se muoio, vendicatemi," in *Oo*, vol. 22, pp. 108, 109.

CHAPTER SIX

Ugo Spirito and the Rationale
of the Corporative State

IN THE DECADE between the March on Rome and the Second Congress of Syndicalist and Corporativist Studies held in Ferrara in May 1932, the features of revolutionary Fascism took on legislative and institutional form. Intimations of those forms had been anticipated in Mussolini's public statements as early as the very birth of the movement.[1] After accession to power, Fascism undertook a series of legislative acts that regularized relations between the various factors of production, acts that Mussolini identified as the "most courageous, most audacious, most innovative and most revolutionary," calculated to further economic growth and industrial development.[2]

Alfredo Rocco argued that because of the arduous tasks Fascism had assumed, it would have "to dominate all the productive forces" of the nation, thereby effecting a "transition from the democratic, liberal, to the national state."[3] What remained uncertain was the precise characterization of the anticipated "corporative state." What was lacking was its detailed rationale. Providing such a rationale was a task history and circumstance would assign to Ugo Spirito.

The legislation governing the national economy had been generated piecemeal and episodically—largely in response to contingencies. Only with the promulgation of the Carta del lavoro in 1927 was an attempt made to inform the processes involved with doctrinal coherence. It was at that time that Spirito assumed the responsibility of giving public expression to that coherence.[4] He sought to make the case for Fascist corporativism by drawing out the implications of Gentile's Actualism.

---

[1] Mussolini's commitments to National Syndicalism and some form of corporativism are well documented. In January 1922, months before the March on Rome, he spoke of organizing the economy through "national confederations of syndical corporations" that would serve to integrate all the forces of production in order to accelerate the nation's agrarian and industrial development. See the discussion in Vincenzo Nardi, *Il corporativismo fascista* (Rome: Istituto Avogradro di Tecnologia, 1974), pp. 16–17.

[2] Mussolini, "La legge sindacale," *Opera omnia* (Florence: La fenice, 1953. Hereafter Oo), vol. 22, pp. 132–35.

[3] Alfredo Rocco, "Discorso al Senato del Regno," in *Scritti e discorsi politici* (Milan: Giuffre, 1938), 3, pp. 998, 999.

[4] Years later, Spirito spoke of committing himself to applying Actualist principles to Fascism's practical efforts—to translate general philosophical principles to immediate national

Making the case for Fascist corporativism—involving the subsumption of all the productive elements of the national economy under the dominance of a single-party state—necessitated a systematic critique of the central convictions of Western political thought. It was argued that at least since the seventeenth century, Western political thought maintained that the solitary, asocial, empirical individual constituted a self-evident reality, while the state, as but a legal fiction—the product of a "contractual" coming together of "atomic" selves—served only as constable, assuring equity and civility. That implied that the state had scant power in undertaking anything other than ancillary activities. It was the "night watchman," and provided for defense of individuals, collectively, against internal and external enemies.

At least since the beginning of the twentieth century, Gentile's Actualism inveighed against just such a conception of individual and collective life.[5] When Spirito took up the responsibility of making the case for corporativism, the singularly Actualist conviction that the state and the individual somehow shared an identity was central to his argument.

Western intellectuals are so accustomed to the liberal conception that the Actualist argument strikes them immediately as incomprehensible. To provide a rationale for Fascist corporativism, Spirito was compelled to make plausible what appeared counterintuitive to most of his audience. As we shall see, he was to argue that individuals took on the fullness of self only in the context created by the state.[6] What that implied, he was to maintain, was that the individual exists as a "concrete" person—one having political, historic, moral, artistic, and religious character—only as a product of interaction within the evolving state. What that signified was that the "concrete" individual was, in fact, somehow inextricably associated with the state, and as such, was critically distinct from the "abstract" individual of traditional liberal political philosophy. Actualists argued that the "true" individual was united with his or her community and its executive expression, the state, in a fashion that liberals did not appear to understand or appreciate.[7] It was that argument that was to be

---

economic concerns. See Ugo Spirito, *Critica della democrazia* (Florence: Sansoni, 1963), pp. 24–36.

[5] See the Actualist discussion in Volpicelli, *Corporativismo e scienza del diritto*, pp. 34–36 and passim.

[6] Arnaldo Volpicelli, "I Fondamenti ideali del corporativismo," *Nuovi studi di diritto, economia e politica*, n.s. 3–4 (1930), pp. 161–72, reprinted in Spirito, *Il corporativismo*, pp. 470–71.

[7] Spirito, "Il Liberalismo," in *Enciclopedia Italiana*, vol. 21 (1934), reprinted in Spirito, *Il corporativismo*, p. 116.

central to the rationale of Fascist corporativism[8]—to be fully drafted by
Spirito in that context—and approved by Gentile.[9] The argument was
complex, but its reconstruction recommends itself.

In 1932, as corporative institutions were given concrete legal character,
discussions devoted to their normative grounds became increasingly intense. Gentile noted that what had been a rather abstruse philosophical
argument had suddenly become a "popular" concern. He wryly noted
that the interest was contemporaneous with the fact that the principle of
the identity of the individual and the state had been proposed as an alternative to traditional liberalism—a proposal that threatened to "touch the
pocketbook" of property holders.[10] The Fascist rejection of liberal political and economic thought was seen as a direct threat to private property.
The totalitarian antiliberal conception of the identification of the individual and the state had become a *practical* concern.

At the center of the practical concern with the security of private property was the argument that the individual could be plausibly "identified"
with the state. The entire notion was a seeming affront to common sense.
Actualism had argued, certainly as early as 1916, that the individual of
common sense could not conceivably be understood as anything other
than as a functional part of the community—whatever historic form that
community assumed (as family, horde, clan, tribe, confederation, city-
state, nation, or empire). Only out of association, and an intricate web of
associations, did the empirical individual of common sense actually
emerge. As Aristotle had long since affirmed, the community, of necessity,
precedes the individual.[11] It is the matrix out of which the empirical person draws substance.

Actualists argued that what had been understood in antiquity had been
lost in the modern era. In our own time, liberals argued that the individual
was to be conceived as given, as an independent and self-contained
monad. Actualists held such a notion to be "abstract and arbitrary"—

---

[8] "The alpha and omega of the idealist theory of politics, formulated before the advent
of Fascism, . . . is the identity of the individual and the state." Arnaldo Volpicelli, *Corporativismo e scienza del diritto*, p. 160.

[9] Gentile was addressing the issue of the relationship between the individual and the state
on the occasion of Ugo Spirito's communication before a meeting of corporativists. See Ugo
Spirito, *Capitalismo e corporativismo* (Florence: Sansoni, 1933), pp. 1–24. For Gentile's
approving commentary, see Giovanni Gentile, "Individuo e Stato e la corporazione proprietaria," *Educazione fascista* 10 (August 1932), pp. 635–38.

[10] Gentile, "Individuo e stato o la corporazione proprietaria," p. 635.

[11] "The state is by nature clearly prior to the family and to the individual, since the whole
is of necessity prior to the part. . . . He who is unable to live in society, or who has no need
because he is sufficient to himself, must be either a beast or a god: he is no part of a state."
Aristotle, *Politica*, bk. 1, sect. 2, ll. 19–20, 28–29.

with the individual a solitary and autonomous entity, who in his self-centered singularity is potentially opposed to all those with whom he co-exists. Within such a conception, the role of the state was reduced to the entirely negative function of controlling the behavior of such individuals in order to protect them from each other.[12]

In opposition, Actualism was to contend that the state was an antecedent and enduring "transcendental reality" in which the abstract individuals of self-indulgent liberalism actually achieved their moral being. It was evident to Actualists that the empirical individual as he was understood by liberalism—independent of the state—was but a "phantom," an unlikely fiction.[13] Individuation—the taking on of the attributes of individuality—was a consequence of the full integration of persons into an organic system of responsibilities in and through which they articulate themselves.[14] The community—as the state—that served as the grounds of individuation for the individual was not a construction that was *inter homines*, between members of the community, but an *immanent* reality that arose out of members themselves. It was *interiore homine*.[15] The community was understood to be at the core of the individual.

For Actualists, the notion that there was an empirical "individual" antecedent to society and the state was not only indefensible; it was inconceivable. For Actualists, the state was the individual writ large—outside of the state the individual was unimaginable. Individuals simply were not found in nature—they emerged out of an organized community. In his first major publication, Gentile had contended that everything that endowed the empirical individual with moral substance—his or her truths, ethical principles, religious beliefs or aesthetic tastes—were products of life lived in community.[16] The true individual was not an empirical reality. The true individual was a "transcendental Ego . . . in which everything is bound up in an indivisible nexus which is the system of consciousness or of thought." That transcendental Ego of Actualism is the "I" at the center of which is a "We"—an ideal community which finds historic expression in the contemporary political state.[17]

---

[12] Volpicelli, "I Fondamenti ideali del corporativismo," p. 468–69.

[13] See the discussion ibid., pp. 12–13.

[14] Spirito, "Regime gerarchico," *Civiltà fascista* 1 (1934), pp. 4–14, reprinted in Spirito, *Il corporativismo*, p. 388.

[15] Gentile, *Discorsi di religione*, 3rd ed. (1920; Florence: Sansoni, 1955), pp. 22–23.

[16] Gentile's argument is available in translation in Gentile, *The Theory of Mind as Pure Act* (New York: Macmillan, 1922), chaps. 1–5, 7, and 8: and *The Reform of Education*, selections from which appear in Gentile, *Origins and Doctrine of Fascism Together with Selections from Other Works*, trans. A. J. Gregor (New Brunswick, N.J.: Transaction, 2002).

[17] These themes are found throughout Gentile's work, but most conveniently found in English in his posthumous work, *Genesis and Structure of Society* (Urbana: University of Illinois Press, 1960), pp. 82–85.

One of the central arguments of Actualism, bearing on that theme, turned on the conviction that the essence of the human being was *thought* and *thinking*—and neither could be conceived, in any real sense, as *private* or *individual*. Thought, as thinking—with all its judgments, convictions, evaluations, conclusions, and confirmations—*intrinsically* involves *language*. And there are no "private" languages. Every so-called private language, like every encryption, is parasitic on public language. "Correct usage" and comprehensibility imply common use. Actualists argued that the criteria governing all such activities are *collective* and *intersubjective*—the product of a common history. They are embodied in inherited speech modalities and in exchanges among the living, and through literature, with the dead. For Gentile and the Actualists there was no "private language," just as there were no uniquely individual judgments. Language, like the individual, was a function of interaction with an historic "audience"—composed of our present interlocutors, together with all those who have gone before, as well as all those who would, one day, come after us and judge our every thought, and the behavior it sponsored.[18]

Each one of us, it was argued, takes pride in our speech, in our prose, and in communication in general. We create ourselves in such exercises of free expression. We conceive of our communication as specifically our own—and yet, no one pretends that any of us has created the vocabulary, grammar, or syntax employed. The language in which we revel, which serves as a vehicle for our "unique" and "free" communication, is an historic, collective product. Without its availability we would all be essentially mute and infinitely less than we are.[19]

In such a conception, the "rules" and "laws" of language are necessary if the individual is to uniquely and freely express him- or herself. The rules and laws become an interior norm, rendering comprehensible the formulations that would otherwise be arbitrary and unintelligible. The individual would have achieved meaningful freedom of expression because he or she would have "identified," become one, with the inherited, collective patterns that govern effective speech.[20]

The notion that the individual might seek and find expession in a "private language" was summarily dismissed—and the general argument was invoked to similarly dismiss the prospect of "private initiative" in the

---

[18] In his first exposition of "the act of thought as a pure act," in 1911, Gentile outlined his argument concerning the collective nature of thought and thinking; see Giovanni Gentile, *L'Atto del pensare come atto puro* (1911; reprint Florence: Sansoni, 1937), paras. 3, 5, 8, and 10.

[19] See the account in Ugo Spirito, "L'identificazione di individuo e Stato," in *I fondamenti dell'economia corporativa* in *Il corporativismo*, pp. 206–8.

[20] See the rendering in Volpicelli, "Individuo e stato nella concezione corporativa," in *Corporativismo e scienza del diritto*, pp. 12–13.

economy. Actualists maintained that there could no more be private initiatives undertaken in economic matters than there could be a private language employed in the individual efforts to communicate. The economy, like speech, was an "organic" product of social history—possessed of rules, laws, and codes of conduct that did not confine or inhibit individuals, but rather supplied the preconditions for their "true" freedom, the achievement of those ends truly chosen.

For Actualists, to *truly choose* a behavior or a goal implied the concrete application of right reason—a reason collaboratively shared by one's community—a reason innocent of prejudice, selfishness, material or logical error. In that sense, individual freedom was understood to be predicated on right reason, itself the historic product of systematic scientific and humanistic education.[21]

These concepts were recognized as the foundations of an inescapably pedagogical, ecclesiastic, ethical, and collectivistically oriented political state. Even in the most pedestrian texts provided for the instruction of students, it was acknowledged that the "atomistic individuality" of liberal economics had to be abandoned because, unlike Fascist corporativist theory, it failed to "include and synthesize" individuals in the economic activities of the state, and thereby failed to create the conditions in which individuals could achieve "their highest human value."[22]

Spirito's efforts turned on making the case for the identification of the individual and the state, drawing out its collectivist implications.[23] He argued that the liberal notion of individuality was indefensible both in terms of social science and morality. However important the atomistic conception of the individual had been in the struggle against the absolute monarchies of Europe, the fact remained that the economy of a community was no more the product of individual initiatives than its language.

Spirito argued that the economies of modern nations had become so enormous, so all-inclusive, and so extensive in scope that no one could convincingly argue that they were the exclusive products of individual enterprise. However unreal the logic of "free enterprise," its convictions

[21] See Gentile, *La riforma dell'educazione: Discorsi ai maestri di Trieste* (Florence: Sansoni, 1955), chaps. 9–11.

[22] A. Serpieri, *Principii di economia politica corporativa*, 2nd ed. (Florence: Barbera, 1944), p. 33. The volume, it will be noted, was published at the end of the Fascist era. By that time, Actualist arguments had become common in the justificatory logic of corporativism. All of that notwithstanding the fact that the author identified himself as a "liberal" by citing Vilfredo Pareto and Maffeo Pantaleoni as his "masters" (p. viii).

[23] Spirito, "Individuo e stato nell'economia corporativa," *Capitalismo e corporativismo*, reprinted in Spirito, *Il corporativismo*, pp. 351–68. The thesis was repreated again in "L'identificaziione di individuo e stato," in *I fondamenti dell'economia corporativa*, reprinted in *Il corporativismo*, pp. 195–208. The implications were drawn out in "Benessere individuo e benessere sociale," in *Il corporativismo*, pp. 219–22.

had produced, over time, a disposition among the denizens of modern industry to organize in exclusive interest groups, united in defense of their special concerns. The result was a contentious, fractious economy with its several component groups each pursuing conflicting, and sometimes mutually exclusive, purposes.

A corporativist economy would recognize the social character of production, with individual initiative governed by social needs and social goals. Like the instructor who tutors individuals in the correct employment of language, thereby enhancing the student's freedom to communicate, the corporative state discharges a similar tutelary function with respect to the economy. In the final analysis, the true freedom of the individual does not find expression in the primitive pursuit of private interests, but in the collaborative effort to achieve collective ends.

Spirito held that the Labor Charter of 1927 implied the Actualist conception of the individual and his or her freedoms. He maintained that, in fact, Actualist "affirmations" concerning the individual and the state had received their "first synthetic formulation" in the Charter.[24] They were implied in the notion that labor was a social responsibility conducted under the tutelage of the state. They were implicit in the contention that both private initiative and the private organization of production were understood to be "functions of national interest."[25]

In Actualism, the distinction between the governed and those who govern is lost. Just as the student, to maximize linguistic abilities, identifies with his or her teacher, the individual, to maximize economic freedom, must identify with the state. The essentially spiritual character of the relationship between the individual and society—in its "concretization" in the state—would become immediately evident.[26]

The inevitable consequence would be that the artificial distinctions between what is conceived "public" and that conceived "private" in the nation's economy would gradually disappear.[27] The social character of property and enterprise would become increasingly apparent. Weakened, equally well and as a consequence, would be the tendency for human beings to identify themselves almost exclusively in terms of material— that is, class distinctions at the expense of the fundamental moral unity of society.

[24] Spirito, "Prime linee di una storia delle dottrine economiche," in *Il corporativismo*, p. l04.

[25] *Carta del lavoro* in *Atti fondamentali del fascismo* (Rome: Nuova editrice Lara, 1969), paras. 2 and 7.

[26] See Volpicelli's specific comments in this respect, "Individuo e stato nella concezione corporativa,"in *Corporativismo e scienza del diritto*, pp. 10–11.

[27] Spirito, "L'identificazione di individuo e stato," *Nuovi studi di diritto, economia e politica* 3, no. 6 (November–December 1930), pp. 373–75.

Ultimately, a community's economy must be seen as a collective undertaking with the "entire life of the individual . . . understood as essentially public or political by definition."[28] Property would no longer count as private. With the dissipation of liberal fictions, the social, and "organic" character of property would became transparent.[29] The ownership of property would no longer be perceived as a reward for individual effort. Rather, property would be understood as eminently an *historical* and *social* product, the result of contributions made throughout the collective history of the community, its defense, the inheritance of inventions, techniques, rules of conduct, and established instruments of transfer.

While the transformation to the new society into its communalist form would necessarily be slow,[30] Fascism had inaugurated the process by creating intermediate agencies between society, its economy, and the political state.[31] Through a chain of interlocking associations, commencing with a variety of youth and student groups, professional, labor, and entrepreneurial organizations, the population of the nation would no longer be composed of those who rule and those who are ruled; everyone would merge into a regime of governance. No longer would the government be distinguished from the general population; everyone would be involved in governance. There is no specific place where government would end and privacy begin.

For Gentileans, the contemporary state was the product of a long historical progression, shaped by the thought and the actions of our forebears. In our own time, the state provides the set of nested associations in which each of us achieves our humanity. As the ultimate repository of collective sovereignty, it is the historic state that fashions the moral and intellectual environment in which each of us achieves reality as a self-conscious individual. It is the state—whatever its institutional permutations—that supplies the formal and informal education that shapes individual consciousness. All the agencies that are seen as contributing to the process—the family, religion, the schools—all exist as a consequence of the sufferance and guidance of the sovereign state. In the modern world, what is permitted and what is proscribed is defined in law, and supplemented by custom and usage—all of which, in the final analysis is controlled, directly or indirectly, by the sovereign state.[32]

---

[28] Volpicelli, "Individuo e stato nella concezione corporativa," p. 18.

[29] See Spirito, "Politica e economia corporativa," in *Il corporativismo*, pp. 60–69.

[30] See Spirito, "Individuo e stato nella concezione corporativa," *Capitalismo e corporativismo*, in *Il corporativismo*, p. 352.

[31] Spirito, "Il corporativismo come liberalismo assoluto e socialismo assoluto," in *Il corporativismo*, p. 378.

[32] See the account given by Gentile, *Introduzione alla filosofia* (Rome: Treves-Treccani-Tumminelli, 1933), chap. 9; and *Discorsi di religione*, pt. 1, sec. 6.

In the effort to translate such arguments into the contemporary reality of the Fascist state, Ugo Spirito and Arnaldo Volpicelli,[33] as Actualists, formulated the philosophical, political, and economic rationale for the "corporative state." In its most rudimentary form, the argument held that as empirical individuals reflect on their lives, rationally anticipating outcomes, calculating probabilities and moral responsibilities, what emerges is predicated on the presence of a *transcendental will*, a general will that is not a simple summing of solitary wills, each in all its particularity—but a will, shaped by historical realities, that reflects a universality possessed of moral character, against which all judgments, are measured. Among Actualists, such a subtending general will looks surprisingly like the general will alluded to by J. J. Rousseau.

Rousseau and many of his contemporaries were convinced that collective exposure to a standard public education, in circumstances as similar as possible, with training in comparable conditions so that each would be exposed to essentially the same stimuli, would tend to render citizens eminently uniform in their values, judgments, and aspirations. That would reinforce the harmony in which the energy of each was united, in liberty, with the will of all—to give rise to a system Fascists identified as "totalitarian democracy."[34] It is "democratic" because it embodies a harmony of sentiments and goals that is not coerced, that externalizes itself as the will of an historic community, finding its executive expression in the state.

When, in 1932, Gentile wrote the preamble to the *Dottrina del fascismo* that was to become the formal statement of Fascist doctrine, he spoke of the "most genuine form of democracy" as that which "finds expression at those times when the consciousness and will of the few, even of one, manifests itself in the consciousness and will of all."[35] In his final apologetic for his life as a Fascist—more than a decade later—Gentile spoke of the ability of one person to speak for an entire political commu-

---

[33] Arnaldo Volpicelli was born in Rome on 30 July 1892. He served as a professor of the philosophy of law and of the doctrine of the state at the universities of Urbino, Pisa, and Rome. His major works include *Pedagogia polemica* (Rome: De Alberti, 1925); *Natura e spirito* (Rome: De Alberti, 1925); *Il Problema della rappresentanza nello stato corporativo* (Florence: Sansoni, 1934); and *Corporativismo e scienza giuridica* (Florence: Sansoni, 1934).

[34] Bruno Spampanato, *Democrazia fascista* (Rome: "Politica nuova," 1933). See the discussion in J. L. Talmon, *The Origins of Totalitarian Democracy* (New York: Praeger, 1960), pp. 29, 43–45.

[35] Benito Mussolini, *La dottrina del fascismo* (Milan: Hoepli, 1935), pp. 14–15. Gentile wrote the first section of the official *Dottrina* entitled "Idee fondamentali." The characterization of the Fascist regime as "democratic" was common among Fascist theoreticians. See, for example, Antonio Navarra, "Governo e governati in regime fascista," in C. Arena, ed., *La Camera dei fasci e delle corporazioni* (Florence: Sansoni, 1937), p. 165, where he speaks of the Fascist government as an "authoritarian democracy."

nity. He spoke unselfconsciously of a *consensus gentium*—the collective voice of a people immanent in the individual—that served to confirm the leader in his leadership.[36]

These general notions were provided support by more empirical accounts that were relatively common among academicians who had become prominent on the Italian peninsula by the end of the nineteenth century. Gaetano Mosca, long before the advent of Fascism, had mounted assessments of political life that provided collateral support for just the kind of elite rule suggested by Actualism.[37] He was followed by Vilfredo Pareto and his notion of the dominance and succession of political elites in the shaping of history.[38]

Within the social science literature of the period that concerns us, one of the central claims, around which most of the discussion gravitated, was that political "democracy," as it was understood in the West, was fatally flawed. The argument was that representative democracy, in the industrialized economies of the West, manifested itself in elections that, at best, reflected the choices of an unthinking mass. More often than not, in such democracies, the choices were really those of monied, political and intellectual interests that succeeded in manipulating those who cast their ballots in good faith, but with precious little security of outcome. Individuals in liberal societies, lumped together geographically for the purposes of exercising suffrage, shared little in common. As a consequence, there was very little unanimity in terms of interests, projects, or intentions that might constitute the "general consensus" that, in turn, could provide the "democratic" support for elite rule. Workers, entrepreneurs, agriculturalists, educators, bankers, professionals of all sorts, would be brought together haphazardly and periodically, and then expected to intelligently "choose" their leaders in what Fascists held to be a meaningless exercise.

Fascists were to argue that citizens in the industrialized democracies really had very little choice in terms of their leaders. Their choices, Fascists argued, were very largely determined by occult and special interest groups, media manipulation, mimetism, suggestibility, and errant influences.[39]

---

[36] Gentile, *Genesi e struttura della società* (Verona: Mondadori, 1954), p. 46, see pp. 44–48.

[37] Gaetano Mosca, *Elementi di scienza politica* (1896; Bari: Laterza, 1953); see Roberto Michels, "Gaetano Mosca und seine Staatstheorien," *Schmollers Jahrbuch* 53, no. 5 (1929), pp. 111–30.

[38] See Roberto Michels, "Literatur zum Problem der Führer und Massen," *Zeitschrift für Politik* 22, no. 7 (1932), pp. 482–84; and Rodolfo De Mattei, "La dottrina della 'classe politica' e il fascismo," *Educazione fascista* 9 (1931), pp. 675–86.

[39] The classic expression of this argument is found in Roberto Michels, *Zur Soziologie des Parteiwesens in der modernen Demokratie* (Leipzig: Hartmann, 1911), translated as *Political Parties*.

The general voter tends to be ignorant of issues, uncertain of his or her interests, incompetent in dealing with them even if known, more comfortable in a disciplined environment that makes few demands on his or her limited capabilities, and, more often than not, subject to the moral suasion of articulate and self-possessed political leaders. The consequence, Fascist theoreticians maintained, was the "incontrovertible scientific fact" that *all* political communities were governed overtly or covertly by one or another "political elite."[40] In times of mortal peril, when a community faces crises that threaten its very survival, a "rotation of elites" takes place—and a revolutionary cadre has the historic opportunity of marshaling populations to their purpose in the effort to resolve challenges. Out of a population in crisis, the new elite collects around itself a revolutionary aristocracy—which serves as the vanguard of systemic change. In such circumstances, the riveting of attention on a critical common concern creates that "harmony of interests" out of which a "general" or "transcendental" will arises—on which a "Fascist democracy" rests.[41]

Italian theoreticians were to make much of these generalizations—most of which predated the advent of Fascist rule.[42] After the establishment of the regime, Fascist intellectuals advocated the creation of a "pedagogical state" that would assume the responsibility of training its citizens from birth to full maturity so that they would participate in a collective "harmony" of shared values, commitments, and projects that was expected to follow the revolution.[43]

Such advocates were to maintain that all "ruling elites," in order to rule, must foster and sustain an irreducible minimum of consensus—by exploiting a popular sense of threat, and appealing to the general thirst

---

[40] Roberto Michels, "Il partito politico," *L'Ordine fascista* 10, nos. 3–4, pp. 183–88; see "Il concetto di partito nella storia italiana moderna," *Università fascista* 1, no. 9 (1930), pp. 33–35.

[41] One of the clearest formulations of this entire argument is conveniently found in Bruno Spampanato, *Democrazia fascista*.

[42] There is a great deal of "protofascist" literature available that gave form and substance to these generalizations. That literature, written by some of Italy's more interesting social science thinkers, was devoted to the psychology of crowds, the suggestibility of groups, and the influence of *meneurs*, leaders, on assemblies. Roberto Michels, among the twentieth century's most celebrated social scientists, contributed to this literature as a Fascist. See the discussion in A. James Gregor, *Phoenix: Fascism in Our Time* (New Brunswick, N.J.: Transaction, 1999), chaps. 3 and 4. Michels was one among many who provided substance to the kinds of generalizations with which we have been here concerned. See Gregor, *The Ideology of Fascism: The Rationale of Totalitarianism* (New York: Free Press, 1969), chaps. 2 and 3.

[43] As we shall see, Sergio Panunzio argued in support of these specific educational responsibilities—in order to provide vindication for Fascism's claims to represent a "centralized and authoritarian democracy." See Panunzio, *Teoria general dello stato fascista* (Padua: CEDAM, 1939), pt. 1.

for security and accomplishment. Carefully orchestrated, such a system produces and sustains compliance behavior—the foundation of a reasoned general consensus—together with a readiness for disciplined collective sacrifice. All of which was understood to give substance to the conception of a Rousseauean "general will."[44]

For Gentileans, the consensus that sustained the "true democracy" toward which they aspired was the product of sentiment, instruction, and entirely rational calculation. True freedom, Actualists argued, would consist of the seamless identification of the individual with his historic community, an identity of interests, emotion, and reasoned purpose. All that, it was argued, must be the result of education, broadly conceived. "The educator," seeking such ends, "must awaken interests that without him would forever lie dormant. He must direct others towards goals which they would be unable to appreciate properly if left alone . . . . The educator must, in short, transfuse into others something of himself, and out of a shared spiritual substance create elements of mind and will" that would make leadership the externalization of a reality already immanent in the community.[45]

These convictions supplied the public vindication of rule by a "dominant party"—a political body that sought to implement the focused policies of an exiguous elite—intended to address the problems of the epoch. Political leadership was understood to arrange itself in a hierarchy in order to discipline and educate the forces available, to unite them to given purposes, and to maneuver them rapidly. This would be particularly true if the community were traversing a demanding and dangerous time.[46]

While most of these accounts were couched in standard social science formulations,[47] they overlapped with the thought of Gentile, who as early as the First World War argued that societies were invariably led by individuals and small groups of individuals who could sense, draw out, and fully articulate prevailing collective sentiments in order to achieve common purpose. Gentile frequently spoke of historic individuals who had im-

[44] See Roberto Michels, "Osservazioni retrospettive sulla democrazia e sul consenso," *La stirpe* 10, no. 12 (December 1932), pp. 533–34.

[45] Gentile, *La riforma dell'educazione: Discorsi ai maestri di Trieste* (Florence: Sansoni, 1955), pp. 30–31. For a discussion of Fascist pedagogical strategies, see Luca La Rovere, *Storia dei GUF: Organizzazione, politica, e miti della gioventù universitaria fascista, 1919–1943* (Turin: Bollati Boringhieri, 2003).

[46] See Roberto Michels, "Le forze essenziali del divenire politico," *L'Ordine fascista* 12, nos. 8–9 (1933), pp. 522–28; and "Il partito politico," p. 184.

[47] Roberto Michels, identified as an important "party comrade," was the most notable of these theoreticians. He published extensively on the subject of political elites. See Carlo Curcio, "L'opera politica di Roberto Michels," in *Studi in memoria di Roberto Michels* (Padua: CEDAM, 1937), pp. 15–76.

pacted their time specifically because they had the faculty of sensing, acting on, and subsequently shaping popular opinion.[48]

However these claims were expressed, in the formulations of social science[49] or via historical example, they provided the rationale for elite rule—and the logic of the transcendental general will that presumably constituted the ultimate support for corporativism. In general, by the time the first institutions of the corporative state made their appearance, few apologists felt it necessary to repeat them. What was clearly understood was that such arguments provided the intellectual justification for corporativism itself, as it transformed itself in its dynamically changing environment. The members of the category syndicates, instead of being animated exclusively by the personal concerns, would find an identity in the larger community—an identity that would enhance their humanity.

In the period between 1927 and the mid-1930s, Ugo Spirito assumed the responsibility of drawing out the implications of just such arguments. Preliminary to the articulation of plausible argument was an extended and relentless critique of anti-Fascist liberal economic thought—which Spirito maintained was derivative of the philosophical individualism that was at its heart.[50]

Spirito held that liberal economic thought, as it evolved—particularly during the nineteenth century—was one expression of an inclusive scientific liberalism. Predicated on the individualism that had been evident in all the activities that defined the Renaissance and the Reformation, the scientific activities of liberal thinkers had early become "scientistic," imagining that human inquiry into nature, society, and humanity could be, in and of itself, "value-free"—and, thereby, entirely "objective." Objectivity had become the twin of individualism.

These were the cardinal features of the cognitive perspective that Actualists identified as "positivistic." The most rigorous positivists sought to provide naturalistic and objective explanations for all manifestations of the human spirit. Human beings were understood to be nothing more than parts of nature, their behavior governed by causal regularities. The inspiration for such positivism was a rigorous Newtonian mechanical atomism in which all of nature was the consequence of the commingling of small, massy particles—"atoms," or "monads"—interacting in a field of forces.

---

[48] Gentile, "Il significato della vittoria (25 October 1918)," *Dopo la vittoria: Nuovi frammenti politici* (Rome: "La Voce," 1920), pp. 5–6.

[49] Characteristic social science formulations are found in the works of Guido Bortolotto; see his *Massen und Führer in der faschistischen Lehre* (n.p.: Hanseatische Verlagsanstalt, 1934).

[50] Spirito, *Capitalismo e corporativismo* (Florence: Sansoni, 1933), p. 28 (origianlly published as "Il corporativismo come liberalismo assoluto e socialismo assoluto," *Nuovi studi di diritto, economia e politica* 6 [1932], pp. 285–98).

Some such notions surfaced at the turn of the century in the formulations of social scientists such as Ludwig Gumplowicz and Vilfredo Pareto. Like the positivists of the period, Pareto sought "to construct a system of sociology on the model of celestial mechanics, physics, [and] chemistry."[51] He was to argue that like celestial mechanics, physics, and chemistry, neither sociological nor economic "laws" admit exception[52]—all of which seemed to imply that the world of human experience was governed by the determinism and the intrinsic amorality of the "objective laws of nature."

Actualism refused to consider the possibility that empirical science could "discover" lawlike regularities that governed the individual and collective conduct of human beings "without exception." Actualists were not only to object to the attempt, by positivists, to rigorously distinguish the "scientific" world of "objective" assessment from what Actualists identified as the total reality of "subjective" human experience; they objected to the conceptual framework that conceived individuals as abstract, solitary, and self-regarding "atoms." For Spirito, the conviction that such distinctions could be entertained constituted the central fiction of the positivism at the turn of the twentieth century.[53]

True to the essentials of Actualist historicism, Spirito held that all science, in some indeterminate measure, was shaped by human values and contingencies prevalent at any given period of time. It was not only the case that whatever natural or social laws empirical science might contrive could only be time and circumstance sensitive;[54] the entire notion that human beings might be meaningfully dealt with as asocial beings was defective.

The conviction that there were immutable and transtemporal general laws governing the behavior of nature as well as that of human beings was part of the irrepressible, if mistaken, positivistic faith that inspired the intellectuals of the nineteenth and early-twentieth century.[55] The notion that scientists "discovered" such laws in an "external nature" that antedated their presence was understood to be one of the unargued, and unarguable, presuppositions of positivistic "empirical science" at the beginning of the century.[56] The other was the conception of individuals as independent, asocial atoms.

---

[51] Vilfredo Pareto, *A Treatise on General Sociology* (New York: Dover, 1935), vol. 1, p. 16.

[52] Vilfredo Pareto, *Manuale di economia politica* (Milan: Libraria, 1919), p. 7.

[53] Ugo Spirito, "La nuova scienza dell'economia secondo Werner Sombart," 1930–1931(?), reprinted in *Il Corporativismo*, p. 329.

[54] Ugo Spirito, "Prime linee di una storia delle dottrine economiche," *Enciclopedia Italiana*, 13 (1932), reprinted in *Il corporativismo*, pp. 98–99.

[55] Ibid., p. 331.

[56] In this context, see the articles on science and philosophy written by Gentile's son, Giovanni Gentile, Jr., in *Scritti minori di scienza, filosofia e letteratura* (Florence: Sansoni,

In general, Actualists conceived *science* not as a unique undertaking, but very much as they conceived *art* and *religion*, as one "moment" within the global totality of human experience. Governed by its own historically relative orientations, standards of competence, and utilitarian purposes, science was seen as a rigorous manner of reordering experience to meet specific time-sensitive standards and in order to discharge specific temporal functions.[57] In that sense, Actualists did not argue that the findings of natural science were untrue. The findings of contemporary empirical science met the requirements of their respective undertakings. But that was always accomplished within a set of historic and philosophical circumstances. However remarkable its contemporary achievements, modern science did not satisfy the specifically *philosophical* requirement that its enterprise be "presuppositionless."[58]

For Actualists, the recognition that all empirical inquiry was predicated on some presuppositions, accepted uncritically as inerrant,[59] identified science, in and of itself and in general, as a "dogmatic" and "intellectualistic" activity.[60] Characteristic of such undertakings, science is "abstract" in its lucubrations, rather than "concrete."[61] Actualists held that positivists were particularly "abstract" and "dogmatic" because they held that their activities were singularly "objective," dismissing the inspection of the epistemological issues that occupied Actualism as "meaningless metaphysics." That, conjoined with the intrinsic atomized individualism that

---

1943), particularly "Il Nuovo panorama della scienza," which appeared in *Leonardo* in April 1934, republished in the above citation, pp. 40–53, in which the younger Gentile refers to "science" as the product of the logical reconstruction, in consciousness, of human experience.

[57] An illuminating discussion of this aspect of Actualism can be found in Pasquale Romanelli, *The Philosophy of Giovanni Gentile: An Inquiry into Gentile's Conception of Experience* (New York: Birnbaum, 1937), chap. 3. During the latter part of the twentieth century a sophisticated argument for the "historicity" of the standards of science was reiterated by Thomas Kuhn, *The Structure of Scientific Revolutions* (Chicago: University of Chicago Press, 1962).

[58] See the discussion in Roger W. Holmes, *The Idealism of Giovanni Gentile* (New York: Macmillan, 1937), pp. 189–91.

[59] A presupposition acknowledged by European thinkers certainly as early as David Hume.

[60] This is the particular meaning given to the term "intellectualistic" so sorely misused by anti-Fascist critics for half a hundred years. "Intellectualism," as used by serious Fascist thinkers, refers to the "dogmatic" readiness on the part of some to consider the "world" dualistically, as a prefabricated "nature" opposing an observing "self." It is nowhere used to suggest that Fascists should be unthinking or irrational. See Gentile, *Teoria generale dello spirito come atto puro*, chap. 15; and the comments of Spirito, "La Nuova scienza," in *Il corporativismo*, p. 331.

[61] See Spirito's discussion in "L'Avvenire della scienza dell'economia," *Nuovi studi di diritto, economia e politica* 6 (1928), reproduced in *Il corporativismo*, pp. 54–55.

animated liberal thought, made prevailing economic theories, in Spirito's judgment, antithetical to Fascism, in general, and Fascist corporativist thinking, in particular.

Spirito, and the Actualists who committed themselves to the defense of corporativism, identified the defeat of the liberal preoccupation with individualism—and positivism's faith in the transhistorical and invariant character of scientific laws—as critical to their task. Both negatively affected the intellectual environment of Fascist Italy and generated much of the resistance to corporativist theory and practice that was evident among professional economists.[62]

Convinced of what was required, Spirito began a systematic methodological critique of liberal economics and positivism as a metatheory of science. His preliminary critique began by calling attention to the fact that much of the vocabulary of classical economics was composed of terms that were loosely framed and ambiguous in reference—making the confirmation of any empirical claims containing such terms difficult, if not impossible.[63] That, together with the fact that conscious and unconscious presuppositions littered its projects,[64] compromised its efforts. Most critical of those presuppositions, of course, was the individualistic biases that shaped much of the substance of liberal—that is, classical—economic theory.[65]

Spirito selected the economic theories of Pareto as a point of departure—and his employment of the term "ophelimity" as an illustrative case.[66] The term was understood to refer to "the individual's satisfaction . . . [of which] *he is the only judge.*"[67] That satisfaction characterized "the relationship between an individual and a given thing"—thereby rendering the individual's satisfaction unique, and impossible to compare over time or intersubjectively. The underlying concept was clearly *asocial*—with the fundamentals of social and economic reality reduced to what could only

[62] Spirito refers to the outspoken academic criticism addressed to the corporativist convictions to which he and his colleagues gave expression during the early and mid-1930s. See Spirito, *Memorie di un incosciente* (Milan: Rusconi, 1977), chap. 3.

[63] Spirito made the point that the intrinsic ambiguities that attended the porous definition of critical terms was often concealed by classical economists by their regular use of statistics to provide a spurious rigor to their work. See Spirito, "Vilfredo Pareto," in *Il corporativismo*, pp. 149–53.

[64] *Il corporativismo*, p. 52. See Vilfredo Pareto's recognition of these disabilities, *A Treatise on General Sociology* (New York: Dover, 1935), vol. 1, para. 119.

[65] Recognizing that the terms "classical" and "liberal" have uncertain referents, it is enough to recognize that Pareto is generally identified with classical economists of the persuasion of M.E.L. Walras, Alfred Marshall, W. S. Jevons and Irving Fisher. See Warren J. Samuels, *Pareto on Policy* (New York: Elsevier, 1974), chap. 1.

[66] See Spirito, "Vilfredo Pareto (1927–1929)," *Il corporativismo*, pp. 129–56.

[67] Pareto, *A Treatise on General Sociology*, vol. 4, para. 2110. Emphasis supplied.

be considered interaction among what used to be identified as "windowless monads" by Cartesians.

Pareto seems to have drawn out the implications. "Between two distinct subjects," he acknowledged, "there can be no rigorous comparison of ophelimities."[68] As a necessary consequence, some of the very fundamentals of his economic notions were emphatically individualistic and fundamentally asocial. His conceptual schemata rested on unexamined individualistic presuppositions.

Spirito insisted that such presuppositions prejudiced any effort to understand the relationship of politics and economics and, in the last analysis, left the enterprise confined to the individual and his or her peculiar interests. Spirito insisted that one of the inescapable implications of such an interpretation of the individual, his interests, and his relationship to the community was that the individual regularly found himself opposed by community interests—that his interests and those of the community were somehow incompatible or antithetical. The very definition of "ophelimity" implied an irreducible tension between the economic utilities of the community and the satisfactions of the atomic individual.

While the utility of the community might "roughly be assumed . . . there is no such thing as the ophelimity of a community." The measure of the utility of the community and the satisfaction of the individual were, by definition, incommensurable.[69] The evident suggestion was that the relationship between the state and the individual could only be adversarial. Spirito argued that such analyses implied the interests of the community could only be served at the cost of the individual. Whatever the case, it clearly appeared to Spirito that liberal economic thought was, in significant part, a function of the interaction of liberal political biases interacting with the atomistic presuppositions of positivistic science.

It was the individualistic bias of liberal economic thought that made of the "individual" of positivism the potential enemy of the community and its executive expression in the state. If the satisfactions of the individual were unique and nonquantifiable, it could never really be argued with assurance that those satisfactions were fully compatible with the interests of the community. The individual always remained, at best, agnostic with respect to the state. More characteristically, the individual was always the potential enemy of the state. The features of that potential enemy of the state were implicit in the classical notion of human conduct being a function of the lawlike behaviors of the hedonistic, self-absorbed, and atomistic *homo oeconomicus*—the "economic man" of free-market liberal economics.

[68] Vilfredo Pareto, *Corso di economia politica* (Turin: Einaudi, 1949), 2, pp. 51–52.
[69] Spirito, "Politica ed economia corporativa," a lecture given at the University of Pisa, 15 February 1932, and reproduced in *Il corporativismo*, pp. 66–67.

The corollary was the conviction that the "unalienable rights" of the individual must forever be protected from the community. The economic and political relationship between the individual and the state would always remain potentially "zero/sum," with the individual's gain being a necessary loss for the state, and conversely the state's gain always a potential loss for the individual.

For Actualists, if corporativism was to be successful, it must of necessity reject the liberal conviction that the state and the individual, and the communities of individuals that composed it, were intrinsically adversarial. It was not enough, in their judgment, to put together the means of mitigating an inevitable and recurrent clash of interests. What was necessary was to create an environment in which individuals, and communities of individuals, would identify their most fundamental interests with those of the state.

For Spirito, Fascist syndicalism and corporativism commenced as "a grand experiment in economic conciliation . . . that is to say, as an effort in the reconciliation of class interests within the superior interests of the nation."[70] It was acknowledged that, at its commencement, Fascist corporativism was an attempt at reconciliation. It did not constitute a *resolution* of differences; it was an effort at reconciliation. For about a decade corporativism had sought to *reconcile* class interests through the intervention of the Labor Courts. In doing that, corporativism had succeeded only in institutionalizing class differences. While it had defended the productive integrity of the nation, individual and class differences continued to separate individuals and classes from their integral unity with the totalitarian state.

Throughout its early years, Fascism understood the corporations to be nothing less that "the instrument which, under the aegis of the state, actuates the integral, organic and unitary discipline of the forces of production with a view to the expansion of the wealth, political power and well-being of the Italian people."[71] Under the aegis of the state, the class struggle had been moderated, and not permitted to undermine the industrializing efforts of the regime—but there were very few who imagined that the system would long remain as it was. It was everywhere recognized as transitional.

If corporativism were to be successful, the sense of separation suffered by individuals and associations of individuals with respect to themselves and the community must be first tempered and then resolved. Individual and parochial interests must find the satisfaction of their most fundamental interests in the interests of the community, the nation, and their execu-

---

[70] *Il corporativismo*, p. 356.
[71] Mussolini, "Dichiarazione per le costituende corporazioni," in *Oo*, vol. 26, p. 85.

tive expression, the state. Individuals, syndicates, categories, confederations and corporations must all find their ultimate identity in the "community of destiny," the nation-state, that defines them and gives substance to their lives.

All of this was transpiring while the international community lapsed into the Great Depression. Industrializing Italy was savagely impacted. Overall production declined precipitously. Unemployment escalated. Mussolini no longer spoke of the dislocation as being "*within* the capitalist productive system," but as being an affliction "*of* the system itself." He refered to the crisis "as no longer a transient disability, but a systemic disease."[72] For Mussolini, the weight of contemporary evidence convinced him that the inherited economic system required radical intervention.

That intervention would be effectuated through syndicates. Through them, workers and employers would directly participate in the nation's productive processes. They would directly collaborate in pursuit of defined ends through means collectively determined. The interventions of the state would no longer count as violations of speculative freedoms. They would be the product of deliberations undertaken by knowledgeable members of associations composed of those involved in every aspect of production.

Within such a conception "corporativism is animated by the possibility of morally and technically unifying social life; it believes in the joy of giving and of sacrifice. It is opposed to every uniquely private goal in life and precisely for that reason, corporativism is not an economic notion, but the unique political, moral, religious, essence of the Fascist revolution."[73]

Until the Great Depression, Fascist Italy had succeeded in rapidly increasing its industrial output. Two years after the succession of Mussolini to power, labor stoppages, which had seriously impaired the nation's productivity, had all but ceased. Output escalated. With the coming of the international economic dislocation, however, plants began to operate below capacity. Concern became insistent.[74] The international economic crisis fueled demands for salvage and increasing state management.

---

[72] Mussolini, "Discorso per lo stato corporativo," in *Oo*, vol. 26, 87.

[73] Spirito, "Il corporativismo come negazione dell'economia," communication before the National Fascist Institute of Culture, 16 June 1934, reprinted in *Il corporativismo*, p. 79. Compare with Mussolini: "There does not exist an economic fact that is of exclusively private and individual interest; from the day in which human beings adapted themselves to community life among their similars, from that day not a single act that the individual undertook developed or concluded with him alone, but that its repercussions extend far from his person." Mussolini, "Discorso al Senato per lo stato corporativo," in *Oo*, vol. 26, p. 147.

[74] See Bruno Caizzi, *Storia dell'industria Italiana* (Turin: UTET, 1965), chap. 5.

In the years after the March on Rome, notwithstanding the modifications in detail and changes in institutional structure, the basic legislation governing Fascist corporativism had remained substantially the same. With the enactment of the basic syndical law of 3 April 1926—through which worker and employer organizations undertook to legally recognize one another as sole bargaining representatives of their respective categories—only operational specifics had altered. Only one syndicate for each category in each district would be recognized by the authorities—each syndicate including at least 10 percent of all workers employed in its category. Labor courts adjudicated issues brought before them by such duly recognized organizations.

By 1930, the labor syndicates were drawn together into confederations to be joined by similar employers' associations. Thirteen confederations representing the major economic activities of the nation were grouped into sections composed of workers and employers. They sent their respective presidents and a given number of delegates to a Consiglio nazionale delle corporazioni (National Council of Corporations). Beneath the National Council there were Provincial Councils of Corporative Economy, charged with the promotion and coordination of economic activities within their respective provinces. Appointees of the Fascist party served in all these organizations as representatives of the state.

The Labor Charter of 1927 had made eminently clear that the organization of labor and the employers of labor taken together constituted "corporations," unitary and integral organizations of the forces of national production, and as a consequence, were "legally recognized as state organs" charged with the responsibilities of imposing discipline on labor and coordinating production. In general, as was reiterated with regularity, the corporations were understood to be "responsible to the state for production."[75]

With the onset of the Great Depression, Spirito was convinced that some discussion concerning forthcoming corporativist developments should be candidly undertaken. He undertook to anticipate the institutional changes that would contribute to the fulfillment of the promise of the "Corporate State"—particularly under the conditions of worldwide economic crisis.

These were the conditions surrounding Spirito's celebrated communication, "The Individual and the State in the Corporative Economy," presented before the Second Congress of Syndicalist and Corporativist Studies held in Ferrara from 5 May through 8 May 1932.[76] The communication

---

[75] *Carta del lavoro*, paras. 6 and 7.

[76] Spirito, "Individuo e stato nell'economia corporativa," in *Capitalismo e corporativismo* (Florence: Sansoni, 1933), pp. 3–24, reprinted in *Il corporativismo*, pp. 351–67.

was prompted by the tensions created by the Great Depression, but turned on what Spirito held to be the fundamental issue of the nature of corporativism itself.

Before delivering his communication, Spirito took the precaution of providing Mussolini himself with a draft copy for review. On 25 March 1932, Spirito met with Mussolini and discussed the substance of his intended address. Mussolini's accord was unequivocal. He seemed to accept the thesis that history has a "logic," and that events, in the immediate past, had so conspired that Italy could ultimately anticipate a "total corporative unification of capital and labor" in terms of its productive system.[77]

In his communication at the Ferrara conference, Spirito argued that the syndicalist and corporativist organization of the Fascist state, if it were to achieve its potential, would have to address unresolved issues within the very institutions themselves. Spirito addressed the fact that corporative organizations were intrinsically dualistic in character—with labor and capital each separately collected in their respective organizations—brought together only to mitigate their differences. An "integral" or "unitary" corporativism would require the supersession of the felt need for separate organizations for labor and capital.

Spirito argued that with the sale of equity through stocks, capital had lost much of its independent productive function. Where, in the past, entrepreneurs had invested in industry and devoted their personal assets and energies to enhance production and improve efficiency—the expansion of industry, with ownership of equity through anonymous stock purchase, had impaired the relationship between ownership and responsible management. Spirito spoke of the circumscribed interests of stockholders—a return on investment—rather than conscientious management of plant and enterprise. He spoke, correspondingly, of the narrowly focused interests of workers—in wages, rather than production.

He argued that these circumstances created a reality in which the atomized elements involved in production had difficulty synchronizing their endeavors because of divergent interests.[78] Since Actualism's rationale in support of Fascist corporativism turned on the identification of individual, group, and state ends,[79] Spirito argued that the refraction of interests produced by prevailing arrangements was not only counterproductive—but, in the last analysis, immoral.

Spirito maintained that the corporativist arrangements still prevailing in the 1930s reflected the individualistic biases of liberal economic theory.

---

[77] Spirito, *Memorie di un inconsciente*, p. 174.

[78] Spirito, "Individuo e stato nell'economia corporativa," in *Il corporativismo*, p. 351.

[79] See, for example, Spirito, "Regime corporativo"; "La crisi del capitalismo e il sistema corporativo"; and "Statalismo corporativo," in *Il corporativismo*, pp. 389, 397, 433.

As a consequence, whatever was attempted in terms of corporativist interventions into the economy almost always had little more than palliative effect on what was a fundamentally dysfunctional individualistic productive system.[80] He held that the corporativism of the beginning of the 1930s was "eclectic" rather than consistently Fascist or Actualist. He alluded to article 7 of the Carta del lavoro, which spoke of private property as a social responsibility—as signaling the end of the liberal conception of private property.[81] He advocated the complete abandonment of the liberal notion of the amoral, hedonistic, and atomistic *homo oeconomicus*, arbiter of himself and the sole judge of his own interests in any struggle against his conationals. He recommended the articulation of a system predicated on *homines oeconomici*, collectively oriented—in search of collective norms and communal moral principles—that would harmonize, foster, and enhance community goals.[82]

Spirito went on to argue that given the social character of property, together with the collectivistic orientation of the state, individual private property could only be an anachronism. Fascism, he continued, was charged by history with the resolution of the antinomies that still afflicted the modern economy of peninsular Italy. Doctrine and practice were beset by manifest inconsistencies. Stockholders pursued narrow private interests. Administrators were preoccupied with special concerns. Workers were occupied almost exclusively with their own welfare.

Should enterprise fail, the state undertakes salvage—because business failure threatens not only individual well-being, but the strength and international stature of the community. Should workers threaten to strike, the state calls upon the courts to mediate. All of which made evident that only the state seemed to bear the responsibility for the most fundamental of collective interests.

Spirito assessed the time as one of transition. Fascist Italy was in the process of creating the modern state.[83] Spirito argued that doctrine, circumstances, and logic recommended the abandonment of the liberal conception of individual private property for the more functional reality of *corporative property*—a gradual fusion of capital and labor in the unitary processes of national production.

Spirito advocated the creation of a system of corporative property in which working members of the corporations would become stockholders. All would become workers and workers would become owners in the

---

[80] Spirito, "Economia programmatica," in *Il corporativismo*, pp. 412–13.

[81] See the discussion in *La concezione fascista dell proprietà privata* (edited by the Confederazione fascista dei laboratori dell'agricoltura. Rome: n.p., 1939).

[82] Ibid., p. 416.

[83] Spirito, "Individuo e stato nell'economia corporativo," in *Il corporativismo*, p. 355.

measure of their place in the organic hierarchy of enterprise. Workers would thus earn a return on enterprise profit and also occupy seats in an adminstrative council for enterprise to collaborate directly in management. The traditional distinctions between entrepreneurs and workers would gradually disappear. The reality of the community would rest on collective interest, collective effort, and collective rewards. "The state, for its part, would no longer undertake control or intervention from without, but would always be present within enterprise, since the corporation would be an organ of the state itself," thereby making manifest the reality of the underlying community of interests uniting all the factors of production. The transformation of private property into corporative property would thereby resolve the unresolved tensions that, in 1932, still separated individual, enterprise, syndicate, corporation, party, and the state.[84]

The argument turned on the Hegelian conviction that moral fulfillment of the individual required the fulfillment of the state in a union of the most fundamental interests of both. In 1932, as acknowledgment of that conviction, Mussolini requested that Giovanni Gentile write the first part, the neo-Hegelian "Fundamental Ideas," of the official *Doctrine of Fascism*—and the totalitarian Actualist argument became a formal part of Fascism's rationale.

Spirito delivered a variant of the Actualist case in the course of the corporativist conference at Ferrara in that same year, to a storm of criticism. Gentile came to his immediate defense, identifying those in opposition—Roman Catholics, political and economic liberals, and unthinking "superfascists"[85]—as the enemies of Fascism.[86] By that time, the more or less formal Actualist arguments, in specific support of the corporativist state, had already begun to make their regular appearance in Fascist literature.[87]

---

[84] Ibid., p. 357.

[85] It seems probable that Gentile was referring to Julius Evola, who, as will be argued, was essentially an anti-Fascist who pretended to "superfascism." See the discussion in H. T. Hansen, "Introduction: Julius Evola's Political Endeavors," in Julius Evola, *Men among the Ruins: Post-war Reflections of a Radical Traditionalist* (Rochester, Vt.: Inner Traditions, 2002), pp. 42–43, 50–57.

[86] Gentile, "Individuo e stato o la corporazione proprietaria," *Educazione fascista* 10 (August 1932), pp. 635–38. Years later, at the close of the Fascist period in Italy, Mussolini himself identified the same contingents as having been enemies throughout his tenure. See A. James Gregor, *Giovanni Gentile: Philosopher of Fascism* (New Brunswick, N.J.: Transaction Publishers, 2001), chap. 7.

[87] See, for example, N. Massimo Fovel, "L'individuo e lo stato nella scienze economica," *Nuovi studi di diritto economia e politica* 3, no. 1 (January–February 1930), pp. 51–67; "L'individuo e lo stato nell'economia corporativa," *Archivio di studi corporativi*, no. 1 (1930), pp. 101–30; "Identificazione dell'individuo e dello stato come attori economici," *Nuovi studi di diritto, economia e politica* 3, nos. 3–4 (March–June 1930), pp. 189–207;

What would emerge out of Spirito's projected "integral corporativism" would be a state economically individuated in and through persons, and collections of persons in syndicates, and corporations—all finding their political identity, as a national community, in the form of a totalitarian state. Historically, such a resolution would satisfy those ideological interests that had animated Fascism since its founding. It would supersede the old socialism—the antinational and antiproductive opponent of nascent Fascism—"to make its own that which remains alive and productive in the Bolshevik experience."[88]

Spirito saw in his proposals the salvage of whatever was alive in revolutionary socialism. Fascist intellectuals of the period echoed that sentiment and saw in some of the institutions of the Soviet Union the empirical confirmation of Spirito's judgments concerning corporativism.

Spirito identified "integral" and "programmatic" corporativism—an evolving corporativism that would transform itself into a "true and effective economic government"—as a form of modern socialism. The corporative pyramidal infrastructure that was being erected, for example, would house those equipped with the expertise necessary to guide the various sectors of the economy. At the pinnacle there would be a "permanent technical office," responsible for program projections—uniting all the elements of production through scientific, indicative planning. Corporativism would unite science with life itself, so that the abstractions characteristic of liberal empirical and academic science would be transformed into an applied and living revolutionary socialism.[89]

Throughout the hierarchy of organized labor, from the lowliest employee to the highest technician and functionary in the productive system, everyone would both contribute to and profit from national enterprise. The state would not be "a centralized bureaucracy, but would be indistinguishable from the organic corporativism which constitutes its substance. . . . The unity of the state would be enriched with all the dynamism of individual initiative . . . expressing itself through the medium of a unitary will."[90] The individual would finally, and effectively, become identified with the state.

What would result would be a "regulated" and "programmatic" economy that was coherent and goal directed, capable of adjusting to, and

---

"Intorno al principio formale della politica economica corporativa," *Archivio di studi corporativi*, no. 1 (1930), pp. 87–100; Spirito, "La riforma della scienza economica e il concetto di stato," *Nuovi studi di diritto, economia e politica* 3, no. 1 (January–February 1930), pp. 68–72.

[88] Spirito, *Il corporativismo*, p. 359.

[89] Spirito, "Economia programmatica," and "L'economia programmatica corporativa," in *Il corporativismo*, pp. 412–32.

[90] Spirito, "L'economia programmatica corporativa," in *Il corporativismo*, p. 424.

mediating, episodic and intersectoral dislocations. It would be a truly *national* economy, serving the vital interests of all in an international environment of challenge. It could not be a *closed* economy—but selectively open to the global community—since the peninsula was dependent on the international markets for at least a substantial part of the resources necessary for its basic industries.[91]

The reaction to Spirito's analysis was immediate. The meeting of some six hundred specialists at Ferrara, devoted to the interpretation of the role and future functioning of the Fascist corporations, was one of the largest gatherings of political thinkers and economic specialists since the March on Rome. It marked the beginning of a new phase of the "Revolution" and clearly engaged the interests of some of Fascist Italy's most important leaders. At the conclusion of Spirito's communication, some of Italy's most prominent industrial leaders rose to voice their objections. Even Giuseppe Bottai, then Fascist Minister of Corporations—obviously discomfited—suggested that Spirito had perhaps allowed his argument to take him beyond the bounds of corporativism.[92]

Others were less circumspect. Some of the more important leaders of industry complained that what Spirito advocated was state socialism at best, or "Bolshevism" at worst. It was said that Spirito had transfigured Fascism and made of it a wretched imitation of "leftist" excess.[93]

Although his argument had been welcomed by notables such as Sergio Panunzio, the response on the part of some distinguished members of the audience left Spirito concerned. He asked for an audience with Mussolini, and Mussolini welcomed him on 13 May, less than a week after the conclusion of the conference.

Spirito wished to know if his communication had been "heterodox." Mussolini replied in the negative. "Your communication was not heterodox," Mussolini insisted, "it was perfectly orthodox, entirely defensible politically and scientifically."[94]

---

[91] Some authors have suggested that Spirito was opposed to the *autarkic* efforts of Fascism. See, for example, Silvio Lanaro, "Appunti sul fascismo 'di sinistra': La dottrina corporativa di Ugo Spirito," in Alberto Aquarone and Maurizio Vernassa, eds., *Il regime fascista* (Bologna: Il Mulino, 1974), p. 387. That does not seem to be the case. He spoke of Fascist Italy operating in international markets in order to supply its needs, but Mussolini himself in speaking of autarky recognized as much. In 1936, responding to the sanctions imposed on Italy because of its aggression against Ethiopia, Mussolini spoke of his conception of autarky as "the maximum degree of economic independence for the nation." Mussolini, "Il piano regolatore della nuova economia Italiana," in *Oo*, vol. 27, p. 242.

[92] Giuseppe Bottai, "Al convegno di Ferrara," in *Esperienza corporativa (1929–1935)*, 2nd ed. (Florence: Vallecchi, 1935), p. 585.

[93] See Guido Cavalucci, *Il fascismo è sulla via di Mosca?* (Rome: Cremonese, 1933).

[94] As cited in Spirito, *Memorie di un incosciente*, p. 177.

As was indicated, Mussolini had approved Spirito's communication before the conference in Ferrara. A few weeks after the conference, Mussolini repeated his judgment once again. The following October, a few short months after Spirito's delivery in May, Mussolini once again spoke of his work on corporativism. He recognized that many had objected to his anticipation of a corporative planned economy. Mussolini acknowledged that Spirito had become a "monster" to all those who insisted on clinging to the remnants of economic liberalism that still survived in the era of the Great Depression. He went on to allude to Spirito's animating conviction—the identity of the individual and the state—as "doctrinally orthodox," and proceeded to send the reader to the *Enciclopedia italiana*, to read the insert devoted to "fascism" in order to establish the orthodoxy of just that conviction. Since the insert appeared over Mussolini's name, the reference confirmed Spirito's Fascist credentials.

Thus, on at least three occasions—one public—Mussolini affirmed his approval of Spirito's assessment, documenting its fundamental doctrinal orthodoxy. "No one," Mussolini insisted, "can deny the clarity of Spirito's historic analysis, the vigor of his argument, or the logic of his conclusions."[95]

In the years that followed, Spirito's sentiments found recurrent expression in Mussolini's prose. Like Spirito, Mussolini spoke of the twentieth century as "the century of power and glory of labor." He spoke of workers entering "more and more intimately into the productive process. . . . When I say producers," he continued, "I do not mean only industrialists or employers, but I also mean workers." It was a development, he argued, that "was imposed by logic and history itself." He spoke of the "end of liberal-capitalistic economy . . . an economy aiming at individual profit." The Fascist economy would be one "concerned with collective interests." In revolutionary Italy, there could be no economic matters that were "exclusively of private or individual concern." The behavior of individuals, and groups of individuals, was to fall increasingly under the discipline of the state. And the state, armed with modern science, Mussolini insisted, would create multifold possibilities for the Italian peninsula—and while Italy's complex economy would have to be managed with prudence, the future was big with the promise of power, glory, and fulfillment.[96]

About a month after he identified himself with the thrust and content of Spirito's intervention in the Congress in Ferrara, in a major address on the corporative state Mussolini spoke unhesitatingly about the passing of capitalism and the abject inadequacy of liberal economic theory. He spoke of the increasing size of enterprise as nullifying all the putative benefits of

[95] Mussolini, "Segnalazione," in *Oo*, vol. 26, pp. 68–69.
[96] Mussolini, "Discorso agli operai di Milano," in *Oo*, vol. 26, pp. 356–57.

private ownership that were supposed to redound to the community.[97] He spoke, without hesitancy, of a planned, regulated and controlled economy for Fascist Italy.[98]

At the same time, he characterized Fascism as a system which fostered and sustained both political and economic discipline through the agencies of a single political party and the totalitarian state. The totalitarian state would "absorb the energy, interests and aspiration of the people, transforming and uplifting them." The people would "live in an atmosphere of strong ideal tension."[99]

It is impossible not to recognize the influence of Actualism and the thought of Spirito in Mussolini's prose. Where, at the founding of Fascism in 1919, he spoke of "capitalism" as having only begun its evolution, of a dogged defense of individuality, and making recourse to the "Manchestrian state" of restricted function[100]—by the beginning of the 1930s, Mussolini spoke of the "totalitarian" state, its anticapitalistic "planned" economy, and the fundamental identity of individual interests with those of the state.

Through the first years of the 1930s, the Great Depression compelled a Fascist response. There was an almost immediate proliferation of *consorzi, enti*, and *istituti*. At first, a number of enterprises came together in defensive voluntary associations—consortia—not unlike German cartels. In June 1932, these consortia were placed under government control. The year before, in November 1931, the Istituto mobiliare italiano (IMI) had been formed, designed to provide financial assistance to those enterprises threatened by bankruptcy as a result of the critical collapse of domestic and foreign demand. Almost immediately, the Società finanziaria italiana (Sofondit) was established, intended to assist the nation's financial institutions to weather the dislocations. In the first months of 1933, the Istituto di ricostruzione industriale (IRI) was created in order to provide long-term loans to industrial undertakings financed with government-guaranteed bonds.

While these were originally salvage operations, with the IRI serving as a transient holding company for industrial equities, very soon the state

---

[97] Mussolini, "Discorso per lo stato corporativo," in *Oo*, vol. 26, pp. 87, 89–90.

[98] Mussolini spoke of the "piano regolatore (the regulative plan)" of the corporative state in a speech before the National Assembly of Corporations on 23 March 1936, "Il piano regolatore della nuova economia Italiana," in *Oo*, vol. 27, pp. 241, 244. Thereafter the terms "plan" and "program" or "programmatic plan" were regularly used to describe the organization and activity of the Fascist economy.

[99] Ibid., p. 96.

[100] See Mussolini, "Il primo discorso alla camera dei deputati," in *Oo*, vol. 16, p. 445; "Il fascismo e gia un partito," in *Oo*, vol. 17, p. 158; "Logica e demagogia," in *Oo*, vol. 14, p. 86; "Tra il vecchio e il nuovo 'navigare necesse,' " in *Oo*, vol. 14, pp. 231–32. See

became majority stockholder in hundreds of diverse enterprises. By 1937, the holdings of both the IMI and the IRI were systematized, allowing the state to control, in large measure, the financial and industrial activity of Italy. Credit was extended by the state, and five major sectors of the economy were drawn together into five parastate entities: Finsider (iron and steel), Finmeccanica (mechanical industries), STET (telephonic communications), Finmare (shipbuilding), and Finelettrica (electricity)

Below the five major sectors perhaps as many as two hundred industrial entities were collected, either directly or partially controlled by the state. These entities shared information with the various corporative agencies already in existence, and they were all supervised by the state, indirectly by the Fascist party, and directly by Mussolini and the Grand Council of Fascism.[101]

By 1938, after Italy, for all intents and purposes, had emerged from the effects of the international depression, the entities under the control of the IRI proceeded to produce 67 percent of Italy's ferrous minerals, 77 percent of its cast iron, and 45 percent of its steel. About 80 percent of all shipbuilding undertaken on the peninsula was done under the auspices of Finmare —and Finmeccanica was producing 40 percent of all machine products. The major part of all infrastructural development was the product of the efforts of similar parastate entities.[102] In effect, by the end of the 1930s, the economy of Fascist Italy was the most extensively state controlled in all of Europe—with the exception of the Soviet Union.

Fascism responded to the rise in unemployment that accompanied the international business depression by undertaking vast public works. The comprehensive land reclamation program together with the expansion of public works devoted to the communications and transportation infrastructure, begun before the depression, were reformulated and expanded in 1933.[103]

While many of the industrialized nations of the West undertook programs of business salvage as a consequence of the Great Depression, Fascist Italy went further and effectively alienated the property of vast sectors of the economy and subjected much of the rest to partial or complete control by the state. By the mid-1930s, almost all credit availability, and almost all heavy industrial activity, was controlled, directly or indirectly, by the state.

A. James Gregor, *Young Mussolini and the Intellectual Origins of Fascism* (Berkeley and Los Angeles: University of California Press, 1979), chap. 9.

[101] See the account in Giulio Scagnetti, *Gli enti di privilegio nell'economia corporativa Italiana* (Padua: CEDAM, 1942).

[102] See Caizzi, *Storia dell'industria Italiana*, pp. 506–12.

[103] See the account in Arturo Tofanelli, ed., *Le opere del fascismo nel decennale* (Milan: Istituto editoriale nazionale, 1934).

While all this transpired, Mussolini gave increasing evidence of an interest in embarking on colonial expansion in East Africa in the search for a secure source of raw materials. The form that expansion assumed was aggression against Ethiopia. The Ethiopian war began in October 1935, to last about seven months. At about the same time, Italy became increasingly involved in the domestic strife in Spain that was to conclude only in 1939. At the same time, Italy became a partner with National Socialist Germany in what was conceived a struggle against the incursion of the Soviet Union into Western Europe.

In the course of all that, Italy was drawn increasingly close to National Socialist Germany and Imperial Japan. The anti-Comintern pact, and the subsequent "Pact of Steel," signaled the imminence of a European war of global impact into which Italy was to be inexorably drawn.

Behind and within all that, the Italian economy underwent substantial change. Those domestic economic changes reflected a great deal of the thought of Ugo Spirito. Private property no longer enjoyed a privileged position in Italy. There was an abandonment of the critical essentials of liberal economic policy. Control over policy more and more emanated from the center—from the Fascist Grand Council and Mussolini himself. The logic of the arrangements, although often precipitated by contingencies, shared obvious features with the rationale provided by Actualism, in general, and Spirito, in particular.

Like all ideological formulations, actualization of the specifics of Spirito's "integral corporativism" was systematically obstructed by events. Nonetheless, Spirito's ideas had resonance not only with Mussolini, but with the youth of Fascism. One could easily see the approximation of those ideas in the developments that followed the conference in Ferrara. The abandonment of liberal economic modalities, the transformation of the purposes of enterprise from private benefit to social utility, the rejection of the essentials of traditional industrial capitalism, the rapid expansion of state influence into all aspects of the economy, all suggested Actualist influence. Whatever Mussolini's relationship to Spirito after the mid-1930s tells us nothing about the enduring influence of Spirito's ideas on Mussolini as well as on a substantial number of young Fascists.

Those Fascists were to carry Actualist ideas into the last tragic months of the Second World War, there to be consumed, together with their ideas about integral corporativism, along with Fascism itself.

CHAPTER SEVEN

Sergio Panunzio and the Maturing
of Fascist Doctrine

IN THE YEARS that were to follow the conference at Ferrara where Ugo Spirito, amidst the challenge of the Great Depression, had attempted to anticipate the future of corporativism, Fascism was to put together the institutions that were to carry it into the Second World War. To Mussolini, whatever its normative rationale, corporativism was essentially an instrument of management and control. Through its instrumentalities, he was to seek to regulate industrial capitalism; to direct its enterprise in the search for surrogates to supply the resources absent from the Italian peninsula[1]—to achieve the "maximum economic autonomy of the nation; a necessary premise and a fundamental guarantee of its political independence and of its strength." He spoke of bringing "key industries" under the ambit of the state. He referred to the provisions of the Carta del lavoro, which provided for state dominance of industry should state interests be engaged. And he spoke of bringing the nation's financial institutions under state supervision. "The great shipping companies," he went on, "have passed under state control." Autarky, he concluded, was necessary for the protection of the nation—to insulate the peninsula from the aggression of those nations rich in both material abundance and arrogance.[2]

No one had foreseen these developments: neither the full extent of the international economic dislocation beginning in 1929, nor the impositions of sanctions on Italy as a consequence of its foray into colonialism in the mid-1930s. Certainly, Spirito's assessment of how corporativism would develop was, in measure, prescient—but major features had eluded him. After 1935, Spirito, for a variety of reasons both political and philosophical, no longer played as public a role in the front ranks of Fascist intellectuals.[3]

---

[1] See Luigi Lojacono, ed., *L'Independenza economica italiana* (Milan: Hoepli, 1937); Angelo Tarchi, *Prospettive autarchiche* (Florence: CYA, 1941).

[2] Mussolini, "Alla terza assemblea generale delle corporazioni," *Opera omnia* (Florence: La fenice, 1953–65. Hereafter *Oo)*, vol. 28, pp. 175, 178–79, 181.

[3] Spirito, *Memorie di un incosciente* (Milan: Rusconi, 1977), pp. 182–85. He continued to work with other intellectuals, particularly the Actualists still prominent in the regime.

Sergio Panunzio, on the other hand, had more closely followed the juridical and institutional evolution of Fascist corporativism. While Spirito's thought was panoramic and anticipatory in character, that of Panunzio was more detailed and meticulous—and by choice, followed, assessed, and influenced, rather than anticipated, developments. He always characterized himself as "pragmatic,"[4] and while always identifying himself as philosphically "idealist" and as antimaterialist, he was content to remain a Kantian of sorts and a more orthodox Hegelian, unprepared or ill-equipped, to fully proceed to Actualism.[5] None of that is to say that Panunzio actively opposed himself to Actualism. Like most intellectuals, he had his reservations concerning particular Actualist formulations—but in essentials, there was remarkable agreement.

Both Gentileans and Panunzio were *statists*—according philosophical and political priority to the state. As a consequence, they were all *collectivists*, opposing the "atomic" individualism of political and economic liberalism that reduced the function of the state to that of a night watchman commissioned to protect life and property. They were all *nationalists* in the sense that they conceived the nation as the contemporary vehicle of individual self-realization. They were all *antiparliamentarian*, holding parliaments to be, at best, ineffectual and, at worst, the source of corruption. They were all emphatic *moralists*, insisting that the state had the pedagogical obligation of training human beings to selfless virtue. As a consequence, Fascist rule was seen as *ecclesiastic, epistemarchic*, and *pedagogic* in essential character.[6] Like religionists, philosophers and pedagogues saw the use of force justified only when in the service of virtue.[7] Panunzio, like the Gentileans, conceived society as *immanent* at the very core of humankind.[8] Actualists and non-Actualists, as Fascists, were all

---

[4] Panunzio, "Il sindacalismo nazionale," *Lavoro d'Italia*, 12 May 1923, reprinted in *Stato nazionale e sindacati* (Milan: Imperia, 1924), p. 115.

[5] Panunzio always held that "facts are superior to ideas." Panunzio, "La rappresentanza di classe," *Rinnovamento* 2, no. 7 (13 August 1919), in *Stato nazionale e sindicati*, p. 46. See Panunzio, "Il sindacalismo nazionale," *Stato nazionale e sindicato*, pp. 102, n. 1; and "Che cos'è il liberalismo?" *Critica fascista* 1, no. 1 (15 June 1923), in *Stato nazionale e sindicato*, p. 195; "Educazione politica," *Popolo d'Italia* (29 March 1916), in *Stato nazionale e sindicata*, p. 29, n.1.

[6] See the discussion in Panunzio, *Appunti di dottrina generale dello stato: Realtà e idea dello stato* (Rome: Castellani, 1934), p. 201.

[7] See Panunzio's comments in "Il sindacalismo nazionale," *Lavoro d'Italia*, 12 May 1923, reprinted in *Appunti di dottrina generale dello stato*, p. 114; and his entire works, *Il concetto della guerra giusta* (Campobasso: Colitti e figlio, 1917); and *Diritto, forza e violenza: Lineamenti di una teoria della violenza* (Bologna: Cappelli, 1921).

[8] See Panunzio's reference to society's very immanence among human beings, rather than as an artefact composed of the "dust of individuals." "Il sindacalismo nazione" in *Stato nazionale e sindacati*, pp. 104–5. Panunzio even uses the characterization of society and the

elitists in the sense that they were "epistemarchs"—advocates of rule by those most gifted, most knowlegeable, and most committed.[9] All subscribed to rule by the hegemonic *single party*, and in appropriate circumstances, rule by a *single, charismatic individual*.

In effect, it shall be argued that, whatever differences marked Panunzio off from Actualism, they were incidental and largely circumstantial. When Western critics suggest that Fascism was informed by a "contradictory" and "inconsistent" doctrine, they expand upon real and fancied differences between ideologues such as Gentile and Panunzio and entirely neglect the central core of beliefs that united everyone around the Partito nazionale fascista and Mussolini.

It is in that sense that the differences between Spirito and Panunzio should be understood. There were, of course, real differences. Spirito addressed himself to the implicit "logic" of corporativism, and sought to anticipate the changes "immanent" in the system. Panunzio, on the other hand and throughout his intellectual life, sought to understand the evolving arrangements, and convey that understanding to those who were to live under Fascism's dominion. His was a more fundamental concern than simply taking the measure of corporativism and anticipating its future. Panunzio had charged himself with the responsibility of providing comprehensive insights into the working of the system.

In fact, by the time of his death on 8 October 1944, Panunzio had delivered the most exhaustive and comprehensive account of the mechanics of corporativism then available. As a consequence, Panunzio has been ranked, by those familiar with Fascist Italy, as a major theorist of corporativism, the equal of Giovanni Gentile in the intellectual defense of the regime.[10]

---

state not being *external* to human beings, but rather *in interiore homine*—the Latin typically employed by Gentile to reflect the same concept.

[9] See Panunzio, "Politica e educazione," in *Stato nazionale e sindacato*, p. 145.

[10] See the comments of Susanna de Angelis, "Il corporativismo giuridico nell'opera di Sergio Panunzio," *Storia contemporanea*, 14, nos. 4–5 (October 1983), pp. 695–96. The relationship between Gentile and Panunzio was complicated on a personal as well as on a theoretical level. With respect to the latter, see the comments by Francesco Perfetti, ed., of Sergio Panunzio: *Il fondamento giuridico del fascismo* (Rome: Bonacci, 1987), pp. 132–33. Panunzio, for example, objected to some of the features of Gentile's conception of the state as "ethical." While accepting the identification of the state as "ethical," Panunzio maintained the necessity of preserving the "juridical moment" distinct from that which was "metajuridical" or "moral" in order to better protect elements of the existing society. He also entertained reservations concerning the "identification" of the syndicates with the state—advocating, instead, their "subordination" to the state. These kinds of differences certainly had implications for conduct, but it would be hard to argue that they were fundamental, or that they rendered the doctrine of Fascism, "contradictory." See the treatment in Perfetti, in *Il fondamento giuridico del fascismo*, ibid., pp. 72 and 96 n. 182. Compare Panunzio, *Lo stato di diritto* (Ferrara: Tadei, 1921), pp. 115–19.

For Panunzio, the First World War had established the contemporary primacy of the nation as the association that could evoke the entire range of sentiments necessary to mobilize human energy to historic purpose.[11] Even before his formal membership in the Partito nazionale fascista, Panunzio had spoken of Italy's underdevelopment, its lack of natural resources and capital; the necessity of the expansion of plant on the peninsula and the encouragement of the nation's industrial production under corporativist auspices.[12] That was the hard issue that faced the revolution—it would have to establish a "new regime of production."[13] Panunzio anticipated that the emerging revolutionary system would meet such demands by putting together arrangements that he identified as a union of "statism and syndicalism—with the first providing the ends, and the second the means."[14]

By the early 1930s, Panunzio was preparing a comprehensive exposition of Fascist doctrine—together with its argued vindication. As an academic, trained in philosophy and social science, he began with a catalog of stipulative definitions of those terms he held to be essential to his exposition. In social science, such stipulative definitions are never held to be true—nor did Panunzio hold them to be so. They were *useful* to his account.[15] They were employed in order to reduce the vagueness and ambiguity of the terms as they are employed in ordinary speech.

Panunzio defined *society* as a collection of persons, arranged in functionally related configuration, engaged in activities governed by some set of explicit or implicit rules of conduct. A society, as a system governed by rules of conduct—sanctioned as laws—provides the material foundation for a *state*. The state—as a politico-juridical reality—is a particular kind of society, one in which a selected minority exercises sovereignty, control, or *imperium*, that is to say, the faculty of issuing authoritative commands.[16] A society, per se, refers to a functional collection of persons that

---

[11] *Lo stato di diritto*, pp. 102–4.

[12] "We are poor in resources, we have very little occasion for savings and capital accumulation . . . and scant capital. We must break out of the cage that renders it impossible for us to develop. . . . We must be frugal, parsimonious, modest in consumption, in pleasures, because without that, we can never achieve greatness. . . . Italy will remain poor, underdeveloped and overpopulated. The axiom of Fascism and Fascist sociology is *production* and its increase." Panunzio, *Che cos'è il fascismo* (Milan: Alpes, 1924), pp. 26, 29, 40, 53; see pp. 24–25. See Panunzio, "Un programma d'azione," *Il Rinnovamento* 1, no. 2 (15 March 1919), pp. 87, 89; and *Lo stato fascista* (Bologna: Cappelli, 1925), p. 67.

[13] Panunzio, *Che cos'è il fascismo*, pp. 63, 64.

[14] Panunzio, "La rappresentanza di classe," in *Stato nazionale e sindacati*, p. 37.

[15] Panunzio, *Appunti di dottrina generale dello stato*, pp. 238–50.

[16] See the conceptual distinctions offered by Panunzio, ibid., pp. 130–31, 249. For the purposes of the present exposition, "sovereignty" is used to signify no more than political power or control.

is innocent of sovereignty, while a state is a particular kind of society—specifically characterized by sovereignty. In effect, it is the state that provides peculiar form to society.[17]

For Panunzio, a *nation* is also a specific kind of society, empirically characterized by an interrelated collection of persons sharing territorial and ethnic origin, a traditional culture, and a common history. A nation is an ordered society—spiritually united by the state. The unity provided by the state is predicated on a shared morality and factually enhanced by a general obedience to law that characterizes its citizens.[18] *Nationality* refers to those persons, united by territory, culture, and spirituality, who are subject to the laws of a given state. They are the *people*[19]—and constitute the *matter* of which the state is the *form*.[20] Even where people do not constitute a nation, the state may rule as the agent, or bearer, of sovereignty. Thus, where diverse peoples are conquered or come together and are governed by a given state, we speak of "empires."[21]

For Panunzio, the state as the bearer of sovereignty was considered an "eternal absolute" in its "spiritual and ideal essence."[22] What that meant was that we are counseled to consider all assemblies of functionally interrelated persons as being, in some real sense, ruled. The agency of sovereign rule—whoever its role-holders might be at any given place, time, or circumstance, or however rule is exercised—is a manifest or implicit "state."[23]

In effect, Panunzio's definition of the state was a theoretical convenience, a term that would be applied in any circumstance when an organized aggregate is subject to command, dominion, or power. The term, although suggested by experience, was not *empirical*. It was a *definition*. It belonged to the philosophical and moral *analysis* of human history. Thus, the term might be applied, in principle, Panunzio affirms, wherever an elite, of whatever kind, exercises sovereign command—in primitive families, tribes, confederations, city-states and/or kingdoms—over any organized body of persons. When such a body is united by history and

---

[17] For Gentile, the "state is the concrete form of the life of a people." Gentile, *Discorsi di religione*, 3rd ed. (1920; Florence: Sansoni, 1955), p. 27.

[18] Panunzio, *Popolo, nazione, stato* (Florence: La nuova Italia, 1933), pp. 17–19.

[19] Panunzio fully recognized the multiple uses of the term "people" (see ibid., pp. 46–49, n. 28). His stipulative use served exposition. It was not designed to reflect "truth."

[20] See the similar analysis in Panunzio, *Il sentimento dello stato* (Rome: Littorio, 1929), pp. 101–8.

[21] See Panunzio's discussion of Austria-Hungary, where he identified the "sentiment of the state," but found the "sentiment of nationality" absent. See Panunzio, *Popolo, nazione, stato*, p. 20.

[22] Ibid., p. 79.

[23] See the discussion and qualifications in Panunzio, *Appunti di dottrina generale dello stato*, pp. 341–43.

culture, and occupies territory of sufficient size, it is identified by the modern term "nation."[24]

Throughout his account, Panunzio employed the terms "spiritual" and "spirituality," intended to sensitize his audience to the fact that he considered obedience to law, however much reinforced by conditioning, to be a fundamentally voluntary, hence moral, act. The state, therefore, was a moral agency—and the nation a "spiritual" product.

All of this was part of the idealist interpretation of individual and collective life for which Panunzio had opted around the time of the First World War. Throughout the remainder of his life he remained influenced by Kantianism, tending to favor some form of neo-Hegelianism in his philosophical interpretation of individual and collective morality.[25] Needless to say, it was that orientation that governed his interpretation of the Fascist state.[26]

Beneath the idealist interpretation, Panunzio entertained standard social science conceptions. He was prepared, as a case in point, to identify what he called "the sentiment of nationality" with the in-group amity concerning which he had written in his youth.[27] Associated, originally, with sociological positivism and Marxist class warfare, Panunzio adapted the notion of "in-group amity" to his idealist analysis of the nationalism and statism of Fascism.

Like Gentile, Panunzio was prepared to acknowledge *sentiment* as an element that underlay moral choice.[28] Thus the sentiment of nationality and of the state were psychological and behaviorial antecedents to mature moral judgment. For Panunzio, nationality was originally associated with an in-group sentiment. Like the sentiment of the state, national sentiment matured—under appropriate circumstances—from sentiment into a fundamental moral commitment. In its first manifestation, that moral commitment was predicated on the cultural unity that initially defined a people.

---

[24] Ibid., pp. 79–82.

[25] As has been suggested, this included a readiness to identify not only with Hegelian, but with Gentilean insights. Panunzio's references to Gentile and Gentile's works are found in all his major works. See, for example, Panunzio, *Popolo, nazione, stato*, pp. 35, 36, 55 n. 39; Panunzio, *Il sentimento dello stato*, pp. 70, 77 n. 36, 86 and 87 nn. 38 and 39, 134, 136 n. 3, 154 n. 9, 230.

[26] Panunzio, *Il sentimento dello stato*, pp. 232–33.

[27] Panunzio speaks of the "natural tendency" of human beings to seek associated life among "similars." See Panunzio, *Appunti di dottrina generale dello stato*, p. 340.

[28] See Gentile, "Il sentimento," *Introduzione alla filosofia* (Rome: Treves-Treccani-Tumminelli, 1931), pp. 38–67; and *Discorsi di religione*, pp. 89–95; A. James Gregor, "Giovanni Gentile, Contemporary Analytic Philosophy, and the Concept of Political Obligation," in *Il pensiero di Giovanni Gentile* (Rome: Istituto della enciclopedia Italiana, 1977), pp. 445–57.

Just as it proved to be the case with Actualists, the entire notion of a national cultural and moral unity provides something like commonsense grounds for Panunzio's discussion of J. J. Rousseau's conception of the "general will"—a will that is that of the national community in its entirety, rather than a summing of its component individual wills. Like that undertaken by Actualists, Panunzio's analysis of Rousseau's general will reveals a great deal about his own, as well as Fascism's, convictions concerning the state.[29] Once again, because contemporary historians of political ideas have largely neglected the relationship to Fascist thought to that of Rousseau, a further review recommends itself.

Since their appearance, Rousseau's works have received disparate treatment at the hands of commentators. For some, the notion of a general will, as distinct from the empirical will expressed in the randomized samples typical of modern polling, has been dealt with as though it were akin to what Christians identify as the "inner voice of conscience." Sometimes the general will is compared to the a priori criteria employed to distinguish good from evil. For some, the general will is evidenced in the behavior of associated human beings—as in the spontaneous obedience to rules that govern all organized associations whether their purpose be piety, charity, war, savagery, or criminal practice. For others, the general will represents a will, immanent in humankind, that underlies the potential for unanimity that, in our own time, provides the "driving force" of totalitarianism.[30]

For Panunzio, Rousseau's general will was conceived a figure of speech having moral reference. It was a term that alluded to a will—a calculated disposition to act—that presumably has the historic community as its subject. It is a will innocent of individual considerations, interests, preferences, prejudices, and passions. It is a *common*, not an *average*, or *modal*, will. It is the product of *moral perfection*—a perfection that assures that however the general will is taken to apply to the individual, it would apply equally to anyone.[31]

The general or common will may be discerned only if a community is prepared to undertake the effort. What is equally clear to Panunzio is that only a few human beings are fully prepared by training and disposition to either identify it or sustain it when identified. Like Rousseau, Panunzio dismissed the notion that such a will can find expression in popular elections in which individuals vote their particular preoccupations, their party affiliations, their ego concerns, and/or their material interests.

---

[29] Most of the following discussion is taken from Panunzio, *Lo stato di diritto*, pp. 102–15.

[30] J. L. Talmon, *The Origins of Totalitarian Democracy* (New York: Praeger, 1960), p. 6.

[31] See Panunzio, *La politica di Sismondi* (Rome: Ugo Pinnaro, 1926), pp. 22–23.

It is in dealing with the attainment of moral perfection that Panunzio refers his reader to Rousseau's general discussion of the moral maturation of individuals.[32] There Rousseau takes his reader through the stages of the individual's moral progression, tracing the infant's love of self as it expands to a broader sense of love that includes all those persons, and all those circumstances, that are life-enhancing.[33] Commencing with the nuclear family, the circle of expanding and enlightened self-interest comes to include the community, the nation, international confederations, and, finally, humanity.[34] Carefully cultivated by both sentiment and reason, the circle of moral identification ultimately comes to include our antecedents and prospective progeny—all of whom, in one sense or another, have influenced, influence or are expected to influence our full moral realization.

Given such an assessment, the disposition to behave in a fashion that satisfies the interests of all—those deceased, living and as yet unborn—finds expression in the morally perfected general will, a will whose imperatives are more demanding than any that might derive from the unanimous interests of any living community of individuals. The general will is therefore fundamentally different from the measured will of any empirical community—sharing its essence with the Gentilean will of the "transcendental self." Understood in such a fashion, Rousseau's entire notion of a general will is ultimately based on an unmistakable form of transcendental idealism—in which the full self-actualization of the individual inextricably involves his or her selfless commitment to a universal community of similars.[35] That community, and those lesser communities of which it is composed, constitute "ethical organisms." In the contemporary world, the agency that provides for the lawful ordering of such "organisms" is the "ethical state."[36]

This analysis, as Panunzio fully acknowledges, is remarkably similar to that of Hegelians, neo-Hegelians, and Gentileans. Panunzio's differences from each and all of them turn on his special analyses of specific concepts.[37] Panunzio insists, for example, on a "moment," or a stage in the

---

[32] See J. J. Rousseau, *Emile; or Treatise on Education* (New York: D. Appleton, 1914), bk. 4.

[33] See Panunzio's reference, *Lo stato di diritto*, p. 109 n. 1.

[34] See the discussion concerning international bodies such as the League of Nations and their moral relevance in this context. Panunzio, *Introduzione alla Società delle Nazioni* (Ferrara: Taddei, 1920), pt. 2.

[35] Panunzio, *Lo stato del diritto*, pp. 111–12.

[36] Ibid., pp. 117–22.

[37] Panunzio does not object to the notion of an "ethical state." What he concerns himself with is a number of distinctions that he feels Hegelians and Actualists fail to consider. See ibid., 134–36, 139–41 and chap. 6.

analysis, when the state is understood, juridically, as the defender of *individual* rights. Below the level of the "ethical organism," the "people" are disaggregated into individual components—each the equal of any other—with each protected by law. This is the *stato del diritto*, the juridical state, an Hegelian moment in Panunzio's entire conception of the more expansive and inclusive ethical state.

Thus, while the nation is treated, juridically, as a functional organism—with each component individual equal before the law—for moral and political purposes, the nation constitutes a single, united community, possessed of a unique state "personality," possessed of a general will, having continuity over time and beyond the lives of individuals. The nation is an "ethical organism," finding expression as an "ethical state," in the Hegelian sense.[38]

Panunzio traced similar concepts in the early-nineteenth-century work of J. C. Sismondi. He held Sismondi's "common" will to be derivative of Rousseau's general will—with both sharing clear affinities with the political and ethical concepts developed in Hegel's idealist doctrine of the state. The common or general will was understood to represent a will that was not only the *immanent, perfected* will of all living persons, but the will of our ancestors and of those as yet unborn. Only such a will would be an "objective" and "moral" will—because only such a will would be impersonal and universal. While the general will is the immanent will of all, discerning the full implications of such a will, with unclouded vision, can only be left to those very few possessed of the training and character sufficient to the purpose.[39]

The discernment involved would be very much like seeing the truth of complex mathematical formulae. Many may fail to perceive such truths, but once seen, such truths are unproblematic. That the many may fail to see such truths in those circumstances cannot count as evidence of the errancy of those truths, but rather of the dullness of the average person.

In that sense, Panunzio was always an "elitist."[40] As a syndicalist during the years before the First World War, he was familiar with all the literature that argued that society was moved, and history was fashioned, by minorities leading masses.[41] As has been suggested, his first works were dedicated to the "aristocracy" that would lead the workers' movement to revolution. After the First World War, one of his first publications as a

---

[38] Panunzio, *Popolo, nazione, stato*, pp. 27–28.

[39] Ibid., p. 22.

[40] See the comments of Susanna de Angelis, "Sergio Panunzio: Rivoluzione e/o stato dei sindacati," *Storia contemporanea* 11, no. 6 (December 1980), p. 971.

[41] For a brief discussion of some of the literature advocating various forms of elitism with which Panunzio must have been familiar, see A. James Gregor, *The Ideology of Fascism: The Rationale of Totalitarianism* (New York: Free Press, 1969), pp. 39–49.

Fascist was a brief political biography of Italo Balbo, the *condottiero* of the Fascist action squads, the conqueror of Ferrara, Bologna, and Rovigo, the leader of men and the master of masses.[42]

Panunzio understood history, in all its complexity, to be a "spiritual" product, a function of singular actors working in singular circumstances. He spoke of heroes and statesmen who shaped events. They did not serve as representatives of individuals or aggregates of individuals; they were the "representatives" of the moral purposes of history.[43] They spoke with the authority of the general will. Possessed of the moral vision implied in Rousseau's notion of an objective and immanent general will, such individuals are the natural leaders of the ethical state.

By the early 1930s, the philosophical rationale for the Fascist state had been completed. The identification of the nation as the vehicle of self-fulfillment[44] left only one further substitution to make the case for Fascist totalitarian rule—-the identification of *one* person as embodying, through his rule, the interests of the entire nation and its informing state.

Gentile was convinced—as were many in his intellectual environment—that history moved through the medium of unique leaders moving masses to moral purpose. Through such leaders, the "particularity" of individuals was to be fused into an "immanence" that gave expession to the culture, economics, politics, and history of a people. The process of fusing a nation into an infrangible unity required the presence of a man, or a minority of men, "who represent the tendencies already apparent in a people, [together with] already operant forces . . . having a solid foundation in political reality."[45] If Italy was to be seen, once more, "as having value in the world," it would require a "sense of religious mission," and a "sense of sacrifice," to be aroused and sustained among the masses by "charismatics."[46]

That necessitated the presence of "intuitive leaders," "geniuses," "heroes," "providential spirits," who "embodied" the real will of an historic people in their leadership—thereby becoming the "conscience and the will

[42] Panunzio, *Italo Balbo* (Milan: Imperia, 1923).

[43] Panunzio, *Lo stato del diritto*, pp. 159–60.

[44] "Whoever sees in corporativism only an economic conception or solely political economy, fails to understand it. . . .This economic revolution completes the spiritual development of the individual and of society." Mussolini, "Corporativism," in *Oo*, vol. 26, p. 173. Panunzio recognized that one of the major functions of the "ethical state" was to cultivate the *development of individuals*. Panunzio, *Teoria generale dello stato fascista*, pp. 66–67.

[45] See Gentile, "Il significato della vittoria" and "L'esempio del governo," in *Dopo la vittoria: Nuovi frammenti politici* (Rome: La Voce, 1920), pp. 5, 9, 71.

[46] Gentile, *Discorsi di religione*, p. 7. Roberto Michels spoke specifically of "charismatic leaders" in speaking of Mussolini. See Roberto Michels, *First Lectures in Political Sociology* (New York: Harper Torchbooks, 1949), chap. 6.

of all."[47] They were capable of correctly assessing the character of their time, and the character of their peoples, in order to effectively mobilize them to their tasks.[48]

Such a unique leader could speak for an entire people in what Fascists were to call an "authoritarian, centralized democracy."[49] The common will would be "democratically" expressed in a series of intersecting economic and political institutions in what Panunzio described as a "popular regime in which the people are *directly*, rather than indirectly, represented."[50]

The fully developed argument was both *philosophic* (or moral) as well as *empirical*. Its critical element, that specific individuals might effectively represent the general will of a given population, was expressed, and defended, by Panunzio in philosophic and empirical argument. He held that it could be expressed and confirmed *empirically*. Some of the most capable Fascist intellectuals agreed, and sought to provide just that.[51] Whatever the case, the proposition was critical to Fascism's rationale.

Thus, by the early 1930s, Panunzio had fleshed out the normative and empirical vindication of the Fascist corporative state. Panunzio could provide expanded meaning and moral character to Fascist doctrinal statements. When the Carta del lavoro affirmed that "spiritually" the "Italian nation is an organism . . . a moral, political and economic unity that fully [*integralmente*] realizes itself in the Fascist state," Panunzio's prose endowed its seeming opacity with more intelligible meaning. When the official *Dottrina del fascismo* appeared in 1932, Panunzio's works—perhaps more than any others—unpacked its central concepts. Panunzio gave public meaning to those parts of the *Dottrina* that remained mercurial. When the *Dottrina* spoke of human beings as "individuals" who are, at once, "the nation and fatherland," bound by moral ligaments to both past and future generations, the meaning was revealed and enlarged by Panunzio's accounts. Compatible with Actualist social philosophy, Panunzio's rendering presented Gentilean concepts in the more familiar language of history and social science.

By the early 1930s, Panunzio had committed himself to writing a "general theory" of the Fascist state—to answer all the questions that re-

---

[47] Gentile, "Idee fondamentali," in *Dottrina del fascismo* (Milan: Hoepli, 1935), para. 9. The section was signed by Mussolini, but was written by Gentile and lightly revised by Mussolini.

[48] Gentile, *Fascismo e cultura* (Milan: Treves, 1928), p. 47; *Origini e dottrina del fascismo* (Rome: Libreria del Littorio, 1929), p. 23.

[49] Typical of this argument is Bruno Spampanato, *Democrazia fascista* (Rome: Politca nuova, 1933); See Panunzio's version, *Teoria generale dello stato fascista*, pp. 29–30.

[50] Panunzio, *Teoria generale dello stato fascista*, pp. 106–7, 136.

[51] See, for example, the effort by Michels, *First Lectures in Political Sociology*, chap. 6; see chap. 4.

mained in the wake of the appearance of the *Dottrina*.[52] Panunzio clearly intended to build on his preceding work, and by the end of the decade published the second, enlarged edition of his *Teoria generale dello stato fascista*.[53]

His *Teoria generale* was perhaps the most comprehensive treatment of Fascism as a social and political doctrine we have available. While there were other major apologetic works,[54] written by authors of competence and integrity, none were as broad in scope, nor as detailed in delivery, as that provided by Panunzio.

In his *Teoria generale*, Panunzio touched on all aspects of Fascist ideology.[55] He made sufficient reference to the *subjective* and *dialectical* process of coming to know the world and its properties as *spirit—consciousness—* to identify him as an epistemological and, perhaps, ontological idealist.[56] Throughout his work, he made regular and affirming references to Hegel and Italian Hegelians, ranging from Bertrando Spaventa to the lesser neo-Hegelians of the end of the ninteenth century.

In his account, Panunzio spoke of philosophy as being the first, and most fundamental, part of his exposition.[57] And while there is little elaboration of the specifically philosophical grounding of his exposition, there are sufficient references to the "formation of the moral consciousness of humankind" to make evident what he conceived to be the ultimate purpose of human communion.[58] He spoke of a spiritual process that informed history and the evolution of the state. He spoke of the historical and "dialectical process of the realization of the Fascist state," as proceeding through a series of "spiritual and ethical moments" that began with the individual, to extend itself to the family, to the communities that composed the nation, until all were incorporated in the state—to ultimately achieve fulfillment in moral perfection for all.[59]

---

[52] Panunzio, *Il sentimento dello stato*, pp. 10–11. One cannot escape the impression that Panunzio sometimes found Gentile's expositions impenetrable, and that he, Panunzio, sought to supply Fascism a more immediately persuasive rationale.

[53] Padua: CEDAM, 1939. 2nd, enlarged edition.

[54] Among the major works, see Carlo Costamagna, *Dottrina del fascismo*, 2nd, enlarged ed. (Turin: UTET, 1940); and Antonio Canepa, *Sistema di dottrina del fascismo* 3 vols. (Rome: Formiggini, 1937).

[55] The term "ideology" is used here to mean "a systematically related set of philosophical, normative and social science propositions that provide a general 'worldview' which, when employed to address some real or fancied problem, delivers doctrinal recommendations concerning individual and collective behavior." See Gregor, *The Ideology of Fascism*, pp. 3–6.

[56] Panunzio, *Teoria generale dello stato fascista*, pp. 452, 474, 508, 561.

[57] Ibid., p. 420.

[58] Ibid., p. 281.

[59] Ibid., p. 334.

Some things become reasonably clear in any review of Panunzio's exegesis of Fascist philosophy. Among them is the fact that Panunzio's emphasis on specifically individual self-realization as the end of history and the purpose of the state— while there—is far less evident than it is in the works of Gentile and Spirito. For Gentile, "the supreme law of the life of the spirit" was self-realization—the moral imperative to be "the ideal self that the individual ought to be."[60]

In the official *Dottrina del fascismo*, in the philosophical portion written by Gentile, it is that conception of self-realization that provides for the moral reaffirmation of the state and its role. The state is characterized as the arena in which the individual becomes his truer, fuller self. Only through an arduous and sacrificial "process of communion with family and social groups, with the nation and with history"—under the aegis of the state—might the individual achieve the promised self-realization.[61]

Panunzio's discussion never achieved the philosophical sophistication that typified that found in the epistemological and ethical works of Actualists. While it was evident that Panunzio's ideas were essentially compatible with those of Actualists,[62] he nowhere gave his convictions the technical philosophical specificity and rigor found in the works of Gentile. The compatibility of his views with those of Gentile is evidenced by Panunzio's emphasis on the idealist roots of Fascism—through references to the works of Giambattista Vico, G.W.F. Hegel, Giuseppe Mazzini, Antonio Rosmini, and Vincenzo Gioberti with impressive regularity—authors with whom Gentile identified his Actualism.[63] He was subsequently to argue that the Fascist corporative state fully satisfied the philosophical and ethical requirements of the generic Hegelian state—requiring some form of Hegelianism as its normative rationale.

---

[60] Giovanni Gentile, *Genesi e struttura della società* (Verona: Mondadori, 1954), pp. 36, 37. This is found in the English edition, *Genesis and Structure of Society* (Urbana: University of Illinois Press, 1960), pp. 75, 76. These references are used because they are easily accessible. Gentile's thoughts on "self-actualization," and the relationship with political and social life, are found in all his major works.

[61] Mussolini, *La dottrina del fascismo* (Milan: Hoepli, 1935), pt. 1, paras. 6, 7. The logic of the *Dottrina* is transparent. Its ethical foundation is that the Fascist state provides the circumstances in which the individual achieves moral fulfillment—and therefore has the right to demand sacrifice, obedience and dedication.

[62] The qualifications that attend this generalization will be dealt with in chapter 8 of this text.

[63] See, for example, Panunzio, *Teoria generale dello stato fascista*, pp. 5, 21, 22–24 n. 1. Gentile wrote his doctoral dissertation on Rosmini and Gioberti, and made Hegel, Vico, and Mazzini critical to the development of Fascist thought. Gentile, *Rosmini e Gioberti: Saggio storico sulla filosofia Italiana del Risorgimento*, 3rd, enlarged ed. (Florence: Sansoni, 1958) and *Origini e dottrina del fascismo* (Rome: Littorio, 1929); and *Giambattista Vico* (Florence: Sansoni, 1936); *La riforma della dialettica Hegeliana*, 3rd ed. (Florence: Sansoni, 1954. Third edition).

The fact is that without some form of Hegelianism, there could be no coherent vindication for paradigmatic Fascism. The nationalism of Corradini and Rocco tended to argue that the individual would have to be somehow subordinated to the political state in order that the *nation* might survive. The Hegelian argument was that individuals could only fulfill *themselves* by growing into their communities—principal among them the nation and the state. Similarly, Panunzio insisted that Fascism never conceived the relationship between the individual and the state as one that could legitimately be characterized as "statolatry, or political absolutism," but rather one in which the state oversaw "the richest possible development of both individual and social forces."[64]

While never totally absent among Italian nationalists, the discussion concerning the self-actualization of the individual was invariably clouded by a focus on the individual's service to the state. Thus, even when Rocco spoke of Fascism's effort to "resolve the fatal tensions between the necessities of political organization and those of the harmonious development of the human personality"—it seemed that he applauded the effort only because he saw an "insufficiency of personality development" as negatively affecting the prospects of the state.[65]

When nationalists spoke of the relationship between the individual and the state, there was a tendency to emphasize sacrifice and obedience to the exclusion of self-fulfillment. Thus, when Rocco spoke of Fascism's inversion of the relationship of the individual to society as that relationship was understood by political and economic liberalism, he could speak of the "total sacrifice of the individual to society."[66] In what was clearly a matter of emphasis, Actualists never spoke of the "total sacrifice" of the individual to the state. They affirmed that sacrifice—even the supreme sacrifice exacted in the defense of the nation—contributed to the individual's achievement of "that spiritual existence in which" each who sacrificed was to find true "value as a human being."[67] For Actualists, in fact, "the state was the true reality of the individual," and its defense was in his or her ultimate interests.[68]

---

[64] Panunzio, *Teoria generale dello stato fascista*, p. 67 n. 1.

[65] Alfredo Rocco, "Tornata parlamentare 9 marzo 1928," *Atti Parlamentari* (Rome: Casa editrice dello stato, 1928), p. 8511.

[66] Alfredo Rocco, *La formazione dello stato fascista (1925–1934)* (Milan: Giuffre, 1938), pp. 1101–2. Mussolini said that "We are among the first to have affirmed, against demoliberal individualism, that the individual does not exist, if not and in so far as he is in the state, and subordinate to the necessities of the state." Mussolini, "Al gran rapporto del fascismo," in *Oo*, vol. 24, p. 145.

[67] In one place Panunzio frames this Gentilean notion in the following fashion: "in defending the state, [individuals] defend themselves, the very profundity of themselves." Panunzio, *Teoria generale dello stato*, p. 61.

[68] Mussolini, *La dottrina del fascismo*, Pt. 1, paras. 2, 7.

For Actualists, the individual, in his or her most profound self, *identified* epistemologically and morally with the community and with the state. Thus, the individual could never be "totally sacrificed" to the community or the state without moral outrage. Whatever sacrifice was demanded from the individual could only be justified if such sacrifice was understood to be a voluntary act in the pursuit of moral perfection. The Gentilean notion of "self-actualization" involved such sacrifices as part of the spiritual process only when such behaviors were understood to be part of a course through which individuals might find their fulfillment.

Similarly, Panunzio always argued that the individual would gradually come to understand just such conceptions by successive approximations—in a process that was at once psychological, moral, and educative. Individuals would learn through education and experience as the Fascist state matured in its practice. The process would involve "the progressive socialization of the individual, through what is essentially moral education."[69]

It is obvious from the entire catalog of Panunzio's works that while his philosophical orientation was compatible with the basic tenets of Actualism, his primary political concerns turned on the juridical character of Fascist institutions and their doctrinal rationale. While relatively insubstantial in terms of epistemology, ethics, and technical philosophy, Panunzio's meticulous juridical treatises distinguish his works from those of other thinkers of the period.

After a perfunctory acknowledgment of the role of philosophy as preliminary to his task, Panunzio carefully followed the evolution of syndicalist and corporativist legislation from the first period of Fascist rule throughout its tenure. In the course of Fascism's evolution, Panunzio identified several phases—empirically observed and empirically confirmed.

The first period he identified as the "movement phase," in which Fascism mobilized the forces and advanced its program—a period begun immediately after the termination of the First World War and continued through the end of 1921—which saw the movement spread through the Po Valley and invest the major cities of the north. The period from the end of 1921 through October 1922, Panunzio characterizes as the "insurrection," the military defeat of the liberal and parliamenary state. The March on Rome on 28 October 1922 marked the commencement of the "revolutionary dictatorship"—in what Panunzio called an "epiphany of history." The revolution was the bearer of a new conception of the state—the resolution of a systemic political and economic crisis.[70] That dictatorship originally featured the concessions implied in Fascism's first commitment to the fabrication of a "Manchestrian state"—an effort to mobilize

[69] Panunzio, *Teoria generale dello stato fascista*, pp. 253, 256.
[70] Panunzio, "Teoria generale della dittatura," *Gerarchia* 14, no. 4 (April 1936), p. 235.

non-Fascist allies in order to undertake rapid economic development and the reestablishment of order on the peninsula as quickly as possible. That period closed with Mussolini's speech on 3 January 1925, when the call was issued for "Fascism as a government and as a party" to assume full, and uncompromising, power.[71]

Commencing in 1926, Fascism entered on a period of institutionalization through which it was to exercise *totalitarian* control over the peninsula— as a "Regime."[72] Panunzio identified the "revolutionary dictatorship," the preliminary to the totalitarian regime, as an entirely modern phenomenon. It was the consequence of a response to singularly modern crises. The revolution and the dictatorship that followed were embodiments of a totalitarian commitment that understood itself to be infallibly enlightened. Panunzio held such a dictatorship to be an irrepressible product of history itself— the consequence of crises that without revolutionary resolution would otherwise be destructive of culture and human potential.[73]

Panunzio argued that the revolutionary party, the revolutionary dictatorship, and its subsequent revolutionary regime were incomparably modern phenomena. They were unique in history. He went on to catalog a series of just such revolutionary parties and their associated dictatorships. Among them, he identified the Bolshevik party of the Soviet Union, the National Socialist party of post-Weimar Germany, the Kuomintang of post-dynastic China, and the Falange of post-Republican Spain.[74] He held that all these revolutionary parties were distinguished by traits that identified them as members of the same classificatory genus: the totalitarian revolutionary party. Because animated by an invincible conviction in the truth of their ideology, such parties, once successful, carry the exclusivist, *unitary party*, and subsequent *party-state* in their train.[75]

Panunzio dealt with what he considered the formal, organizational, or institutional similarities of such parties—characteristics that were the product of their organizational features rather than their specific ideological beliefs. For example, he maintained that the conviction in their own infallibility bred in each a typically *ecclesiastical* character. Their unrelieved conviction in the truth of their respective belief systems generated

---

[71] Mussolini, "Discorso del 3 Gennaio," in *Oo*, vol. 21, p. 240.

[72] Panunzio briefly summarizes this trajectory in *Teoria generale dello stato fascista*, pp. 430–31.

[73] Panunzio, "Teoria generale della dittatura," pp. 305–10.

[74] Panunzio, *Teoria generale dello stato fascista*, pp. 459–63, 513–14, 523, 557, 564, 579; and Panunzio, *Spagna nazionalsindacalista* (Milan: Bietti, 1942), pp. 46–51, 79, 89–90, 103–11.

[75] Panunzio had some reservations about the "purity" of the form of totalitarianism to be found in the Spanish Falange and the Chinese Kuomintang. See A. James Gregor, *Phoenix: Fascism in our Time* (New Brunswick, N.J.: Transaction Publishers, 2001), pp. 131–37.

responses that were typically religious—ritualistic, liturgical, jealous, and exclusionary.[76] Members of such parties proved to be intransigent in their convictions, intolerant of alternative ideologies, and punitive toward out-group members. Panunzio went on to argue that those dispositions generated the need for an aggressive defense against nonbelievers in the form of *military ancillaries* to the party—the "action squads" and the voluntary militia of revolutionary Fascism, the Bolshevik Red Guards, the Sturmabteilungen, and the subsequent Shutzstaffel, of the National Socialists.[77] By entailment, such dispositions found expression in ready recourse to violence to protect the integrity of their doctrinal convictions.[78]

Given the character of their commitments, and the circumstances in which they are forced to operate, such parties take upon themselves *pedagogical* responsibilities—as evangels of the truths they were prepared to defend with arms.[79] Together with such traits, the revolutionary parties and the regimes they precede are fundamentally *political* in essence.[80] However they commence, perhaps with an ideology that is economic and materialist in inspiration, modern revolutions and the regimes they create emphasize the *supremacy of politics* and the subordination of all else.

While perfectly content with his account of their formal similarities, Panunzio went on to outline their substantive ideological differences. Almost all were found to be critically wanting in coherence and normative effect.

With respect to the Soviet Union, Panunzio was dismissive of the Marxist-Leninist claim that they possessed an ideology that could be considered, in any sense, impeccable. He maintained that belief to be either simple pretense, delusionary, or the result of theoretical confusion. Marxism, Panunzio contended, had committed itself to ontological and epistemological materialism. No matter how "dialectical" that materialism, Panunzio held it to be beset by fundamental difficulties. Among those difficulties was an inability to discuss its conceptions without massive confusion. The concept "class," for example, which was presumably at the center of the system,[81] was nowhere defined with any precision—a singular failure for a system that claimed to be an infallible social science.[82]

---

[76] Panunzio spoke of totalitarian beliefs as religious in character. With respect to such beliefs, "one cannot be neutral." See Panunzio, *Il sentimento dello stato*, pp. 20–21.

[77] See Panunzio's comments, ibid., p. 462.

[78] Panunzio spoke of the revolutionary dictatorship as employing "the violence of the idea in the service of the idea." Panunzio, "Teoria generale della dittatura," p. 306.

[79] Panunzio, *Teoria generale dello stato fascista*, pp. 5, 19, 59–60, 64, 109, 253, 261, 275, 278, 456, 462, 471, 483, 501–3.

[80] Ibid., pp. 557–63.

[81] Ibid., pp. 25–26.

[82] Ibid., p. 246.

In terms of the reality within which the Bolsheviks found themselves compelled to operate, the failure of the international revolution left the Russian revolutionaries not in possession of a worldwide industrial system capable of generating the liberal abundance anticipated by Marx and Engels, but in possession of an economically retrograde *nation*. Other than rule a fractious and grievously wounded system, the Bolsheviks were driven to mobilize and organize workers in order to restart, maintain, and foster the *national economy*. To speak of the "dictatorship of the proletariat" in such an environment was an absurdity. A nation so circumstanced could hardly be composed of a single class, much less be ruled by one.

A nation is a *system*, made up of functionally related categories of persons; and so it was in the Soviet Union.[83] Every class was represented in the Stalinist totalitarian system—and the system was a dictatorship not *of*, but *over* the proletariat (however "proletariat" was, in fact, defined). The inconsistent system generated a new bureaucratic "class" (actually a stratum or a category) that acceded to dominance, with Josef Stalin, as the Vohzd, the Leader, becoming the capstone of the system.[84]

Panunzio argued that the rationale of the Soviet totalitarian state was based on a collection of fictions having very little to do with classical Marxism—the Marxism of Karl Marx and Friedrich Engels. Classical Marxism was fundamentally anarchic with respect to the state.[85] All the revolutionaries active in Italy before the First World War understood that perfectly well. All, almost without exception, including Mussolini and Panunzio, himself, were initially intrinsically and unalterably opposed to the state.

That had been true in Russia as well. It was as true of Lenin as it was for any other. His *State and Revolution*, written immediately before the Russian revolution, was basically antistate, antimilitary, and antipolice— anticipating the "withering away" of the state, and all its agencies, immediately on the successful accession to power by the Bolsheviks. In light of that, Stalin could only describe the subsequent creation of the Soviet state—"the mightiest and strongest state power that has ever existed"— as one of the "contradictions" of "dialectical development" intending, as Communism did, to accomplish the very "withering away" of the state.[86]

Panunzio cited these kinds of confusions as contributing to the inability of the Communist party to rule without the massacre of millions of inno-

---

[83] See Panunzio's comments in *Il sentimento dello stato*, pp. 139–40.

[84] See Panunzio's comments, *Teoria generale dello stato fascista*, p. 558.

[85] Ibid., pp. 565–67; and *Il sentimento dello stato*, pp. 42–47, n. 18.

[86] J. Stalin, ""Political Report of the Central Committee to the Sixteenth Congress," *Works* (Moscow: Foreign Languages, 1952), vol. 12, p. 381. See Panunzio's comments, *Il sentimento dello stato*, pp. 235–36.

cents.[87] If the revolution was destined to produce revolutionary dictator-ship, and a regime that enjoyed unqualified sovereignty over its citizens, any ideology that was inconsistent and unpersuasive would most likely have to sustain its authority with naked violence.[88]

Thus it is interesting to note that Panunzio held Hitler's National So-cialism to be apparently as mistaken in its ideological commitments as Stalin's Marxism-Leninism. Thus, as late as 1936, when Fascist Italy and National Socialist Germany were gradually approaching each other in political and military alliance, Panunzio noted that the rationale of "the Hitlerian revolution brings nothing with it other than the notion of 'race,' which literally has nothing to do with the concept 'nation.' "—a concept critical to modern revolution.[89]

As cautious as Panunzio was, he repeated the same reservations con-cerning National Socialist ideology in 1939, even after the publication of the official "Fascist Doctrine of Race," and the international pacts that united Fascist Italy with National Socialist Germany.[90]

In retrospect, the implications are eminently clear. National Socialism was animated by a seriously flawed ideology, intrinsically incapable of convincing anyone not already committed by self-interest, sentiment, or simple emotion.[91] If that were the case, the analysis of Bolshevik failures offered by Panunzio carried ominous entailments for those who lived under the revolutionary dictatorship of National Socialist Germany.

For Panunzio, Fascism was paradigmatic of revolutions in the twentieth century. Any substantial departure from its ideological, doctrinal, or insti-tutional properties could only threaten its revolutionary performance. The central issue that immediately arises in such an account turns on the ability to identify the fundamental "principles" of the revolutionary and

---

[87] Panunzio, *Teoria generale dello stato fascista*, p. 565.

[88] These implications surface throughout Panunzio's exposition—hence his emphasis on the credibility of Fascism's justificatory rationale. Thus Panunzio insisted, shortly before his death, that the entire structure of Fascism rested on "the Fascist conscience"—on the "collection of persuasive convictions and beliefs that live in each of us"—in much the same manner as the Gentilean Actualists. He held that the "first principles" were immediate and self-affirming data of consciousness. See Panunzio, *Motivi e metodo della codificazione fas-cista* (Milan: Giuffre, 1943), pp. 168–69.

[89] Panunzio, "Teoria generale della dittatura," p. 309.

[90] Panunzio, *Teoria generale dello stato fascista*, p. 32.

[91] Thus, in 1937, Julius Evola, a marginal thinker in Fascist Italy, published his *Il mito del sangue* that was presumably read and approved by Mussolini himself. Evola wrote that "the theory of race," which inspired National Socialist Germany, was not a "concept" that could be evaluated employing "properly scientific, philosophic, or historical" criteria. Evola identified National Socialist race theory as a "myth"—not a fiction, but a nonrational de-vice, which through "suggestive force" would be capable of moving persons to action. He reminded his audience that Mussolini had always insisted that race was a "matter of senti-ment, not a reality." Julius Evola, *Il mito del sangue* (Milan: Hoepli, 1937), pp. ix, x.

totalitarian regime. The issue, which is fundamentally philosophical, engaged Panunzio. In his response, Panunzio appealed to "Fascist conscience, that collection of persuasions and beliefs that live in each of us . . . [as] immediate data of consciousness." He addressed himself to the epistemic nature of just those "first principles": they could not be derived, because they were logically primary. He concluded that they must be matters of "belief, faith . . . and persuasion."[92]

It is at that point that an appeal to Actualism recommended itself. Panunzio had himself recognized that philosophy provided the necessary intellectual foundation for Fascism both as an ideology and as a revolutionary doctrine of the state. Such an argument could only conclude in some variant of the first principles of ontological and epistemological Actualism.

In general, it can be argued that the major claims found in the work of Panunzio were all but fully compatible with Gentilean Actualism. Only if one were to carefully pursue Panunzio's arguments would the suggestion of differences make themself apparent.

For one thing, Panunzio had made evident his objection to the "absolute immanence" that was central to Gentile's epistemology and ontology. Gentile proposed an epistemology that was "presuppositionless"—a theory of knowledge that commenced with the self-affirming awareness of consciousness—that drew "reality," and all its myriad distinctions, out of the immediacy of its own experience.[93] Gentile argued that an ultimate *unity* was a cardinal necessity for the intelligibility and the moral meaningfulness of the world as it emerged from immediate experience. Experience, in the final analysis, could not be divided, intelligently or morally, into separate and distinct "subjects" and "objects"—each forever separated and distinct. In some sense, subjects and objects, whatever the commonsense distinctions that marked them out in the empirical world, were *one*. They both arose out of a transcendental, sensing, and thinking subject. Objects were immanent in that "universal thinking subject"—distinctions having been made, and defended, in thought.[94]

Whatever this meant for common sense, it had major significance for organized religion. For Gentile, religion as a system of belief, and

<hr>

[92] Panunzio, *Motivi e metodo della codificazione fascista*, pp. 168–69. This is a repeat of the account in "I principi generali del diritto fascista (Contributo alla loro determinazione)," in *Principi generali dell'ordinamento giuridico fascista* (Pisa: University di Pisa, 1940), reprinted in Perfetti (ed.), Panunzio, *Il fondamento giuridico del fascismo*, p. 322.

[93] A convenient English treatment of the epistemological issues of Actualism can be found in Pasquale Romanelli, *The Philosophy of Giovanni Gentile: An Inquiry into Gentile's Conception of Experience* (New York: Birnbaum, 1937).

[94] See the discussion in A. James Gregor, *Giovanni Gentile: Philospher of Fascism* (New Brunswick, N.J.: Transaction, 2001), chap. 3.

God, as the object of those beliefs, were understood to be immanent in, and not external to, humanity. Actualism was a radical form of humanism—the kind of philosophical humanism that had been the acknowledged opponent of organized Roman Catholicism for at least half a thousand years.

By the early 1920s, the Church had identified Actualism as a solipsistic or pantheistic heresy—and when Mussolini decided to have Gentile write the "Idee fondamentali" of the official *Dottrina del fascismo*, the Church broadcast its objections to "the diabolic philosophy of the ethical state."[95] A substantial number of important Fascists—who were Roman Catholics—found themselves entertaining grave reservations concerning the official character of Actualism.[96] They correctly anticipated the objections of the Vatican—and, in fact, by the mid-1930s, the Catholic Church had placed all of Gentile's works on its Index of proscribed literature. That together with the much heralded Concordat with the papacy made the issue of Actualism's political and intellectual role in the defense of Fascism increasing sensitive.

Panunzio's position in all of this was eminently clear. In the first place, he emphasized the importance of the Concordat from the point of view of the moral integrity of Fascism. More than that, he maintained that Fascism was "intrinsically Roman Catholic."[97]

The difficulty, of course, was that it really was impossible to affirm with any conviction that Mussolini himself had taken an unequivocal position on the issue. Initially, Mussolini was indifferent to the Roman Catholic objections to Actualism. In fact, the position he originally assumed was immediately objectionable to the Church. In explaining the implications of the Lateran Accords to his followers, Mussolini maintained that while "the Fascist state . . . is Roman Catholic," according to his agreements with the Vatican, it was "in fact and above all, exclusively and essentially Fascist."[98]

Thus, in 1932, against the explicit objections of the Vatican, Mussolini assigned Gentile the task of articulating the fundamental philosophical principles of Fascism. To this day, the official *Dottrina del fascismo* has Gentile's "fundamental ideas" as its necessary preamble; it constitutes the official foundation of Fascist thought.

---

[95] See H. S. Harris, *The Social Philosophy of Giovanni Gentile* (Urbana: University of Illinois, 1960), p. 205.

[96] See Gregor, *Giovanni Gentile*, pp. 63–65, 69–80.

[97] Panunzio, *Teoria generale dello stato fascista*, pp. 281–82, n. 1.

[98] Mussolini, "Relazione alla Camera dei deputati sugli accordi del Laterano," in *Oo*, vol. 24, p. 89.

For all that, by the mid-1930s, the issue of Roman Catholic objections to Actualism created controversy everywhere in Fascist Italy. For Panunzio, it created significant intellectual, political, and moral problems.

In the 1920s, he had made his neo-Hegelianism transparent. As has been indicated, his basic agreement with the substance of Actualism as a system of thought can be demonstrated. The one objection that he made explicit was the issue of "transcendence." Actualism insisted on thought, spirit, consciousness as the reality of the world. It reserved no place for a thought, spirit, or consciousness that "transcended" that of human beings. The world must be immanent in the only thought we, as human beings, knew. In such a construal of the world there could be no place for the traditional deity, standing outside human thought. It was that radical humanism that made Actualism anathema to the Roman Church.

It was clear that Panunzio could not accept such an interpretation of the world. As a consequence, Panunzio was reluctant to cite Actualism, even when direct allusion to Actualism would have intellectually strengthened his argument. Although his publications are dotted with references to the works of Gentile, Panunzio never really specifically mobilized Actualism to the argument. As has been suggested, references to the works of Vico, Rosmini, Spaventa, Mazzini, and Gioberti appear throughout Panunzio's texts—all thinkers who provided the intellectual background for Actualism—but there are few direct citations to Gentile's publications themselves. The cost that Panunzio was to pay included an inability to carry his argument to a persuasive conclusion.

As has been suggested, Panunzio acknowledged that his arguments required ultimate recourse to "first principles."[99] In his *Teoria generale dello stato fascista*, he maintained that those principles were to found in the "philosophical premises of idealism." He immediately added, however, that the neo-Hegelianism that would supply those premises would be an idealism that allowed for a "transcendent" God.[100] Panunzio had allowed himself to be put in a position from which he might have to argue that the first principles of Fascism came from the God of Roman Catholicism.

As we have seen, when he was asked, shortly before his death, to supply the "first principles" of Fascist thought, Panunzio made recourse, without argument, to the "immediate data and the immediate intuitions of consciousness, to the data of faith . . . and persuasion."[101] This was a minimalist account of the "presuppositionless" epistemology and moral phi-

---

[99] Panunzio, *Teoria generale dello stato fascista*, pp. x, xiii.

[100] Ibid., pp. 5, 22–24, n. 1.

[101] Panunzio, "I principi generali del diritto fascista," *Principi generale dell'ordinamento giuridico fascista*, in *Il fondamento giuidico del fascismo*, p. 322.

losophy of Actualism. Panunzio might have put together another account, drawing on Hegel or Spaventa. He did not. It was left to his readers.

The fact is that, for whatever reason, the relationship between Panunzio and Gentile had always been acrimonious. Gentile never cited any of Panunzio's works and apparently never allowed his name to be cited in any of the volumes of the *Enciclopedia italiana*. All of that has no real relevance in taking the measure of the intellectual defense of Fascism or in judging the competence of its apologists.

By the mid-1930s, the ideology of Fascism was essentially complete. The Actualist rationale was conjoined with that typical of Panunzio's account of the institutional properties of Fascism. Panunzio spoke of *philosophical idealism* as the normative foundation of the state,[102] and then proceeded to argue how a neo-Hegelian vindication provided the moral grounds for the Fascist party's control of the political infrastructure of the nation. On the basis of those neo-Hegelian concepts, the local, provincial and national party organizations provided the critical membership of all the highest legislative, executive, and economic organs of the state.[103]

By the end of the 1920s, the Gran consiglio (Grand Council of Fascism), composed of the senior leaders of the Partito nazionale fascista, was recognized in law as the highest political organ of the state, in effect controlling the entire nation. The officiating officer of the Grand Council was Mussolini.

Parallel to the specifically political structure of the state, the several syndicalist and corporativist bodies were united in "category" councils, in which representatives of the agricultural, industrial, and service sectors were vertically congregated in a Consiglio nazionale delle corporazioni (National Council of Corporations), to provide their expertise and counsel in fashioning the nation's economic goals. This was the analogue of the "technical committees of competence" spoken of by Panunzio at the very founding of the Fascist movement—only one aspect of the many prefigured in his initial conceptions of national syndicalism as early as 1921.[104]

Since the meetings of the Assembly of the National Council of Corporations, given the large membership involved, were cumbersome, a Central Corporative Committee—composed of ministers and their more important subsecretaries, the secretary and vice-secretaries of the Fascist party, the chief officers of the *Dopolavoro* (the organization devoted to general labor interests and recreation), and the vice presidents of the category corporations—became the most active agency of the entire system.

---

[102] Panunzio, *Teoria generale dello stato fascista*, pp. 5–6.

[103] As early as 1929, Panunzio outlined the central dominance of the state. See Panunzio, *Il sentimento dello stato*, pp. 101–2, 107–9.

[104] Panunzio, *Teoria generale dello stato fascista*, p. 242.

Mussolini retained the power to determine its composition.[105] Together with his control of the "omnicompetent and sovereign state,"[106] and the party, Mussolini controlled what Panunzio correctly described as a neo-Hegelian "monistic state."[107]

The syndicalist and corporativist institutions, while directive in terms of the economic interests of the nation, were clearly understood to be fundamentally political. The institutions were understood to be "political-ethical" in intrinsic character. Their intent, beyond their function as state agencies of economic counsel and control, was the political "socialization" of the population in order to effect their moral identification with the "omnicomprehensive unity of the state."[108]

By the mid-1930s, convinced that the international liberal economic system had lapsed into a fatal torpor, the Fascist regime was preparing the entire corporative structure to serve as "an instrument under the aegis of the state," to carry out "the complete organic and totalitarian regulation of production with a view to the expansion of the wealth, political power and well-being of the Italian people."[109] Ultimately, those evolving economic institutions would substitute for the "anachronistic" traditional Camera of the parliament.[110]

By that time, Fascism had essentially concluded its institutionalization, together with the articulation of the philosophical rationale that would serve as its vindication. It had overcome some of the major economic disabilities suffered in the course of the Great Depression, to recommence its disciplined growth and expanding industrialization. Heard, more and more frequently, were those foreign policy themes that had accompanied Fascism at its birth.[111] There was increasing talk of territorial expansion to meet the nation's resource and settlement needs—and there was talk of strategic initiatives calculated to allow the nation free access to the oceans of the world.[112] Fascism was preparing to embark on its final, fateful course.

---

[105] Panunzio spoke of Mussolini as the "logical center" of the entire system. Ibid., pp. 336, and 295–96, 312, 335–36, 339, 349, 366.

[106] Ibid., pp. 40–43.

[107] Ibid., pp. 299–300.

[108] Ibid., pp. 125–26, 134, 154, 175.

[109] Mussolini, "Dichiarazione per le costituende corporazioni," in Oo, vol. 26, p. 85.

[110] Mussolini, "Discorso per lo stato corporativo," in Oo, vol. 26, p. 94.

[111] See the discussion in Giorgio Rumi, *Alle origini della politica esterna fascista, 1918–1923* (Bari: Laterza, 1968).

[112] See Robert Mallet, *The Italian Navy and Fascist Expansionism, 1935–1940* (London: Frank Cass, 1998); C. Terracciano, G. Roletto, and E. Masi, *Geopolitica fascista: Antologia di scritti* (Milan: Barbarossa, 1993), particularly Carlo Tetracciano, "Direttrici geopolitiche coloniali dell'Italia nell'era fascista," pp. 5–20.

In the course of those final turbulent and tragic years, Fascism's increasingly intimate relationship with Hitler's Germany —together with the tensions generated by a conflict that clearly exceeded its powers— influenced the regime to assume doctrinal theses fundamentally alien to its ideological integrity. At the same time, it will be argued, the central developments of the system remained consistent and its political and economic efforts coherent.

What is clear is the fact that the ideology of Fascism had achieved maturity by the end of the 1930s. The final years of the regime were consumed in the catastrophe that was the Second World War. It was in those years that the intellectuals who had collected around Fascism were to deliver themselves of their final judgments.

CHAPTER EIGHT

Camillo Pellizzi, Carlo Costamagna, and the Final Issues

IN JANUARY 1934, Giovanni Gentile wrote, "A period has closed and another opens. Every Italian senses that . . . the Fascist revolution has attained maturity . . . [The] period of transition between the old liberal, and the new Fascist, civilization is now over."[1] As a consequence of that conviction, Gentile changed the title of the journal of the Institute over which he presided from *Educazione fascista*, to *Civiltà fascista*—from reference to a tentative "Fascist education" to invocation of a presumably fully emergent "Fascist civilization."

Years later, Camillo Pellizzi, the last effective president of the institute Gentile founded, suggested a very similar assessment of the period traversed. After 1932 and 1933, Pellizzi maintained, there was little in Fascist Italy that could pass as specifically corporative doctrinal development. Most debate turned on the institutionalization of decisions already made. Fascism had entered into a phase dominated by foreign policy concerns—ranging from responses to the global economic crisis now identified as the Great Depression, to war in Ethiopia and Spain—to a growing rapprochement with Adolf Hitler's Germany.[2]

Domestically, the ideology of Fascism had attained those qualities that heralded its maturity. Fascism's primary interest, after 1934, was the pursuit of its foreign policy objectives—objectives that had been largely fixed, in a generic sense, before the March on Rome.[3]

In 1937, the institute founded by Gentile changed its title from the "National Fascist Institute of Culture" to the Istituto nazionale di cultura fascista, the "National Institute of Fascist Culture." The original title announced the Fascist intention of dealing with the prevailing culture. The new title conveyed the assurance that a distinctive and fully

---

[1] Gentile, "Parole preliminari," *Civiltà fascista* 1, no. 1 (January 1934), pp. 1–3.

[2] See his comments in Camillo Pellizzi, *La tecnica come classe dirigente* (Rome: Frattina, n.d.), pp. 17–18. The comments were probably made in 1949.

[3] See the discussion in Carlo Terracciano, "Direttrici geopolitiche coloniali dell'Italia nell'era fascista," in C. Terracciano, G. Boletto, and E. Masi, *Geopolitica fascista: Antologia di scritti* (Milan: Barbarossa, 1993), pp. 5–20.

articulated Fascist culture had been contrived and was to be disseminated and fostered.[4]

It was at that juncture that Achille Starace, then national secretary of the Partito nazionale fascista, sought to bring Gentile's institute under direct political control of the party as part of a systematic program of "fascistizing" the nation. The effort provoked Gentile's resistance. Gentile's concept of education was vastly different, in principle and spirit, from that of Starace. In the institutional struggle that followed, Gentile tendered his resignation. On 7 March 1937, he surrendered the leadership of the institute he had founded in 1925.

Between 1937 and April 1940, the National Institute of Fascist Culture was essentially presided over by place-holders. At that point, immediately prior to Italy's intervention in the Second World War, Camillo Pellizzi assumed the presidency. He had been specifically selected by Mussolini himself.[5]

Born in Collegno, Turin, on 24 August 1896, Pellizzi was an accomplished intellectual. After active service in the First World War, he pursued his academic interests in England, where he lived for long periods of time between 1920 and 1939, remaining forever occupied with Italian affairs and the Fascism with which he had early identified. He became a recognized journalist, a literary critic, and a university professor who served in both English and Italian institutions of advanced learning. Throughout his foreign residency, he continued to regularly contribute to Italian newspapers and journals. Two of his earliest works, *Problemi e realtà del fascismo* and *Fascismo-aristocrazia*,[6] both Fascist apologetics, marked the parameters of his political thought—from which he was not ever to really deviate.

In his twenties, Pellizzi saw in the *squadristi*—the Fascist foot soldiers of the revolution—the promise of a new political "aristocracy" that would secure both the nation's unity and its independence from foreigners. It would rescue Italy from its long degradation and restore it to the first rank among modern nations. He argued that for too long Italy had remained a servile inferior to those industrialized nations that turned to

---

[4] For decades after the passing of the regime, some intellectuals chose to discuss whether there had ever been a "Fascist culture." If one understands a culture as being defined in terms of a coherent collection of reasonably specific normative, philosophical, political, and economic principles that inform a system, then there was a Fascist culture.

[5] See the excellent discussion of this period in Gisella Longo, *L'Istituto nazionale fascista di cultura: Gli intellettuali tra partito e regime* (Rome: Antonio Pellicani, 2000) and Danilo Breschi and Gisella Longo, *Camillo Pellizzi: La ricera delle elites tra political e sociologica (1896–1979)* (Soveria mannelli: Rubbettino, 2003).

[6] Pellizzi, *Problemi e realtà del fascismo* (Florence: Vallecchi, 1922); and *Fascismo-aristocrazia* (Milan: Alpes, 1925).

her only as a market supplement where they might profitably dispose of their excess products.[7]

In effect, immediately after the First World War, the young Pellizzi was animated by that same tissue of convictions that succeeded in making Fascists of so many Italians. He, like them, rejected parliamentary institutions, international organizations, utopian notions of universal harmony, socialist nostrums, class warfare, political passivity, and moral indifference. By the time he became politically active, he was a convinced "Mussoliniano"—a dedicated admirer of the man with whom he associated the revolutionary promise of a new, and more imposing, Italy.

More to our purpose, Pellizzi was an Actualist of sorts—a principled follower of Gentile. For Pellizzi, Gentile was "the first philosopher of Fascism." In his judgment, it was "in no way accidental" that Gentilean idealism shared "resonance in, and a moral affinity with, the actions of Fascism."[8]

Throughout his service as a Fascist intellectual, Pellizzi remained, in critical measure, an Actualist. In fact, those with whom he most intensively interacted were almost all Actualists. He shared the intellectual persuasions of Ugo Spirito and Arnaldo Volpicelli, themselves Actualists.[9] Pellizzi distinguished himself from rigorous Actualism insofar as he was a practicing Roman Catholic.

The relationship of Actualism and institutional Roman Catholicism, as has been indicated, remained a troubling question throughout the history of the Fascist regime. Even though Gentile's proposed reform of Italy's educational system in 1923 reintroduced Catholic religious teaching in the public elementary and secondary schools from which they had earlier been excluded by liberal sensibilities, the Catholic Church continued to object to his Actualism. Gentile's conviction that religion was an intrinsic and valuable part of the nation's history was not considered sufficient. The Church's objections turned on the *immanentism* of philosophical Actualism—in which all reality, all ideas, all knowledge, all perceptions, all beliefs, and all sentiments found their ultimate source in consciousness—and left no room for the *transcendent*, personal deity of orthodox Roman Catholicism.[10]

The modal response of active Fascists, in the concerted effort to avoid overt conflict with the Church, was a readiness to sacrifice Actualist philosophical rigor for "collaboration" with established Catholicism—in the somewhat forlorn hope that the totalitarian "interests of the state [might]

---

[7] Pellizzi, *Fascismo-aristocrazia*, pp. 76–77, 80–81, 109, 147, 156, 194.

[8] See ibid., pp. 25, 30, 40–41, 49.

[9] See, for example, Longo, *L'Istituto nazionale fascista di cultura*, pp. 181–82.

[10] William A. Smith, *Giovanni Gentile on the Existence of God* (Paris: Beatrice-Nauwelaerts, 1970).

coincide with those of the Church."[11] Most argued that the issue was not so unequivocal as to render conflict unavoidable. Moderation, it was argued, recommended itself in dealing with the question.[12] A moderate Actualism, as a form of "spiritualism," might serve Fascism as a "bridge" to Catholicism. For Pellizzi such a strategy was perfectly acceptable. For him, Gentilean dialectics allowed sufficient latitude to permit the insinuation of some form of Catholicism into that Actualism that was so central to the rationale of Fascism.[13]

For an intransigent Fascist minority, on the other hand, Actualism was either a form of humanistic atheism or an heretical pantheism—neither of which could be tolerated by serious Roman Catholics. In their judgment, Actualism was nothing less than a major political disability for Fascism. That was the position assumed by at least several prominent Fascist theoreticians: including Roberto Farinacci, Paolo Orano and Carlo Costamagna.

For Orano, one of the more interesting of the early syndicalists-cum-Fascists, "in the truths of Catholicism . . . all the fatuous subtleties of Actualist immanentism . . . [together with all its] sophisms are annihilated."[14] The position of Farinacci, and Costamagna in turn, were hardly any less dismissive.[15]

Pellizzi himself was numbered among the more moderate Actualists. In his exchanges with dissident Fascist youth, who insisted on both their anti-idealist "realism" and their atheism, in order to distinguish themselves from institutional idealism as well as Roman Catholic conformity, he counseled that they had only begun to consider the philosophical issues. He maintained that they were hardly equipped to make decisions concerning such difficult and significant matters. That they were not Catholics prompted Pellizzi to candidly confess that he sometimes preferred their innocent atheism to *official* Catholicism.[16] In effect, Pellizzi's Actualism and his Catholicism were both sufficiently flexible to accommodate each other.

As proved to be the case, just such properties recommended him to Mussolini for the post vacated by Gentile in 1937. In 1940, Mussolini had neither time nor patience to deal with the issues that turned on Actu-

---

[11] Roberto Pavese, "Filosofia e religione di fronte al fascismo," *Gerarchia* 14, no. 8 (August 1934), p. 670.

[12] See the discussion in Delio Cantimori, "Chiarificazione di idee," *Vita nuova* 8, no. 7 (July 1932), pp. 623–26.

[13] Longo, *L'Istituto nazionale fascista di cultura*, p. 191 n. 29. Gentile saw no difficulty as an *immanentist* remaining a Catholic.

[14] Paolo Orano, *Il fascismo* (Rome: Pinciana, 1940), vol. 2, p. 281.

[15] Carlo Costamagna, *Dottrina del fascismo* (Turin: UTET, 1940), pp. 9, 31, 33, 275–89.

[16] Pellizzi, "Sul manifesto realista," in Diano Brocchi, ed., *L'Universale* (Rome: Del Borghese, 1969), pp. 44–46.

alism's philosophical humanism and its apparent Catholic heterodoxy. Throughout his active life, Gentile had remained intransigently opposed to *institutional* Catholicism as an infringement on the inviolable, totalitarian sovereignty of the state.[17] Whether or not he considered himself, in whatever sense, a Roman Catholic was irrelevant to what was a critical and complicated *political* issue.[18]

Pellizzi had skirted just those issues for fifteen years—and in that sense, could effectively represent the culture of Fascism as it had matured. While Fascism always found itself uncomfortable with respect to official Church doctrine, members of its hierarchy, more often than not, made efforts to avoid direct confrontation. In that sense, Pellizzi was admirably equipped, by disposition, to function in the intellectual environment of the early 1940s.

By the time Pellizzi assumed the responsibility of the presidency of the Istituto nazionale di cultura fascista in April 1940, he was singularly well suited to further represent the regime with respect to other matters—corporativism and imperialism principal among them. In the few remaining years left to Fascism, both issues were to be addressed.

While in 1933, Pellizzi had referred to corporativism as a system in the process of articulation,[19] by 1938, he was prepared to enter into the animated discussion that surrounded what was considered, at that juncture, a "pause" in its slow, but ongoing, evolution. By that time, he was prepared to maintain that the system was not involved in temporary inactivity. It was not showing signs of change because, for all intents and purposes, it had achieved effective maturity.[20]

Fascist journals of the period were filled with exchanges concerning developments in corporativist institutions. Some of the most searching discussions turned on the purported functions of corporativist agencies. Out of all the excitement, it became evident that the more sophisticated of the discussants recognized that whatever had been proposed in the heady years of the 1920s, the characteristic functions of corporative organs were, and had always been, *consultative*—essentially intended to convey a sense of efficacy, of participation, to all the elements active in the

---

[17] Gentile, *Fascismo e cultura* (Milan: Treves, 1928), p. 175.

[18] See Gentile, *La mia religione* (Florence: Sansoni, 1943); see Ugo Spirito, "La religione di Giovanni Gentile," in Ugo Spirito, *Giovanni Gentile* (Florence: Sansoni, 1969), pp. 97–123.

[19] See Pellizzi, "Ancora sulle 'formule,' " *Critica fascista* 11, no. 8 (15 April 1933), pp. 154–55.

[20] See the opposing comments by Agostino Nasti, "Corporativismo concreto," *Critica fascista* 14, no. 6 (15 January 1936), pp. 81–82, in which he suggests that there has been too much discussion concerning corporativism and too little concrete activity. This was typical of the disputes that surrounded Fascist corporativism in general.

nation's economy. Whatever legislative or executive functions had been suggested, over time, as the proper concern of syndicalist and corporativist agencies, were never really in the offing. Pellizzi held that the system was, in effect, what it was intended to be. It was consultative.

Pellizzi reminded the discussants that the initiatives that had first shaped Fascist syndicalism and then the corporativist system, in its entirety, had come almost exclusively from the state. It had been the state, in fact and over time—irrespective of the intensity of the discussions conducted by corporativist theorists—that had discharged all the critical, concrete economic social, and political functions that the new corporativist institutions were purportedly, and ultimately, to perform.

Commencing with the rescue of industries threatened by economic collapse after the First World War through the efforts to remedy the effects of the international depression, it was the state alone that had assumed complete responsibility and had itself intervened. In the decades that followed the March on Rome, corporativism had gradually become, and remained, what was essentially a control system dominated by the political leadership of the Fascist state.

After the Ethiopian war and the internationally imposed punitive sanctions, the drive for national autarky had further activated the state—and it was the state, not any of its constituent agencies, that governed the domestic economic enterprise. Corporativist agencies had been the "transmission belts" of state decisions. This had become evident over the years. Very few serious analysts had been confused. Fascists themselves regularly described the system in something like the following fashion: "The state . . . proceeded to absorb the economic life of the nation. Central organs, possessed of irresistable political power, dominate productive activity. . . . Not a single sector of the national economy has been able to resist the state. . . . The result has everywhere been the same, the national economy has been put in service to the state . . . so that the institutional results remind one of state socialism."[21]

In contributing to the discussion, Pellizzi made little effort to qualify such an assessment. Instead, he expanded on the role of "authority" in the process of corporative development. He reminded his audience that in Fascist Italy, authority specifically emanated from the nation's leaders. His audience was reminded that Mussolini had initiated the processes out of which corporativism had emerged. Corporativism had grown "out of the rich soil of idealism"—and all of it had its ultimate vindication in the totalitarianism of that idealism.

---

[21] "Erba," "Corporativismo e autarchia," *Critica fascista* 16, no. 9 (1 March 1938), pp. 132–34.

Corporativism, for Pellizzi, was essentially a means of bringing the working and productive classes into the circumference of the totalitarian state—to infuse them with a consuming sense of participation in the fateful drama of national life. In such a system, neither individuals nor unattached groups of individuals, were expected to undertake independent initiatives in political and economic circumstances characterized by one, all-inclusive, executive will.

That will was the will of the Duce. Prior to the Second World War, what all that meant to Western political liberals was that the Fascist system was, at best, "authoritarian," but more likely, "dictatorial." And yet, as has been suggested, one of the central arguments of Fascism's rationale was that the system was a "centralized, organized, and unitary democracy."[22] For Panunzio, the corporativist arrangements he had done so much to foster and shape had helped create "a new, organic and harmonious democracy" out of what had been the ineffectual forms imposed on Italy and the world by the "false, capitalistic and plutocratic so-called democracies" of the Anglo-Saxon world.[23]

Fascist intellectuals did not deny that the state was the executive will of an integrated, self-conscious, and active population conscious of its goals and the conditions requisite to their achievement. They spoke of the system as "hierarchical," and Gentile recognized it as an expression of the unitary, collectivist, higher self that was gradually achieving conscious expression—"the unification of all citizens in one consciousness and in one political and universal will."[24]

Thus, at about the same time that Pellizzi engaged himself in the discussions concerning the functions, and the intrinsic character, of the corporative state, Gentile himself described what he understood to be the essentials of "Fascist democracy." It was a conviction he had consistently held both before and throughout, the Fascist period.

It was in that context that one is to understand Pellizzi's references to the development of corporativism as "democratic," in the sense of being governed by a the political leadership of a "given person or persons" whose ideas were the incarnation of the will of an entire society. Historic circumstances "had conferred authority" on that person or those persons—and it was that authority, and those persons, that informed the entire corporative system—of which corporative agencies were to serve

---

[22] Mussolini, "Il discorso dell'Ascensione," *Opera omnia* (Florence: La fenice, 1953–65. Hereafter Oo), vol. 22, p. 389. In 1936, Mussolini maintained that Italy "was a true democracy." "Discorso di Milano," in *Oo*, vol. 28, p. 70.

[23] Panunzio, "L'Impero italiano del lavoro," *Gerarchia* 9, no. 9 (September 1940), p. 462.

[24] Gentile, *Dottrina politica del fascismo* (Padua: CEDAM, 1937), p. 7.

as extensions.[25] What Pellizzi provided, on such occasions, was a synoptic expression of the rationale of the Gentilean "democratic ethical state,"[26] whose fully articulated rationale was to be found in the technical works of Actualism.

It was clear that Pellizzi expected Fascism, as a political system, to work because it had its source among "a new class of youthful heroes and thinkers" who had survived the sacrifices and carnage of the First World War—and in whom the people of Italy could see themselves at their best. As an aristocracy, the survivors of the trenches had been "selected" through the very carnage of the war. They were to "initiate a new epoch" in the history of Europe. Pellizzi argued that each significant period in history is initiated by just such "a new and heroic minority"[27] in whom the masses find their truest selves reflected.

The First World War had created circumstances in and through which Italy, "as a poor, oppressed and friendless" nation, might seek its redemption through "internal unity and independence from foreigners." In 1925, Pellizzi had spoken of that redemption as coming through a state, led by the "aristocracy of the trenches," that enjoyed "priority before and above all else"—a state that would render all the productive forces of the nation its "direct organs," a state that, as a consequence, would be capable of "guaranteeing security against all domestic and foreign aggression."[28] The rapid industrial development that would result would supply the arms that would render Italy, once again as it had been in antiquity, one of the "great powers."

The argument, of course, was familiar and orthodox. It followed that put together by Mussolini in the years that preceded the March on Rome and was, in large part, anticipated by Gentile.[29] Everyone among the national syndicalists was accustomed to calling upon revolutionary "elites" to resolve the crises that had settled down upon Italy at the turn of the twentieth century.[30] No one had been particularly specific concerning the criteria for admission into that aristocracy that would determine the future. They had all charged history with the responsibility of identifying

---

[25] Pellizzi, "Corporazioni e autorità," *Critica fascista* 16, no. 13 (1 May 1938), pp. 197–200.

[26] Gentile regularly spoke of the Fascist state as "democratic" in precisely the sense indicated. See Gentile, *Origini e dottrina del fascismo* (Rome: Libreria del Littorio, 1929), sec. 13.

[27] Pellizzi, *Fascismo-aristocrazia*, pp. 21, 22, 35.

[28] Ibid., pp. 55, 77, 83.

[29] See the account in A. James Gregor, *Young Mussolini and the Intellectual Origins of Fascism* (Berkeley and Los Angeles: University of California Press, 1979); and Gregor, *Giovanni Gentile*, chaps. 4 and 6.

[30] See the account in A. James Gregor, *The Ideology of Fascism: The Rationale of Totalitarianism* (New York: Free Press, 1969), chaps. 2–3.

those who would serve as the envisioned ruling "class." Pellizzi wrote that they would be "independent, inflexible and creative, finding within themselves the inspiration, and the principles that govern their conduct." They would be "astute, strong, just, and of determined will," capable of anticipating futures with critical intelligence.[31]

Over time, it became evident to Pellizzi himself that if Fascism was to generate and sustain such an "aristocracy," it would be necessary to fashion some procedure that would assure the regular and predictable production of suitable candidates. Allusion to the personal properties he would have such an elite evince was clearly not enough. He became involved in a sustained exchange with other Fascist intellectuals concerning what might be an appropriate selective procedure to accomplish Fascism's self-sustaining purpose.[32] Formal education, and institutional syndicalist and corporativist organization, would provide the test beds for the selection of those who would serve as the ruling political class.

By the time Fascism, as a system, had fully matured, its properties were evident and all but universally recognized. That some expected corporative institutions to take on the democratic features familiar in a liberal political environment was, at best, curious. In Fascist Italy, corporative institutions were agencies of control—and Sergio Panunzio, about a year before his death, was content to so describe them.

In 1943, Panunzio expected the workers' and employers' syndicates to become more active in the economic undertakings of the state—but he did not expect them to independently undertake initiatives. They were consultative resources for the state, involved as the state was in a program of projected economic self-sufficiency for the nation. The entities created in the efforts at corporative arrangement of the economy interacted among themselves and with the executive Ministry of Corporations. Of all the corporative structures that had been been put together, a Comitato corporativo centrale, a "Central Corporative Committee," had been selected to serve as directive. Composed of few members, it operated with far greater dispatch than the more cumbersome National Council of Corporations—and would, Panunzio suggested, probably be more effective

---

[31] Pellizzi speaks of the expected ruling elite as "heroic, energetic and faithful." Pellizzi, *Fascismo-aristocrazia*, pp. 93, 101, 103, 113.

[32] See Pellizzi, "Educazione fascista e classe dirigente," *Critica fascista* 15, no. 16 (15 June 1937), pp. 275–78; "Educazione fascista e classe politica," *Critica fascista* 15, no. 19 (1 August 1937); and the response Agostino Nasti and Bruno Fattori, "Obiezioni a Pellizzi," in *Critica fascista* 15, no. 17 (1 July 1937), pp. 291–94; Nasti, "Conclusione con Pellizzi," *Critica fascista* 15, no. 21 (1 September 1937); and Nasti and Fattori, "Codicillo a Pellizzi," *Critica fascista* 15, no. 24 (15 October 1937), pp. 405–7. In this context, see Luca La Rovere, *Storia dei GUF: Organizzazione, politica e miti della gioventu universitaria fascista, 1919–1943* (Turin: Bollati Boringhieri, 2003).

than the new representative body, La Camera dei Fasci e delle corporazioni, that was to serve as a substitute for the original, pre-Fascist Camera, the body that once included all the political parties, special interests, and subgroups of the old liberal system.[33]

Panunzio saw the new economic control system as paralleling that of the political control system that culminated in the Grand Council of Fascism—and was intended to accomplish the same results in the economic that the Grand Council had achieved in the political arena. It would be "institutionally representative" of the economic interests of the population in the same sense that the Grand Council would institutionally represent the political convictions of the general population.

The role of the Grand Council in the political system had been regularized only in 1928—after six years of its de facto rule. As the control arm of the Partito nazionale fascista, it had become the principal political organ of the state. Panunzio saw in the Central Corporative Committee the economic counterpart of the Grand Council. Essentially all professional economic reflection would be conducted within the evolving corporative agencies gradually put together over almost two decades of Fascist rule. Like the Grand Council that politically represented the masses, the Central Corporative Committee represented the workers and employers in the national economy.[34]

Both the Grand Council and the Central Corporative Committee were dominated by Mussolini and the leaders of the party. They constituted the "aristocracy" that Pellizzi had left to history and national challenge to select. That such an aristocracy was representative of the nation's masses was confirmed, Fascist intellectuals maintained, by acclamation, the consensus enjoyed by the regime.[35]

One sees in the system identified by Panunzio, and inferentially by Pellizzi, in 1943, at the close of the Fascist experiment, all the major elements they had anticipated two decades before. In the very first years after the revolution, Panunzio, like Pellizzi, saw the nation's regeneration in the restored strength of executive power—the power of "a modern sovereign state, politically superior to everything" within its reach. At the very commencement of corporativism's institutionalization, Panunzio told his audiences that Fascism filled the spaces between the individual and the state

---

[33] Panunzio was prepared to countenance the prospect of the merger of the Central Corporative Committee with a "junta" of the emerging corporative Camera. See the discussion in Carlo Costamagna, "Ancora su 'Gli sviluppi corporativi,'" Lo stato 14, no. 1 (January 1943), pp. 20–22.

[34] See the entire discussion in Panunzio, "Le corporazioni e la camera," Lo stato 14, no. 3 (March 1943), p. 79–89.

[35] See the discussion in Bruno Spampanato, Democrazia fascista (Rome: Politica nuova, 1933), pt. 3.

with representative socioeconomic bodies that must be legally recognized and sustained, but reabsorbed, and rendered "subordinate to the state."[36] The continuity was palpable.

In effect, the major theoreticians of Fascism (with some notable exceptions)[37] recognized in the arrangements of the late 1930s and the early 1940s the full political and economic maturation of the system. They had never suggested that Fascism was anything other than hierarchical in structure and authoritarian in form. The corporative system never had any specific legislative function because it was never expected to have such responsibility. It could, and did, provide norms for the behavior of syndicates and did settle disputes between labor and capital—but its essential activities were consultative. It provided the occasion for drawing all the active elements of the productive system into the process. It provided the opportunity for interaction at a level that would otherwise be unavailable. Thus, during the first years of Fascist rule, Panunzio spoke, as did Pellizzi, of "a strong state . . . an organic, powerful, active . . . state, surrounded by a rich and varied architecture of classes organized in syndicates and corporations of syndicates . . . with the entire state a great army, a great discipline, a living hierarchy"—all in the service of mobilizing all resources to the task of finally making Italy—a wretched and underdeveloped nation—a great power, no longer to suffer the shame of the past.

At the same time, participants in the process would develop a sense of involvement, of efficacy. Italy was to proceed along its path of development employing a program of rapid economic growth and industrial expansion, whose very "postulate, whose axiom . . . production and expansion," was to be achieved through the activation of all the "forces of production under the direction of the sovereign state."[38] That was the system created by the Fascist revolution. Few, if any, serious Fascist theoreticians expected anything else.

The suggestion frequently tendered by commentators on the history of Fascism that corporativism had either proved a failure or a fraud is arguable at best. Corporativism served Fascism as it was meant to serve: as a control mechanism for an economy that was in the process of expanding and deepening in order to provide the material foundation for a "new civilization"—one in which labor was not undertaken solely for material rewards, but to contribute to the creation of a new world system that

---

[36] See Panunzio, *Lo Stato fascista* (Bologna: Cappelli, 1925), pp. 56–57, 80, 87; and the entire discussion in Vincenzo Zangara, *La rappresentanza istituzionale* (Bologna: Zanicelli, 1939).

[37] The most important of whom was Ugo Spirito, whose ideas resurfaced later in the Republic of Salò.

[38] Panunzio, *Che cos'è il fascismo* (Milan: Alpes, 1924), pp. 14–16, 19, 24–25, 26, 53.

would reflect all the complex virtues of a Third Rome. Once Italy committed itself to involvement in the Second World War, Panunzio identified
Fascism's mission as creating a corporativist, organic, centralized and authoritarian "empire of labor," destined to replace the "empire of gold"
created by the advanced capitalist, plutocratic Anglo-American powers.[39]

Dismissed as simple "rhetoric" by commentators at the time, such convictions revealed, in fact, the logic of the system. Elite rule, corporativism,
economic development, the generation and maintenance of popular consensus through "representative institutions" were all elements of a reasoned, if antiliberal and antidemocratic program of revolutionary transformation. It was a transformation intended to change the course of
Italian, European, and perhaps world history. All of this was duly recognized by its principal advocates—and, toward the end of Fascist rule, its
implications were transparent.

Pellizzi had always been aware of what the more remote policy implications of Fascist doctrine had been. He foresaw that Italy, for centuries
servile and humbled, emerging regenerate out of the crucible of the First
World War, could not be confined within the limits of the *nation*. A re-
newed Italy would transcend the territorial confines of a specific geographic place and extend itself over an *empire*, the geographic and political basis of a new world *civilization*. Pellizzi had long maintained that
Fascist Italy's destiny was not specifically national, but imperial.[40] The
aristocracy that would arise out of centuries of oppression, the carnage
of war, and the transformative tempering of revolution would be animated by a morality and a courage that could not be confined within the
egocentric, restrictive limits of family, corporation, or nation. The ultimate purpose of Fascism "could only be historic and moral," to participate in the drama of the modern world: the ineluctable conflict of empires—that between the "industrial and colonial empire of Great Britain,
of the monetary and financial empire of the United States, and of a Germany that [had] embarked on an imperial course that will inevitably cast
it athwart that of the others."[41]

Pellizzi went on to argue that while Fascism appeared inspired by an
idealism that was initally essentially nationalistic, the fact was that Actualism, understood in the fullness of its convictions, was not so privative.
For Gentile, while it was perfectly clear that the *state* was the informing
spirit of territoriality, language, customs, and subjects by virtue of which
we empirically distinguish nations—in the dialectic of world history, spirit

[39] Panunzio, "L'Impero italiano del lavoro," *Gerarchia* 19, 9 (September 1940), pp.
462–63.

[40] See Pellizzi, *Fascismo-aristocrazia*, pp. 157, 164–65, 168.

[41] Ibid., p. 173.

could not be confined to the nation as an exclusive vehicle. In the emerging revolutionary reality of the mid-twentieth century, Pellizzi reminded his readers that its past suggested that the form Italy might responsibly assume would be imperial. In his judgment, that ultimate form would be animated by the same sustaining, evolving, and transcendental spirit identified by Actualism as informing the national state. For Pellizzi, the Fascist state was destined to re-create the analog of the ancient empire of Rome—as a new civilization in a new institutional form.

Pellizzi argued that the Rome of antiquity had not been a nation in the generally recognized sense. He proceeded to point out that the subsequent empire of the universal Church was not a nation either. The universal Church that arose out of dying Rome was born as a *faith*—not a nation. Out of its resurgent civilization and its rekindled faith, Fascism was destined to ultimately create not simply a nation animated by revolutionary impulse, but an empire.[42]

Pellizzi early argued his case in Gentile's *Educazione politica*, returning to the theme with some regularity.[43] The fact was that throughout the late 1920s and the years of the 1930s, the foreign policy orientations of Fascism became increasingly apparent. As early as 1931, Fascist intellectuals took up, in earnest, specific geopolitical themes that had been given currency as early as the turn of the century.[44]

Nationalists, before the First World War, had referred to overseas colonies as necessary for the rebirth of the nation and the rehabilitation of the peninsula. In the course of the maturation of the Fascist regime, there were regular references to "strategic colonies" that assured access to, and security of, waterways for both commercial and military purposes. There were references to territories that would serve as habitable lands for excess populations; and there were allusions to territories possessed of raw materials essential to the development of Italy's industrial potential.[45]

All of this had been implicit and explicit in Mussolini's public statements both before and after the March on Rome. The Fascist movement had arisen in a world dominated by the advanced industrial powers. To survive, the argument proceeded, Italy would have to develop major in-

---

[42] Pellizzi, "Lo stato e la nazione," *Educazione politica* 4, no. 6 (June 1926), pp. 317–20.

[43] See Pellizzi, "Rinascimento politico," *Educazione politica*, 4, no. 7 (July 1926), pp. 389–92.

[44] Ernesto Massi and Giorgio Roletto made direct and indirect references to Mario Morasso, *L'Imperialismo nel secolo XX (La conquista del mondo)* (Milan: Treves, 1905); and Edoardo Scarfoglio, *Guerra della sterlina e del marco* (Rome: Quattrini, 1915) who addressed some of the central issues of imperial expansion.

[45] See Paola Maria Arcari, *Le elaborazioni della dottrina politica nazionale fra l'unità e l'intervento (1870–1914)*, 3 vols (Florence: Marzocco, 1934–1939).

dustrial capabilities—and to do that, it would have to establish access to industrial raw materials. To successfully transport those resources, it would have to secure robust sealines of communication.

By the advent of the First World War, the advanced industrial powers controlled more than 43 million square miles, or 84.4 percent of the Earth's surface. Locked within the confines of an inland sea, with egress and entry controlled at Gibraltar and Suez by Great Britain, and its southern littoral dominated by both France and England, Italy's sealines, over which necessary raw materials made transit, were potentially subject to the control of others.

Without resources, burdened by a population that exceeded the support capacity of the soil, generating a fraction of the per capita income of the advanced industrial nations, Italy had been a marginal country that, for centuries, had been subject to the occupation and control of others. At the conclusion of the First World War, Fascists were to call for equity in both the distribution of the world's material resources and its opportunities. Even before his accession to power, Mussolini was prepared to argue that "the political independence of a nation is a direct function of its economic independence." Without that independence, Italians would "remain slaves. They were hostages to those who would provide them coal; hostages to those who would provide them grain."[46] Mussolini called for rapid industrialization —a program that would occupy Italians for decades—in order that Italy might develop the capabilities necessary to attempt the restoration of national lands lost to privileged powers during the eighteenth and nineteenth centuries. The call would then be made for control of Italy's interior seas, the Tyrrhenian, Adriatic, and the Ionian—as well as the sealines of the Mediterranean[47]—so that the nation might have ready access to sources where it could satisfy its raw material requirements.

Such a program implied an assertive and capable Italy. It implied expansion into ill-defined space beyond the boundaries of the peninsula. What seemed clear, even during the first phases of Fascist rule, was that nationalism shaded off into a commitment to imperial design.

In a world controlled by the advanced industrial "plutocracies," Fascist intellectuals made the case for Italy's expansion into areas where its meager natural resources might be supplemented[48]—and where it might find and secure some strategic geographic advantage from which to defend the sea routes, and gain access to the oceans, over which those resources

---

[46] Mussolini, "Per essere liberi," in *Oo*, vol. 16, pp. 105–6.

[47] See the entire discussion in Glen Barclay, *The Rise and Fall of the New Roman Empire* (New York: St. Martin's Press, 1973).

[48] See, for example, Vito Beltani, *Il problema delle materie prime* (Rome: Tupini, 1940); and Fernando Gori, *Roma nel continente nero* (Rome: Tupini, 1940).

might be transported.[49] It was in that environment that Pellizzi's early call for Fascist imperial enterprise was welcomed—it was a freshet that, by 1941, made its contribution to what had become a tide.

It was in that year that Pellizzi's National Institute of Fascist Culture published an Italian translation of Carl Schmitt's *Völkerrechtliche Gross-raumordnung mit Interventionsverbot für raumfremde Mächte*[50]—a brochure that addressed the issue of the status of empire, and related political configurations, in contemporary international law—marking, as well, the increasing influence of National Socialist thought on Fascist intellectual development.

Schmitt's long essay on the status of "Extended Space" (*Grossraum*) was to address an issue that occupied an important place in the development of Fascist doctrine through the trying years of the Second World War. Italy had begun to put its proposed empire together by the middle years of the 1930s. By 1940 it was enmeshed in the conflict that was to see its destruction.

In June 1940, Italy declared war on France and Great Britain, and almost from its first involvement in the conflict, it had suffered reverses. As a result, Italy became abjectly dependent on German assistance from the very commencement of hostilities. Together with National Socialist material assistance came intellectual influence that previously had been almost absent.

The case of Carl Schmitt is of some consequence to those who would understand something of the history of Fascist political thought during the years of the Second World War. Some of Schmitt's major essays, including his *Der Begriff des Politischen*, were translated into Italian as early as 1935. In that year, Gentile's publishing house, Sansoni, published translations of several of Schmitt's more important political essays as *Principii politici del Nazionalsocialismo* (The political principles of national socialism).[51]

At the time, the reception received by the collection provided evidence of the ideological differences that separated Fascist Italy and National Socialist Germany. In the preface to the collection, Arnaldo Volpicelli made his objections known without reluctance. As a Fascist intellectual and a Gentilean, he felt compelled to speak of Schmitt's "grave theoretical errors" that could only culminate in equally grievous "errors in

---

[49] See the discussion in Giuseppe Maggiore, *Imperialismo e impero fascista* (Palermo: Arceri e Agate, 1937).

[50] Carl Schmitt, *Il concetto d'impero nel diritto internazionale: Ordinamento dei grandi spazi con esclusione delle potenze estranee*, translated by L. Vannutelli Rey and with an appendix by Franco Pierandrei (Rome: Biblioteca dell'I.N.C.F., 1941).

[51] Carl Schmitt, *Principii politici del nazionalsocialismo*, selected and translated by D. Cantimori, with a preface by A. Volpicelli (Florence: Sansoni, 1935).

practice."[52] What some of those theoretical errors were, in Volpicelli's judgment, not difficult to determine. The discussion requires only some preliminaries.

The differences that marked the reception of Schmitt's essays in 1935 and that extended in 1941 indicated the extent of change that had taken place in the intervening years. Schmitt's long essay on the concept of "extended space" in international law was accorded an entirely different reception when it appeared in 1941 than had his essays of 1935.

In Schmitt's essay on extended spaces, published by Pellizzi through the agency of the National Institute of Fascist Culture in 1941, neither the preface by L. Vannutelli Rey nor the appendix by F. Pierandrei pretended to any criticism of the author's complex claims. As will be contended, some of the very ideas that provoked the critical response of Volpicelli in the publication of 1935 were allowed articulation in 1941 without the least negative response.

Schmitt's brochure occupied itself with the juridical status of "hegemonic" states in international law. It addressed an issue that had been made of emphatic interest by the conflict then raging. By 1940, it was clear that the Axis powers—upon their anticipated victory—would seek not only a redistribution of territories that would far exceed the simple restoration of lands they might have lost in precedent wars, but they expected to exercise dominant influence over politically independent nations.

It was reasonably plain that the Axis powers would each seek not only to secure adequate "living space" (*Lebensraum*)—territory sufficient to settle surplus population, provide necessary raw materials, and assure free access to, and security of, sealines of communication—but would also expect to exert hegemonic influence over lesser nations within their respective proximities. While such arrangements had traditionally been considered empires, Schmitt addressed himself to a more complex notion.

Schmitt spoke of "extended spaces" (*Grossraüme*) rather than "empires." He sought to distinguish the two through juridical and political features. He held extended spaces to be fundamentally different from traditional empires, blocs, confederations, alliances, or simple living space. Extended spaces shared features with all such entities, but were different in critical ways.

For the purposes of his exposition on extended spaces, Schmitt emphasized the importance of the Monroe Doctrine of 1823—a piece of American public law that unilaterally sought to control relations between Europe

---

[52] Arnaldo Volpicelli, "Prefazione"; Schmitt, *Principii politici del nazionalsocialismo*, p. ix.

and the independent political nations of the Western hemisphere.[53] In the Monroe Doctrine, the government of the United States held that the Western hemisphere, and all the independent nations and territories therein, be closed to both further colonization and European interference. Schmitt held that the Monroe Doctrine produced an uncommon international "political space"—*defined by a particular political idea*—that was prototypic of those unique political arrangements that he spoke of as "extended spaces." Such spaces, at the core of which might be a nation-state (as was the case with the Monroe Doctrine),[54] could extend over entire hemispheres and have only some of the defining properties of traditional empires or any of the other familiar politico-juridical international bodies.

In the course of his discussion, Schmitt reminded his readership that it was still uncertain what the international legal status of the Monroe Doctrine was at its initiation, or what that status might be at the time of his inquiry. Originally advanced as a piece of United States public law, and sometimes defended as "not depending on technical legal right, but upon policy and power," and at other times, cited as a derivative of the international "right of legitimate defense,"[55] the Monroe Doctrine of 1823 simply announced, unilaterally, that the Western hemisphere was no longer open to European colonization nor European interference. Since its promulgation, until the time of Schmitt's writing, the Doctrine served to restrict the extension of European influence into the American hemisphere.

Schmitt pointed out that not only had the United States insisted on a reserve clause in international treaties that allowed its government to exclude any foreign intervention in the Western hemisphere, but at times, the Washington foreign policy establishment urged other nations to each formulate and implement their own "Monroe Doctrine."[56] At those times, the United States seemed to favor an international community parsed into defined extended spaces, each animated by an exclusive *political idea*.

Schmitt found in such delimitations of secured space the intimation of an international principle, some fundamental premise that might constitute the legal framework for future international behaviors. He argued

---

[53] On 28 April 1939, Hitler announced that National Socialism supported a policy like that of the Monroe Doctrine for the new Germany. As cited in Kevin Coogan, *Dreamer of the Day: Francis Parker Yockey and the Postwar Fascist International* (New York: Autonomedia, 1999), p. 78.

[54] This is clearly implied in Schmitt's discussion of the Monroe Doctrine of the United States. The Monroe Doctrine served Schmitt as a model instantial case of "extended space" acknowledged in the behavior of international powers, and yet the space involved did not constitute, in law, an empire. See Schmitt, *Il concetto d'impero nel diritto internazionale*, pt. 2.

[55] Ibid., pp. 30 n. 2, 31, 33.

[56] See ibid., p. 43.

that variants of expanded spaces might come to constitute major components of a postwar international system.

Schmitt argued that a similar process could be observed throughout
history. There were arrangements in antiquity—"spheres of influence,"
"blocs," and "contiguous territories" that, in our own time, are acknowledged as legally recognized entities. He was to argue that "extended
spaces," distinguished by distinctive political doctrines, would constitute
international legal personalities in the future.

Schmitt anticipated that entities very much like his "extended spaces"
would soon make their appearance in the modern world. The modern
world required some principle of international law that would indulge
the political reality of hegemonic nations extending their influence over
geographic regions, regularizing its practice, in order to foster and sustain
peace. He expected that the future would see a polyarchic world system
composed of a still indeterminate set of polycentric extended spaces—and
that if the world sought peace, there should be international law governing their interaction.

The extended spaces Schmitt anticipated would involve peoples, each
politically conscious and possessed of a given political worldview and—
like the authors of the Monroe Doctrine—morally committed to the exclusion of any intervention on the part of representatives of alternative
doctrinal persuasion.[57] Each such relatively closed system would be sustained by an inclusive "planned economy" governing both production
and distribution. Implicit in the conception of extended space is the supposition that such space would encompass an adequate material foundation for the survival of the populations involved. Schmitt's notion of
Grossraum thus explicitly included the lesser notion of *Lebensraum*. It
is hard to convince oneself that Schmitt's conception of a future world
composed of an international arrangement of mutually exclusive extended spaces did not involve a concern for the future of National Socialist Germany. It seemed reasonably clear that if Germany were to win the
war, it would be a hegemonic power that would dominate most of Europe
and perhaps a considerable part of Africa, and possibly Asia, as well. If
such an arrangement were to have anything more than the most temporary existence, it would have to evince all the properties of Schmitt's extended space as well as possess an established international legal personality. It would have to be legally sustained by something more than the
happenstance and ad hoc qualities of the British Empire. An internation-

---

[57] See ibid., pp. 38–40; and Alessandro Campi, "Introduction," in Carl Schmitt, *L'unità
del mondo e altri saggi* (Rome: Antonio Pellicani, 1994), pp. 34–40. No attempt has been
made here to translate the typically Germanic title of Schmitt's work. The Italians simply
translated it, inadequately, as "The Concept of Empire in International Law."

ally recognized legal principle of "extended space" would provide such arrangements legitimacy.[58]

Fascist thinkers seemed to have found Schmitt's ideas of interest, but they clearly were not matters of immediate concern. While Schmitt's views were accorded significant space in Fascist publications, there seems to have been very little explicit support for them by Fascist theoreticians.[59] Most of the Fascist literature that sought to provide a rationale for Italy's intervention in the Second World War alluded to those reasons that could be identified with Italy's "vital," rather than those associated with Schmitt's "extended," space needs.[60] Little argument was specifically devoted to the advocacy of extended space aspirations.

All the arguments employed by Fascist apologists for Italy's involvement as an ally of Germany in the Second World War invoked claims long since made by Mussolini and identified by Schmitt as specifically "living space" demands,[61] rather than those made for an Italian "extended space."[62] For all intents and purposes, those expectations that were to figure as Fascist wartime incentives had already been made, in principle, long before the advent of the Second World War. Even Schmitt specifically identified them as *Lebensraum*, rather than *Grossraum*, claims.[63] When Fascist authors referred to "extended space" at all, they more frequently than not spoke of "extended *living* space," that is to say, a living space of imperial dimension.[64]

---

[58] Schmitt was suspected of ideological indifference by the SS. His views were not held to be sufficiently National Socialist. This was apparently the reason Schmitt chose to concentrate on international affairs. His concept of "extended *Grossraum*" was the consequence. Schmitt went on to make the case for internationally recognized extended spaces during the "Cold War." See Schmitt, "L'ordinamento planetario dopo la seconda guerra mondiale (1962)," in *L'Unità del mondo*, pp. 321–44.

[59] Roman Catholic publications were emphatically opposed to Schmitt's conception. See A. Messineo, S.J., *Spazio vitale e grande spazio* (Rome: Civiltà Cattolica, 1942).

[60] See, for example, Lauro Mainardi, *Nazionalità e spazi vitali* (Rome: Cremonese, 1941); Domenico Soprano, *Spazio vitale* (Milan: Corbaccio, 1942); Virginio Gayda, *Perchè l'Italia e in Guerra* (Rome: Capriotta, n.d.).

[61] Schmitt, *Il concetto d'impero nel diritto internazionale*, p. 49.

[62] Mussolini regularly referred to free passage through the Mediterranean and the Straits of Gibraltar and the Suez Canal as vital issues for Italy, while they were matters of convenience for Great Britain. See Mussolini, "Discorsi di Milano," in *Oo*, vol. 28, pp. 70–71. In the Italian translation, Schmitt refers to Mussolini's statement as alluding to "uno spazio vitale." Schmitt, *Il concetto d'impero nel diritto internazionale*, p. 42, n. 2.

[63] See the discussions in Virginio Gayda, *Profili della nuova Europa: L'economia di domani* (Rome: Giornale d'Italia, 1941); F. S. Orlando, *L'economia bellica ed i problemi della nuova Europa* (Milan: Bocca, 1941); and Gori, *Roma nel continente nero*. There is no reference to "extended spaces" as part of the rationale for the war in any of these texts.

[64] See Soprano, *Spazio vitale*, pp. 71, 72. Soprano was fully familiar with Schmitt's notion of *Grossraum*, and speaks of specifically *Lebensgrossraum*, "economic extended space,"

Although there clearly were instances of more systematic allusions to Schmitt's "extended space," the more frequent Fascist appeal was made to what is easily identified as traditional empire and spheres of influence. As early as 1922, Mussolini described the projected Fascist foreign policy as predicated on a "civilizing national or imperial society . . . informed by a state."[65] Out of that traditional conception, Fascist ideologues characteristically anticipated the advent not of anything that had the appearance of Schmitt's extended space, but of a traditional empire.[66] Over the Balkans, and parts of Eastern Europe, for example, Fascist Italy expected to project a presence in the manner of a traditional sphere of influence.

It is not that Fascist doctrine could not accommodate Schmitt's conception of a pluriform international system of extended spaces. It was simply the case that Fascist intellectuals, like Pellizzi, had already outlined a future for Italy that was captured in the traditional conception of empire and spheres of influence. There clearly were not many Fascist thinkers prepared to embrace Schmitt's notions. Among Fascist thinkers, Schmitt's notion of extended space was superfluous. Fascist doctrine found expression in the standard Fascism geopolitical conception of empire.[67] Most Fascist intellectuals, when they referred to Schmitt's notion of "extended space" at all, simply reduced it, explicitly or implicity, to the dimensions of what had become known to National Socialist thinkers as *Lebensraum*, "living space."

For Fascist intellectuals, the material necessity of living space was enhanced by a conviction in the spiritual, imperial, "civilizing" mission of their revolution. That had been part of Fascist doctrine since its first appearance. Pellizzi had given it expression, and in its general outline, the concept of an imperial, civilizing mission was fully compatible with the sustaining thought of Gentile's Actualism.

In one of the journals of the time most favorably disposed to Schmitt's ideas, the effort to make the case for the creation of a postwar system of extended spaces quickly dissolved into what was clearly a reaffirmation

---

and of "securing economic spaces." See pp. 6, 17, 57, 59, 60, 67, 71–73. The elements of such spaces are demographics, raw materials, ocean access, and marketing requirements.

[65] See Mussolini, "Dal malinconico tramonto liberale all'aurora fascista della nuova Italia" and "Stato, antistato e fascismo," in *Oo*, vol. 18, pp. 260, 439. See the reference in Mainardi, *Nazionalità e spazio vitale*, p. 101.

[66] See, for example, Giuseppe Maggione, *Imperialismo e impero fascista* (Palermo: Arceri e Agate, 1937).

[67] In fact, among German theorists speculating on future international arrangements, there was a tendency to limit their discussion to what was called "living spaces." Works like Paul Schmidt's collection, *Revolution im Mittelmeer: Der Kampf um dem italienischen Lebensraum* (Berlin: Volk und Reich, 1940), simply repeated standard Fascist arguments concerning the "empire."

of Fascist Italy's claim to an adequate living space, together with some trappings of a more-or-less standard sphere of influence arrangement established by voluntary association.[68] This was, by and large, the general reception Schmitt's ideas were accorded by Pellizzi and most other Fascist intellectuals.

In retrospect, however interesting, Schmitt's concept of extended spaces was not really the most arresting feature of his writings. In general, Fascist intellectuals digested the account without difficulty. By and large, Schmitt's reflections on that subject were treated as peripheral to Fascist interests. There was, however, a minor theme in Schmitt's thought that was to create very special problems for Fascist intellectuals.

Until 1938, the notion of biological racism played a minor, and relatively benign, role in the formulations of Fascist ideology. Even with the promulgation of the "Manifesto of Fascist Racism" in that year, and the formal character that the issue thereby assumed, most Fascist intellectuals managed it without serious doctrinal dissonance.[69]

Even in that more formal context, the nature of "Fascist racism" was fundamentally different from that of Hitler's Germany.[70] It was that difference that was to make of Schmitt's writings a matter of considerable importance. The occasion of Schmitt's essays precipitated discussions that were to have portentous consequences for Fascist Italy.

That should not be understood to suggest that Schmitt was a racist of the sort one would expect to find among National Socialists. Schmitt's role in the ensuing discussion was not a consequence of his specific racism. Whatever racism was to be found in his work was marginal. The theme had been given vast currency in the Germany of his time, and it would have been most unusual if no mention at all of biological race appeared in his work.

In an earlier work, Schmitt had spoken of a kind of "*Gleichartigkeit*," a "homogeneity," that assured affinities between a ruler and those he

---

[68] See Pier Silverio Leicht, "Osservazioni sul problema del grande spazio e spazio vitale," *Lo stato* 14, no. 4 (April 1943), pp. 97–110.

[69] This was not true of Gentile. Gentile was alienated by the "Manifesto." He considered the effort by the Fascist government to attempt any accommodation whatever with racism to be a gross moral infraction. See the discussion in Gregor, *Giovanni Gentile*, chap. 8. For the nature of Fascist racism, see the discussion in A. James Gregor, *The Ideology of Fascism*, chap. 6. The antimiscegenation laws of the late 1930s, dealing with Italian relations with the population of Ethiopia, were prompted by political, rather than biological, concerns. See appendix A of *The Ideology of Fascism*, pp. 383–86.

[70] In this context, see the discussion in Renzo De Felice, *Fascism: An Informal Introduction to Its Theory and Practice* (New Brunswick, N.J.: Transaction, 1976), pp. 40–41, *Interpretations of Fascism* (Cambridge: Harvard University Press, 1977), pp. 10–11; and *Storia degli ebrei italiani sotto i fascismo*, new enlarged ed. (Turin: Einaudi, 1993), pp. 27–77.

ruled. That homogeneity rendered governance possible.[71] In his *Staat, Bewegung, Volk*, translated into Italian in 1935, Schmitt spoke more expressly of those affinities. They were apparently attributed to a shared racial heritage.

In the text, he speaks of National Socialist leadership predicated on the "equality of race"—with minority leadership of a nation legitimized by the "shared and infallible contact between the leader and his followers"— its shared and infallible quality, the product of racial homogenity.[72]

It was that element of racism to which Volpicelli and Delio Cantimori had objected in their respective introductions to *Staat, Bewegung, Volk* in 1935.[73] Fascist doctrinal objections to biological racism as a determinant in the political history of communities were, at that time, general and emphatic. By 1941, by the time Schmitt's essay on extended spaces appeared, the situation had dramatically altered.

By that time, Fascist Italy was abjectly dependent on National Socialist Germany for the arms and collateral support without which the nation could not survive. The Fascist–National Socialist alliance had become a matter of simple survival for Italy. Circumstances thus militated against continued Fascist criticism of National Socialist doctrine. As a consequence neither Pellizzi, Vannutelli Rey, nor Pierandri, in dealing with Schmitt's ideas, raised any objections to anything said in the essay of 1941.[74] Those were the conditions that rendered it possible for the racist conjectures of National Socialist theoreticians to insinuate their way into academic and popular literature in Fascist Italy without difficulty.

At about the time that Pellizzi's National Institute of Fascist Culture published Schmitt's brochure on the international juridical status of extended spaces, Carlo Costamagna's journal *Lo stato* began publishing, with some regularity, Schmitt's essays on a variety of subjects.[75]

With the appearance of Schmitt's essay on extended spaces, Carlo Costamagna, the editor of *Lo stato* and an important Fascist ideologue, proceeded to expand the discussion beyond the specific issues joined in the text. In an essay of his own, in attempting a credible response to Roman Catholic criticism[76] of the entire thesis of extended spaces, Costa-

---

[71] See the discussion in Carl Schmitt, *Verfassungslehre* (Munich: Duncker und Humblot, 1928), pp. 234–37.

[72] Schmitt, *Principii politici del nazionalsocialismo*, pp. 176, 191–92, 226–27.

[73] Arnaldo Volpicelli, "Preface," and Delio Cantimori, "Note sul nazionalsocialismo," in Schmitt, *Principii politici del nazionalsocialismo*, pp. v–x, 1–42.

[74] L. Vannutelli Rey "Preface" and F. Pierandri, "Appendice: La politica e il diritto nel pensiero di Carl Schmitt," in Schmitt,*Il concetto d'impero nel diritto internazionale*, pp. 1–12, 95–143.

[75] These essays have been conveniently collected as Schmitt, *L'Unità del mondo*.

[76] The earlier cited volume by Father Messineo, *Spazio vitale e grande spazio*, was specifically referred to by Leicht, "Osservazioni sul problema del grande spazio e spazio vitale,"

magna gave it a special emphasis that did not even appear in Schmitt's original discussion. Costamagna, in discussing the human character of the projected extended spaces, spoke of them as involving "cognate peoples" (*popoli affini*). He argued that the subject peoples in any extended space would have to somehow share "affinities"—apparently in order to assure their "harmonious and fruitful collaboration."[77] He went on to speak of a consequent "organic" collaboration of such peoples throughout Italian history, first in the early years of the making of the Roman empire, and subsequently in the making of the universal Roman Catholic Church.

He went on to suggest that that such collaboration could only be the product of the working together of cognate peoples of "Aryan race."[78] Costamagna went on to speak of "ethnic" and cultural affinities as though true collaboration in the anticipated extended spaces would require that the peoples involved share some discriminable biopsychological similarities.[79] There was the evident suggestion, although significantly qualified, that the requisite collaboration was the result of unspecified biological factors.

Costamagna was familiar with Schmitt's work, and in one place referred to the necessity of preserving the "spiritual forces" that sustain a "nation's identity"—immediately thereafter alluding to Schmitt's *Verfassungslehre*, where we find Schmitt speaking of the "homogeneity" of a population as the necessary condition for the integrity of any political arrangement.[80] There is little doubt that the homogeneity to which Schmitt alluded on that occasion was biological or racial. In 1933 and 1934, Schmitt's characterization of the *Volk*—one element of the trinity of "state, movement, people" of which Germany's National Socialist ideological persuasion was composed—was clearly biological and racial. Those Fascist intellectuals who commented on the Italian translation of Schmitt's *Der Begriff des Politischen* and his *Staat, Bewegung, Volk* clearly recognized as much. The homogeneity that assured the harmonious compatibility of the governed and their leaders, as well as the affinities that bound peoples together in extended spaces, was conceived to be biological.[81]

---

p. 102. Messineo made himself an informed critic of Schmitt's theses and had published several pieces of criticism prior to the publication of the cited volume.

[77] Carlo Costamagna, "Grande spazio e etnarchia imperiale," *Lo stato* 13, no. 1 (January 1942), p. 3.

[78] Ibid., p. 4.

[79] See ibid., pp. 9 and 12.

[80] Schmitt, *Verfassungslehre*, pp. 234–35.

[81] See the entire discussion in Schmitt, "I caratteri essenziali dello stato nazionalsocialista," in *L'Unità del mondo*, pp. 175–80.

Costamagna was circumspect in dealing with Schmitt's conjectures concerning the factors that rendered leaders and followers, and associated peoples, "organically compatible." He warned his readers, for example, not to accept any simplisms concerning the "racial character" to be attributed the "Aryan" populations of proposed extended spaces. He maintained that he would ascribe the "ethnic affinities" to which he made reference in his exposition more to a "spiritual," than to a simple biological, source. He seemed prepared to ascribe those affinities to which he alluded to the effects of a life shared in a "determinate civilization."[82]

For his part, Schmitt recognized that the biological racism that served as a linchpin of National Socialism was absent from Fascist doctrine.[83] Costamagna's tentativeness in discussing the racism of Schmitt's account suggested that he was well aware of the sensitivity of the subject.

Over the years, Costamagna had come to serve as a member of a nationalist-Catholic faction among Fascist intellectuals. An early collaborator of Giovanni Gentile, he had become increasingly alienated over time—first because Gentile had proven more a statist than a nationalist, and later because the Church of Rome identified absolute idealism as heretical.

Costamagna was born in Quiliano, Savona, on 21 September 1881. He trained as a jurist and served as a judge in the Italian courts. He early joined the Fascist movement and after the March on Rome served with Gentile as Secretary of the Council of Eighteen, charged by Mussolini with the Fascist reform of the Italian constitution. Costamagna continued to serve the regime, throughout its tenure, by assisting in the drafting of corporative legislation and as a professor of corporative law at the University of Ferrara.

Costamagna's alienation from Actualism probably arose primarily out of his commitment to Roman Catholicism. By the last years of the regime, Costamagna's opposition to the philosophy of Gentile was both transparent and categorical. He employed every opportunity to cite what he took to be evidence of Fascism's ultimate commitment to something other than Actualism—to "the traditions of Italian civilization," for example, and "to Christian and Roman Catholic spiritualism."[84]

---

[82] Costamagna, "Grande spazio e ethnarchia imperiale," p. 12. It is not clear how this is made compatible with the distinction Costamagna makes between "ethnicity" and "culture," since in the immediately subsequent sentence he quotes Adolf Hitler referring to Europe as a "racial and cultural expression" as though the two concepts were separate and distinct.

[83] Schmitt, "Faschistische und Nationalsozialistische Rechtswissenschaft," *Deutsche Juristen Zeitung* no. 13 (1936), pp. 787–89.

[84] See the unsigned review of Stefano Mazzilli's *I caratteri e l'originalità della filosofia del fascismo* (Florence: La Vela, 1943) in *Lo stato* 14, no. 4 (April 1943), p. 125.

In 1940, in one of his last major works, Costamagna's rejection of Gentile's Actualism, as a Fascist philosophy, was explicit.[85] More interesting for our purposes is the fact that, like the first organized Italian nationalists of the Nationalist Association, Costamagna conceived Italians defined, in part, by virtue of their "ethnicity." As early as 1905, Enrico Corradini had spoken of the nation being composed of "ethnographic" material. More emphatically still, he identified the nation as an "ethnarchic" polity.[86] Apparently still resonating with such notions, Costamagna, in 1942, was to identify the anticipated Fascist extended space he found suggested in Schmitt's work as "an *ethnarchic* empire."[87]

Gentile, convinced as he was of the irreducibly "spiritual" essence of the state—and that it was the state that informed nations or empires—refused to identify any material properties as necessary to establish their coherence. Costamagna had no such reservations. He was prepared, without hesitation, to consider ethnicity as a factor in the shaping of the nation in a fashion totally unacceptable to Gentile. For Gentile, one was as responsible for one's nationality as one was responsible for one's allegiance. Neither biology, anthropology, nor ethnicity altered that. Nationality was, for Gentile, a moral choice.

Very early in his career, when the suggestion was made that *race* might be an historical determinate, Gentile forthrightly dismissed the possibility.[88] However "ethnicity" was to be understood, Gentile dismissed as "naturalism" any appeal to its efficacy as an historic agent. The notion that a human being's biology might shape his or her nationality or moral allegiance was rejected by Actualists as not only epistemologically objectionable but morally repugnant.

As a case in point, there is no evidence and much counterevidence that Gentile ever entertained any form of anti-Semitism. The entire notion was contrary to his philosophical and ethical convictions.[89] Costamagna, on the other hand, was prepared to fulminate against Jews whenever the occasion presented itself. He made a special point of publishing anti-Semitic literature,[90] and in his own doctrinal statements, while he granted that the Jews, as a group, did not demonstrate a "racial identity in the

---

[85] Costamagna, *Dottrina del fascismo*, pp. 31, 33, 149.

[86] Enrico Corradini, "La vita nazionale" and "Nazionalismo e democrazia" in *Discorsi politici (1902–1923)* (Florence: Vallecchi, 1923), pp. 36, 43, 159.

[87] Costamagna, "Grande spazio e etnarchia imperiale," pp. 1–18.

[88] Gentile, *Teoria generale dello spirito come atto puro* (Bari: Laterza, 1924), p. 171.

[89] See Gregor, *Giovanni Gentile*, chap. 8.

[90] See, for example, the review in *Lo stato* of Siro Conti, *Pervertimenti giudaici nella filosofia* (Milan: Criterion, 1942) in *Lo stato* 13, no. 11 (November 1942), p. 299.

anthropological sense," they did "constitute a serious threat to the spiritual integrity of the people of Europe."[91]

All of that was intolerable to Actualists—and never supported by Pellizzi. Costamagna, unconstrained by the philosophical tenets of Actualism, proceeded to make political and moral distinctions predicated on "ethnic" differences. Throughout the discussions that were to follow among Fascist intellectuals, "ethnicity" remained a term intrinsically vague and ambiguous. It was to perform, nonetheless, in critical fashion in Costamagna's interpretation of Schmitt's conception of extended and living space.

The Fascist responses to the entire notion that enlarged or extended living spaces might in any way be influenced by "biological determinants" is instructive. It was not uncommon for Fascist commentators to object to the suggestion that biology might be a factor in the formation of extended or living spaces—on the grounds that Fascist doctrine was based on principles that were "spiritual" and "ethico-political" rather than "material."[92] In the months and years that were to follow, those convictions were to be sorely tested.

All the questions prompted by such matters were to torment Fascist doctrine through the last years of the regime. They were to involve Fascist intellectuals in complex and painful doctrinal disputes that were to savage some and alienate more. They were to make the final tragic years of Fascism more tragic still.

---

[91] Costamagna, *Dottrina del fascismo*, p. 198.

[92] See Gelsy Coppiello, "Grandi spazi reali e falsi," *Lo stato* 14, no. 2 (February 1943), pp. 52–53.

CHAPTER NINE

Doctrinal Interlude: The Initiatic Racism of Julius Evola

By the late 1930s, Fascist Italy, having established itself as a serious actor on the European continent, turned its attention almost exclusively to foreign affairs.[1] It was during the years of the late 1930s that Italy attempted to establish its place among the constellation of European powers. Mussolini sought to engage Germany as a dissatisfied power—in an effort to respond to its demands—in an attempt to stabilize Europe. It quickly became evident that Germany could not be satisfied—and that the major powers of Europe were disposed to appease Adolf Hitler's aggressive initiatives at what appeared to Mussolini to be Italy's expense. Mussolini's efforts, however unrealistic, were an attempt to contain National Socialist Germany. By the mid-1930s, it became increasingly clear that Germany was not to be contained.

It was within that fateful context that Mussolini sought to make evident to the advanced industrial powers that Fascist Italy, whatever the circumstances in continental Europe, would seek "living space" in Africa. He was convinced that both England and France had implicitly acknowledged the justice of his case. Italy had one of Europe's highest population densities, and a dearth of subsoil resources; Mussolini was convinced that both France and England could not fail to see the merits of Italy's colonial claims. Pre-Fascist Italy had long evinced interest in expansion in the Mediterranean and Africa—at a time when other European nations had all but occupied the entire African continent.[2] Whatever Mussolini's convictions, however, the position of both France and England, should Italy embark on aggression anywhere in Africa, was ambiguous.

Mussolini had long argued that without secure access to raw materials, a developing Italy would be denied political and economic independence and political equality.[3] Ethiopia had been long considered just such a

---

[1] See the account in Renzo De Felice, *Mussolini il duce: Gli anni del consenso, 1929–36* (Turin: Einaudi,1974), chap. 4.

[2] See, for example, Mussolini, "Discorso di Piazza Belgioioso," *Opera omnia* (Florence: La fenice, 1953–65. Hereafter *Oo*), vol. 16, pp. 300–1, "Italia e Mediterraneo: L'Egitto indipendente?" in *Oo*, vol. 18, p. 77.

[3] See Mussolini, "Per rinascere e progredire: Politica orientale," in *Oo*, vol. 14, pp. 225–27; "Per essere liberi," in *Oo*, vol. 16, pp. 104–6, "Manifesto dei fasci per le elezioni generale," in *Oo*, vol. 16, pp. 264–65.

source of those resources required by Italian industrial expansion.[4] After long and complex negotiations, Mussolini proceeded with his war against Ethiopia—possessed of a certain understanding that the undertaking would not be strenuously resisted by either France or England. Whatever Mussolini believed, the aggression in Ethiopia was to prove fateful.

The war in Ethiopia saw Great Britain leading the demand for League of Nations' sanctions against Fascist Italy. Britain's actions against Italy seemed to confirm Mussolini's long-held conviction that Italy's interests, as a "proletarian nation," would always be obstructed by those powers that were "sated."[5] Only Germany, of all the major European powers, was prepared to assist Italy in the pursuit of what Mussolini had long considered the just interests of a resource-poor, late-developing industrial aspirant.[6]

The immediate consequence was an increasing rapprochement between National Socialist Germany and Fascist Italy. With the outbreak of the civil war in Spain in 1936, their bilateral relations intensified. Both Germany and Italy provided material assistance to the Spanish nationalists, while the Soviet Union and the activists in France and England supported the leftist government. By that time, Fascist Italy and National Socialist Germany were almost universally considered antidemocratic political and military allies.

In October 1936, Germany and Italy signed a secret protocol that outlined their common foreign policy objectives. In November, Germany and Imperial Japan entered into an anti-Comintern pact directed against the Soviet Union. A year later, Italy acceded to the pact.

At the same time, Hitler pursued his policy of seeking to integrate Austria into the new Reich. Once again he courted Mussolini. With Fascist Italy finding itself obstructed in its foreign policy objectives by Britain and France, Hitler considered the time propitious to attempt a military and political alliance with Mussolini. In September 1937, Mussolini accepted Hitler's invitation to visit resurgent Germany.

Both the reception and the impressive display of German arms clearly overwhelmed Mussolini. Fewer and fewer differences separated Italy and Germany in terms of foreign policy. On 29 September 1937, Mussolini announced that Fascism and National Socialism shared much in terms of a worldview—a rejection of "historical materialism" and a corresponding commitment to the efficacy of determined, courageous, and tenacious

---

[4] See Mussolini, "Il discorso della mobilitazione," in *Oo*, vol. 27, pp. 159–60; see "La necessità di espanzione dell'Italia in Africa," and "Politica di vita," in *Oo*, vol. 27, pp. 160–65; and Carlo de Biase, *L'Impero di "facetta nera"* (Rome: Il Borghese, 1966), chap. 1.

[5] See Mussolini, "Noi e l'estero," in *Oo*, vol. 18, pp. 274–75.

[6] Mussolini always identified Italy as a "late developing nation," having emphatic needs that the "plutocratic nations" were not likely to respect. See Mussolini, "La riforma della scuola," in *Oo*, vol. 20, pp. 129–30.

will. He alluded to their joint emphasis on the dignity of labor, and the role of youth in restorative revolution. He spoke of the necessities of economic independence and corresponding military preparedness that characterized both revolutionary regimes. As a consequence, Mussolini committed himself to "a firm solidarity between the two revolutions" in an "Italo-German friendship consecrated both in the policies and in the hearts of both nations."[7] In November 1937, Mussolini indicated that Fascist Italy would no longer obstruct Germany's efforts to incorporate Austria into the Reich. After that, developments proceeded very rapidly.

By the beginning of 1938, Italian and German intellectuals were meeting with greater and greater frequency in discussions concerning economic, cultural, military, and political matters. In the course of those meetings extraneous National Socialist ideological material was introduced that began to influence the character and content of Fascist doctrine.

Issues that involved the worldview of National Socialism more and more frequently impinged on Fascism. The most irritating incidents turned on the fact that many Italian Jews, serving in the ranks of the Partito nazionale fascista, were interacting with their National Socialist counterparts in symposia and conferences—to everyone's discomfort. The Fascist foreign ministry requested that Jews absent themselves from such encounters—in the first semiofficial act of anti-Semitism in Fascist Italy.[8]

Until that time, official anti-Semitism was unknown in Fascist Italy. In 1933, Mussolini told Emil Ludwig that anti-Semitism did not exist in Italy. "Italian Jews," he went on, "have comported themselves well as citizens, and as soldiers they have fought courageously. They occupy the most prestigeous positions in our universities, in the military, in our financial houses. Many are general officers."[9]

That was a position Mussolini had consistently held throughout his public life. A. O. Olivetti, one of his close associates, a syndicalist, and subsequently a national syndicalist, who clearly contributed to Mussolini's ideological maturation in the period before the First World War, was Jewish. Over the life span of the regime, there were proportionately more Jews in the Partito nazionale fascista then there were in the general population.

Fascist "racism" throughout the period between 1922 and 1938, however distinctive, was essentially benign—and shared little, if any sub-

---

[7] Mussolini, "Il discorso di Berlino," in Oo, vol. 28, p. 251; and "Riporto dalla Germania. . . . Un'impressione profonda e ricordi indelebili," in Oo, vol. 28, p. 253.

[8] The entire history of the Italian Jews under Fascism is detailed in Renzo De Felice, *Storia degli ebrei italiani sotto il fascismo*, new enlarged ed. (Turin: Einaudi, 1993).

[9] Mussolini, in Emil Ludwig, *Colloqui con Mussolini* (Verona: Mondadori, 1933), p. 72.

stance, with the malevolent racism so prevalent across the Alps.[10] None of the major Fascist intellectuals were racists of the sort one found in National Socialist environs. In fact, since many, if not most, of the principal ideologues of Fascism were Actualists, they had principled objections to attributing human behavior to material—that is, biological—causes. They simply could not accept the proposition that an entire population, characterized by ill-defined "racial" traits, could be held, as a body, guilty of anything.

After considerable resistance, National Socialist influence began to penetrate some circles in Fascist Italy. Anti-Semitism and forms of biological racism began to surface in some publications. In general, however, there was a concerted effort to distinguish Fascist "racism" from that emanating from the north. It was not unusual, before the outbreak of the Second World War, for Fascist intellectuals to oppose themselves to some of the major elements of National Socialist racism.[11]

Until the actual publication of the official "Manifesto of Fascist Racism," biological racism, as it was understood by National Socialist theorists, had literally no place in Fascist doctrine. Thereafter, the Fascist position became increasingly confused.

It was clear to anyone who understood Fascism as a doctrine that Gentile, and most Actualists, were opposed to any racism that shared significant properties with the racism of Hitler's Germany.[12] In that context, marginal persons, who had long been dismissed as lacking any significance whatever, made their reappearance among Fascist intellectuals. Giovanni Preziosi, Italy's only committed anti-Semite, suddenly resurfaced together with Julius Evola, whom serious Fascists were to forever dismiss as the "Magic Baron."[13]

It was into that tumult that the ideas of Carl Schmitt were introduced. When his discussion of the imperialism of "extended spaces" somehow invoked the vague suggestion that the populations of such spaces might

---

[10] See Mussolini's comments ibid., pp. 70–72. An account of Fascist racism is provided in A. James Gregor, *The Ideology of Fascism: The Rationale of Totalitarianism* (New York: Free Press, 1969), chap. 6.

[11] As late as 1941, one can find in Fascist doctrinal literature the insistence that National Socialist racism was "antithetical" to that of Fascism. Enzo Leoni, *Mistica del razzismo fascista* (Rome: Quaderni del Scuola di mistica fascista Sandro Italico Mussolini, 1941), pp. 29–40, 63. National Socialist racism is identified as "primordial and absolute"—while Fascist racism "contains, at its very foundation, the germs of a new humanism . . . necessary . . . to resolve the moral crises of our time" (p. 54).

[12] See the discussion in A. James Gregor, *Giovanni Gentile: Philosopher of Fascism* (New Brunswick, N.J.: Transaction, 2001), chap. 8.

[13] See the account in H. T. Hansen, "Introduction: Julius Evola's Political Endeavors," in Julius Evola, *Men among the Ruins: Post-war Reflections of a Radical Traditionalist* (Rochester, Vt.: Inner Traditions, 2002), p. 91.

conceivably share some important "racial affinities," those Fascist intellectuals long opposed to Actualism for a variety of reasons seized the opportunity to attempt its definitive displacement by making appeal to biological racism.

By 1941, it had become transparent to everyone that Fascist Italy found itself in desperate military circumstances. On the battlefield, Fascist forces were in retreat everywhere. Only German intervention might recover the situation.

The consequence was that a closer, more intimate union with National Socialist Germany recommended itself. Some intellectuals urged the abandonment of what had been ideological orthodoxy. To close the distance between Fascism and National Socialism, they advocated an infusion of "hard" racism into what was perceived as an ideological system that was too "humanitarian." One of the consequences produced by those most singular circumstances was the reappearance of that eccentric intellectual who had early been dismissed by every Fascist critic as a person of no consequence: Baron Julius Cesare Andrae Evola.[14]

Evola was born in Rome on the 19 May in 1898, scion of an old aristocratic family. On his return home after service in the First World War, he was to try to find himself in poetry, in Dadaism, and in nonrepresentational art in general—in Futurism, theosophy, anthroposophy, and philosophical solipsism. For a brief while, immediately after the succession of Mussolini to power, Evola identified himself with political anti-Fascism. At the same time, he became more and more involved in the intensive study of Far Eastern "spiritual," "metaphysical," and "initiatic" thought.[15]

By 1925, Evola was attempting to resolve the problems of philosophical idealism by pursuing epistemological problems into ontological conclusions that made the "Absolute Individual"— initially understood as the sensate self—somehow "responsible" for all "reality."[16] What resulted was a more than quaint "magic idealism"—part Tantric, part primitive Buddhist, part pre-Christian pagan, and part medieval alchemy. Ugo Spirito, one of the most prominent of the Fascist intellectuals of the time,

[14] The best intellectual biography of Evola is that of H. T. Hansen, cited in Evola, *Men among the Ruins.* A bibliography of the works of Evola is available in Renato Del Ponte, "Julius Evola: Una bibliografia, 1920–1994," *Futuro presente* 3, no. 6 (Spring 1995), pp. 27–70.

[15] Evola was early identified as a representative of the "most rigorous and most extreme position in all of European dadaism"—at the same time that he was an express anti-Fascist. See Marco Rossi, "Evola e la pubblicista antifascista liberal-democratica; 1924–1925," ibid., p. 98 and pp. 97–106.

[16] The most easily accessible arguments are to be found in Julius Evola, *Saggi sull'idealismo magico* (Rome: Antanor, 1925); *L'individuo e il divenire del mondo* (Rome: Libreria di scienze e lettere,1926); and *L'uomo come potenza: I tantra nella loro metafisica e nei loro metodi di autorealizzazione magica* (Rome: Atanor, 1927).

called it a product of "a mania for originality at whatever cost, a vanity for new formulations, and a poorly concealed inability to suffer the moral discipline of an idealism that is adequately understood." He dismissed the young Evola as a pretentious poseur who had given himself over to a Europeanized version of Eastern mysticism—a kind of fictive "anti-intellectualism" that, in fact, revealed itself as nothing other than an exotic and stilted intellectualism.[17]

It was during this period that Evola, for reasons that cannot be determined with any confidence, decided to attempt to insinuate himself into the intellectual ranks of institutional Fascism. At almost the same time, he attempted to ingratiate himself with Giovanni Gentile—whose Actualism all but dominated the cultural landscape.[18]

Whatever Evola's motivation, in 1928 he published his first overtly political work, *Imperialismo pagano: Il fascismo dinnanzi al pericolo Euro-Cristano,*[19] a volume that contained many of the ideas he had already advanced in an article published the year before in one of the official journals of Fascism.[20] The sentiments contained in *Imperialismo pagano* were painfully clear.

Fascism, for Evola, as it had manifested itself in Mussolini's revolution, was a *material* thing, without a *soul*. It was a revolution that had mobilized to its standards some of the dregs of society. It had been "born of compromise, fed on rhetoric and the petty ambitions of petty people. The state system it fabricated [was] uncertain, ill-conceived, violent, unfree, and subject to equivocations." What Fascism needed was a soul—to be governed not by leaders chosen by chance or popular appeal, but by those animated by the "true Wisdom" of "cosmic Masters." Only in those circumstances would people spontaneously sort themselves into castes—as they had in the antiquity of China, Persia, and Egypt—to thereby provide structure for a "true state." A caste arrangement would provide "uncon-

[17] Ugo Spirito, "L'idealismo magico," *L'idealismo italiano e i suoi critici* (Florence: Felice le Monnier, 1930), pp. 192, 204–5.

[18] See the discussion in Stefano Arcella, "L'epistolario Evola-Gentile: Tra *Weltanschauung* 'traditionale' ed idealismo attualistico," *Futuro Presente* 3, no. 6 (Spring 1995), pp. 79–88. For an account of Gentile's influence, and that of Actualism, in the Fascist culture of the period, see Gregor, *Giovanni Gentile.*

[19] Rome: Atanor, 1928.

[20] Julius Evola, "Fascismo antifilosofico e tradizione mediterranea," *Critica fascista*, 5, no. 12 (15 June 1929), pp. 227–29. Giuseppe Bottai, who as editor of *Critica fascista*, occasionally (seven times over twenty years) published essays by Evola, published them, he admitted, as an act of friendship. Bottai and Evola had served together in the Great War. Bottai, as arbiter of Fascism as a doctrine, identified Evola's notions as "an arbitrary coupling of a mass of ill-digested notions." As cited in Mario Giovana, *Le nuove camicie nere* (Turin: Edizione dell'Albero, 1966), p. 7.

ditional freedom" for those infused with cosmic wisdom and unlimited power—thereby to capture the "rational essence" of "true liberalism."[21]

The entirety of then contemporary politics was to be abjured. Evola advocated the rejection of *nationalism* together with the *secular state*. He deplored the violence of the *squadristi*, the armed militia of Fascism. He condemned the "socialistoid" and "demogogic" character of Fascist corporativism. The only way Fascism could hope for deliverance was to be infilled with the "calm illumination" of that true "Wisdom" arising out of Mediterranean "hermetic and pythagorean silence"—finding confirmation of its "Truth" through "acts of power," resonating with "vibrations in the blood," rather than via the provision of pallid "arguments and the writing of books." Only if Fascism succeeded in finding its "light" in the *Bhagavad-gita* might it be made truly revolutionary—to restore the "traditional order of things"[22] to a decadent modern world.

In all of this, little of Mussolini's Fascism, other than some of its vocabulary, escaped unscathed. Almost four decades later, Evola was to repeat the same roster of objections—and convey his conviction that Mussolini had never been sufficiently "spiritual" to understand any of it.[23] In effect, for the youthful Evola, Fascism, as it was, had precious few immediate and evident virtues. Early in 1925, his intention had been to convey all that by undertaking efforts that were expressly anti-Fascist.[24] He soon reconciled himself to Fascism, however, apparently in order to employ it as a vehicle to bring to its elite the "traditional wisdom" of his "invisible Masters"[25]—in order that they might assist him in mounting a revolution against the antitraditional decadence of the postmedieval "modern world."

In retrospect, it appears evident that Evola was never particularly interested in Fascism, as such.[26] In effect, he actually has no place in any history of Fascist social and political thought. He is accorded a place because,

---

[21] Evola, *Imperialismo pagano*, pp. 11–17 and part 3.

[22] For Evola, the "traditional order of things" apparently ceased with the close of the Middle Ages; see Evola, *La tradizione ermetica nei suoi simboli—nella sua dottrina—nella sua "arte regia"*, 2nd ed. (1931; Bari: Laterza, 1948, second edition of the 1931 volume), p. 24.

[23] See Evola's postwar critique of Fascism in his *Il fascismo: Saggio di una analisi critica dal punto di vista della Destra* (Rome: Volpe, 1964), In his *Il cammino del cinabro* (Milan: Al'insegna del pesce d'oro, 1963), pp. 96–97, he told his readership that Mussolini was not sufficiently "spiritual" to understand "magic idealism."

[24] Marco Rossi, "Evola e la pubblicistica antifascista liberal-democratica: 1924–1925," *Futuro presente* 3. no. 6 (Spring 1995), p. 103.

[25] Philippe Baillet, "I rapporti di Evola con il fascismo ed il nazionalsocialismo," *Futuro presente* 3, no. 6 (Spring 1995), p. 142. See Evola's discussion of the "invisible masters" in *La tradizione ermetica*, pp. 226–28.

[26] In this context, see Hansen's "Introduction," in Evola, *Men among The Ruins*, pp. 1–104. In the foreword to that same volume, Joscelyn Godwin correctly identified Evola as "a fearless critic of the Fascist regime" (p. x).

years after the passing of fascism, discussants have chosen to identify him as the "fascist" source of the irrationalism and antihumanism of contemporary "extremism." He presumably provided the meaning of fascism for modern revolutionaries.

In fact, Evola was never a fascist, however the term is understood. He provided idiosyncratic meaning for all its principal concepts in his candid effort to further the interests of that arcane Tantric and Vedic Wisdom that he had made his own.

With respect to Fascism, he advocated a total rejection of any notion of a "totalitarian state" that rested on a nationalism that required obedience and commitment. Terms that had become familiar to Fascists, such as "hierarchy," "leadership," "elitism," the "state," "imperialism," and "myth" all had their meanings transmogrified in the lexicon of Evola's "traditional Mediterranean vision."[27]

Evola was the advocate of an anti–Roman Catholic pagan imperialism.[28] The Roman Church was an obstacle to his purposes—and revolutionary responsibility cried out for the Church's "subjugation." According to his account, Christianity had destroyed the imperial universality of the Roman Empire by insisting on the separation of the secular and the spiritual. Out of that unnatural bifurcation arose all the decadence of the modern world. Out of Christianity's implacable opposition to the healthy paganism of the Mediterranean world arose the secularism, democracy, materialism, scientism, socialism, and the "subtle Bolshevism" that heralded the final age of the current cosmic cycle: the age of "obscurity," the *kali-yuga*.[29]

During 1927 and 1928, while Mussolini was negotiating his historic Concordat with the Papacy, Evola persisted in his public attacks on the Church until they appeared to constitute a serious impediment to improved Church-state relations. Giovanni Battista Montini, the future Pope Paul VI, condemned Evola as a fevered anticlerical whose obstructionist, anti-Catholic works were all but entirely devoid of meaning—but which were nonetheless creating Church-state tensions. Montini proceeded to lodge formal complaints against him with the Fascist authorities.[30]

---

[27] Evola, *Imperialismo pagano*, pp. 48–49.

[28] Ibid., pt. 5, pp. 96–123.

[29] Ibid., pp. 19–21.

[30] Montini identified Evola as suffering from "those strange forms of cerebralism and neurasthenia, of intensive cultivation of incomprehensibility, of the metaphysic of obscurity, of cryptology of expression, of pseudo-mystical precosity, of cabalistic fascinations magically evaporated by the refined drugs of Oriental erudition. " As cited by Richard Drake, "Julius Evola, Radical Fascism, and the Lateran Accords," *Catholic Historical Review*, no. 74 (1988), p. 411.

In retrospect, it is clear that Mussolini allowed Evola to continue a diversionary controversy with the Church in order to drive the Papacy into the most accommodating arrangement he could. Mussolini recognized Evola as just that kind of anticlerical "hysterical fanatic"[31] who could best serve his purpose.[32] And serve he did. Faced by the apparent threat of a violent anticlerical "fascist" opposition, the Church concluded its negotiations with Mussolini. With the Lateran Accords, the Church agreed to a form of recognition that left it with a very distinctive sovereignty—a sovereignty that was, according to Mussolini, "neither sovereign nor free."[33] In part through his deft manipulation of Evola, Mussolini had won what was perhaps his greatest single political success. As we shall see, that was not to be the last time Mussolini was to press Evola into service.

Irrespective of his contribution to Mussolini's purpose, Evola was never accorded any respect in Fascist intellectual circles. Almost every Fascist intellectual of the period identified Evola as the author of "formless and unsophisticated" polemics—the framer of works "every line" of which "conceals a coarse error"—of publications that were not serious, meriting only "to be put aside and thought no more about."[34]

It is important to recognize that at the time of the writing of *Imperialismo pagano*, there is little evidence that Evola had any real interest in race as an intellectual and political problem.[35] Given those circumstances, it cannot be said that anyone would have anticipated his interest in the subject per se—or in Adolf Hitler's National Socialism, when it later burst upon the scene.[36] Nonetheless, at about the time of Hitler's accession to

---

[31] See ibid., p. 414; and D. A. Binchy, *Church and State in Fascist Italy* (London: Oxford University Press, 1941), p. 119.

[32] The Church opposed the neo-Hegelian philosophy of Gentile's Actualism as well, but Mussolini's treatment of Gentile was vastly different from that accorded Evola. Evola always remained marginal to Fascism. His prominence increased, as shall be argued, only when Mussolini had some tactical use for him and his ideas.

[33] Benito Mussolini, "Relazione alla Camera dei deputati sugli Accordi del Laterano," in *Oo*, vol. 24, p. 44.

[34] Ugo d'Andrea, "Imperialismo pagano," *Critica fascista* 6 (15 August 1928), pp. 319–20; Luigi Volpicelli, "Imperialismo fascista," *Educazione fascista* 6 (September 1928), p. 561.

[35] There are some few and nonessential references to "race" as *sangue* (blood) and *stirpe* (which can mean "race," or "people") throughout the text, but they are not really essential to his argument.

[36] Nor were major representatives of National Socialism particularly interested in Evola except as a useful functionary for their purposes. They correctly perceived Evola as a representative of the "old aristocracy against the modern world." He was considered a "reactionary" who was a "dilettante and pseudoscientific." They further acknowledged that since Evola had only been "tolerated and hardly supported by Fascism," there was little reason to "treat him seriously." The report on "Baron Evola" is contained in a dossier maintained

the chancellorship in Germany, when Fascist doctrine uniformly opposed biological racism and anti-Semitism,[37] Evola authorized a revised German translation of *Imperialismo pagano* as *Heidnischer Imperialismus*[38]—characterized by significant and portentous changes in the text.

In reading the German translation, one is immediately struck by the excision from the text of almost any reference to Fascism. In fact, the term disappears from the very title of the translation with the suppression of the subtitle.[39] All the subheadings within the text that contained the term were altered. Almost the entire discussion concerning Fascism was suppressed. In the translation, Evola's seeming concern with the prospects of Fascism enjoyed none of the prominence it had in the original publication.

More important than the deletions is the reformulation of entire sections of the original argument—in order to introduce systematic and emphatic references to race and the theory of race. Along with all references to Fascism, almost all mention of the "pagan Mediterranean tradition" vanishes as well. What suddenly appears in the revised rendering is a distinguished place for recurrent allusions to an "Ur-Aryan" and "solar-Nordic" race. Evola argues that it is out of the creativity of that "blood" that world culture emerges. Conversely, culture decline is a function of the feckless mixture of Aryan, with lesser "animalistic," blood—notions almost entirely absent from the original Italian edition.[40]

More significant, perhaps, is the emphatic appearance of an explicit anti-Semitism in the translation. In the revised text, Evola considered principled *anti-Semitism* one of the essentials of a salvific "racial rebirth" in the modern world. Not only did Evola make a point of identifying Karl Marx, one of the architects of the modern world of materialism, inferiority, pretended equality, and cultural decay, as a Jew—but he

---

by the staff of Heinrich Himmler. As cited in H. T. Hansen's "Introduction" to the English translation of *Rivolta contro il mondo moderno, Revolt against the Modern World* (Rochester, Vt.: Inner Traditions, 1995), p. xviii. Evola was convinced he could use National Socialism in order to rally support for his war against the "modern world." See Elemire Zolla, "The Evolution of Julius Evola's Thought," *Gnosis*, no. 14 (Winter 1990), pp. 18–20.

[37] Bruno Brunello, a student of Gentile, in a review of a book on "Fascist racism," identified German racism as a "most flagrant negation of historicistic immanentism." *Giornale critico della filosofia italiana* 18 (1937), pp. 202–5.

[38] Leipzig: Armanen Verlag, 1933, trans. Friedrich Bauer.

[39] The subtitle read: "Fascism Facing the Euro-Christian Threat." Later, Evola spoke candidly of suppressing any discussion of Fascism in the translation. See Evola, *Il cammino del cinabro*, p. 149.

[40] Compare Evola, *Heidnischer Imperialismus*, pp. 1, 2–3, 5–7, 11, 12, 51–53. References to "blood" appear in the original *Imperialismo pagano*, but those references carry little theoretical weight. Later, Evola referred to the changes in the German translation as a response to "contingent" influences. See Evola, *Il cammino del cinabro*, p. 160.

spoke of a "Jewish capitalistic yoke" that obstructed every effort at racial regeneration.[41]

As a reflection of those changes, the entire section "The Preconditions
for Empire" was rewritten.[42] According to the modified version, the "natural" and endogamous caste system of antiquity that sustained the "purity" of the culture-creating "Hyperborean Nordics" slowly disintegrated
over time under the corrosive influence of Semitic religion and the "Semitic spirit." That spirit, incorporated in the Catholic Church, precipitated the decomposition of the true, hierarchical, and Leader- (Führer-)
dominated Roman, and Germano-Roman, empires. The Germanic leadership of the Holy Roman Empire resisted the "negative and Semitic"
sources of systemic decay throughout much of the Middle Ages with "a
spirit of freedom, independence and individuality—that found its origin
in the fundamental ethos of the original Germanic tribes."[43]

The changes that occurred in the text of Evola's *Imperialismo pagano*
in its translation as *Heidnischer Imperialismus* five years later were neither subtle nor unimportant. The core concepts that made up the substance of Evola's thought remained substantially the same, but a number
of critical elements were introduced or modified that were to have serious
consequences. The "Mediterranean tradition" of the earlier text becomes,
more consistently, the "Nordic-solar tradition" in the translation.
"Aryan-German" and "Nordic-German" appear with insistent regularity
in the place of "Mediterranean."

Evola's shift of emphasis, together with the suppression of some, and
the modification as well as the introduction of other, concepts, transformed his *Imperialismo pagano*. It became, in part, a poor rationale for
National Socialist race theory. All the features that had made the work
non-, not to say anti-, Fascist in 1928 remained and were emphasized.
Nation, as a mobilizing myth, was abjured. *Social concerns*, the doctrinal
and juridical commitment to the syndicalist and corporativist organization of labor, was deplored. *Populism* was decried. *Hierarchy* and *leadership*, on any grounds other than mystic selection from "on high," were
renounced as a perversity of the natural order of governance. While it was
clear that the core concepts of Evola's "transrational" and transcendent
conception of the world had not significantly altered, it became manifestly
evident that his worldview had never been Fascist.

---

[41] *Heidnischer Imperialismus*, pp. 11, 56, 59, 63. Whatever references are made to Jews
in the original version trace their origin back to Giovanni Preziosi, the anti-Semitic with
whom Evola had early established an intellectual relationship.

[42] Compare the entire section "The Preconditions of Empire" in *Imperialismo pagano*
(pp. 18–35) with the same section in *Heidnischer Imperialismus* (pp. 14–18).

[43] Evola, *Heidnischer Imperialismus*, p. 19.

By the time of the translation of his *Imperialismo pagano* into German, the overt form assumed by Evola's "mysteriosophic" notions were superficially rendered compatible with at least some of the public formulations of Hitler's National Socialism. Very much the same might be said of Evola's *Rivolta contro il mondo moderno*[44]—which appeared a year after the German translation of *Imperialismo pagano*.

At the time he published his *Imperialismo pagano*, Evola exploited the entire vocabulary of Fascism to cloak the features of his "Pythagorean" and hermetic Wisdom. It was all part of his effort to reveal the "transhistorical Wisdom" of what Evola had originally identified as the "Homeric and Hellenic . . . Mediterranean solar tradition" that in the German translation became the "Nordic- or Aryan-solar tradition." Evola seemed prepared to employ whatever his environment made available in an effort to convey the Wisdom of a "race of invisible and irresistible leaders" who, as "demi-gods . . . outside of space and time" were capable of accomplishing all things.[45] In his exaltation, it is clear that Evola considered neither Mussolini's Fascism nor Hitler's National Socialism as "true." They were to be used as conveyances for his "higher" purposes.

By 1934, with both *Imperialismo pagano* and *Heidnischer Imperialismus* behind him, Evola devoted himself entirely to conveying an account of the "supernatural, invisible and intangible forces" of "*primordial hyperborean Aryanism*"—the "source of the principles of true life," employing concepts familiar to National Socialists but almost entirely unknown to Mussolini's Fascism.[46] While he continued to employ the solar symbols and the deities of old, the bearers of light were no longer denizens of the Mediterranean. They had become generic "Nordic-Aryans"—a stock of primordial "Hyperboreans"—cosmic representatives of that "metaphysical Reality" that sustained the world. The existence of Hyperborea (or Ultima Thule) was a "superrational" conviction common among German mystics and occult racists certainly as early as the turn of the twentieth century.[47] It seems evident that Evola recognized that the concepts he chose to employ in the German translation would be familiar to his audience.

By the time he produced *Rivolta contro il mondo moderno* in 1934, all of Evola's culture creators had become, as descendents of Hyperboreans,

---

[44] Milan: Hoepli, 1934.

[45] Ibid., sec. 1.

[46] See ibid., pp. 21, 45–46, 66–72, 88–94, 243–60, 407–25.

[47] The range of German mysticism is reviewed in Louis Pauwels and Jacques Bergier, *The Morning of the Magicians* (New York: Avon, 1968). While the Germans were responsive, Evola complained that *Rivolta contro il mondo moderno* was entirely overlooked in Italy. Whatever the case, the book had nothing whatsoever to do with Fascism. See Evola, *Il cammino del cinabro*, p. 150.

generic "Aryans."[48] We are told that they originated, in primordial times, in Hyperborea—that fabled land presumably located in the artic regions. Over time, Evola informed his readers, the Hyperboreans migrated south, to remain for some indeterminate time in Atlantis—yet another fabled land—until its destruction prompted their further trek—in the course of which they created all the grand cultures of North and South America—including those of the Aztec and the Maya. In their migrations from east to west, they fashioned the historical cultures of East and South Asia—together with those of the Fertile Crescent and Egypt as well.[49]

By 1934, Evola was prepared to deliver himself of these accounts of vast migrations and culture creation without the least hesitation. He was distainful of the objections raised by "positivistic" historians—who insisted on physical "confirming evidence" for any of his omnibus claims. In fact, he was proud to reject the methodology of "modern" inquiry.[50] He was fond of repeating Laotze: "He who possesses the Truth does not discuss it; he who discusses it, does not possess it."[51] A sympathetic commentator characterizes the historiography of Evola's "Secret Wisdom" in the following fashion: "We must, for once, turn off the continual din of reason and listen with the 'ear of the heart' if we want to have the symbols strike responsive chords in ourselves." What we presumably have in Evola's account is "a timeless world lying beyond reason, prehistorical, and beyond history."[52] For Evola, "Truth" had an exclusively "celestial" origin and any demand for historical evidence or logical validation was not only profane and plebeian, but blasphemous as well.

Evola was convinced that there was nothing that could count as "objective" science. What there was, was a traditional "Wisdom," "superrational, superbiological and superindividual," infinitely superior to anything generated by empirical science—having nothing to do with the "mundane intellect and still less with the thin world of 'thinkers.' "[53] He argued that not only were all contemporary sciences predicated on sys-

[48] He regularly reminded his readers that the term "Aryan" had clear racial connotations. See, for example, Julius Evola, *La dottrina del risveglio* (Milan: Scheiwiller, 1942), p. 23, n. 2.

[49] Evola, *Rivolta contro il mondo moderno*, pt. 2, chaps. 4 and 5; and *Sintesi di dottrina della razza* (Milan: Hoepli, 1941), pp. 70–77. Chinese civilization may have originated among the Nordic-Aryan race as well. Evola cites the discovery of blonds among the earliest human remains in China. See *Rivolta contro il mondo moderno*, pp. 304–5.

[50] See the discussion in Titus Burckhardt, *Mirror of the Intellect: Essays on Traditional Science and Sacred Art* (Albany: State University of New York Press, 1999), pp. 68–74.

[51] Evola, *Rivolta contro il mondo moderno*, p. 9, n. 7.

[52] H. T. Hansen, Foreword to Evola, *The Hermetic Tradition: Symbols and Teachings of the Royal Art* (Rochester, Vt.: Inner Traditions, 1995), p. xii.

[53] Evola, *Sintesi di dottrina della razza*, p. 46.

tematic "materialistic"[54] presuppositions, with the individual sciences each based on fundamentally different assumptions, and therefore intrinsicably incommensurable, but he also held that there was "Hebraic" as distinct from "Aryan-Nordic" science.[55] Anyone who did not intuitively understand that was hopelessly and irretrievably impaired.[56] If there had ever been anything of Fascism in the thought of Evola, it had long since disappeared into the mists of "transrational Wisdom."

Evola's "supreme Wisdom" found expression in, and was exclusively recoverable through, those myths and symbols that positive science was content to treat only as primitive fantasies and distortions of half-remembered events. For Evola, myths and symbols contained the ineffable truths of human and superhuman history—revelatory of the most profound realities. Only if one were infilled with the proper physical and spiritual racial heritage—been initiated into the mysteries of "supernatural" and "supercorporeal" reality, and been suitably trained in esoteric ritual and ceremony—might one become privy to the most profound Truths of Evolian metaphysics.[57]

Evola's definitive statement of the racism that first found expression in his *Rivolta contro il mondo moderno* was fully articulated in his *Sintesi di dottrina della razza* that appeared seven years later, in 1941, and four years after the publication of his *Il mito del sangue*.[58] In that latter work, he provided a more or less synoptic rendering of the works of race theorists such as Joseph Arthur de Gobineau, H. S. Chamberlain, Georges Vacher de Lapouge, Ludwig Woltmann, and Hans F. K. Günther—to conclude with an entirely uncritical chapter on the racial notions of Adolf Hitler.[59] Evola treated all these individuals as dealing with a "materialistic," and hence entirely inadequate, inquiry into "truth."

The volume that followed in 1941, *Sintesi di dottrina della razza*, provides Evola's account of a theory of race he held to be both credible and revolutionary. It contained his views on "spiritual racism" and cosmic philosophy. Whatever else it was, it was a book that was neither Fascist

[54] *Ibid.,* p. 45.

[55] Julius Evola, "Andare avanti sul fronte razzista," *La difesa della razza* 4, no. 8 (20 February 1941), p. 19, and "Panorama razziale dell'Italia preromana," *La difesa della razza* 4, no 16 (20 June 1941), p. 9, reprinted in *La razze e il mito delle origini di Roma* (Monfalcone: Sentinella d'Italia, 1977).

[56] Evola, *Rivolta contro il mondo moderno,* pp. 7–12.

[57] Evola, *Sintesi di dottrina della razza,* pp. 148–50.

[58] Milan: Hoepli, 1937. That it was more "orthodox" than other of his works does not mean that *Il mito del sangue* did not contain a long exposition of Hyperborea and the "primordial Nordic-Aryan race." See chap. 7. It also contains suggestions concerning an "occult war" conducted by Jews against the modern Aryan nations. See chap. 9.

[59] Evola considered his exposition as entirely descriptive, serving his audience as an "objective" source of information. See Evola, *Il mito del sangue,* pp. 263–64.

nor National Socialist. Evola was a "believer" in neither.[60] For his own purposes, Evola used the book to introduce his views into both Fascist and National Socialist doctrine. In 1941, he was prepared to use, to the same ends, the views of Carl Schmitt—which had been insinuated into Italy via the increasingly intense discussions that collected around the concept "imperialism."

Schmitt's views, in general, were moderate. Evola used the occasion of the discussions initiated by Schmitt to attempt to envelop Fascist doctrine in a kind of mystical anti-intellectualism it had previously scant acknowledged. As has been indicated, Evola consistently imagined truth to be a "celestial and supermundane" product made available to humankind through a "superior and transcendent Tradition" embodied in myth and symbol, to be interpreted by initiates sensitized by occult ritual. He told his audience that initiatic science revealed the truth of racism to be superbiological, nondeterministic, and supernatural. He insisted that any subordinate truths that dealt with race as *physical*, were far from the "Truths" with which he was concerned. Such "material" or "positivistic" truths dealt with race in terms of inferior "natural" anthropological and genetic factors. It was that form of racism Evola disdained. He chose, rather, to point to "higher" forms: racism of the *soul*, and racism of the *spirit*. The "Truths" of that complex racism could be provided only by "Transcendent Wisdom." Privileged by his special access to the "Silent Wisdom of Tradition," Evola proceeded to outline the principal features of his comprehensive racism in his *Sintesi di dottrina della razza*.

The racism for which Evola made himself virtually the sole spokesman was a racism composed of special insights into human beings. Evola saw the human being as a complex entity composed of three elements: first, the corporeal body; the second, what Evola spoke of as the "racial soul"; and third, that of the "racial spirit."

Physical race corresponded, by and large, to that studied by physical anthropologists, biologists, and geneticists. Evola held their findings to be of meager interest and even less merit. The physical study of race was afflicted with all the cognitive impairments Evola attributed to modern empirical science. Anthropologists, biologists, and geneticists dealt with race as though races were "natural" phenomena. Worse still, modern ma-

---

[60] National Socialist authorities recognized as much. Evola was dismissed as a simple "anti-revolutionary reactionary" who identified himself with the "decadent nobility." SS officials saw no point in assisting him in any way, particularly because "Fascist officials rejected him." See Giorgio Galli, "Evola e la Germania national-socialista," in Mario Bernardi Guardi and Marco Rossi, eds., *Delle rovine e oltre* (Roma: Antonio Pellicani Editore, 1995), pp. 199–217.

terialists, Darwinists all, imagined that mankind had evolved from lower forms of life. All of which Evola held to be profoundly mistaken.[61]

Evola was prepared to concede that there was, in fact, hereditary transmission of certain physical properties that established the continuity of races (however defined by anthropologists). Such properties, however, were of peripheral importance and served largely as limiting conditions for the terrestrial activity of "spiritual races."

Whatever relationship they had with the material world, spiritual races had superterrestrial and transtemporal origins. The principal function of the material races, the races studied by physical anthropologists and geneticists, was to provide a medium through which the "superbiological" spiritual forces of the "transcendent" race would find expression. Equally clear was the conviction that only specific material races could serve in such capacity. Those were the races identified as "Aryan"—non-Jewish and apparently of "Hyperborean" extraction. Evola spoke of "Aryans" as "all the major indoeuropean races that shared a common Hyperborean element that traced its prehistoric origins to the Artic regions of the North."[62] Evola was convinced of the Hyperborean origins of most Europeans, the indigenous peoples of North and South America, as well as those of the Indian subcontinent—making it exceedingly difficult to identify his potential Aryan host races with any specificity.[63]

---

[61] Ibid., pp. 44–47, 51, 64, 92.

[62] Julius Evola, "Dell'Italia preromana," *Difesa della razza* 4, no. 16 (20 June 1941), p. 9. He specifically maintains "grave reservations" concerning the meaning attributed to the term "Aryan" in "certain modern racist ideologies." See Evola, *Rivolta contro il mondo moderno*, p. 302, n. 1.

[63] *Rivolta contro il mondo moderno*, pp. 81, 75. It is impossible to trace many of the citations to the English translation of the *Rivolta contro il mondo moderno*. In the English translation, some of the edge of Evola's racism is blunted. For example, on page 36 of *Revolt against the Modern World* (Rochester, Vt.: Inner Traditions International, 1995) there is simply talk of "pre-Aryan races" rather than "the black non-Aryan race" as it is found in the original Italian version (*Rivolta contro il mondo moderno*, p. 59). Similar instances recur throughout the translation. Instead of "the Nordic-Atlantic race" in the Italian edition (p. 252), for instance, we find "races of the second cycle" in the English translation (p. 195). "Nordic-Heroic" in the Italian (p. 344) becomes "heroic Aryan-Western" in English (p. 264) and the "Nordic-Aryan" becomes simply "Aryan." The "pure Aryan race" referred to in the Italian edition as originally of "Nordic stock" (p. 253) becomes a "first major group" in English (p. 197). None of these changes conceal the fundamentally racist character of the text, of course, but there seems to be a tendency to suppress its "Nordic" emphasis—as perhaps too reminiscent of National Socialism. (Compare, for example, pages 230 and 231 in the English to pages 302 and 303 in the Italian.) While Evola was clear about the relative insignificance of the physical attributes of race, he did acknowledge that the "original Hyperboreans," with which he was critically concerned, were probably "dolicocephalic (long-headed), tall and slender, blond, and blue-eyed." (Evola, *Sintesi di dottrina della razza*, p. 67). He seemed to identify them with the "pure Nordics" of National Socialist doctrine. In what seems to be a further attempt to dilute the racism, there is an alteration of the Italian

Evola held that the physical mixture of races, particularly between Aryans and races that were "alien" (i.e., non-Aryan), was always hazardous—but mixture between "related" races, under ill-defined circumstances, might produce hybrid vigor.[64] Given his generous notion of what constituted an Aryan race, those candidate races Evola considered to be truly "alien" were never really explicity cataloged—except in terms of Semites (although that proscription seems to have been restricted specifically to Jews) and the deeply pigmented peoples of sub-Saharan Africa.[65] What seemed eminently clear, for all the qualifiers, was that all the material races that Evola identified as capable of serving as hosts for the extrabiological and supernatural spiritual elements were purportedly biological descendants of the "Aryan-Nordics" of Hyperborea. Some of the Aryan peoples seem to have somehow become increasingly pigmented in the course of their migrations—distinguishing them from contemporary Nordics—but that was only incidental to Evola's account. Rather than their physical traits, he was more concerned with their properties of soul and of spirit.

Evola's discussion of the racial *soul* followed the account provided by the German writer Ludwig Ferdinand Clauss, author of a number of books on what Clauss variously called "racial character" or "racial soul."[66] Clauss's studies were "empirical" in the sense that they were

---

text where Evola speaks of the Jews as bearers of "a ferment of decomposition" (p. 314)—an Hitlerian phrase familiar to National Socialists. It appears in much milder form in the English translation (p. 242). In the Italian, Evola charges Jews with fostering anti-Traditional ideologies (p. 421 and n. 9)—all of which seems to disappear in the English version (p.324). A review by Ugoberto Alfassio Grimaldi di Bellino, "Ai margini di una polemica sulla validità di un esoterismo razzista," of Evola's work in *Civiltà fascista* 9, no. 10 (August 1942), pp. 647–52, excoriated Evola and his work, dismissing it as "pseudoscience," at best, and intrinsically anti-Fascist (see p. 652).

[64] Evola, *Sintesi di dottrina della razza*, p. 85.

[65] See Evola, "Psicologia criminale ebraica," *Difesa della razza* 2, no. 18 (20 July 1939), pp. 32–35. His specific objection to African Blacks is expressed in many places, but see, for example, *Sintesi di dottrina della razza*, pp. 74, 237. At times, Evola seemed to indicate, with qualifications as indicated, that "true Aryans" were blond, dolicocephalic, slender and tall—what National Socialist theorists identified as "Nordics." See *Sintesi di dottrina della razza*, pp. 67, 140–41. How different Evola's views on race were from those of other Fascist thinkers is made evident by statements that characterize many of them. In 1938, for example, in the same volume of *Difesa della razza* in which the Fascist "Racial Manifesto" appeared, Quinto Flavio could write, "Every people, every racial type, is, in one or another respect, a masterwork of creation, and can consider itself a chosen people. . . . The notion of election becomes . . . absurd and inhuman when it pretends to an *absolute* character. . . . It takes on the character of megalomania and makes little ethical sense." "Il razzismo e la pace," *Difesa della razza* 1, no. 3 (5 September 1938), p. 38.

[66] Ludwig Ferdinand Clauss, *Rasse und Seele: Eine Einführung in den Sinn der leiblichen Gestalt* (Berlin: Gutenberg, 1937); and *Rasse und Charakter* (Frankfurt am Main: Moritz Diesterweg, 1938).

based on some sort of systematic observation. He selected persons possessed of reasonably specific somatic racial traits and observed their behaviors in order to typify the various racial "souls" those behaviors exemplified.[67] Thus, in Clauss's judgment, Nordic man is driven by a racial necessity to "achieve," while Mediterraneans, not particularly serious, are dispositionally "histrionic." For Clauss these were the discernible properties of "soul (*Seele*)" to which Evola refers.

To carry the account further, Evola argued that in unmixed types, the "racial soul" somehow conforms to the overt somatotype. In some racial mixtures, however, the body and soul are disparate, incompatible. Thus, a "physical" Nordic may harbor a Mediterranean, or even a Hebrew, "soul."[68] Individuals of this kind, however much they may physically resemble their parent race, fail to comprehend, or be comprehended by, members of that parent community. "A boundary separates their souls, their manner of sensing and seeing is different and opposed to those who may share their outward racial traits. There exists the possibility of comprehension, and therefore of real solidarity, of profound unity, only where there exists a common 'race soul.' "[69] Thus, Jews, no matter how long resident in Italy, would still manifest those differences of soul that render them truly corrosive of the unity of the non-Jewish community.[70]

Evola explained that the "racial soul" was not that studied by modern psychology. Rather, Traditional Wisdom informs those who are adepts that the racial soul, identified as a *daemon* by the Ancients, is an entity in and of itself—a "subtle body, having its own proper existence, its own forces, its own laws, and its own heredity, distinct from those that are physiobiological."[71] Precisely how such an independent soul—which survives the material body at its death—worked together with the flesh was unclear, and Evola spent little time trying to relieve the obscurity. Those who possessed the "transcorporeal" properties necessary for full comprehension would duly understand.

Evola dismissed the notion that the study of the racial soul could be an empirical physiobiological or psychological inquiry. True knowledge could come only from the wisdom "adumbrated" in the cryptic myths, evanescent symbols, and obscure rituals we inherited from Hyperborean antiquity. Beyond the racial "soul," the "primordial Sacred Science" pro-

---

[67] See Clauss's discussion in *Rasse und Seele*, pt. 2.

[68] Evola, *Sintesi di dottrina della razza*, pp. 79–80, 119.

[69] Ibid., p. 119.

[70] See Evola, "Inquadramento del problema ebraico," *La vita italiana* 25, no. 293 (September 1937), pp. 266–72; and "Ebraismo distruttivo: Scienza, letteratura, musica," *La vita italiana* 26, 301 (April 1938), pp. 440–52.

[71] Evola, *Sintesi di dottrina della razza*, pp. 116, 118–19, 120.

vided insights into the "spirit" that, beyond body and soul, animated the races of humankind.[72] Beyond the body and soul of modern races, Evola addressed himself to what he considered its most important component: the transcendent cosmic *spirit* that infuses each individual at birth.

If Evola's treatment of the racial soul leaves one uncertain, his account of "racial spirit" seems even more opaque. Of the trinity of elements that make up the human being, the spirit is apparently an aspect of an *eternal race* that lives its eternal life in cycles.[73] In Evola's account, each such racial cycle has four "ages" or "epochs": golden, silver, bronze, and iron, each defined by virtue of the increasing degeneration of the initial "celestial race."[74]

In the golden age, the celestial race was spiritual—only gradually, over time, taking on material properties. The original celestials could command all the tangible and intangible forces of the cosmos—and left behind, as evidences of their presence, gigantic megalithic and pyramidal structures, which are still to be seen in Europe, in Egypt, on Easter Island, and in the high plateaus of South America. Where others have since discerned evidences of the "gods," traveling in flying saucers from distant galaxies to Earth, Evola perceives the faint footprints of the unadulterated celestial "super race."

At least part of the reason for the decline of that race was its mating with lesser creatures,[75] the fossils of which are produced by "positivistic" scientists in their efforts to establish the credibility of human ascent from lower forms of life.[76] Evola employs the fossils of primate humanoids to support his claims of the misalliance of the celestial race with those of lesser "animalistic" breed.

As a necessary consequence of miscegenation, there was a continual and irreversible decline of the celestials throughout ancient times,[77] a tenuous revival under the Romans, and another by the Nordic-Germans during the course of the Holy Roman Empire—but by the time of the Renaissance, with its humanism, rationalism, universalism and its gradual submission to the theses of the equality of all humans, humankind had reached *kali-yuga*, the terminal age of "obscurity," the end of this current

[72] See Evola, *La tradizione ermetica*, pp. 1–3.

[73] Evola, *Sintesi di dottrina della razza*, p. 153.

[74] See the discussion in Evola, *Rivolta contro il mondo moderno*, pt. 2, chaps. 1–7.

[75] See ibid., p. 285. Since the four ages followed the cosmic "laws" of *dharma*, it would seem that decline was fated, so that mismating could have only been the mechanism that produced the predetermined result.

[76] Ibid., pp. 233–37.

[77] Evola identifies the Jews as providing a "ferment of decomposition, dissolution and corruption" in antiquity; see Evola, *Sintesi di dottrina della razza* p. 160; *Rivolta contro il mondo moderno*, p. 314.

race cycle. For Evola, given the fateful path traversed by history, there remained only one course for contemporary humanity: an attempt at re-constitution of the primordial celestial race, amid the debris of previous race cycles, employing the racial remnants of the Hyperboreans.

While Evola was not sanguine concerning the prospects of that under-taking, he argued that some of the prevailing conditions might well foster such an outcome. First of all, he was convinced that the cosmic spirit governing the fate of races, under present world conditions, might well contribute to the enterprise.

Evola was prepared to accept some of the conclusions of the "positive" science of genetics, acknowledging the influence of the "materialistic" laws governing the Mendelian transmission of hereditary traits from par-ents to subsequent filial generations, but he was to make an emphatic point of what he called "idiovariations"—unpredictable genetic muta-tions in hereditary transmission between generations—to make a case for the influence, from "on high,"[78] of "superbiological" and "spiritual" forces in the shaping of races. For Evola, spiritual forces shaped races for their own inscrutable purposes.[79]

Geneticists, Evola argued, failed to provide a compelling account of how mutations occur. He maintained, as a consequence, that "the cause is to be found elsewhere, in the actions of a superbiological element not reducible to the determinism of the physical transmission of genetic mate-rials." The true cause of hereditary variation was to be found "rather by starting from another point of view that affords one an entirely different set of laws" than those of empirical science.[80]

Given that entirely unsupported supposition, Evola proceeded to argue that Fascism or National Socialism—with their heroism, their sacrificial and ascetic ethic, their authoritarian and hierarchical order, together with their appeal to myth and ritual—provided an environment compatible with the "spirit" of the celestials. That might be enough to prompt a cosmic, if gradual, reemergence of the celestial race. In such circum-stances, the formative spiritual principle that, in the ultimate analysis, governs the transcendent "superhistory" of humankind might literally re-constitute the individuals of the primordial creative race of Hyperborea. Evola sought to show that such an outcome would not be essentially de-

---

[78] See Evola, "La razza e la guerra: La concezione Ariana del combattere," *La difesa della razza* 3, no. 4 (20 December 1939), p. 34.

[79] The notion that mutations, governed from "on high," might be the source of raciation was a relatively common conviction among German esoterics. See Pauwels and Bergier, *The Morning of the Magicians*, pp. 400–5.

[80] Evola, *Sintesi di dottrina della razza*, p. 79; see pp. 77–79, and Evola, "Critica della teoria dell'eredità," *Regime fascista*, 13 December 1934, reprinted in *Diorama: Problemi dello spirito nell'etica fascista* (Rome: Europa, 1974), vol. 1, pp. 191–96.

termined by biology, but by the cosmic spirit —that its formative influence could transform individuals into persons accommodating a properly corresponding soul and spirit—to render them once again "pure."[81] None of this has anything to do with Fascism as a doctrine—except as a caricature.

In general, this was the "racial theory" Mussolini purportedly read, and of which he is said to have approved.[82] If there ever was such an approval, it clearly was significantly qualified. There is no doubt whatsoever that Mussolini, for a variety of reasons, objected to National Socialist race theory—and Evola's original statements, as early as 1935, expressed explicit opposition to its "materialism."[83] It was in that limited and specific sense that Mussolini, given that he had long since raised emphatic objections to what he identified at the time as "pan-Germanic racism,"[84] welcomed Evola's book.

It was evident that Mussolini had no intention of allowing National Socialist race theories, as such, to find a place in Fascist doctrine. Mussolini *never* identified Fascism with National Socialist racial theories—and Evola's book (apparently one of the very few of Evola's publications he had apparently read) served his purposes. To effectively serve that end, Mussolini permitted the publication of a translation of the *Sintesi* to appear in Germany with the title *Fundamentals of Fascist Race Theory*,[85] in what was clearly an effort to indicate that Fascism had its own distinctive views concerning the race issue—and they bore scant resemblance to those notions found in National Socialism. Within the covers of an easily available single publication, it would demonstrate to National Socialists that their preoccupations concerning Aryanism and anti-Semitism were being addressed by Fascism. Evola's pages were dotted with references to both issues—something that was not true of standard Fascist discussions of race.

By the mid-1930s, Fascist intellectuals had already articulated coherent and sophisticated conceptions of raciation and human evolution that many were prepared to identify as a "Fascist racial doctrine."[86] The formulations included a thesis of race formation that conceived endogamous

[81] Evola, *Sintesi di dottrina della razza*, p. 82.

[82] See the discussion in Evola, *il cammino del cinabro*, pp. 160–74 and the quotation reported in Gianfranco de Turris, *Omaggio a Julius Evola* (Rome: Volpe, 1973), p. 76.

[83] In the *Sintesi di dottrina della razza* (p. 17), Evola explicitly abjures "materialistic" racism, identifying it with "certain extremist racist tendencies from beyond the Alps."

[84] See the section entitled "Il pangermanismo teorico," in *Il Trentino veduto da un socialista (note e notizie)*, in Mussolini, *Oo*, vol. 33. pp. 157–61.

[85] Evola, *Grundrisse des Faschistichen Rassenlehre*, trans. by Annamarie Rasch (Berlin: Runge, 1943).

[86] See, for example, Giacomo Acerbo, *Fondamenti della dottrina fascista della razza* (Rome: Ministry of Popular Culture, 1940).

groups gradually taking on relatively uniform physical and perhaps psychological characteristics that would identify them as "neo-" or "mesodiacritic" races—as "races in formation." Such races in formation could be found, at various stages of development, in any community maintaining relatively strict endogamy over long periods of time. Geographically or politically isolated communities such as tribes, city-states, confederations, or nations might serve as just such "race-cradles." The group-building psychology—which Fascist thinkers identified with nationalism—would foster the entire, complex workings of population genetics that rendered endogamous communities "races in formation."[87] The entire conceptual framework that gave expression to what might legitimately be identified as "Fascist race theory" involved a process that had been early suggested by the generalizations of "protofascist" social scientists such as Ludwig Gumplowicz, Alfredo Niceforo, and Vilfredo Pareto.[88] In the years that followed, Fascist intellectuals built upon that foundation.

What "orthodox" Fascist race theory did not include were speculations concerning racial superiority and inferiority—nor did it characteristically include anti-Semitism—features prominent in Evola's work. Those were the features—not their mystical rationale—that made Evola's work eminently serviceable for Mussolini's political purposes.

The fact is that at the time of the publication of Evola's *Sintesi*, the most serious students of raciation and comparative psychology in Fascist Italy dismissed his ideas as "bizarre . . . occult anti-scientific fantasies."[89] Evola had early been identified by Fascist critics as a "lucid madman," who was not to be taken seriously. Even granted his tactical utility, it is difficult to entirely understand Mussolini's readiness to allow the publication of Evola's book in National Socialist Germany as a rendering of "Fascist" doctrine.[90]

Mussolini had a fairly sophisticated conception of science and epistemology. In the mid-1930s, he said, "If one understands by 'mysticism' the ability to apprehend truths *independent of intelligence*, I would be the first to declare my opposition."[91] He was clearly convinced that human

---

[87] For a more complete account of the orthodox version of Fascist race theory, see Gregor, *The Ideology of Fascism*, chap. 6.

[88] See ibid., chap. 2.

[89] Mario F. Canella, *Principi di psicologia razziale* (Florence: Sansoni, 1941), pp. 59, 61, n. 1, 203, n. 2. See the similar, but more intense criticism in the official Fascist monthly, *Civiltà fascista* 9, no. 10 (August 1942), pp. 647–52.

[90] For a more nuanced view of Evola's relationship with Mussolini, see Marco Rossi, "L'avanguardia che si fa tradizione: L'itinerario culturale di Julius Evola dal primo dopoguerra alla metà degli anni Trenta," in Guardi and Rossi, *Delle rovine e oltre*, pp. 37–120.

[91] Mussolini, as quoted in Yvon de Begnac, *Palazzo Venezia: Storia di un regime* (Rome: La Rocca, 1950), p. 186. Emphasis supplied.

beings, possessed of limited capabilities, found themselves compelled to labor assiduously to meet the most "rigorous of scientific and rational criteria" in their pursuit of truth.[92] There was, in fact, very little that could qualify as "mystical" or "transintellectual" in his political thought.[93] To say that he found something other than tactical utility in invoking Evola's work is most implausible.

It is evident that Mussolini was convinced that for the vast majority of those subject to rule, ritual affirmations, symbolic speech, mobilizing myths, and hyperbole served an evident and useful purpose. To foster and sustain conviction, inspire enterprise, and motivate effort, omnibus injunctions and dramatic exaggerations might well serve.[94] All that was recommended not because of mystic inspiration from "on high," but as a consequence of perfectly rational calculation.

It is clear, therefore, that Mussolini would not be averse to using "mystic musings" to foster political ends—without himself subscribing to mysticism. The problem then becomes one of attempting to determine what possible Fascist ends might be served by the official or semiofficial publication, with whatever qualifications, of the works of Evola.

The "orthodox" theory of race that had become a functional part of Fascist nationalism had simply accommodated itself to doctrine as doctrine developed in Italy through the late 1920s and early 1930s. By the mid-1930s, Mussolini was convinced that Fascism, as the senior of the two revolutionary movements that had appeared in Western Europe after the First World War, was required to take a position on the specific issue of race that had come to preoccupy all of Europe at the time. But more than that, the increasing interaction of German and Italian political, military, and intellectual representatives generated a number of problems that complicated the entire issue.

What Mussolini needed, as the military and political alliance between Fascist Italy and National Socialist Germany became more and more intimate, was an account of how Fascism dealt with the race issue that might placate Hitler and his followers. Mussolini was always mildly contemptuous of National Socialist race theory. He mocked all of its intellectual

<hr/>

[92] As cited ibid., p. 644.

[93] The "anti-intellectualism" of Fascism is generally misunderstood. See Gregor, *Giovanni Gentile*, chap. 3; and Gregor, *Ideology of Fascism*, chap. 5.

[94] See, for example, Mussolini's comments in de Begnac, *Palazzo Venezia*, p. 652; and Ludwig, *Colloqui con Mussolini*, pp. 119–20, 125. Roberto Michels gave a perfectly rational account of Fascist myth and invocation. See Roberto Michels, *First Lectures in Political Sociology* (New York: Harper, 1949), chaps. 6 and 8; and "Psychologie der antikapitalistische Massenbewegungen," in *Grundriss der Sozialökonomik* (Tübingen: Mohr, 1926), pt. 7; and Gregor, *Phoenix*, chaps. 3 and 4.

sources and insisted that a healthy nationalism had no need for the "delirium of racism" that afflicted his German counterparts beyond the Alps.[95]

By 1938, however, Mussolini sought to reduce any distance that separated him from his National Socialist allies.[96] Convinced since the very foundations of his movement that the "plutocracies"[97] would never allow Italy its sought-for "place in the sun," and given Italy's meager military capabilities, Mussolini believed that he had no option but to follow Germany into a conflict that he hoped would be of very short duration.[98] Under the circumstances, it became critical to reduce the ideological distance between the two regimes. Fascist race theory would have to speak to the issues of Aryans and Jews—something, until that time, that standard race theory in Mussolini's Italy did not do. Mussolini, by overtly addressing issues that were central to National Socialist thought, sought to have Hitler's Germany take Fascist Italy more seriously.[99] That would serve Fascism's immediate and general purposes.

As has been suggested, prior to 1938, Fascist criticism of National Socialist race theory was all but universal. As late as 1932, Mussolini himself dismissed National Socialist race theory as "hysterical." He was fully aware of the implications of Hitler's race theories: "they tended more or less explicitly to underline the superiority of the German race with respect to all the other races—including the Italian."[100]

As Italy moved closer and closer to military alliance with National Socialist Germany, the importance of an accommodating race theory increased in significance. In mid-1938, the "Manifesto of Fascist Racism"[101] was formally issued and was calculated to address all the tensions the alliance with a racist National Socialism had provoked. In itself, the Man-

---

[95] Mussolini, in Ludwig, *Colloqui con Mussolini*, pp. 71–72.

[96] See Andrew M. Canepa, "Mussolini's Racist Politics: Half-Hearted Cynicism," *Patterns of Prejudice* 13, no. 6 (November–December 1979), pp. 18–27.

[97] In 1919, Mussolini identified the "plutocracies" as England, France, and the United States. See Mussolini, "Il discorso," in *Oo*, vol. 14, pp. 30–31.

[98] See the account in De Felice, *Mussolini il duce: Lo Stato totalitario, 1936–1940* (Turin: Einaudi, 1996), note pp. 286–88.

[99] It is also recognized that, at the same time, Mussolini felt that some sort of racial legislation should be invoked in order to stop Italians from consorting with the native population of Ethiopia. Mussolini was convinced that such relations between Italians and the indigenous population would undermine the political security of Italian rule. The consequence was antimiscegenation legislation, which contributed to the evolving pro-racist intellectual environment. See the comments in Ciano, *Ciano's Hidden Diary, 1937–1938*, pp. 62, 141, and De Felice, *Storia degli ebrei italiani sotto il fascismo*, pp. 237–38, n. l.

[100] S. de Martino indicated that some ill-informed Italian intellectuals sought to "construct the Italian doctrine of race on the anti-Roman principles of Nordicists." Salvatore de Martino, *Lo spirito e la razza* (Rome: Signorelli, 1940), p. 183; and Renzo De Felice, *Mussolini il duce*, p. 595.

[101] A translation is available in Gregor, *The Ideology of Fascism*, app. A, pp. 383–86.

ifesto was a relatively inoffensive document, apparently largely the work of Mussolini himself.[102]

Long before political concerns prompted the official issuance of a peculiar sort of racial doctrine, Mussolini had used the characterization "Aryan" to identify Italians—and had often spoken of Italians as a "race" (*stirpe*), frequently using the terms "race" and "nation" interchangeably.[103] All of that was commonplace among intellectuals during the first four decades of the twentieth century. As had been indicated, what was notably absent from Mussolini's writings and speeches were expressions of "Aryan" racial superiority and ideological anti-Semitism.[104] Early in the history of Fascism, he asserted that "Italy has never known anti-Semitism, and I believe it never will."[105]

As has been indicated, until the middle of the 1930s, Mussolini rejected any form of official anti-Semitism. In fact, he advised Hitler to minimize his overt anti-Semitism on the grounds that it would create unnecessary repugnance on the part of foreign powers. Only with Hitler's refusal, and after the political and military circumstances of the late 1930s left Italy, in his judgment, no alternative but alliance with National Socialist Germany, did he decide to render the alliance "totalitarian" by adopting his own variant of official anti-Semitism.

The official "Manifesto of Fascist Racism" abjured any a priori distinctions of superiority and inferiority between races.[106] It spoke of major and minor races, geographic and local, each sharing some nonspecific constellation of heritable traits. While making clear distinctions between nationality and race, it did speak of an "Italian race"—alluding to an "historic race,"

[102] See Ciano, *Ciano's Hidden Diary, 1937–1938*, p. 136.

[103] See the interesting discussion "Genesi del razzismo fascista," in Enzo Leoni, *Mistica del razzismo fascista* (Varese: Tipografia Varese, 1941), pp. 19–27.

[104] Clearly, Mussolini touted the creativity of the "Italian race," but there is literally no evidence that he conceived that creativity to be biologically or genetically based. Mussolini, like Josef Stalin, entertained a form of vulgar anti-Semitism in private (see, for example, his comments in Ciano, *Ciano's Hidden Diary, 1937–1938*, pp. 9, 47, 75). The public anti-Semitic legislation he ultimately allowed after 1938 was to be used to "discriminate, not persecute." (See p. 137). Early in the regime, long before the alliance with National Socialist Germany, Mussolini spoke of "the great Jewish bankers," and their control of "world finance"—power they employed in supporting the rise of communism in an effort to exact "revenge against the Aryan race." (See Mussolini, "I complici," in *Oo*, vol. 13, pp. 169–70). A year later, however, Mussolini made it clear that he was convinced that "Bolshevism, as it is thought, is not a Jewish phenomenon" (Mussolini, "Ebrei, Bolshevismo, e Sionismo Italiano," in *Oo*, vol. 15, p. 269). During the last six hundred days of the Republic of Salò, he made references to the perfidy of Jews. Whatever the case, the notion that he ever considered their mass immolation can be confidently dismissed.

[105] Mussolini, "Ebrei, Bolscevismo e Sionismo Italiano," in *Oo*, vol. 15, p. 270.

[106] This was a position consistently held by Mussolini since his tenure, as a socialist, in Austria-Hungary before the First World War.

the product of a relatively long period of endogamy among members of a politically defined population on the Italic peninsula.[107]

The closing claims of the Manifesto were more clearly tactically political than scientific.[108] There was talk of "sharp distinctions" between Continental "Mediterraneans" and "Eastern and African Mediterraneans," with Italians entertaining an "Aryan-Nordic orientation" in order to foster a "normative ideal" indisputably "European."[109] The Jews were spoken of as unassimilable—and intermarriage between Jews and "Aryans," as well as between members of "non-European races" and "Aryans," were proscribed. Corresponding discriminatory legislation followed.[110]

It became evident almost immediately to the Fascist hierarchy that Italians, apparently in their majority, were uncomfortable with the new legislation.[111] Many Fascist intellectuals, represented at their best by Giovanni Gentile, found the legislation morally objectionable.[112]

However serviceable the anti-Semitic legislation may have been for Mussolini's tactical purposes, it was undertaken with bad conscience. It involved regulations manifestly different from those of National Socialist Germany. It was, for one thing, "more moderate and 'civil,' " allowing those Jews who had served in the Italian armed forces in any of Italy's wars in the twentieth century, together with their immediate families—as well as those who had been members of the Fascist party, together with their families—to escape discrimination.[113]

Nicola Caracciolo has written that "Italian society, more so than any other under the hegemony of the National Socialists (with the exception of Holland and Denmark), facing the prospect of their extermination, chose, as a community, to protect 'its' Jews."[114] That "protection" proceeded under Fascist auspices.

---

[107] That thesis was fully compatible with the "race theory" characteristic of Fascist doctrine. See Gregor, *The Ideology of Fascism*, chap. 6.

[108] That was specifically acknowledged by Fascist intellectuals, see Giuseppe Maggiore, *Razza e Fascismo* (Palermo: Agate, 1939). Maggiore's volume is among the more interesting expositions.

[109] Mussolini had already blamed social and political unrest in Ethiopia on social and sexual contact between the indigenous peoples and Italians. Prior to the "Manifesto of Fascist Racism," those contacts were increasingly proscribed by Fascist authorities.

[110] See the discussion in Antonio Banzi, "Documenti e legislazione," in *Razzismo fascista* (Palermo: Agate, 1939), pp. 209–69; Luciano Elmo, *La condizione giuridica degli ebrei in Italia* (Milan: Baldini e Castoldi, 1939).

[111] See the comments in Ciano, *Ciano's Hidden Diary, 1937–1938*, p. 151.

[112] Gregor, *Giovanni Gentile*, chap. 8.

[113] De Felice, *Gli ebrei italiani sotto il fascismo*, pp. 349–50. Because of the legal exceptions provided, about 20 percent of all Jewish-Italian families escaped virtually all discrimination. See Luigi Preti, *Impero fascista africani ed ebrei* (Milan: Mursia, 1968), pp. 154–58.

[114] Nicola Caracciolo, "Introduction," in *Gli ebrei e l'Italia durante la guerra, 1940–1945* (Rome: Bonacci, 1986), p. 17.

The form of anti-Semitism adopted by Fascist Italy, as a consequence, was singularly different from that of National Socialist Germany. However indecent, it shared few of the genocidal traits that have horrified the civilized world. Italian Jews suffered innumerable indignities and material losses, but there is scant, in any, evidence that between 1938 and 1943, any Jews died at the hands of Fascists simply for having been Jewish.

From 1938, when the first formal anti-Semitic legislation appeared in Italy, through 1943, Mussolini retained power over the disposition of Jews under Fascist control. As long as that remained unchanged, thousands of Jews, with Fascist assistance, escaped destruction at the hands of National Socialists.[115] Until July 1943, when, for all intents and purposes, Fascism collapsed, Mussolini—made increasingly aware of the National Socialist "final solution" to the Jewish question—communicated to Italian diplomatic, military, and police entities that not a single Jew in Italian occupied France, Croatia, Yugoslavia, Greece, Albania, or North Africa should be surrendered to National Socialist forces.[116]

All of this provides something of the context in which Fascist racism manifested itself. The original racism that had been intrinsic to Fascist doctrine was uniquely its own. It was a racism that entertained scant conviction in the superiority of one or another race.[117] Its subsequent anti-Semitism, after 1938, was to be temporary and was understood to be tactical. Even at its most vicious, during the last six hundred days of its existence, Fascism anticipated that anti-Semitism would persist only as long as the war in Europe continued.

In retrospect, and considered in context, it appears that Mussolini used Evola's *Sintesi di dottrina della razza* exclusively in an attempt to serve Fascism's tactical purposes. Nothing of Evola's exotic ruminations appeared in any official Fascist doctrinal pronouncements. Much the same

---

[115] In very many cases, Fascist authorities allowed, and frequently assisted, Jews to escape from Europe through Spanish ports on the Atlantic. Many Jews escaped German apprehension by traveling from North Africa, Greece, and Yugoslavia through Italian territory to ports of embarkation. See the account in Leon Poliakov and Jacques Sabille, *Gli ebrei sotto l'occupazione italiana* (Milan: Comunità, 1956). The most comprehensive book on the subject remains that of De Felice, *Storia degli ebrei italiani sotto il fascismo*. A convenient summary of the entire period can be found in Caracciolo, "Introduction," and Mario Toscano, "Gli ebrei in Italia e la politica antisemitica del fascismo" in Caracciolo, *Gli ebrei e l'Italia durante la guerra, 1940–1945*, pp. 17–34.

[116] The Fascist resistance caused extraordinary difficulties for the Italians. Nonetheless, it continued until Fascist Italy no longer controlled its own policies. See Renzo De Felice, "Preface" to Caracciolo, *Gli ebrei e l'Italia durante la guerra 1940–45*, pp. 8–9, and De Felice, *Gli ebrei italiani sotto il fascismo*, pp. 456–67.

[117] In September 1940, Mussolini affirmed, "races exist . . . that is an undeniable fact. There are no superior or inferior races." Mussolini, as cited, De Begnac, *Palazzo Venezia*, p. 642.

had been the case at the time of Mussolini's negotiations, concerning the proposed Concordat, with the Catholic Church. Evola's writings were to be used exclusively, as they had on that occasion, to serve Mussolini's tactical purposes and then be allowed to fade away.[118]

In dealing with National Socialist Germany, Mussolini needed a convenient, and well-publicized, expression that might persuade the Germans that Fascist Italy entertained "appropriate" racial views. Once again, Mussolini used Evola's writings for his own purposes. As has been indicated, he early decided that Evola was an hysteric—but that his views might serve to convey, to equally hysterical fanatics in National Socialist Germany, Fascism's seriousness of purpose.[119]

What seems evident is the fact that by 1941 Mussolini had every reason to seek to ingratiate himself to his German ally. By that time, the war had gone very badly for Fascist Italy. Singularly inferior to their opponents in terms of ground forces, airpower, armor, antiaircraft and antiarmor capabilities, the Fascist military had become almost abjectly dependent for their ultimate survival upon direct German support, transferred from the Continent to the Balkans and North Africa. Mussolini urgently needed something to convince the Germans that Fascist Italy was a serious ally. He employed Evola's volume to that end.[120] As has been indicated, Evola's *Sintesi* of 1941 was replete with references to "Aryan-Nordics" and their intrinsic superiority as well as to threats emanating from their "antithesis"—the Jews.[121]

Beyond that, it is not clear how carefully Mussolini read Evola's crabbed and vatic exposition. Given his convictions concerning race, anti-Semitism, and epistemology, it would be hard to imagine that his "recommendation" (if, in fact, one had actually been made) of Evola's works rested on any notion of the book's intrinsic merits. As suggested, the recommendation was more than likely prompted by transient and tactical considerations. From an "orthodox" Fascist perspective, almost everything was wrong with Evola's views.

---

[118] There are reports that some of Evola's publications were used in the political training schools of the Republic of Salò. Their titles have not been made available, and I have not been able to confirm any such use.

[119] In fact, there appears to have been but few members of the intellectual hierarchy of the National Socialist German Workers Party who found much cognitive merit in Evola's work. See H. T. Hansen, "A Short Introduction to Julius Evola," in Evola, *Revolt against the Modern World*, p. xviii. Evola sought to ally himself with the old German aristocracy. See Evola, *Il cammino del cinabro*, pp. 151–52.

[120] Throughout the period of increasing Fascist military defeats Mussolini became increasingly submissive to German influence. See the discussion in Renzo De Felice, *Mussolini l'alleato: Part 2. La guerra civile, 1943–1945* (Turin: Einaudi, 1997), passim.

[121] Evola, *Sintesi di dottrina della razza*, p. 172.

Evola clearly held Mussolini and Fascism to have been nothing other than a "hypnotic" side show that might be conveniently employed as a means of communicating the profound realities of a transcendent world to those capable of understanding.[122] It seems clear that throughout his life, Evola sought to use Fascism's instrumentalities to educate a truly "spiritual" elite who would undertake the restoration of the "Traditional" virtues of the ancient world. All that notwithstanding, by 1943 Mussolini's tactical decision to allow Evola to masquerade as a Fascist intellectual bore bitter consequences.

By that time, with the collapse of the Fascist military, the king had asked for Mussolini's resignation—and upon his refusal proceeded to depose and arrest him. Mussolini's rescue by German commandoes led to the tragic effort to reestablish a Fascist presence in the north of Italy. Under German auspices, Mussolini was installed as the head of the Fascist Social Republic of Salò.

As was to be fully expected, Evola maintained his distance. He rejected, in its entirety, the ideology of the Social Republic—and while he drew a stipend from the Fascist republican government, refused to reside within its political confines.[123] At the same time, he continued to identify himself with a number of marginal political persons, including Giovanni Preziosi, the spokesman for Italy's small coterie of committed anti-Semites, and Roberto Farinacci, an anti-Semite and an outspoken ally of National Socialist Germany[124]—all political and doctrinal opponents of Mussolini.

During the final six hundred days of republican Fascism, Evola remained in Rome until the city was threatened by imminent occupation by Allied forces. There, as he later affirmed, he worked not for Fascism, or National Socialism, but to create a political movement that, at the conclusion of the conflict then in progress, would continue the struggle against the "modern world." Neither Fascist nor National Socialist, Evola sought to create a movement that would labor for neither Fascism nor National Socialism—but for a "truly Traditional Right."[125] That was the political movement that survived the war. It had precious little to do with Fascism.

For the history of Fascist doctrine, it is of some significance that virtually all the intellectuals with whom Evola associated explicitly opposed Giovanni Gentile, both as a political figure and as the "philosopher of

[122] Ibid., p. 130.

[123] See Evola's comments on Fascist ideology in general, and that of the Republic of Salò in particular in Evola, *Il cammino del cinabro*, pp. 82–89, 175–76.

[124] See the account in Aldo Mola, "Giovanni Preziosi," in Fabio Andriola, ed., *Uomini e scelte della RSI: I protagonisti della Repubblica di Mussolini* (Foggia: Bastogi, 2000), pp. 157–78; and Gianfranco de Turris, "Un tradizionalista nella RSI: Julius Evola, 1943–1945," *Nuova storia contemporanea* 5, no. 2 (March–April 2001), pp. 79–86.

[125] Andriola, *Uomini e scelte della RSI*, pp. 175–76.

Fascism." As anti-Gentileans, Evola and those with whom he most readily identified rejected the humanism of Gentile's Actualism, as well as its moral opposition to anti-Semitism and biological racism.[126] Roberto Farinacci, Carlo Costamagna, and Preziosi were all anti-Actualists and anti-Semites.[127] All exercised some influence over developments during Fascism's end days in the Republic of Salò. One of the consequences was the creation of an intellectual and political environment that was to ultimately render Fascism complicit in the murder of Jews.

No longer in control of his government, Mussolini was compelled to accommodate political and doctrinal influences not of his choosing. As a result, the malevolence of Preziosi and Farinacci shaped something of the reality in which Jewish Italians found themselves. During the final days of Fascism, Jews suffered mounting indignities, and their circumstances became increasingly perilous. Their property was confiscated and they were collected in significant numbers by the Fascist Black Brigades to be surrendered to National Socialist forces in Italy—a consignment that was tantamount to a death sentence.[128] Renzo De Felice has written, "the RSI (*Repubblica sociale italiano*) assumed an official position with respect to the Jews that was different than that of the Germans. It was undoubtedly more humane, and distant from any idea of mass extermination. In practice, however, the RSI found itself compelled to tolerate and assist in the indiscriminate arrests, in the massacres, and the deportations undertaken by the Germans, often in violation of Italian law."[129]

Fascism's unhappy misalliance with National Socialism had culminated in those tragic consequences—but the way was facilitated by elevating Julius Evola to the totally unwarranted level of an intellectual "spokesman" for Fascism. He had early allied himself with those persons who

---

[126] See Gregor, *Giovanni Gentile*, chap. 8.

[127] After his first efforts to ingratiate himself with Gentile (see Stefano Arcella, "L'epistolario Evola-Gentile," *Futuro Presente* 3, no. 6 [Spring 1995], pp. 79–88), Evola became his dogged opponent. See, for example, his explicit rejection of "neo-Idealism," whose doctrines opposed "true racism." His most fundamental objections turned on the "rationalism" of Actualism (Evola, "Filosofia etica: Mistica del razzismo," *Difesa della razza* 4, no. 11 [5 April 1941], pp. 12–15). After the Second World War, Evola was very explicit in his objections (see Evola, "Gentile non è il nostro filosofo," *Minoranza* 2, nos. 5–7 [1 August–20 October 1959], pp. 22–27). Farinacci was both anti-Gentilean as well as expressly anti-Semitic (see Roberto Farinacci, *Realtà storiche* [Cremona: "Cremona nuova," 1939], pp. 81–169). It is interesting to note that other important Fascist anti-Semites were also anti-Gentilean (see Paolo Orano, *Il fascismo* [Rome: Pinciana, 1940], pp. 229–97; and *Gli ebrei in Italia* [Rome: Pinciana, 1938]). Carlo Costamagna, who provided Evola considerable space in his publication, *Lo stato*, was similarly opposed to Gentile (see Gregor, *Giovanni Gentile*, pp. 73–75), as well as a defender of a qualified form of racism (see Costamagna, *Dottrina del fascismo*, pp. 185–209).

[128] Responsible estimates put their number at about seven thousand.

[129] De Felice, *Gli ebrei italiani sotto il fascismo*, pp. 518–19.

would be instrumental in burdening Fascism with an ill-contrived and immoral racism and an equally repugnant anti-Semitism that violated almost every principle of integral nationalism, revolutionary syndicalism, corporativism, and Gentilean Actualism that had given form and substance to historic Fascism. Mussolini's tactical decision to reduce the ideological distance between Fascist Italy and National Socialist Germany through the employment of the work of Julius Evola was paid for at exorbitant cost.

CHAPTER TEN

Doctrinal Continuity and the
Fascist Social Republic

THROUGH ITS final years, Fascism struggled to survive in a whirlwind of destruction. With the devastating losses suffered on the Russian front and, after 1942, the loss of its African empire, dissent mounted throughout Fascist Italy. The war itself generated doctrinal cross-pressures that produced anomalies such as the emergence of the mysteriosophic racism of Julius Evola[1] together with the rise of a vicious Fascist intransigence.

Fascist Italy had entered the Second World War as an ally of National Socialist Germany in June 1940.[2] Almost from the very first day of its involvement, the war went badly. Ill-equipped and indifferently led, the Italian armed forces, in general, performed poorly.[3]

---

[1] There can no longer be any doubt of the anomalous nature of Evola's racism. His "mystic Traditionalism" was no more Fascist than it was National Socialist. National Socialists and Fascists alike did not take him seriously. See the discussion in H. T. Hansen, "Introduction: Julius Evola's Political Endeavors," in Julius Evola, *Men among the Ruins: Post-war Reflections of a Radical Traditionalist* (Rochester, Vt.: Inner Traditions, 2002), pp. 50–95.

[2] Mussolini had informed Hitler early in 1939 that because of its inadequacies and weapons shortfall, Italy was not prepared to enter into a sustained conflict against Great Britain and France before 1942. In August 1939, when it became evident that Hitler intended to invade Poland, Mussolini reaffirmed the inability of Italy to directly participate unless Germany could make available major resources. The Germans did not have the required supplies available, and Italy was charged with the responsibility of holding down the forces of France and Great Britain in the Mediterranean while Hitler "resolved" the problem of Poland. On 18 March 1940, Mussolini met Hitler at the Brenner Pass and committed Italy to entry into the conflict. The swift and successful German invasion of France gave the appearance that Fascist Italy entered the war only when the defeat of France was assured. Actually, Fascist Italy had committed itself months earlier.

[3] At the commencement of the Second World War, the military commanders of the Italian armed forces gave every evidence of incompetence. General Pietro Badoglio is reported to have said that battles "are fought with infantry, rifles, mules and some machine guns—but not too many machine guns." The Chief of the Army General Staff, General Alberto Pariani, held that "It is spirit that transforms an idea into conviction, and it is the spirit that makes faith of a conviction. And when there is faith, there is animating force for every undertaking." To which the Fascist, Luigi Federzoni, remarked, "Pariani is a person bereft of a sense of reality." Among the six hundred generals of the Italian armed forces (one general for every thirty-five officers) there was little talk of the availability of heavy equipment. War was a matter of "spirit." In 1940, its lack of artillery, antitank weaponry, heavy armor, aircraft of sufficient speed, range and armament, as well as the absence of antiaircraft capa-

At the end of 1941, in accordance with its treaty obligations, Fascist Italy declared war against the United States. The defeats that previously had been disheartening became catastrophic. The difficulties rapidly accumulated. In a desperate move, Mussolini urged Hitler, in the spring of 1943, to seek a separate peace with the Soviet Union in the effort to dispel the shadow of ultimate defeat that increasingly collected around the conduct of the war—only to be rebuffed. By the summer of 1943 all of Italian East and North Africa had been lost to Anglo-American arms—the defenses of the Italian offshore islands of Pantelleria and Lampedusa had been compromised and the territories occupied. Anglo-American forces had begun an invasion of the Continent through Sicily with the intention of proceeding upward into the heart of Europe through the peninsular corridor.[4]

Through July, the military situation continued to deteriorate. Anglo-American attacks on Italy increased in fury, and it was clear that enemy invasion threatened the survival of the nation. The members of the Grand Council of Fascism, led by Dino Grandi, proposed a meeting in which the situation would be reviewed. A session was fixed for the late afternoon of 24 July, at which time a proposal was submitted that urged Mussolini to invite the king, Vittorio Emmanuele III, to assume the responsibility of military leadership. Mussolini immediately intuited that such a request would be tantamount to a surrender of political power and the disintegration of his regime.[5]

In fact, with the Grand Council's approval of the Grandi proposals—equivalent to a vote of no confidence in Mussolini—the king requested that Mussolini step down. Marshall Pietro Badoglio, already groomed to assume the responsibilities of Head of the Government, did precisely that—and Mussolini was placed under arrest.

There was some sporadic reaction by individual Fascists, and Fascist groups, to what was seen to be a palace coup,[6] but by and large the trans-

---

bilities, clearly identified Fascist Italy as an inferior military power. That understood, Field Marshal Erwin Rommel, as well as the British commanders in Italian East Africa and El Alamein, testified to the courage and initiative of the individual Italian soldier. What the Italian military needed were the instruments of war. See Carlo De Biase, *L'Aquila d'oro: Storia dello stato maggiore italiano (1861–1945)* (Milan: Il Borghese, 1970), pp. 403–38.

[4] See Mussolini's discussion in *Storia di un anno*, in *Opera omnia* (Florence: La fenice, 1953–65. Hereafter *Oo*), vol. 34, pp. 305–44.

[5] See the account in Giorgio Pini and Duilio Susmel, *Mussolini: L'uomo e l'opera* (Florence: La fenice, 1963), vol. 4, chap. 5; as well as those in Ruggero Zangrandi, *1943: 25 Luglio 8 Settembre* (Milan: Feltrinelli, 1964); and Pino Romualdi, *Dossier: 25 Luglio 1943* (Rome: Ciarrapico, 1978).

[6] Manlio Morgagni, Director of "Stefani," the official information agency of the Fascist government, committed suicide upon being informed of Mussolini's dismissal. He wrote, "The unbearable pain of being an Italian and a Fascist has overwhelmed me. . . . For more

fer of power was effected without major political difficulties. Given the fact that the king and Badoglio announced that both Fascism and the war would duly continue, Fascists were uncertain as to what behaviors recommended themselves. As a consequence, there was great confusion. Mussolini, for "his own safety," was transported, under guard, to several different locales, to be finally deposited on a mountain site at Gran Sasso.

In retrospect, it is clear that the intention of the monarchy and its allies was that neither the war nor Fascism would continue. Almost immediately after the coup, the Badoglio government began secret negotiations with the representatives of the Anglo-American allies to arrange an armistice. On 8 September, the Badoglio government announced what was to be an unconditional surrender to the Allied forces. The entire Italian military collapsed, with commanders abandoning their troops in the field—and troops laying down their weapons in a disorderly scramble to return home.

Confused and uncertain, many in the military turned to their German allies for direction. Moved largely by patriotism, rather than Fascist commitments, many of those in the Italian armed forces, holding that the surrender of Italy to the allies was an unconscionable betrayal of trust, took up arms, under German leadership, against the Anglo-American invaders.[7]

At the same time, Fascists throughout the nation began to organize. Even before the announcement of the armistice on 8 September, young Fascists in Rome had begun initiatives against the "Badogliani" in the first attempts to reestablish a properly Fascist government. In Trieste, the offices of the Party were reopened. In Padua, Verona, Brescia, Perugia, and Ancona, similar efforts were undertaken.

On 12 September, Mussolini was liberated from Italian custody by German special operations units. There is every indication that Mussolini, physically and morally exhausted, sought nothing more than to be allowed to disappear into history.[8] Equally evident was the fact that Italy's German allies had absolutely no intention of allowing that to happen.

Adolf Hitler had decided that a committed Fascist Italy was necessary if the conduct of the war was not to be impaired.[9] On the fourteenth, Hitler, with almost his entire General Staff, met a thin and tragically distracted Mussolini in order to inform him that he was to assume command of a restored Fascist government—the ally of National Socialist Ger-

---

than thirty years you, Duce, have received all of my fidelity. My life was yours. I ask for your forgiveness if I depart." Giorgio Bocca, *La repubblica di Mussolini* (Rome: Laterza, 1977), p. 3.

[7] The SS division "Italia" was subsequently organized to host over ten thousand Italian volunteers.

[8] See Renzo De Felice, *Mussolini l'alleato: Part 2* (Turin: Einaudi, 1997), chap. 1.

[9] The German military was equally convinced that it would serve their cause better if Italy were simply occupied. A Fascist government would limit Germany's freedom of operation.

many—in a war that clearly threatened to destroy them all. On the fifteenth, the dialogue continued—with Mussolini fully aware, by that time, that he was there to attempt to placate the leaders of a powerful and vengeful army that occupied all of Italy north of Rome. No one, least of all Mussolini, believed that the Axis powers could win the conflict then in what was clearly its final phase. The real question for Mussolini was, how might Fascism most credibly conclude its historic parabola?[10]

Required by circumstances to attempt to revive Fascism, Mussolini immediately made clear what his intentions concerning such a reborn Fascism were to be. On the eighteenth, in a broadcast from Munich to the Italian people, Mussolini announced the formation of a provisional Fascist government that would return Italy to the side of its German ally. The armed forces of the nation were to be reconstituted. Perhaps more surprising still, he announced that Fascist Italy, irrespective of the difficult times it was to traverse, intended to pursue the course of social revolution it had initiated on its succession to rule in 1922. Fascists would diminish the influence of domestic "plutocratic" elements—the major Italian industrial and financial agents—in the process.

Mussolini argued that the "plutocratic bourgeoisie," together with the monarchy and some elements in the military, had compromised not only the conduct of the war, but Fascism's revolutionary course as well. With the suppression of the monarchy together with some of the major leaders of industry and their allies, Fascism intended to make labor the "infrangible foundation of the state."[11] There was no longer time for circumspection. Fascism would pursue its social revolution.

In the existing environment, and given the obligations he had assumed, Mussolini's position was eminently clear. Fascism had been encumbered by a variety of extraneous elements. "Bourgeois" conservatives had impaired the evolutionary development of corporativism. The abiding concern for the rapid industrialization of the peninsula had counseled caution in the past. The time for caution had passed.

Together with all that, the increasingly intense relationship with Hitler's Germany fostered a penetration of a form of racism into Fascism that was completely extraneous to its ideology. The anti-Semitism and the

---

[10] Giovanni Dolfin, Mussolini's director of his Secretariat, in daily contact for much of the final six hundred days, maintained that Mussolini never "appeared concerned with his own life. He never considered death as the most grievous of evils." Mussolini outlined his concerns (1) for Italy's very survival as an essentially unarmed dependent, incapable of defending itself, and (2) the entire loss of its revolutionary heritage. Giovanni Dolfin, *Con Mussolini nella tragedia: Diario del Capo della Segreteria Particolare del Duce, 1943–1944* (Cernuseo sul Naviglio: Garzanti, 1949), pp. viii, 26–27, 54–55, 118–21, passim. See Ermanno Amicucci, *I 600 giorni di Mussolini* (Rome: Faro, 1949), chap. 11.

[11] Mussolini, "Il primo discorso dopo la liberazione," in *Oo*, vol. 32, pp. 4–5.

initiatic racism of Evola had distorted the ideology of Fascism to the extent that its foremost exponents, like Giovanni Gentile, Sergio Panunzio, Ugo Spirito, and Camillo Pellizzi, had been, for the most part, alienated.

Tragically, there was no possibility that Fascism could abjure the alien elements of racism that had collected around it. Given his abject dependence on National Socialist Germany, Mussolini could do very little more than he did. He acted to contain its worse excesses. Even though what he did manage was, at best, immoral and cruel, the racism of Fascism's final years was something substantially different from that of Hitler's "final solution."[12]

In that doleful mix, nothing of Evola's mystic racism survived, and very little of the fanatic anti-Semitism of Giovanni Preziosi was permitted to act out its savagery. Jews were harassed and defamed and their property pillaged, but Hitler's "final solution" exacted its victims (numbering about seven thousand)[13] only over and against persistent Fascist obstruction.[14]

It was within this evolving tragedy that Mussolini sought to create a republican Fascism that would not only attempt to defend the nation from Anglo-American invasion, but would pursue, as well, the revolutionary ends that inspired and informed it throughout its history. Mussolini's first task was to engage those prepared to serve in what was, at best, a government involved in a devastatingly one-sided conflict. It would be a government without the traditional support of the familiar monarchy—threatened with destruction from an irresistible enemy from without, opposed with arms by domestic enemies from within, and constrained by the presence of an "ally" that was ill-disposed, vengeful, and suspicious. The reconstitution of the military, in the course of a war that was going very badly, was itself an unforgiving task. Reorganizing and controlling the members of a wrathful reborn Fascism was perhaps more difficult still.[15]

[12] See the account of the Fascist treatment of the "Jewish question" during the Repubblica sociale italiano, 1943–1945, provided by Renzo De Felice, *Storia degli ebrei italiani sotto il fascismo* new enlarged Ed. (Turin: Einaudi, 1993), pp. 446–86.

[13] Fascists were complicit in the murder of Jews to the extent that Italian Jews had been herded into camps where SS troops might retrieve them. Italians were under orders not to release Italian Jews to their tormentors—but eventually German orders prevailed. For a discussion of the camps under Fascist control see the personal memoirs of Salim Diamand, *Dottore! Internment in Italy, 1940–1945* (London: Mosaic Press, 1987).

[14] For a general discussion of Fascist racism, see A. James Gregor, *Giovanni Gentile: Philosopher of Fascism* (New Brunswick, N.J.: Transaction, 2001), chap. 8; and Gregor, *The Ideology of Fascism: The Rationale of Totalitarianism* (New York: Free Press, 1969), chap. 6.

[15] There are several excellent sources for this period. See F. W. Deakin, *The Brutal Friendship: Mussolini, Hitler and the Fall of Italian Fascism* (New York: Harper and Row, 1962); and Renzo De Felice, *Mussolini l'alleato: Part 2.*

As soon as the new Fascist republican government was established in Northern Italy, the bureaucracy,[16] the technical intelligentsia, the clerical and communications technicians, the engineers and designers, the supervisors and educators, made themselves available, in very substantial numbers. In the North, scientists and instructors remained at their posts. Few explicitly identified with the new government and few inscribed themselves in the new Partito fascista repubblicano, but very many of those who had devoted their lives to the nation's working institutions never seriously considered abandoning their posts.[17]

Those traditionally considered "intellectuals"—the scholars, literary figures, artists, and journalists—also made themselves available, in substantial measure, as well. Notable figures, like Filippo Tommaso Marinetti, the founder of twentieth-century Futurism, together with many of his followers, directly or indirectly became involved with the new Fascist government. They were joined by some of the foremost architects and artists of Italy.[18] Internationally famous intellectuals like Giovanni Gentile, Ardengo Soffici, and Ezra Pound assumed official obligations in the new system. Many, like Giovanni Papini and Gioacchino Volpe, while not officially enlisted in either the party or in specific public service, clearly favored the new government.[19] Sergio Panunzio, active during the first years of the war, already afflicted with his last illness at the time of the armistice of 8 September 1943, died in early October 1944.

Many of the ministers and subsecretaries of ministries of the regime through July 1943 adhered to the emerging Fascist government, officially identified as the "Italian Social Republic" (La repubblica sociale italiano [RSI]). Some of the most prominent ministers of the old regime, having been involved in the 24–25 July meeting of the Fascist Grand Council and the subsequent coup, disappeared. Others, important and politically untarnished, together with still others who were marginal figures, made their appearance, either as extensions of German influence—like Roberto

---

[16] See a typical statement in Vito Saracista, *Con la Repubblica sociale italiana al servizio del paese* (Milan: Cerea Manara, 1950), chap. 1.

[17] See the fuller account in De Felice, *Mussolini l'alleato: Part 2*; chap. 3.

[18] See Carlo Fabrizio Carli, "Filippo Tommaso Marinetti: Destini italiani: Artisti in RSI," in Fabio Andriola, ed., *Uomini e scelte della RSI: I protagonisti della Repubblica di Mussolini* (Foggia: Bastogi, 2000), pp. 227–33.

[19] Some of the most prominent Fascist intellectuals died before a decision had to be made concerning adherence to the new government. Enrico Corradini had died in December 1931, A. O. Olivetti in November 1931, Alfredo Rocco in August 1935, Roberto Michels in May 1936, and Sergio Panunzio in October 1944. Ugo Spirito had distanced himself before the advent of the Second World War, but as late as 1941 defended Italy's participation on what he held to be a "revolutionary war." See Danilo Breschi, "Guerra rivoluzionaria," *Mondo Operaio*, no. 6 (November–December 2002), pp. 177–83.

Farinacci, Giovanni Preziosi, and Julius Evola—or as advocates of non-Fascist aspirations—like Edmondo Cione, the democratic socialist; Nicola Bombacci, the heretical Marxist; and Vittorio Rolando Ricci, the conservative liberal.[20]

However disheartened he may have been, Mussolini undertook the creation of the new Fascist republican state with almost frenzied application.[21] While it is manifestly evident that his foremost intention was the protection of the peninsula and its population from Anglo-American and German predation, equally clear —recognizing that the war was lost— was his concern with leaving behind a doctrinal and institutional legacy of his rule. Against very firm German opposition, Mussolini embarked upon a revolutionary program of "socializing" the Italian economy. In the midst of a war the imminent loss of which loomed ominously over everyone, and against the resistance of his only ally, Mussolini committed himself and the Fascist Republican Party to the socialization of Italian industry and agriculture.

Many factors influenced that decision. Mussolini was convinced that the "bourgeoisie," Italian financial and business interests, allied with the Catholic Church and the monarchy, had undermined the regime, impaired its war effort, and thwarted its social and economic programs.[22] What did *not* appear to influence his decision was a simple desire to remain in power. His resumption of leadership was insisted upon by Hitler—and his position was secured by German arms. He was in power and would remain in power—whether he or anyone else did, or did not, like it—as long as the Germans dominated the scene. From the very moment of his return to the leadership of the Fascist Social Republic, it was absolutely

---

[20] See Edmondo Cione, *Storia della Repubblica Sociale Italiana* (Casterta, "Il Cenacolo," 1948); Guglielmo Salotti, *Nicola Bombacci da Mosca a Salò* (Rome: Bonacci, 1986) and Guglielmo Salotti, "Nicola Bombacci," in Andriola, *Uomini e scelte della RSI*, pp. 235–46; Franco Franchi, *Le costituzioni della Repubblica Sociale Italiana: Vittorio Rolandi Ricci il "Socrate" di Mussolini* (Milan: Sugar, 1987); and Fabio Torriero, "Vittorio Rolandi Ricci," in Andriola, *Uomini e scelte della RSI*, pp. 209–16. The Andriola collection addresses itself to the motivations of these major figures. Clearly there were many whose motivations were venal, but among the major actors their behavior was largely inspired by a defense of country and its honor.

[21] The Germans, who occupied virtually all of Italy not under Allied control, made it clear that unless a Fascist authority could be reestablished, and Italy were an ally, its population and resources, at the very best, would be treated as booty. As early as 24 September, only twelve days after his liberation by the Germans, Mussolini could announce that a Fascist republican government had been formed. By 3 October, all the ministries were in place. See the account to be found in Pini and Susmel, *Mussolini, l'uomo e l'opera*, vol. 4, chap. 6 and p. 334 together with that of De Felice, *Mussolini l'alleato: Part 2*, chap. 4, see also p. 373, n. 1.

[22] See Mussolini's own discussion in *Storia di un anno (Il tempo del bastone e della carota)*, in Oo, vol. 34, pp. 339, 345, 410–11 and Amicucci, *I 600 giorni di Mussolini*, p. 143.

clear that he would remain in power as long as Germany controlled what remained of the Italian peninsula. Whatever the appearances and whatever the judgments of those inflexibly opposed, there can be little doubt that, within the tragedy that was unfolding, Mussolini sought to achieve the "logical" conclusion of the social and economic program he had initiated in 1919—as a legacy to those who would succeed him.[23]

During the first weeks of November 1943, the newly reconstituted Fascist Republican Party held its first assembly in Verona—and formulated the initial statement of its provisional program for the reconstituted "Social Republic."[24] With the guidance of Mussolini, ten of the eighteen points of the program were dedicated to the completion of the social and economic revolution commenced with the March on Rome in 1922.[25] The point was made that "manual, technical and intellectual labor in every form" was to constitute the "basis of the Social Republic." While private property was to be "guaranteed by the state," it was affirmed that property would not be allowed to "undermine the physical and moral personality" of citizens through exploitation or alienation. Workers and technicians would participate in decisions concerning "the fair apportioning of wages and the distribution of profits." More than that, it was clearly intimated, in the course of the exposition, that the existing leadership of industry might be displaced by some form of workers' councils.[26]

The Verona program suggested the full participation of labor in the management of industry and the economy in general. The subsequent elaboration of the program was the product of the collaborative effort of a number of persons—but primarily Mussolini and Nicola Bombacci, the intellectually independent revolutionary compatriot of his youth.

Mussolini and Bombacci had been prominent figures in the socialist movement in the years before the First World War, and Bombacci was subsequently to go on to serve as cofounder of the Italian Communist party.[27] Bombacci was only one of the number of revolutionary socialists

[23] See Mussolini, "Ventennale sviluppo logico della dottrina fascista," in *Oo*, vol. 32, pp. 316–18.

[24] Mussolini was disposed to call it the "Socialist" Republic, others the "Proletarian" Republic, but finally the republic was identified as the "Social" Republic in order to satisfy the sensibilities of some Fascists. See Dolfin, *Con Mussolini nella tragedia*, pp. 55, 118.

[25] An English language translation of the Program of Verona is available in Gregor, *The Ideology of Fascism*, pp. 387–91.

[26] For the original Italian, see "Il 'Manifesto' di Verona," in Bruno Spampanato, *Contromemoriale: L'ultimo Mussolini* (Rome: Poligrafica italiana, n.d.), vol. 2, pp. 441–43. See the comments of Roberto Bonini, *La repubblica sociale italiana e la socializzazione delle imprese dopo il codice civile del 1942* (Turin: G. Giappichelli, 1993), p. 15.

[27] See De Felice, *Mussolini l'alleato, Part 2*, p. 539, n. 1; and Guglielmo Salotti. "Nicola Bombacci," in Andriola, *Uomini e scelte della RSI*, p. 240.

who entered the ranks of republican Fascism, in 1943, to cooperate with Mussolini during Fascism's last fateful six hundred days.

Like many revolutionary socialists, Bombacci saw Fascism as the redemption of a flawed Marxism that failed to appreciate the role of nationalist sentiment in the mobilization of masses. He argued that the Marxist canon did not seem to appreciate the psychosocial impact of the pretensions of the advanced industrial powers on those communities languishing in underdevelopment. He clearly appreciated the psychology of peoples confined to circumstances of retarded industrialization. They were "proletarian peoples," and "proletarian nations," in arduous conflict with those peoples and nations that were "bourgeois." Like many of the national syndicalists, Bombacci early reflected on the inability of Marxism, as a theoretical system, to answer any of the major concerns of less-developed economies in the competitive and dangerous modern world.

Bombacci, like many Marxists before him, and "left-wing" revolutionaries of the interwar years, saw Fascism as a credible answer to many of the problems of orthodox socialism[28]—as the world-historical resolution of many of the problems of "proletarian nations," rather than those of an uncertain, and historically fanciful "proletarian class."[29] Bombacci saw in the relationship between the "plutocratic" and "proletarian" *nations* of the post–World War One era the same relationship that Marx hypothesized with respect to the proletarian and bourgois *classes*.

In the anticipated Social Republic, both Bombacci and Mussolini saw the culmination of the revolutionary process commenced in 1919 with the foundation of revolutionary Fascism. On 13 January 1944, the republican Council of Ministers approved the "fundamental premises for the creation of a new structure for the Italian economy."[30] On the foundation of the Labor Charter of 1927, the decree-legislation of 13 January 1944 addressed itself to the socialization of all the nation's productive establishments.

The "fundamental premise" of the new economy was its "socialization." The state was to assume management and control over all enterprises essential to the nation's economic independence: raw materials and energy supplies, for example, criticial to industrial growth and stability. Becoming agencies in public law, the capital of the socialized establishments would be transferred to a single *Istituto di gestione e finanziamento* (Institute of Management and Finance)—an institute that would absorb the functions of the Istituto mobiliare italiano (established in 1931), and the Istituto di

---

[28] See the insightful discussion of Zeev Sternhell, *Neither Right nor Left: Fascist Ideology in France* (Berkeley and Los Angeles: University of Californa Press, 1986).

[29] See Salotti, *Nicola Bombacci da Mosca a Salò*, pp. 139–49.

[30] "Premesse fondamentale per la creazione della nuova struttura dell'economia italiana," in De Felice, *Autobiografia del fascismo: Antologia di tesi fascisti, 1919–1945*, pp. 480–81.

ricostruzione industriale (established in 1933), created during the Great Depression to provide financial assistance and long-term financing to those sectors of the economy that had suffered most grievously.

The owners of the capital of those nationalized firms, whose management and control passed to the state through the Istituto di gestione e finanziamento, would receive the value of their capital in the form of state credits that were interest bearing and fully negotiable. Management and control, while passing to the state, would be effectuated through councils of management, elected by all workers—simple and skilled laborers, technicians, and clerical workers. The responsibilities of such a council would be to deliberate all issues inherent in maintaining and enhancing production within the parameters of the "unitary national plan formulated by the competent organs of the Social Republic."

The enterprise councils of state firms would determine wages by having individual firms contract with labor associations covering entire sectors. Firms that remained in private hands, employing at least fifty workers, would be socialized by creating an administrative council, charged with management, composed of both workers and the representatives of stock owners in equal number. In establishments that remained privately owned, the owner, who performed productive technical and/or managerial tasks, would assume, as director, political and juridical responsibilities to the state for the maintenance of production and enterprise discipline. Failing to perform, an owner could be divested of his position. The issue of successful enterprise management and control might be raised by the enterprise councils of either state-owned or privately owned firms. The state would then nominate a successor, with the Istituto di gestione e finanziamento assuring professional (and presumably political) suitability. Workers' councils would then either accept a new director or subject him to the scrutiny that displaced his predecessor.

The Council of Ministers of the Social Republic expected that the details of the new economic structure would be subject to scrutiny and refinement through a series of individual pieces of legislation. A great deal of proposed legislation was generated— some of it abandoned in course—particularly a projected program of reconstruction of the provincial and national corporative organs that would interface with enterprise workers' council and discharge information gathering, control, and consultative functions in formulating the republic's economic plans.[31] The projected legislation was considered far too cumbersone to undertake in the circumstances that prevailed during the first months of 1944, but it made clear what the ultimate configuration of the Social Republic was anticipated to be.

---

[31] "Schema di decreto legislativo concernente la istituzione degli organi corporativi," in Bonini, *La Repubblica sociale italiana*, pp. 347–60.

Because the structure of the "new corporativism" anticipated that socialization included only workers, managers, and technicians per se, there was no longer any institutional reason to maintain two separate national confederations, one reserved for workers and the other for owners of industrial plant and financial institutions—as though some fundamental "class" interests distinguished them. Under the conditions stipulated in the legislation governing socialization, only those employers who functioned as technicians or administrators might serve in the councils of management—to count as "workers." As Ugo Spirito had anticipated in his presentation in Ferrara in 1932, it would no longer be necessary to institutionalize the difference between "workers" and "owners." Two national confederations were no longer necessary, one that included only "workers," and the other only "owners" of property, plant, and financial agencies.

Already addressed in the "provisional program of the Manifesto of Verona" (in para. 16), and presented in Decree legislation (no. 853) on 20 December 1944, a single national confederation was proposed—identified as the Confederazione generale del lavoro, della tecnica e delle arti (General Confederation of Labor, Technology and the Arts), that would end "the dualistic system" that had prevailed in the past—to be exploited for their own purposes by the owners of large enterprise and financial institutions. Together with all that, it was made evident that the political control of the new unitary confederation would "devolve," in the last analysis, upon the leadership of the Partito fascista repubblicano, while the ultimate technical and administrative national control would be that of the Minister of the Corporative Economy.[32]

The rationale advanced to support the new legislation addressed itself to precedent doctrinal and legislative enactments that had early intimated just such an ultimate socialization of the nation's means of production. It was affirmed that as early as 20 March 1919, for example, Mussolini had addressed the workers of Dalmine and insisted that they, the direct producers, were to be the equal of the owners and managers of industry.[33] On 9 October, that same year, Mussolini spoke at the first national assembly of Fascists in Florence, where part of the preliminary party program read that Fascism ultimately intended to have "workers representatives as members of the technical and administrative management of indus-

[32] See "La costituzione della Confederazione general del lavoro, della technica e delle arti (Decr. del Duce 20 dicembre 1943, n. 853) and its accompanying political and juridical rationale, in Bonini, *La Repubblica sociale italiana*, pp. 216–17.

[33] See the full account of the decree-legislation in Bruno Spampanato, *Contromemoriale*, vol. 2, pp. 452–54. The entire speech is contained in Mussolini, "Discorso di Dalmine," in *Oo*, vol. 12, pp. 314–16. See the comments of the Minister of Corporations under the Fascist republican government. Angelo Tarchi, *Teste dure* (Milan: S.E.L.C, 1967), pp. 114–16.

try."[34] On that occasion, Mussolini warned his audience that, confronted as Italy was by the Western plutocracies, the promised direct participation of labor into the managerial and directive processes of industry would necessarily entail an extended period—in order not to disrupt the rapid development of the nation's industries—necessary for national defense.[35]

In April 1927, the Charter of Labor was promulgated, containing the premises of the anticipated corporative economy. In the preambulatory work leading to the actual formulation of the Charter, Italians were reminded that given the world situation, with the nation facing increasing foreign challenge, nothing could be undertaken that would threaten the nation's steady industrial growth or competitiveness. At the same time, labor organizations became public institutions in anticipation of their consultative participation in the governance of industry. There was no anticipation that workers' organizations would immediately and entirely substitute themselves for the existing leadership of industry—since it was held that such a change, at that time, would threaten the drive to maximize the nation's productivity.[36] The national interests required economic and industrial discipline—through collaboration, social welfare initiatives, and legal parity among all the elements of production, if Italy were to successfully compete with the advanced industrial powers.[37] The direct participation of labor organizations in the govenance of industry would be gradually accomplished only as circumstances allowed.

The anticipated process was interrupted by the advent of the Great Depression of the 1930s, into which Italy was inextricably drawn. The economic crisis precipitated Mussolini's decision to embark on the effort to create a "living space" for the nation—a space that would allow Italy to develop in relative autarky, substantially free from the constraints of being resource dependent in a world dominated by the advanced industrial powers.

In the early 1930s, Mussolini addressed all these issues. At the same time, he continued his general program for involving Italian workers in

---

[34] Mussolini, "Ventennale sviluppo logico," in *Oo*, vol. 32, p. 317.

[35] Mussolini, "I diritti della vittoria," in *Oo*, vol. 14, p. 53. Mussolini always argued that while political revolution might be undertaken very quickly, economic change necessarily would involve an extended period of time.

[36] Mussolini made his thinking public in that regard. He held that the Bolsheviks, with their untimely experiments, had destroyed their economy and brought ruin and death on Russians. See, for example, Mussolini, "Posizioni," "Non subiamo violenze!" in *Oo*, vol. 13, pp. 29, 65; "La fine di una illusione," "Alla moda Russa?" in *Oo*, vol. 15, pp. 97–99, 178–81.

[37] See the entire discussion in Giuseppe Bottai, *La Carta del lavoro* (Rome: "Diritto del lavoro," 1928), pp. 21–39. See Mussolini's comments on the critical role of increasing productivity in order to compete with the advanced industrial powers. See, for example, Musso-

the processes of production. He called for workers to "enter more and more intimately into the productive process" because it had become clear that while "the past century was the century of capitalist power, the twentieth century would be the century of the power and glory of labor."[38] Concurrently, he began to speak more insistently of the economic independence of Italy—of the necessity of providing "a maximum degree of economic independence for the nation"—in order to provide for the "possibility of an independent foreign policy."[39]

All of this created the circumstances, and the attendant limitations, within which Fascist corporativism developed. Whatever the real or fancied constraints, Mussolini never surrendered the notion of workers' participation in the governance of the economy. During the winter of 1941, for example, in the midst of the war for the nation's survival, he spoke unequivocally of a program of socialization that would see labor participating in that governance. At that time, he anticipated the program to commence at the successful conclusion of the conflict then in progress.[40] In the service of that anticipation, he had the constituent pronouncements of the Fascist Labor Charter formally identified by the Royal Declaration of 5 February 1941, as the "general principles of the juridical organization of the State" and as constituting "the directive criterion for the interpretation and application of the law."[41] At the foundation of the Labor Charter was the repeated conviction that the twentieth century would see labor at the very core of production and the center of the state.

After the events of 25 July 1943, and his restoration to power; in September, Mussolini committed himself to following to its conclusions the revolutionary political and economic commitments made even before the March on Rome and the promulgation of the Labor Charter. As has been suggested, the decision to undertake such manifestly revolutionary changes in the economy—in the course of a desperate war being fought on Italian soil—was not governed by a venal search for personal power; it was a forlorn and desperate attempt to leave a revolutionary legacy. The rationale for the radical changes in the economy had long since been articulated by some of Fascist Italy's most profound intellectuals—intellectuals whose work was publicly recommended and fostered by Mussolini himself.

---

lini, "L'Adriatico e il Mediterraneo," "Chi possiede, paghi!" and "Cifre da meditare," in *Oo*, vol. 13, pp. 142–43, 224, 284. The theme surfaces regularly.

[38] Mussolini, "Discorso agli operai di Milano," in *Oo*, vol. 26, p. 357.

[39] Mussolini, "Il piano regolatore della nuova economia italiana," in *Oo*, vol. 27, p. 242.

[40] See Amicucci, *I 600 Giorni di Mussolini*, pp. 142–43.

[41] Vittorio Emanuele III, "Valore giuidico della Carta del lavoro," in Bonini, *La Repubblica sociale italiana*, p. 69.

It is relevant that in his last book, completed about the time of Mussolini's liberation by the special forces of Hitler's Germany, Giovanni Gentile had already spoken of the spiritual realization implicit in the "humanism of labor" that Fascist corporativism anticipated. Gentile had entertained special convictions concerning the critical role labor was to play in the economy of the twentieth century. The first elements of such a view are to be found in his writings as early as the years immediately following the First World War—some considerable time before the appearance of revolutionary Fascism.[42]

Gentile conceived the modern world attaining a sense of the spiritual importance of labor, just as it had long acknowledged the spiritual significance of culture. He saw in labor, in work, an activity that shaped the individual. Echoing much of the philosophical and ethical convictions of the early Sorelian syndicalists, Gentile gave specific form to the "heroic and proletarian morality" of Georges Sorel.

Opposed, as were later Fascist thinkers, to a culture that remained far too "intellectualistic," Sorel anticipated that the increasingly complex character of modern industry could only foster the evolution of social and cognitive consciousness among workers. He was "persuaded that work can serve as a basis for a culture" that would shape society into a vehicle for the elevation of humanity.[43] It was an essentially idealistic conviction that was to find its place in the revolutionary syndicalism that occupied a place among the revolutionaries of Italy.

Gentile articulated very much the same conception as early as 1920, in his *Discorsi di religione*.[44] As has been indicated, between 1908 and 1920, many of the revolutionary syndicalists—Sergio Panunzio and A. O. Olivetti among them—made the transition from a form of materialism associated with Marx to antipositivistic idealism increasingly associated with Gentile's "humanism of labor."

Years later, Gentile acknowledged that the Fascist "State of Labor" followed a trajectory begun in the nineteenth century by socialism, which ultimately culminated in the conviction that only the "humanism of labor" could provide the most suitable foundation for the Social Republic of Salò.[45] Shortly before his death, Gentile maintained that the full freedom of humans could be achieved only with their organic integration into

---

[42] See Gentile, *Genesi e struttura della società* (Verona: Mondadori, 1954), pp. 146–47. Gentile had spoken of the spiritual essence in the humanization of labor even before the Fascist March on Rome. See Gentile, *Discorsi di religione*, 3rd ed. (1920; Florence: Sansoni, 1955), p. 26.

[43] Georges Sorel, *The Illusions of Progress* (1908; Berkeley and Los Angeles: University of California Press, 1969), p. 157.

[44] Gentile, *Discorsi di Religione*, p. 26.

[45] Gentile, *Genesi e struttura della società*, p. 146.

the infrastructure provided by the evolving corporativism of the Fascist ethical state.[46]

In Italy, it had long been held that only the activity of intellectuals and artists were matters of "culture." What Gentile argued was that labor, increasingly involving cerebration and creative activity, was also a matter of culture, an evolving process through which individuals might develop into that which they could, and should, be.[47] He saw Fascist corporativism as an arena in which that process might be increasingly realized.

Those were among the normative concepts that influenced the thought of some of Fascist Italy's most important thinkers—all, in some measure, Gentileans. Ugo Spirito, Luigi Fontanelli, and Camillo Pellizzi all were advocates of a Fascist "socialism"—a socialism that would see the direct engagement of workers in the self-developmental process of labor. They had all consistently held that just such a form of Gentilean "socialist humanism" would gradually emerge from the revolution of 1922.[48]

Those doctrinal convictions animated Spirito's delivery before the syndical and corporative conference that took place in Ferrara in May 1932. As has been argued, his entire delivery was predicated on Gentilean Actualism. In his exposition at Ferrara, Spirito applied Actualist convictions to the political and economic circumstances of Fascist Italy. He argued that its very logic dictated that Fascist corporativism, then passing through a transitional phase, would eventually have to transcend economic individualism, and its attendant capitalist commitment to "private property," with which it was burdened, in order to "socialize" the economy. He understood the transition would, of necessity, be gradual—if for no other reason than the fact that rapid change might further destabilize an already impaired economy—given the international depression then raging.

Granted that, he maintained that Fascist corporativism remained confounded by the legacy of liberal economic thought. The structure of corporativism embodied all the critical elements of a bifurcated productive system. There was labor institutionalized in the Confederazione del sinda-

---

[46] Gentile, "Discorso agli italiani," in Benedetto Gentile, ed., *Giovanni Gentile dal discorso agli italiana alla morte* (Florence: Sansoni, 1951), p. 71.

[47] See the discussion in Gentile, *Genesi e struttura della società*, pp. 146–47; and H. S. Harris, *The Social Philosophy of Giovanni Gentile* (Urbana: University of Illinois Press, 1960), p. 273. For an interesting account of how "labor" as "activity" would function in "self-development," see Vito A. Bellezza, *L'Esistenzialismo positivo di Giovanni Gentile* (Florence: G. C. Sansoni, 1954).

[48] Their convictions were constantly evolving. See, for example, Danilo Breschi, "Technica e rivoluzione: Il fascismo nel pensiero di Ugo Spirito," in *Annale della fondazione Ugo Spirito* (Milan: Luni Editrice, 2000). vol. 9, pp. 337–410. See the discussion in Daniele Gaudenzi, "Dal sindacalismo eroico all'umanesimo del lavoro," in Vittorio Vettori, *Giovanni Gentile* (Florence: La fenice, 1954), pp. 163–70.

cati industriali on the one hand, and the owners of plant and the employers of labor in the Confederazione dell'industria—with the political state attempting to act as a "neutral mediator" of their respective interests.[49]

Spirito maintained that, in principle, Fascism sought not to institutionalize the differences between the factors of production, but to accomplish their ultimate identity. Given that intention, Spirito argued that what Fascism was obliged to achieve was the gradual disassembly of the economic corporations of the early 1930s, and create one single organization that involved all the active constituents of production.

Spirito contended that the two then existing confederations, even if only temporarily, reflected the prerevolutionary duality of the nation's productive processes. In 1932 and 1933, he advocated the construction of a *single* confederation made up of all elements involved directly in the maintenance and increase of production. He pointed to the seventh article of the Carta del lavoro, which affirmed that private property in the Fascist state found legitimacy only as an instrument of the state. If private property failed to satisfy the needs of the community, it was to be controlled and administered by the state. He proceeded to argue that in those circumstances, capital might be effectively subsumed by the corporation, with workers enjoying the rewards of ownership. That would eliminate the distinction between workers and employers—between workers and capitalists.

Out of the new relationship to be achieved in an anticipated "integral corporativism," plant, syndicates, corporations, and the state would unite, to resolve all the antinomies that characterized the first stages of the Fascist social and economic revolution. Given the changes he advocated, a unitary national economic plan would be the capstone of the emerging "new corporativism." The Fascist state, possessed of efficient agencies that systematically collected industrial, agricultural and census statistics of all kinds, would formulate a programmatic, indicative, national economic plan that would make manifest the union of all interests in the reality of the nation—a reality already given substance in the regional and circumscribed plans involved in the "battle for grain," the vast reclamation programs in the rural areas, and the systematic expansion of hydroelectric production.[50] In effect, almost all the elements of the social and economic changes implemented in the Social Republic after 1943 were anticipated in the early 1930s in the work of Ugo Spirito, Gentile's most gifted representative among Fascist intellectuals.

---

[49] See the discussion in Spirito, "Verso la fine del sindacalismo," reproduced in *Il corporativismo*, pp. 436–39.

[50] See the account given in 1933 in "L'Economia programmatica corporativa," in Spirito, *Il corporativismo*, 421–52.

As has been indicated, as Fascism reached its doctrinal maturity in the 1930s, Spirito was at the very center of a dispute that turned on the issue of what Fascist corporativism was becoming and what it was to become. His opponents at the time were representatives of big business, orthodox Catholicism, economic liberalism, and anti-Marxism in a number of variants—all elements Mussolini identified as obstructing the free passage of the Fascist revolution.[51]

Spirito was the most prominent of the Gentilean idealists who provoked the acrimonious discussion concerning an emerging Fascist socialism. It was he who sought to distinguish between those elements in Fascism that would only survive during the period of transition and those that constituted Fascism's "living and vital" essence. Spirito specifically identified as "living and vital" Fascism's increasing appeal to national planning, its emphasis on the identification of the individual with the community, and their totalitarian inclusion in the historic and dynamic institutional reality of the state.[52]

Spirito spoke of the productive role of managers as distinct and independent of the passive role of capital in industry, which argued that they, as distinct from those who simply owned capital assets, should be incorporated into the ranks of labor. Technological and managerial activity were to be understood as integral parts of productive labor to the exclusion of capital per se.[53]

That constituted part of the rationale for a unitary confederation of labor and technology operating within a planned national economy. As a Gentilean, Spirito identified the individual with the state. A single organization of all productive factors would make a structured reality of that identification. An organization of workers in an institution that represented only labor as distinct from capital could only compromise that identification. For Spirito, corporativism was intended to transcend the antinomy that characterized labor and capital in liberal economic systems.[54] For Spirito, to achieve that identity of purpose, the duality represented by the corporative system of the early 1930s would have to be resolved. The arrangements anticipated that while capitalists would continue to receive compensation for delaying the gratification that would

[51] See the discussion in A. James Gregor, *Giovanni Gentile: Philosopher of Fascism* (New Brunswick, N.J.: Transaction, 2001), chap. 7; and Spirito's response to Gino Olivetti's criticisms after the conference at Ferrara in "Riposte alle obiezioni," in Spirito, *Il corporativismo*, pp. 361–67.

[52] Ugo Spirito, "Introduction" to *Capitalismo e corporativismo* (Florence: G. C. Sansoni, 1933), pp. xi–xx.

[53] Ibid., pp. 7, 9

[54] Spirito, "Verso la fine del sindacalismo," in *Capitalismo e corporativismo*, pp. 119–23.

attend their immediate use of funds, the role of capital would become increasingly passive, a contingent concern for the totalitarian community.

In the mid-1930s, the "integral corporativism" that Spirito anticipated would see unskilled and skilled workers, plant employees, technicians, and managers all represented at the plant level, rather than in national category confederations. All would benefit through wage and profit increments that would result from expansion in production. The simple ownership of capital assets would also deliver benefits, but stock owners would have only passive involvement in the productive process itself.[55] The purpose of such a "totalitarian" arrangement was to foster the increasing spiritual fulfillment of workers—skilled or unskilled, technicians or managers—as part of the Actualist program of individual actualization.[56]

Throughout his delivery, Spirito had made evident his conviction that Fascism recognized the positive features of "socialism," "Bolshevism," and/or theoretical "communism" in the process of self-actualization that was at the center of Gentile's thought. Spirito contended that both capitalism and liberal economics, as the material and ideological foundation of political and economic individualism, had run their course. In the world of the mid-1930s, they had been revealed as increasingly dysfunctional, sustaining political and economic systems that impaired both the viability and development of humanity—as well as the survival capacity of the communities that were their hosts.

Concerned as it was with rapid industrialization, Fascism had retained some features of economic liberalism during its first revolutionary phase (1922–25), to be followed thereafter by a form of "state capitalism" (1926–29), that sought to gradually transform the economy into a planned "integral corporativism" expected to function at the level of the individual enterprise rather than through nationwide category confederations.[57]

As has been indicated, in the course of the discussions that followed the meetings at Ferrara, Mussolini both read and approved of Spirito's exposition.[58] It reflected much of his own thought.[59] There is persuasive

---

[55] See "Individuo e stato nell'economia corporativa," in *Capitalismo e corporativismo*, pp. 3–24.

[56] *Capitalismo e corporativismo*, pp. 31, 33.

[57] Ibid., pp. 21, 42, 47, 52, 56–57, 85, 88; and "L'economia programmatica corporativa," pp. 96–109; and "Statalismo corporativo," pp. 113–16. See Spirito's comments in *Il corporativismo nazionalsocialista* (Florence: G. C. Sansoni, 1934), pp. 12–13, where he argues for the corporativism of the individual factory, rather than through confederations of category syndicates.

[58] See Spirito, "Benito Mussolini," in *Memorie di un incosciente* (Milan: Rusconi, 1977), pp. 173–87.

[59] See, for example, Mussolini, "Discorso per lo stato corporativo" and "Discorso agli operai di Milano," in *Oo*, vol. 26, pp. 86–96 and 355–59.

evidence that had not the necessities of autarky, and the preparation for the wars associated with creating an adequate resource base for the economic development of Fascist Italy, not intervened, the institutionalization of integral corporativism would probably have been made manifest by the late 1930s—by the time Fascist doctrine had achieved maturity.[60]

The themes that were to directly govern the political activity of the Fascist Social Republic after 1943 were thus to be found in the writings of many of the Fascist intellectuals of the early and mid-1930s. In January 1933, as an illustrative case, Luigi Fontanelli, like Spirito, addressed himself to the issue of the intrinsic "logic" of Fascist corporativism—before the Assembly of the National Council of Corporations, chaired by Mussolini himself.

In his presentation, Fontanelli acknowledged Spirito's priority and essentially expanded his arguments. He held that the duality represented in the confederations of labor and industry not only threatened the totalitarianism of the Fascist state, but allowed self-serving elements a staging area for the pursuit of their parochial interests—at the cost of collective national purpose.[61] He argued that production in modern industry actively involved skilled and unskilled labor—with technical competence critical among its skill requirements. Workers and technicians were the "true protagonists of production."[62] Money remained, at best, a passive prerequisite—a prerequisie that was being increasingly supplied by the state in Fascist Italy.

Fontanelli went on to argue that it was labor, in all its forms, that provided the dynamic force of production. More than that, he went on to argue that it was industry's ethical responsibility to provide labor the occasion for self-actualization through the prospect of upward mobility.

In an expanding and increasingly sophisticated productive system, the acquisition of skill by individual workers furthered the purposes of industry as well as the self-realization of all participants. The possibilities of upward mobility provided the occasion for labor to make of itself what it could be, and to thereby enhance the total body of skills and expertise

---

[60] In retrospect, it is clear that Ugo Spirito continued as an adviser to Mussolini until the collapse of the regime in 1943. In 1977, years after the end of the war, Spirito maintained that he had distanced himself from Fascism around 1935 (see Spirito, *Memorie di un incosciente*, p. 186). The fact is that at least until late 1942, Spirito continued to advise Mussolini and contribute to the discussions that involved Fascist intellectuals (see Ernesto Massi, "Le intuizioni geopolitiche di Ugo Spirito," and Gaetano Rasi, "Significato storico dell'inedito spiritiano" in *Guerra rivoluzionaria* (Rome: Fondazione Ugo Spirito, 1989), in *Il pensiero di Ugo Spirito* (Rome: Enciclopedia Italiana, 1988), pp. 509–12, 125–66).

[61] Luigi Fontanelli, *La logica della corporazione* (Rome: "Novissima," 1934), pp. 28–34, 50–51.

[62] Ibid., pp. 37, 39.

that would, in turn, contribute to national output as well as the increasing sophistication of production. Efforts at self-development would be rewarded by movement through the levels of skills essential to the productive maturation of the industrial system.

Such an arrangement would tend to satisfy not only the productive needs of a less than fully developed industrial economy, but would address, as well, the moral issues Gentilean Actualism had made prominent. Spirito had made the point that the very logic of Mussolini's political convictions emanated from the principles of the thought of Giovanni Gentile.[63] Fontanelli's exposition was its implicit confirmation.

On 3 October 1933, Mussolini called the attention of Italians to Spirito's exposition, identifying its theses with those of the offical *Dottrina del fascismo*, the philosophical portion of which was the work of Gentile.[64] In a retrospective, years later, after Fascism had receded into history, Spirito could affirm, with some persuasiveness, that Mussolini, as a Gentilean of sorts, rather than a "philo-capitalist, a reactionary or an anti-socialist," had always been a revolutionary, disposed to a qualified socialist solution for Italy's social and economic problems.[65] In substance, both Spirito and Fontanelli, inspired by Actualism, proposed some of the same features of "integral corporativism" advanced by Mussolini upon his resumption of the leadership of republican Fascism in 1943.

That none of this was casual is indicated by the doctrinal thought of Camillo Pellizzi, who since April 1940 served as president of the Istituto nazionale di cultura fascista, selected specifically by Mussolini to educate Italians to their national responsibilities. As a qualified Gentilean,[66] Pellizzi was a critical supporter of Spirito's programmatic economics—which he did not hesitate to call "Fascist communism."[67]

As the prime mover of the Istituto nazionale di cultura fascista after Gentile's departure, Pellizzi's responsibilities expanded geometrically with Italy's entry into the Second World War. Both Sergio Panunzio and Spirito worked with Pellizzi on projects that were considered essential to

[63] See the discussion in Spirito, "Benito Mussolini," in *Memorie di un incosiente*, pp. 173–80.

[64] Mussolini, "Segnalazione," in *Oo*, vol. 26, pp. 68–69.

[65] Spirito, *Memorie di un incosiente*, pp. 182–87.

[66] Pellizzi made his Actualist commitment evident in his first major work. See Pellizzi, *Fascismo—aristocrazia* (Milan: Alpes, 1925), pp. 30–31, 36–37, 40–41, 48–49, 170–71, 189.

[67] Pellizzi had converted to Roman Catholicism in 1925. That created some considerable tension in the coherence of his Actualism. Many Gentileans attempted to reconcile their Actualism with orthodox Catholicism—a daunting task. See the account in Gisella Longo, *L'Istituto nazionale fascista di cultura: Gli inellettuali tra partito e regime* (Rome: Antonio Pellicani, 2000), pp. 177–85. See R. Suzzi Valli, *Il "fascismo integrale" di Camillo Pellizzi* (Rome: Annali della Fondazione Ugo Spirito, 1995).

the maintenance of mass allegiance. That included the publication of *Civiltà fascista*, which anticipated many of the problems that would collect around the government and the party as the war drew on. There was talk of a rigorously planned economy in which labor would finally find its place. All of this was understood by Fascist intellectuals to represent the reality of the existence of a class of similar modern economic regimes—the product of historic circumstances—that included Soviet communism.[68]

In the course of the discussion concerning the future of Fascist corporativism, *Civiltà fascista* carried articles directly and indirectly calling attention to the Gentilean concept of the cultural character of modern labor. The argument was that as labor became increasing sophisticated, it would assume something of the traditional character of culture, assuring modern labor a place in society commensurate with its individualizing and developmental potential.[69]

Pellizzi recognized that steady increments in production were essential to developing Italy,[70] but he insisted—as did Sorel and Gentile before him—that production, and the processes it entailed, also provided the occasion for the working out of moral issues. Production was not only the source of commodities; it also, and primarily, afforded labor opportunities for self-development. Modern workers could form part of a labor aristocracy that, in turn, would constitute part of the political elite that would govern the nation.[71] As we have seen, in the years that were to follow, Fontanelli, like Spirito, would develop the argument and anticipate the self-development of workers through initiatives that would lift them above the level of ordinary unskilled labor to the rank of skilled technical enterprise.[72]

While Pellizzi had anticipated all this almost two decades before the legislation that sought its realization in the Social Republic, he was equally clear that he had not expected the maturation of Fascist corporativism to be rapid. In 1925, he held that the fulfillment of its promise might take half a century. He was convinced that the revolutionary

---

[68] See, for example, Guido Carli, "Dell'economia pianificata," *Civiltà fascista* 9, no. 11 (September 1942), pp. 680–86 and no. 12 (October 1942), pp. 757–63, as well as Pellizzi, "Ordine corporativo e programmazione sociale," *Civiltà fascista* 10, no. 6 (April 1943), pp. 351–55.

[69] See Luigi Volpicelli, "Natura e funzione del lavoro scolastico," *Civiltà fascista* 9, no. 4 (February 1942), pp. 239, 243, and "Premesse per una cultura operaia," *Civiltà fascista* no. 7 (May 1942), pp. 430–38.

[70] Fontanelli was equally aware that production and its increase was essential to the survival and enhancement of the nation. See Fontanelli, *La logica della corporazione*, p. 130.

[71] Ibid., pp. 118–21.

[72] See ibid., pp. 73–78.

changes implicit in Fascism required time if Italy was not to follow the tragic path of the Soviet Union—which saw the collapse of industry and agriculture and the attendant famines that drove Russians, Ukrainians, and Georgians to absolute despair. To avoid the horrors that afflicted the Bolshevik revolution, Fascism sought the same radical changes through systematic, if gradual, reform.[73]

In his exposition of 1925, Pellizzi identified Fascism with Gentilean Actualism and correspondingly saw it as an "engine" of change. Italy, like the Soviet Union, sought to address the social and economic issues of the modern world.[74] The critical difference was that Fascism saw those issues as fundamentally ethical rather than simply materialistic.

Almost a decade later, Fontanelli repeated the same theses. Like Bolshevism, Fascism addressed modern problems. That they would share similarities simply meant that the character of revolution in the twentieth century was shaped by a set of common concerns—the industrialization of retrograde economies. That, together with the crisis of industrial capitalism that afflicted the entire globe after 1929—signaling the passing of market capitalism—meant that the state, whatever its political persuasion, would become increasingly involved in national production. Production would become increasingly planned, with increasing participation by skilled workers, technicians, and trained managers. That would render workers, once simple vendors of labor, *conscious* agents in the making of their own lives and circumstances.[75]

When Fontanelli was criticized for presumably anticipating that labor would dominate the system, he responded that while labor, skilled and fully conscious of both its involvement and its moral responsibilities, was required to have a detailed and particularistic vision of its tasks, only a *political* leadership was possessed of that "panoramic" oversight that ensured the gradual realization of both national productive and normative goals. In effect, under the arrangements of the anticipated "state of labor," he expected the political leadership of a corporativist Italy, a minority, to be ultimately responsible for the general planning of the national economy.[76]

The discussion devoted to the final realization of Fascist corporativism continued throughout the war. Until 1943, both Pellizzi and Fontanelli continued their programmatic recommendations. What appears evident,

[73] Pellizzi, *Fascismo—aristocrazia*, pp. 150, 153–54.

[74] Ibid., pp. 124, 157, 169, 197.

[75] Fontanelli, *Logica della corporazione*, pp. 28–29, 30–31, 67–69, 81–83.

[76] Fontanelli responded in that fashion in 1941, two years before the advent of the Italian Social Republic. Once again, he had fully anticipated the subsequent development of Fascist corporativism. See Fontanelli, *Logica della corporazione e relative polemiche* (Rome: U.E.S.I.S.A., 1941), pp. 203–9.

given the pervasive similarities one finds in their work and in the legislation passed during the tenure of the Fascist republican government, is that
Mussolini, and significant members of the Fascist elite, continued to find
inspiration in the discussion.[77] In fact, the entire discussion that turned
on the issues of integral corporativism and Fascist socialism created an
intellectual environment in which some Marxists and independent socialists found a place. Both Nicola Bombacci and Edmondo Cione, together
with a surprisingly large number of intellectuals—some with a lifetime
identification with socialism in one or another form—could find moral
and intellectual affinities in the Fascism of the last six hundred days.

Gentile had long since identified socialist values as elements inherent in
Fascism since its conception. He recognized some of his own inspiration
in the early writings of Marx—when Marx was largely under the direct
influence of Hegel. Toward the end of his life, Gentile acknowledged the
socialist origins of Fascism when he identified Italian communists as "im-
patient corporativists" who failed to understand the logical and "dialectical" development of an historic social and philosophical idea.[78]

The effort to actually accomplish the socialization of the Italian economy involved, of course, factors having very little to do with the origins
of Fascism's ideological commitments. After July 1943, Fascist Italy was
no longer master of its own house. When the government of Pietro Badoglio undertook to surrender to the Anglo-Americans, the Germans occupied all of Italy not yet under Allied control. The creation of a republican
Fascist government, largely the creature of the German military, became
subject to German arbitration and control. As soon as the Germans heard
of Mussolini's decision to embark on the socialization of the economy,
they immediately signaled their concern that such initiatives might negatively impact war production. General Hans Leyers was charged with the
responsibility of assuring that Italian war production continue without
interruption even during the trying times generated by the political, economic, and military confusion following the July coup and the Italian
surrender in September 1943.[79]

Leyers, in discharging his obligations, was in charge of a commission
entitled Rüstungs und Kriegsindustrie, or RUK, that extended "protec-

---

[77] The clear evidence is that Mussolini would not accelerate the changes anticipated by
intellectuals like Spirito and Fontanelli—even though they conformed to his ideological convictions—because he anticipated the advent of conflict on a world scale, which required
that he do nothing that might threaten heavy industrial production. After the events of
1943, it was clear that the war, for all intents and purposes, was lost. Socialization became
a concern for a Fascist "legacy." See the account in Tarchi, *Teste dure*; and Giuseppe Pardini,
"Angelo Tarchi," in Andriola, *Uomini e scelte della RSI*, pp. 129–45.

[78] Gentile, "Discorso agli italiani," in *Giovanni Gentile*, p. 72.

[79] See the discussion in Deakin, *The Brutal Friendship*, pt. 3, chap. 8.

tion" to all and any armaments and support industries on the peninsula—in order to insulate them from any civil or political interference that might negatively affect output committed to war production.[80] Leyers entertained grave misgivings concerning any effort to embark on any form of experimentation in industry. Together with General Karl Wolff, commander of all SS forces in Italy, and Rudolph Rahn, the German ambassador to the republic, he impeded almost every effort to socialize the economy. The Germans made common cause with major Italian industrialists, who were more than dubious about the Fascist experiment.[81] Representatives of Swiss financial institutions, particularly important in the funding of hydroelectric installations in Italy, warned the Fascist government that socialization would dampen enthusiasm for investment among Swiss financiers.

Against all this dedicated opposition, Mussolini persisted in his efforts. In a period of about sixteen months, against the resistance of the Germans, some major Italian industrialists, as well as some of the most important financial houses of Europe, republican Fascists substantially socialized about seventy-six regional industries involving perhaps as many as 126,000 workers. The bulk of the socialized enterprises were publishing and paper manufacturing establishments, but some were critical industries. Alfa Romeo, Motomeccaniche, Fiat, Acciaierie e Ferriere Lomabarde, Puricelli, Olivetti, Ansaldo, and Montecatini were among the largest in which socialization was undertaken.[82]

Among all the obstructions to socialization, the general indifference and/or hostility of Italian workers played a significant role. Public sentiment was largely determined by the continued defeat of Fascist and German forces in the air and on the ground. By the turn of 1945, Italian workers had become hostile and generally refused to cooperate in the election of workers' councils.[83] By the time that Fascists were prepared to embark upon general socialization of the economy, there was no longer time. Anglo-American forces had broken through the last organized resistance in Northern Italy. Only Fascist irregular warfare slowed, for a brief time, the Allied forces flooding into the Po Valley. By the end of April, Mussolini, together with most of the political leadership of the Social Republic, had fallen before the guns of anti-Fascist Italians. The Fascist experiment was over.

---

[80] See the comments in Dolfin, *Con Mussolini nella tragedia*, pp. 119–20; and Piero Pisenti, *Una repubblica necessaria (R.S.I.)* (Rome: Volpe, 1977), pp. 100–8.

[81] See the discussion in Rocca, *La repubblica di Mussolini*, pp. 171–78.

[82] See the discussion in Cione, *Storia della Repubblica sociale italiana*, pp. 308–9.

[83] See Bocca, *La repubblica di Mussolini*, pp. 165–68.

CHAPTER ELEVEN

Conclusions

THE END OF Mussolini's Fascism came amid mountains of ruins and the unnumbered dead that haunted the final days of the Second World War. The Italy that Fascism imagined would be the seat of a new civilization lay prostrate, not even a shadow of the nation that had embodied the dreams of a generation and that had impressed half a world. It is the crushed and tattered image of those final days, thrashed out under the shadow of the swastika, that remains in the collective memory of the last half of the twentieth century. We are left with an impression that all those lost and beaten creatures who had followed the siren call of Fascism were, at best, to be pitied. They could only have been impelled by an unimaginable foolishness or an otherwordly malevolence to have allowed themselves to become involved in so mad an enterprise.

Those who had identified with so distracted an undertaking could only have been mad themselves, devoid of judgment and moral principle. Fascists must have simply not calculated probabilities. They must not have thought things through. Worse then that, they must not have considered the wickedness implicit in the words of their leader or in the formulations of his ideologues.

And yet, there was more to Fascism than its final days. There was a time when its call to revolution awakened a response among the youth of Italy, and the veterans who had served its flag. There was a time when intellectuals, old and young, spoke of its goals in books and articles as carefully crafted as any books and articles written to vindicate any revolution, anywhere and at any time. Mussolini's intellectuals were no better and no worse than any intellectuals who ever sought to promote their cause through violence and war.

To begin to appreciate that, one must be somewhat familiar with the thought of those charged with accounting for Fascism. That is what has been attempted here. There is no way that one might reconstruct the excitement, the passions, the desperation, and the aspirations that animated those who sought to foster, sustain, influence, and defend Fascism. We are left only with the echo of those times—and the lifeless prose of some singular persons. To maintain that there was no thought in that prose is untrue. To insist that it addressed itself only to the celebration of violence and war is equally untrue. That all that is untrue is evident in some of the works we have here considered. That those works contain errors and that their appeal may have led many to death and dishonor seems equally clear—but then, it is a singular doctrine, secular or religious, that has not done any of that.

Some of that seems to become evident when we allow ourselves to read something like Curzio Malaparte's volume, *L'Europa vivente*, devoted, as it is, to Fascist thought and its history—written in his youth, in the very heat of events, when he was a committed follower of Benito Mussolini.[1] Almost everything is there in that one volume: an account of the history of humiliations that infilled the first nationalists with the passion that carried them into the maelstrom of the First World War, and from there into nascent Fascism—to the union of nationalism and revolutionary syndicalism, all combined in that "atmosphere of the highest moral tension" of which Mussolini spoke.[2] It was that moral tension that Giovanni Gentile sought to employ to unite all the components of Italy into a seamless totalitarianism that would be instrumental in the creation of a new civilization. Malaparte understood all of that. He understood Fascism in its adolescence and first maturity as few other commentators understood it then or now.

Malaparte was a superlative craftsman, and manages to convey, through his masterful prose, some of the emotion that Fascism evoked among the young. He supplies dimension not to be found in the writings of Gentile, or Panunzio, or Spirito. While artful, his account remains thoughtful. What becomes evident to anyone not unalterably biased is that the "fascist thought"—filled only with emotion and devoid of critical reflection—about which many contemporary commentators still speak with such conviction, has very little to do with the ideology of historic Fascism that Malaparte knew so well. Malaparte spoke of the ideas that made up the substance of the Fascism he knew. Those ideas came together as a consequence of historic circumstances that made economic growth and industrial development goals that were compelling for both nationalists and revolutionary Marxists. For nationalists, the nation could not achieve greatness without rapid economic development and the ability to project its power. For revolutionary syndicalists, the material and proletarian base that was the prerequisite of revolution would not obtain without industrial expansion. Futurists, machine fetishists, and modernizers, of all and sundry persuasion, collected themselves around the guidons of

[1] Curzio Malaparte, *L'Europa vivente: Teoria storica del sindacalismo nazionale* in *L'Europa vivente e altri saggi politici* (Florence: Vallecci Editore, 1961), pp. 315–77.

[2] Benito Mussolini, "Discorso per lo stato corporativo," *Opera omnia* (Florence: La fenice, 1958. Hereafter *Oo*), vol. 26, p. 96.

the first Fascism.[3] War veterans and adventurers of all varieties filled the ranks of a popular movement led by skillful orators and manipulators of public sentiment. Gifted intellectuals supplied the rationale that inspired it all.

Over the next two decades, Italy was bundled through a series of crises and developments scant ever experienced by a less-developed, newly united nation. There were a series of challenges that tested the mettle of the new nation. There was the recovery from the ravages of the First World War, followed by a major surge of economic growth and industrial expansion—interspersed with major political conflicts—before the Great Depression brought everything to a ruinous halt. There were then the great transatlantic crossings and the adventures in exploration. And then there were instances of international violence and increasing demands for "living space"—until it all found outlet in the second world conflict that brought destruction to the entire experiment.

Taken together, all of that made of Mussolini's Fascism an enormously complex and consequently unique historical phenomenon.[4] What has been attempted here has not been an effort to understand so complex a totality of events, or to explain its unfolding, but rather to deliver something of the history of an evolving body of thought produced by intelligent and articulate spokesmen for the regime. The history that accompanied the development and expression of that thought has been alluded to only insofar as it was assessed to be necessary for exposition.

Given the obligations attendant upon such an exposition, recourse has been made to primary sources, to the writings of a chorus of selected intellectuals. The principal thrust of the exposition has been to pursuasively portray what is taken to be the coherence and relevance of Fascist social and political thought in its temporal context.

Clearly, what is required to capture a sense of the fullness of historic reality is that a distinction be made between Fascist thought and Fascist behavior—just as one must distinguish Marxist or democratic thought from Marxist or democratic behavior. Just as gulags, mass murder, and slavery mar the history of Marxist and democratic regimes respectively, and urge us to distinguish behavior from ideological commitment, so Fas-

---

[3] See the interesting account in Antonio Vinci, *Prefigurazioni del fascismo* (Milan: CELUC Editrice, 1974), pp. 81–144.

[4] This is, of course, the position assumed by Renzo De Felice. For De Felice, given the uniqueness of the constellation of properties identified with the historic realities of Fascism, there could be only one Fascism. See Renzo De Felice, *Fascism: An Informal Introduction to its Theory and Practice* (New Brunswick, N.J.: Transaction Books, 1976), chaps. 2 and 3. De Felice was chary of any attempts at historic or social science generalizations. See A. James Gregor, "Autopsia di una intervista," in *Sei risposte a Renzo De Felice* (Rome: Volpe Editore, 1976), pp. 129–44.

cist behaviors must be distinguished from Fascism's argued beliefs. Not to recognize the differences between behavior and beliefs would be to falsify reality.

To attempt to credibly relate doctrinal thought to behavior would be, of course, a daunting task, requiring both rare skill in making distinctions as well as employing reasonably sophisticated social science insights— necessitating, moreover, access to an enormous fund of documentary and trace evidence. It would require an encyclopedic grasp of a dense history of events as well as impeccable understanding of human motives and personal deliberations.[5]

Acknowledging that, the present exposition attempts none of it. The present effort is calculated to partially answer but one question: was Italian Fascism subtended by a reasonably coherent and relevant ideology, composed of both rational normative and empirical convictions? To that question, an answer has been conscientiously attempted. That has been the relatively modest task of the present enterprise.

The obligation has been to provide a reasonably objective and accurate account of the public thought of selected members of that class of thinkers who legitimately might be counted among "Mussolini's intellectuals." They have been allowed, in the measure possible in a work of this sort, to speak for themselves.

Clearly, the class of intellectuals treated might have included others. Without question, it might have included Curzio Malaparte and Roberto Michels.[6] It might have included A. O. Olivetti—and probably Edmondo Rossoni—among a number of others. The decision to limit the number of intellectuals considered was governed almost exclusively by the limitations of space and energy. Should others have been encompassed, their addition would not have significantly altered the outcome, or changed the argument in any significant measure—but would accomplish little more than increase the bulk of the exposition. The account provided above has gone into sufficient detail, by appeal to primary sources, to make the case that Italian Fascism was animated by a rationale that its authors imagined rendered its behaviors both comprehensible and moral.

The narrative provided is intended to serve cognitive ends. By pretending that Mussolini's regime found support in nothing other than irra-

---

[5] The person who has come closest to that accomplishment was Renzo De Felice in his massive biography of Mussolini. He did not spend much time on an account or an analysis of Fascist thought.

[6] I have elsewhere briefly reviewed the voluminous works of Michels in an introductory essay to selections from his works in A. James Gregor, ed., *Roberto Michels e l'ideologia del fascismo* (Rome: Volpe, 1979), pp. 5–69; and *Phoenix: Fascism in Our Time* (New Brunswick, N.J.: Transaction Publishers, 1999), chaps. 3 and 4.

tionality and violence, some contemporary commentators have delivered only a parody of Fascist thought. They have left us bereft of any real understanding of one of the major revolutions of our immediate past. That not only affects our comprehension of the past, but may very well impair our understanding of the revolutions in our future. To imagine that the Fascism of the twentieth century was inspired and vindicated by an appeal to simple violence, and hatred is not only a fiction—but may very well be a significantly misleading fiction as well.

As a case in point, the number of Fascist intellectuals who advocated war, violence, and hatred for their own sake were both few and marginal.[7] As we have seen, Julius Evola, who might conceivably be counted among them[8]—was not a "fascist" thinker in any meaningful sense of the term. He himself, both implicitly and explicitly, rejected such a characterization.[9] That he remains identified as a fascist thinker by many contemporary commentators tells us more about contemporary discussions than it does about Fascism.

A better candidate for the role of a Fascist advocate of violence for its own sake might be Filippo Tomasso Marinetti, born in Alexandria, Egypt, on 22 December 1876—the founder of Futurism, the radical artistic movement that provided color to the world of art at the turn of the twentieth century. Marinetti early married his movement to Mussolini's Fascism—and, if nothing else, the presence of Futurists in the ranks certainly contributed to the political theater of the period. Irrepressibly given to hyperbole, very little Marinetti or the Futurists said or did was either measured or reasonable in any conventional sense.

When Marinetti founded Futurism in 1909, he called for "incendiary violence" that might drive Italy and Italians out of the "fetid somnolence" of *dolce far niente*. He incited Futurists and their allies to the destruction of museums, monuments, and universities—to decimate everything that

---

[7] See the account in Zeev Sternhell (with Mario Sznajder and Maia Asheri), *The Birth of Fascist Ideology: From Cultural Rebellion to Political Revolution* (Princeton: Princeton University Press, 1994), particularly the "Epilogue," pp. 233–58.

[8] Even that is debatable. Inner Traditions Publishers, purveyors of "New Age" thought, have insisted that none of that is true concerning Evola—and they may very well be correct. See H. T. Hansen, "A Short Introduction to Julius Evola," in Evola, *Revolt against the Modern World* (Rochester, Vt.: Inner Traditions International, 1995), pp. ix–xxii; and "Julius Evola's Political Endeavors," in Evola, *Men among the Ruins: Post-war Reflections of a Radical Traditionalist* (Rochester, Vt.: Inner Traditions, 2002), pp. 1–106.

[9] In his response to the charge that he "glorified Fascist ideas," Evola maintained that such was never his concern. "I have defended," he correctly affirmed, "and I still defend, 'fascist ideas,' not inasmuch as they are 'fascist' but in the measure that they revive ideas superior and anterior to Fascism." Evola, in effect, was never a "fascist" thinker. He identified himself as a "radical traditionalist," rejecting all the political ideas not those of Greco-Roman and medieval antiquity.

"stank of the past." He cried out for a New Italy, one alive with massive engines of production, commerce, and travel; he spoke of aircraft filling the skies with the thunder of their motors, of automobiles challenging space with "eternal and omnipresent velocity," and of steamships, like sharpened steel, slicing across far horizons. He spoke of the tall smoke-stacks of factories piercing the clouds, and of electricity sparking life into inanimate matter.[10] All this was suffused with aggression and violence, with an appeal to slaps and blows, to culminate in an invocation to what he called the "beauty of battle," and the "hygiene of war."[11]

Marinetti and his followers rejected everything featured in the "old Italy," the Italy of literary ruminations, of meaningless and ineffectual parliamentary rule, of tour guides, ruins, and amorous preoccupations. Futurists spoke of vast economic and industrial development, of trade schools, and of training engineers, chemists, and mechanics. They spoke of rapidity of movement, of intuition rather than lucubration.[12] What that required, they insisted, was agitation, provocation, a rejection of tradition and rules, and, ultimately, violence.

By the end of the First World War, the images of death and violence, of bravery and commitment, were common fare among the survivors of the trenches, where hundreds of thousands of young men had faced brutal death and experienced the exhilaration of victory. The Futurists them-selves had fought, and many had died. For them, the talk of violence and victory took on an emphatic and immediate quality.

Marinetti imagined himself the spokesman for all these men—and for an emergent Italy for which they had fought. He spoke of an Italy that was youthful, self-confident, assertive, and energetic, indifferent to dusty history and nostalgia about the glories of ancient Rome. He was the advo-cate of energy, of Italy's entry into the competitive world of the industrial-ized and industrializing twentieth century—a century of arms and arma-ments—to earn its place among the advanced nations of the world through enterprise, the assumption of risk, and a commitment to personal responsibility.[13]

[10] There are many anthologies of Futurist writings, both by Marinetti and his followers, that speak to all these elements of Futurist thought. Among the better is Luciano De Maria, ed., *Marinetti e il Futurismo* (Verona: Arnoldo Mondadori Editore, 1973).

[11] F. T. Marinetti, "Fondazione e Manifesto del futurismo," *Figaro*, 20 February 1909, in Luigi Scrivo, ed., *Sintesi del Futurismo: Storia e documenti* (Rome: Mario Bulzoni Edi-tore, 1968), pp. 2–3.

[12] Marinetti, "Contro Firenze e Roma, piaghe purulente della nostra penisola," "Contro l'amore e il parlamentarismo," "Manifesto tecnico della letteratura futurista," and "Pro-gramma politico futurista," in Scrivo, *Sintesi del Futurismo*, pp. 23, 24, 53, 86.

[13] Even before the First World War, Marinetti had spoken of the requirements of gran-deur, of earning a place among the advanced industrial nations, in "Contro la Spagna passa-tista," *Prometeo*, June 1911, in Scrivo, *Sintesi del Futurismo*, pp. 38–39, where he spoke of

On the surface, all of this was generally compatible with the political intentions of the first Fascism as it emerged from its founding meeting in the Piazza San Sepolcro in March 1919. At that time, Marinetti duly brought his followers into the movement.

More than that, and in many ways, Futurism was compatible with the revolutionary movements of the time. In Russia, the Futurists, bringing their appeals to violence and war, identified with the revolutionary Bolsheviks.[14] In fact, the appeal to violence did not really distinguish Futurism, nor Fascism, in any absolute sense.[15] Revolutionary syndicalists and Lenin's Bolsheviks were all convinced of the strategic and tactical necessity of revolutionary violence. The entire atmosphere of the time crackled with appeals to violence, warfare, and bloodshed. Revolutionary Marxists, no less than Futurists or syndicalists, invoked violence without hesitation. V. I. Lenin not only conceived violence a necessary revolutionary weapon; his prose was filled with the language of warfare, battles, and violence. In 1918, Lenin affirmed, without hesitation, that Marxist revolution required "revolutionary violence of the proletariat against the bourgeoisie and the latter's destruction. . . . The revolutionary dictatorship of the proletariat is rule won and maintained by the use of violence . . . unrestricted by any laws."[16]

There seemed to be, however, an enthusiasm for the employment of violence in Marinetti's effusive prose that was not readily to be found in the prose of Lenin or many other revolutionary theorists. That having been said, it seems equally apparent that a similar enthusiasm is not to be found among the major spokesmen of national syndicalism and Fascism. It certainly was not found in Sergio Panunzio's volume, written about the same time, devoted to a "theory of violence"—in which he builds upon the distinction urged by Georges Sorel between conservative *force*

---

defense of the Fatherland, a strong military, and the possibility of achieving international stature through victorious war.

[14] See Vladimir Markov, *Russian Futurism: A History* (Berkeley and Los Angeles: University of California Press, 1968). In "Al di là del comunismo," Marinetti was pleased that the Russian Futurists had identified with Lenin's Bolshevism. Marinetti, "Al di là del comunismo," in *Teoria e invenzione futurista: Manifesti, scritti politici, romanzi, parole in libertà* (Verona: Arnoldo Mondadori Editore, 1968), p. 418.

[15] This was not only true during the first quarter of the twentieth century. Mao Zedong did not conceal his enthusiasm for war and violence. He was convinced that "only with guns can the whole world be transformed." He went on to argue that "some people ridicule us as advocates of the 'omnipotence of war.' Yes," he went on, "we are advocates of the omnipotence of revolutionary war; that is good, not bad, it is Marxism." Mao Zedong, "Problems of War and Strategy," *Selected Works* (Beijing: Foreign Languages Press, 1965–1967), vol. 2, p. 225.

[16] V. I. Lenin, "The Proletarian Revolution and the Renegade Kautsky," *Collected Works* (Moscow: Progress Publishers, 1965), vol. 28, pp. 236, 242–43.

and innovative *violence*, the first embodied in the coercive power of the establishment and the latter providing the transformative power of revolutionary energy.[17]

There is little readiness to invoke violence for its own sake in Panunzio's studied exposition. In the course of revolution, he maintained, violence is notable, organized, physical resistance to the force of the established state. It becomes necessary only when certain conditions render it absolutely unavoidable—and, he continued, its proper objects are *never* innocents. As a consequence, Panunzio drew a consistent distinction between carefully calculated revolutionary *violence* and the thoughtless and immoral appeal to political *terror*. For Panunzio, violence must always be ethical, serving the higher ends of justice—terror was a blunt weapon that was not only immoral, because directed against the innocent, but ineffectual as well, because it was, more frequently than not, counterproductive.[18]

Given such an analysis, it seems evident, in retrospect, that Fascism could not domesticate Futurism. Futurism and Futurists were essentially anarchic in disposition, and antinomian by conviction. They were devoted, as they insisted, to the "dignity and liberty of the individual"[19]— and that seemed to mean that one was not required to obey prevailing law nor submit to convention. There was more than a suggestion that Marinetti's political ideals included an individualism predicated on an undefined conception of unconstrained "total liberty."[20] Equally evident was the fact that whatever the compatibility of its call to rapid economic growth and industrialization of the Italian peninsula, and its insistence that the nation win a place at the table of the "Great Powers," Futurism would have more than a little difficulty accommodating itself to the authoritarian rigors of Mussolini's Fascism.[21]

Even before the March on Rome that brought Fascism to power, Mussolini directly addressed the issue of political violence. At the very beginning of 1921, Mussolini insisted that "for Fascists, violence is not a caprice. . . . It is not art for art's sake. It is understood to be a surgical necessity. A doleful necessity. . . . For us, violence is an exception, not a

---

[17] Sergio Panunzio, *Diritto, forza e violenza: Lineamenti di una teoria della violenza* (Bologna: Licinio Cappeli-Librio Editore, 1921).

[18] Ibid., pp. 40–44, 46 n.1, 55–56, 131–34.

[19] Ibid., p. 39; see "La pittura Futurista: Manifesto tecnico," in Scrivo, *Sintesi del Futurismo*, p. 13.

[20] Luciano De Maria, "Marinetti poeta e ideologo," in Marinetti, *Teoria e invenzione futurista*, p. xxviii.

[21] Futurism was to have the same difficulty with Lenin's Bolsheviks. By the late 1920s, few Futurists remained active in the Soviet Union, and certainly none were permitted to represent the thought of the Communist party.

method, or a system. For us, violence . . . is part of our defense of the nation."[22]

In April of the same year, Mussolini reaffirmed the differences between the views of Fascism and those of Futurism in terms of political violence. There was no mistaking the intent of his speech. In the course of his delivery, he obliquely referred to the Futurists by acknowledging their objections to "pastists" (*passatisti*)—those whose vision is fixed exclusively on the past. At the same time, Mussolini made evident his differences with Futurists by insisting that the Rome of antiquity, which they rejected, was the normative model for the emerging, modern Italy—and by repeating his rejection of any violence that was avoidable, stupid, or lacking in chivalry.[23]

By that time, it was clear that Futurism and Fascism would part political company. It was not a simple question of their different conceptions of violence that determined the rupture. Marinetti and the Futurists had published a "Program Manifesto of the Futurist Political Party" in September 1918, in which they called not only for an industrial Italy sovereign over its own future in its own space, but for unrestricted universal suffrage, the socialization of land, the unbridled freedom of workers to strike, the rejection of organized religion, and the substitution of only one commanding faith: that of "the Italy of tomorrow."[24]

In 1920, Marinetti had published his "Al di là del comunismo," in which he affirmed his continued commitment to one or another form of anarchic individualism.[25] He continued to insist on his antimonarchism and his anticlericalism—postures that an expanding Fascism found increasingly difficult to accommodate.

By the time of the Second Congress of the Fasci in Milan, in May 1920, Marinetti, and his immediate lieutenants, resigned from the political leadership of the Fasci di combattimento and remained alienated until 1924. Whatever the reconciliation that followed at that time, Marinetti never became a member of the Partito nazionale fascista.[26] Thereafter, Marinetti absented himself entirely from any doctrinal concern with Fascism.

---

[22] Mussolini, "In tema di violenza," in *Oo*, vol. 16, pp. 181–82.

[23] Mussolini, "Discorso di Bologna," in *Oo*, vol. 16, pp. 239–46.

[24] "Manifesto-programma del Partito politico futurista (settembre 1918)," in Renzo De Felice, *Mussolini il rivoluzionario, 1885–1920* (Turin: Giulio Einaudi Editore, 1965), pp. 738–41.

[25] In the course of the exposition, Marinetti affirmed that the kind of individualism he advocated was actually "the maximum extension of the individual, a greater individual." See F. T. Marinetti, "Al di là del comunismo," in *Teoria e invenzione futurista*, p. 412.

[26] See F. T. Marinetti, *Futurismo e fascismo* (Foligno: Franco Campitelli Editors, 1924). The Fascist party was formally established at the end of 1920. Marinetti never joined. See Carlo Fabrizio Carli, "Filippo Tommaso Marinetti: Destini italiani, artisti in RSI," in Fabio

After 1924, Marinetti occupied himself exclusively with literary activity. He remained steadfast in his loyalty to Mussolini until the very end of the Fascist experiment, but he was not to publicly address specifically ideological issues ever again.[27] He exercized some literary and artistic influence over Fascist Italy, he served with considerable courage in its wars, but he did not ever influence the development of its formal ideology.

Given all that, it is very difficult to cite Futurist notions concerning violence and its employment as evidence of Fascism's unqualified commitment to its use—to the exclusion of thought and morality. Like the thought of Julius Evola, the thought of F. T. Marinetti had very little to do with the formal ideology of Fascism. Fascism, like any revolutionary ideology of the twentieth century, sought a moral and empirical rationale for its undertakings and legitimation for its rule.

The failure to understand that has produced a woeful tendency in some contemporary discussions to identify fascist thought with any and every notion found indefensible by contemporary sentiments of "political correctness." Thus, anyone whose views are, in any fashion, antiintellectual, antihumane, antifeminist, and antidemocratic—sadistic, insensitive, homicidal, xenophobic, racist, genocidal, psychopathic, "totalitarian," and lacking in charity—is identified as a fascist thinker. That inevitably leads to the extravagance of identifying soccer thugs, members of the Ku Klux Klan, as well as all and sundry sociopaths and terrorists—together with their lunatic advocates and apologists—as fascist thinkers. All of which must strike one not only as silly, but intellectually privative as well.

More productive of consequence is the treatment of Fascist thought as a time- and circumstance-specific historic product—as informed by a rationale composed of relatively distinctive themes: (1) the felt need to restore a humiliated and diminished community to its "appropriate" historic station; together with (2) the conviction that, in our own time, the politically defined nation serves as such a community; and (3) only through restoration and renewal might the nation provide for the "self-actualization" of its denizens; and finally, (4) that instrumental to all that is the availability of a "strong state," a state capable of decisively commanding all the human and material resources of the developing community understood to be facing challenge.

Given that, there are relatively informal "entailments" that follow: (1) to achieve its ends, the nation must be capable of not only defending itself, but projecting its power into what is understood to be a threatening

---

Andriola, *Uomini e scelte della RSI: I protagonisti della Repubblica di Mussolini* (Bastogi: Editrice italiano, 2000), p. 225.

[27] See the account in Luciano De Maria, "Marinetti poeta e ideologo," in Marinetti, *Teoria e invenzione futurista*, pp. xxxiv–xliv.

international environment as well; (2) to achieve those capabilities would necessitate the rapid expansion and maturation of its economic power, in general, and its industrial base, in particular; and that (3) in order to achieve such ends, it is conceived necessary to diminish what are generally held to be individual political and civil rights, so that the behavior of all taken together would be "single-willed" or "totalitarian," heroic, committed and sacrificial—prerequisites to the accomplishment of the revolution's omnibus purpose.

Such a catalog of primary and derivative descriptive criterial traits is composed of both normative and empirical elements. Some are more fundamental, while others are understood to be derivative and instrumental. Among the body of elements, that which serves as primary could only be the unproblematic normative enjoinment that each of us seek to "fulfill oneself as a human being" (sii uomo). Fascist thinkers occupied with fundamental philosophical and essentially ethical questions held that community and its fullness were absolutely essential to the achievement of that end.[28] How the fullness of community was understood, how that fullness was achieved, and how all that affected the realization of self were not only normative, but analytic as well as empirical issues. Granted that, the public doctrine becomes a function of still further and increasingly complex derivations that require definitional and empirical grounds for their support.

It cannot be our purpose here to pursue an analytic reduction of Fascist doctrine. More to our purpose is the provision of a criterial list of properties that might help us to appreciate what Fascist thought was not. For one thing, it is manifest that Fascist thought was not fundamentally irrational nor intrinsically inhumane. Whatever irrationality or inhumanity was advocated was generally held to be instrumental to other ends— sharing much the character that such advocacy does in non-Fascist environs. Where some one or another Fascist advocated violence and inhumanity for their own sake, he would qualify, among Fascists as well as non-Fascists—then, as now—not as an apologist of the system, but as either incompetent to deal with normative and empirical issues and/or clinically disturbed.[29]

---

[28] "Within the soul of man there is a still small voice that is never silent, and will not let him rest, but incessantly spurs him onward. Onward toward what end? Toward himself— toward the ideal self that he ought to be. . . . In seeking to define the moral law . . . I expressed it as strictly as possible in the admonition: Be man." Giovanni Gentile, Genesi e struttura della società: Saggio di filosofia pratica (Florence: G. C. Sansoni, 1946), pp. 7–8, 44; see chap. 2, para. 2.

[29] Gentile and Gentileans regularly abjured anti-Semites and biological racists with just such dismissals. See A. James Gregor, Giovanni Gentile: Philosopher of Fascism (New Brunswick, N.J.: Transaction Publishers, 2001), chap. 8.

There is very little in the historic Fascist doctrine produced by academicians and social scientists that might so qualify. Much, if not most, of the most execrable elements in Fascist doctrine were episodic, contingent, and instrumental—as they tend to be in any revolutionary system. A similar case can be made for the enormities that have stained the history of alternative revolutionary systems—whatever their respective ideologies. The massacre of Kulaks and the Great Terror under Stalin and the horrors of the Great Proletarian Cultural Revolution under Mao Zedong qualify as illustrative cases.

Fascist anti-Semitism, for example, however despicable, was recognized even by the most intransigent Fascists as a contingent, rather than an essential, component of doctrine—often administered with uneasy conscience.[30] There was little pretense in any serious Fascist literature that anti-Semitism was central to Fascist convictions.[31] True anti-Semites, in fact, were rare among Fascist thinkers.[32] Paolo Orano's *Gli Ebrei in Italia*, typical of much of Fascist literature on the subject, was an account of what was held to be the empirical circumstances that made anti-Semitism

[30] In this respect, there is an entire library of literature that attests to the differences between Fascist and National Socialist anti-Semitism. Anti-Semitism defined Hitler's National Socialism, and mass murder was the inevitable consequence of holding the view that whatever disabilities were attributed to the Jews were biological and unalterable. None of that was the case with Fascist anti-Semitism. See the entire discussion in De Felice's *Storia degli ebrei italiani sotto il fascismo* (Turin: Einaudi, 1993) and the discussion and the sources in Gregor, *Giovanni Gentile*, chap. 8. Not only had Fascist Italy provided qualified protection to Italian Jews from their National Socialist oppressors, but even when the situation had so radically changed that Mussolini had few opportunities left to defy Hitler, the Fascists of the Republic of Salò, identified anti-Semitism as a contingency, attendant upon the war then in process. See "The Program Manifesto of the Fascist Republican Party," in A. James Gregor, *The Ideology of Fascism: The Rationale of Totalitarianism* (New York: Free Press, 1969), p. 387, para. 7. Consult, in this context, the account provided by Giorgio Israel and Pietro Nastasi, *Scienza e razza nell'Italia fascista* (Bologna: Il Mulino, 1998). Rehearsing the coarse stupidities and unspeakable violations of human decency that were the consequences of Fascist anti-Semitism serves little purpose—any more than recounting the human degradations and needless suffering that accompanied the institution of black slavery tells us much about the belief system of North American democracy.

[31] The defense of such a claim would require a detailed assessment of apologetic Fascist literature, particularly that which appeared in the most scurilous state-sponsored publications like *La difesa della razza* that commenced publication about the time of the publication of the "Fascist Racial Manifesto" in 1938, when Mussolini had wedded Fascism's future to that of National Socialist Germany. All of that must be put into context. See Gregor, *The Ideology of Fascism*, chap. 6 and appendix A.

[32] Giovanni Preziosi was among the very few Fascists who were committed anti-Semites. He was almost always considered a marginal person among Fascists until Mussolini's abject dependence on National Socialist Germany provided him tactical advantage among those who disdained him. See the discussion in De Felice, *Storia degli ebrei italiani sotto il fascismo*, pp. 446–63.

an apposite response to political contingencies.[33] As Fascist Italy became increasingly dependent on National Socialist Germany, its anti-Semitism, which formally appeared for the first time in 1938, became correspondingly insistent and morally objectionable.[34] For established Fascist thinkers the entire issue was more than problematic.

Whatever it became, Fascist anti-Semitism was never a question of *biological determinism* among those who spoke most authoritatively.[35] Unlike National Socialist theoreticians, the issues of race and anti-Semitism never became one involving genetic determinism for Fascist intellectuals—a notion violative of every principle of Fascist idealism. Like the anti-Semitism of the Soviet Union, anti-Semitism in Fascist Italy never became an inextricable component of its doctrine.[36] It was a tactical posture largely dictated by the association with Hitler's Germany.

For almost all major Fascist thinkers, any flirtation with biological determinism and anti-Semitism remained, at best, marginal. Whenever such elements surfaced, they can easily be traced to contingencies, precipitated by historic and political circumstance.[37] There was never *doctrinal* substance that might provide them vindication.

As such, Fascist arguments never provided a rationale for the mass murder of members of the Jewish community.[38] Racism never succeeded in

[33] Paolo Orano, *Gli Ebrei in Italia* (Rome: Casa Editrice "Pinciana," 1938).

[34] In August 1938, the journal *La Difesa della razza* appeared. It contained material that emphasized biological determinants of behavior, assessments that conflicted with what had been standard Fascist judgments concerning human responsibility. Few, if any, major Fascist intellectuals contributed to its pages, and when they did, it was to qualify the biological determinism prevalent. The anti-Semitism in its pages was of the vilest sort and found scant support among established Fascist intellectuals.

[35] Even among the most culpable, such as Roberto Farinacci, the argument against the Jews was not predicated on biological determinism. It was grounded in what were taken to be the anti-Fascist postures of Jewish organizations or on the alleged wickedness of Talmudic counsel concerning treatment of non-Jews. None of this constituted a rationale for mass murder. See Roberto Farinacci, "La Chiesa e gli Ebrei," "I non Ebrei e il Talmud," and "La Francia e gli Ebrei," in *Realtà storiche* (Cremona: Società Editoriale, 1939), pp. 81–169. See the account in Roberto Maiocchi, *Scienza italiana e razzismo fascista* (Florence: La Nuova Italia, 1999), pp. 187–210.

[36] Fascist anti-Semitism was exorbitantly expensive for Italy as it was to be for the Soviet Union (not to speak of National Socialist Germany). See the discussion on Fascist Italy in Israel and Nastasi, *Scienza e razza nell'Italia fascista* and that concerning the Soviet Union, in Gennadi Kostyrchenko, *Out of the Red Shadows: Anti-Semitism in Stalin's Russia* (Amherst, N.Y.: Prometheus, 1995); and Arkady Vaksberg, *Stalin against the Jews* (New York: Alfred A. Knopf, 1994).

[37] See the discussion in Sergio Panunzio, *Teoria generale dello stato fascista*, 2nd enlarged ed. (Padua: CEDAM, 1939) paras. 6 and 12.

[38] The logic of the National Socialist argument apparently took the following form: the Jewish deficits (whatever they were imagined to be) were *biological* and fixed. In order to

supplanting the principal elements of Fascist doctrine. Unlike National Socialism, biological determinism and anti-Semitism remained transient and indigestible constituents of Fascist doctrine. That any such racism and anti-Semitism should survive as definitive of Fascist thought is, at best, unpersuasive. However offensive to moral sensibilities both the Fascist racism and anti-Semitism that did influence political behavior might be, they never took on the determinate doctrinal properties featured in National Socialism.[39]

As intimation of its essential respectability, much of the rest of Fascist thought, disaggregated into its components, has by and large passed into contemporary thought. Giovanni Gentile's "anti-intellectualism" and his notions of a self-generative collective and transcendental consciousness, for example, have been represented as a "positive existentialism" and an "absolute humanism," comparable to the European existentialism that became popular after the Second World War.[40] Further, not a few of Gentile's ideas resurface in the "postmodernism" of contemporary "social constructivism"—in which an external material reality, independent of consciousness, is treated as nothing more than a useful fiction.[41]

Beyond that, Ugo Spirito, who survived the Second World War, went on to bring Gentile's ideas forward into postwar Europe as a "neo-idealism" that he identified as a "new humanism."[42] Like many other formerly Fascist thinkers, Spirito carried what were essentially Fascist ideas into the new Europe that emerged after the war. After the destruction of the Italian Fascism they had so long served, for example, Camillo Pellizzi and Luigi Fontanelli continued to advocate a new form of national syndicalism, and an attendant "viable corporativism," to serve a postwar "new man" who, after Italy's defeat in the Second World War, might

---

expunge the deleterious worldwide effects of those disabilities, one would have to physically expunge the "race." That argument was apparently held to be the vindication for genocide. Such an argument rarely, if ever, appeared in the public statements of any Fascist thinker. Even the writings of Giovanni Preziosi, the most committed of anti-Semites in Italy, never rested on the grounds that the "Jewish problem" was of biological origin. See the discussion in Aldo A. Mola, "Giovanni Preziosi," in Fabio Andriola, ed., *Uomini e scelte della RSI*, pp. 157–78.

[39] Fascism became complicit in the murder of Jews when the Fascist Black Brigades rounded up Jews and allowed German SS units to take them for what was, in effect, murder. About seven thousand Jews perished under those circumstances.

[40] See Vito A. Bellezza, *L'Esistenzialismo positivo di Giovanni Gentile* (Florence: G. C. Sansoni Editore, 1954).

[41] See A. James Gregor, *Metascience and Politics: An Inquiry into the Conceptual Language of Political Science* (New Brunswick, N.J.: Transaction Publishers, 2003), Postscript.

[42] See Ugo Spirito, *Nuovo umanesimo* (Rome: Armando Armando Editore, 1964); see the commentary, Roberto Mazzetti, *Quale umanesimo? Ipotesi su Croce, Gentile, Ugo Spirito, Mussolini* (Rome: Armando Armando Editore, 1966).

bring the nation back from "the abyss" of disillusion, corruption, and abject failure.[43]

For years after the end of the Second World War, "corporativism," in one form or another, continued to be a matter of serious reflection.[44] Of the constellation of themes that together provided Fascism its substance, nationalism, and irredentism—of one or another variety—resurfaced in Eastern Europe, the Balkans and in South, Southeast and East Asia, after the Second World War—and have remained influential, and probably will continue to influence events in the future. For at least some of these reasons, some have seen "fascism" reappearing in less-developed, reactive nationalist communities pursuing programs of rapid economic, industrial, and technological growth under authoritarian and single-party auspices.[45]

Out of all this, several defensible propositions seem to emerge: (1) Most of the central doctrinal convictions of Fascism were largely inoffensive in their simple affirmation. (2) Taken together, however, the ideas are, on their face and in fact, rather more irrelevant than offensive to modern Europeans, North Americans and Japanese. There are few, if any, nations in the European Union, for example, that conceive themselves oppressed, and held inferior by their neighbors. The nations that harbored such sentiments before the Second World War are now among the wealthiest and most dynamic of the Union. In those circumstances it would seem very unlikely that thematic Fascism would find a place anywhere in the Union or among industrially advanced democracies.

The evidence seems to suggest that all the themes that characterize interwar Fascism are all but completely irrelevant to Europe, North

[43] See Camillo Pellizzi, *La tecnica come classe dirigente* (Rome: Libreria Frattina Editrice, n.d., but probably 1963) and Luigi Fontanelli, "Per un nuovo ruolo del sindacato," as appendix to Pellizzi, *La tecnica come classe dirigente*, pp. 71–104. See the more ample discussion of Pellizzi's postwar position in Danilo Breschi and Gisella Longo, *Camillo Pellizzi: La ricerca delle elites tra politica e sociologia* (Soveria Mannelli's Rubbettino Editore, 2003), pp. 235–54.

[44] In reformist China, the Communist party has fostered the growth of a "corporatist" structure for the economy. See the discussion in Bruce J. Dickson, *Red Capitalists in China: The Party, Private Entrepreneurs, and Prospects for Political Change* (Cambridge: Cambridge University Press, 2003), pp. 23–26. More than that, "corporativism" remained a matter of discussion in Italy and elsewhere after the passing of Fascism. See, for example, the publications of the Istituto di studi corporativi in Rome, particularly works like Gaetano Rasi, *La società corporativa: Partecipazione programmazione* (Rome: Istituto di studi corporativi, 1973), 2 vols., and Raffaele Delfino, *Programmazione corporativa* (Rome: Volpe, 1967). In the 1970s, Fedrick B. Pike and Thomas Stritch, eds., spoke of *The New Corporatism: Social-Political Structures in the Iberian World* (Notre Dame: The University of Notre Dame Press, 1974).

[45] See the discussion in A. James Gregor, *A Place in the Sun: Marxism and Fascism in China's Long Revolution* (Boulder, Colo.: Westview Press, 2000).

America, and Japan after the developments that followed the termination of the Second World War. Reactive nationalism no longer appears to find a place among them. Irredentism no longer seems to command the passions it did during the interwar years. Economic and industrial development no longer generate the commitment they once did, in those environs, three-quarters of a century ago. For Europeans, political authoritarianism and dictatorship elicits little of the favor it did in the 1920s and early 1930s. As a consequence, none of the real or imagined "fascisms" of the interwar years have resurfaced with any credibility in any nation of the European Union. Even the most successful, the "neofascism" of the Italian Movimento sociale italiano, was largely Fascist in name only. While the initial phases of the Movement were large with nostalgia, with Fascist songs, and the presence of Fascist paraphernalia, there was very little, if anything, like a Fascist program. Whatever Fascism there was in the Movement was the product of the presence of survivors of the Fascist republic of Salò.[46]

Once all of that is understood, one easily comprehends why the Movement gradually shed most of the identifiable features of interwar Fascism until, in the 1990s, it entirely abjured "totalitarianism" in any form, and explicitly denounced any expression of racism. The reality is that Fascism no longer appears to constitute an issue for contemporary Italians, in particular, or Europeans in general.

What commentators almost invariably identify as "fascist" activity in contemporary Europe is the product of individual and group activity that advocates, or engages in, violence against immigrants and/or Jews—and/ or which denies the reality of the mass murder of Jews during the Second World War—and/or trashes graveyards and/or supports Arab fundamentalists in their opposition to Israel and the West.[47] To call such posturing "fascist" might be useful in mobilizing sentiment in day-to-day political contest, but it hardly tells us much about historic Fascism—and prepares us even less for any cognate fascisms that might appear in the future.

It seems very unlikely that entertaining and/or disseminating any peculiar constellation of ideas might re-create "fascism" in Europe. Like all revolutions, Fascism was the product of an array of historical circumstances that in their specifics can never appear again. Nonetheless, that

---

[46] See the informed discussion in Ludovico Garruccio (Ludovico Incisa di Camerana), "Fascismo, Pseudofascismo e MSI," *La Discussione* 19 (1035), 4 (November 1971), reprinted in Ludovico Incisa di Camerana, *Fascismo, Populismo, Modernizzazione* (Rome: Antonio Pellicani Editore, 1999), pp. 135–41.

[47] See the account in Glyn Ford, ed., *Fascist Europe. The Rise of Racism and Xenophobia* (London: Pluto, 1992). The confusion arises out of the fact that many in the radical European left support the Palestinian resistance against Israel, probably for reasons having nothing to do with anti-Semitism.

there will be revolutions in the future, and that they may take on some of the traits we have associated with Mussolini's Fascism can hardly be gainsaid. That those traits, together with the historic conditions that generated them, might foster the re-creation of features of Fascism that proved exceedingly dangerous, is equally possible. That possibility recommends that we equip ourselves to recognize the traits and the conditions that evoke and sustain them. As has been suggested, that cannot be an easy task.

Actualism: and Carta del lavoro, 117; *Ideas in:* collectivity, 141; democracy, 107; economy, 116, 139, 141; elite, 120; freedom, 122; history, 124, 125; human beings, 124; humanism, 161, 168; immanence, 161; individual, 97, 124, 141; individual and community, 113, 128; individual identification with state, 154; interaction with others, 98; liberalism, 97, 126, 141; morality, 124, 141; nationalism, 141; national syndicalism, 109; objectivity, 124, 126; parliament, 141; politics, 141; positivism, 123–25, 126; profound self, 96; race, 189, 190, 194, 195; religion, 125, 167–68; sacrifice, 153; science, 123–25, 126; self, 109; self-actualization, 96–97, 98; self-realization, 109; society, 141; spirituality, 168; state, 141; subjectivity, 124; syndicalism, 85; transcendence, 161, 167; truth, 93; will, 146; *In relation to:* Costamagna, 168, 188; Evola, 196, 220; Farinacci, 168; Fascism, 86, 88, 97, 98, 99, 133; Mussolini, 86, 98, 110, 137, 168–69; Orano, 168; Panunzio, 83, 86, 88, 89, 141, 142, 150, 152, 159, 161–62; Pellizzi, 167, 168, 172, 176, 177, 243; Roman Catholic Church, 160–61, 167–68; Spirito, 92, 93, 94, 97, 99, 109, 111, 133, 236. *See also* Fascism; Gentile, Giovanni
actualization. *See* self
Africa, 139, 191, 223
agencies, intermediate, 118. *See* institutions
agriculture/agrarian population, 12, 20–21, 45, 56, 99, 105, 228
Albertine Constitution, 88
Alfieri, Vittorio, 22
anti-Comintern pact, 139
anti-Semitism: in Costamagna, 189–90; in Evola, 200–201, 212, 219, 221, 225–26; in Fascism, 193, 194, 211, 212, 217, 220, 257–59, 261–62; in Hitler, 215, 257n; in law, 216; in Mussolini,

193, 215; in National Socialism, 217, 257n, 259; in Preziosi, 226. *See also* Jews; race
Ardigo, Roberto, 62, 69
aristocracy: and Associazione nazionalista italiano, 34, 49; government by, 27; landed, 44; as leader of masses, 32; in Olivetti, 52; in Panunzio, 66, 76, 88; in Papini, 27; in Pellizzi, 172, 173, 174, 176; productive, 49; squadristi as, 166; workers as, 242. *See also* elite
Aristotle, 113
Aryans/Aryanism, 187, 188, 200, 201, 202, 203, 206, 207, 211, 214, 215, 216, 218
Assembly of the National Council of Corporations, 240
associations/organizations: employer, 130, 173; and Great Depression, 137; in Mussolini, 90; private for production, 117; single for production, 237, 238; and state, 90, 118; of workers, 35, 76, 108, 130. *See also* corporations
Associazione nazionalista italiano (ANI), 49, 56, 89; aristocracy in, 34, 49; corporativism in, 98; Corradini's domination of, 41; in Costamagna, 189; democracy in, 41; economy in, 49; education in, 49; elite in, 49; first congress of, 35, 38, 40; and Gentile, 91; industry in, 34, 49, 50; and List, 48; Marxism in, 50; and Panunzio, 89; production in, 50; proletariat in, 50; revolution in, 50; and Rocco, 42, 43; and Roman Catholic Church, 58–59; second congress of, 40; socialism in, 50; society in, 50; state in, 58; and syndicalism, 57
Austria, 193
Austria-Hungary, 77, 78
autarky, 135n, 140, 170
authoritarianism: contemporary relevance of, 261; in corporativism, 175; and democracy, 150; in Evola, 210; in Italian Nationalist Association, 58; in List, 46; in Panunzio, 73, 86, 176; in Rocco, 51

authority, 240; of law, 77; in Panunzio, 70, 71, 73, 74–76, 75, 77; in Pellizzi, 170; of state, 75
Avanguardia socialista, 66
Axis powers, 180

Bacon, Francis, 92
Badoglio, Pietro, 223, 224, 244
Balbo, Italo, 149
Baldazzi, Giovanni, 53
Balkans, 184
Bedouins, 47
Belgium, 24
Bergson, Henri, 54, 90, 92
Berkeley, George, 92
Bernstein, Eduard, 61
Blanqui, August, 53
Bolshevism, 9; economic and industrial failures of, 100, 102, 104; in Evola, 198; in Panunzio, 155, 156, 157; in Pellizzi, 243; sources of support for, 21; in Spirito, 134, 135, 239; state-controlled economy in, 101; violence in, 252. *See also* Soviet Union
Bombacci, Nicola, 228, 229, 244
Bombrini, Alberto Maria, 59
Bottai, Giuseppe, 135
Bradley, F. H., 92

Camera dei Fasci e delle corporaziani, La, 174
Cantimori, Delio, 186
capitalism: in Bernstein, 61; in Corridoni, 56–57; in Engels, 63; and Fascism, 1, 7, 13, 18–19; and fascism, 5–6, 8; Gramsci on, 10, 11; in Italy, 6; Marx on, 6–7; in Marxism, 6; middle class in, 6, 7; in Mussolini, 104, 140; in Panunzio, 69–70; profit in, 12–13, 18; and revolution, 18; in Rocco, 44; and socialism, 50; in Spirito, 131, 238–39
Caracciola, Nicola, 216
Carta del lavoro, La, 108, 110, 111, 117, 130, 132, 140, 150, 233, 234, 237. *See also* workers
Central Corporative Committee. *See* Comitato corporativo centrale
Chamberlain, H. S., 204
Cione, Edmondo, 228, 244
Civiltà fascista, 165, 242
civilization, 65, 176, 177, 184, 188, 246

class: in corporativism, 128; in Corradini, 27, 31, 33, 34; in Fascism, 89, 128; Gramsci on, 10; individual identification with, 39, 55; in Italian Social Republic, 232; in Marxism, 27, 68–69; in nationalism, 36; in Panunzio, 68–69, 72, 78, 156, 157; in socialism, 25; state as mediator of interests in, 53; in syndicalism, 32, 36, 55
class conflict: in Corradini, 33, 49; in Fascism, 128; in Gumplowicz, 67, 68; and industry, 128; in Marxism, 27, 28, 63, 67; in Panunzio, 66, 67, 68, 72, 145; in Pellizzi, 167; in Sorel, 65, 66, 68
Clauss, Ludwig Ferdinand, 207–8
Colajanni, Napoleone, 62
collective/collectivity: in Actualism, 141; in Corradini, 39; democracy in, 58; and economy, 118, 132; in Fascism, 89, 97, 99; in Fontanelli, 240; in Gentile, 86, 87, 96, 110, 112, 122–23, 171; harmony in, 121; List on, 46; in Mussolini, 136; in nationalism, 38, 41; in Panunzio, 67, 68, 73, 90, 103, 141; and personhood, 87; in Rocco, 43; sacrifice for, 122; in Spirito, 110; in syndicalism, 55; totalitarian, 87. *See also* community; corporativism; society
colonialism, 25, 41, 139, 177, 191–92. *See also* expansionism; imperialism
Comitato corporativo centrale (Central Corporative Committee), 162, 173, 174
Committee of Eighteen, 108
community: in Actualism, 113, 128; from association of similars, 39; choice in, 116; common destiny of, 74; in Corradini, 27–28, 39; of destiny, 39, 129; and economy, 132; in Fascism, 255, 256; in Gentile, 114; and individual, 116, 127, 153; individual identification with, 79, 109, 122, 147; individual as protected from, 128; individual sacrifice to, 154; as individual's core, 114; law in, 74; and leader, 122; in Mussolini, 137; nation and, 255; in nationalism, 38, 39; in Panunzio, 71–72, 74, 75, 76, 79, 151; right reason in, 116; in syndicalism, 31, 32; syndicates in, 123. *See also* collective/collectivity; society
Confederation generale du Travail, 81
confederations, 129, 130, 237
Confederazione dell'industria, 237

Confederazione del sindacati industriali, 236–37

Confederazione generale dellavoro, della tecnica e delle arti (General Confederation of Labor, Technology and the Arts), 232

consciousness, 94, 95–96, 259

consensus, 122, 176

Consiglio nazionale delle corporazioni (National Council of Corporations), 130, 162

consumption, 44

corporations: in Fascism, 128–29; labor and employer organizations as, 130; in Mussolini, 90; in Spirito, 132–33; as state organ, 133; in totalitarian state, 134; workers as stockholders in, 132–33. See also associations/organizations

corporativism: in Associazione nazionalista italiano, 98; authoritarianism in, 175; and Carta del lavoro, 233; class in, 128; consultative institutions of, 169–70, 173, 175; control by, 140; in Corradini, 35; duality in production system of, 236, 238; economy in, 116, 117, 128, 173–74, 175, 233, 237; in Evola, 197, 201; as failure, 175; in Fascism, 97, 99, 239; Ferrara conference on, 133, 134, 135, 136, 140, 232, 236; in Fontanelli, 240, 241, 243, 259–60; and general will, 123; in Gentile, 113, 235, 236, 244; hierarchy in, 175; and hierarchy of organized labor, 134; individual in, 117; individual as adversary in, 128; and industry, 59, 175, 233; institutions of, 113, 123, 169–70, 173, 174, 231, 232, 240; integral, 131, 134, 139, 237, 239, 240, 241; in Italian Social Republic, 231, 232; and law, 113, 130, 175; manager in, 239; in Mussolini, 110, 111n, 131, 136, 140, 149n, 225, 233, 244; and owners, 232; in Panunzio, 73, 76, 79, 141, 142, 143, 173, 174, 176; in Pellizzi, 165, 169, 170–71, 173, 242–43, 259–60; in Rocco, 59–60; and Roman Catholic Church, 59; and science, 134; and socialism, 134; in Spirito, 98, 111, 112–13, 116, 119, 129, 130, 131–36, 140, 141, 142, 237, 238, 239, 241; and state, 35, 59–60, 110, 123, 170; syndicates in, 175; in Volpicelli, 119; workers in, 59, 134, 232, 238, 239. See also collective/collectivity; Consiglio nazionale delle corporazioni (National Council of Corporations)

Corradini, Enrico: and domination of Associazione nazionalista italiano, 41; and first nationalist congress, 35; Ideas on: class, 31, 33, 34; collectivism, 39; community, 27–28, 39; corporativism, 35; democracy, 30–31, 32, 41; economy, 29, 48, 49; elite, 32; heroes, 32; history, 29, 48, 49; human beings, 29; imperialism, 48, 48–49; individual, 153; industry, 41, 49; leaders, 32; liberalism, 49; masses, 30; military, 49; modernity, 33; nation, 31–32, 49; nationalism, 25–26, 27, 30, 37, 39, 41, 108; national syndicalism, 36, 83; parliament, 30–31, 32, 49; plutocracy, 33–34; production, 32, 48, 48–49; proletariat, 27, 33; revolution, 27, 32; socialism, 28; soldier-producer, 34; state, 153; syndicalism, 28, 29, 30, 31–32, 37, 57; workers, 31, 33; World War I, 49; In relation to: Corridoni, 57; Gentile, 85; List, 48, 49; Marxism, 27, 28, 29; Olivetti, 54; Orano, 54; Rocco, 42, 48, 49, 57; Sorel, 28; Valli, 38

Corridoni, Filippo, 56–57, 58, 101

Costamagna, Carlo, 168, 186–88, 189–90, 220

Council of Eighteen, 188

Croce, Benedetto, 26, 75, 82, 91

crowd. See masses

culture: and Associazione nazionalista italiano, 34; in Costamagna, 187; in Evola, 201, 202, 203; Fascist, 165–66; foreign, 42–43; in Gentile, 86, 236; and international survival, 40; Italian inferiority in, 25; in List, 46; in Panunzio, 79; in Rocco, 43; of workers, 236, 239

custom, 74

Cyrenaica, 35

Davanzati, Roberto Forges, 37

De Felice, Renzo, 220, 248n

De Man, Henri, 17

democracy: abandonment of, 58; in Actualism, 107; and Associazione nazionalista italiano, 41; authoritarian, 150; and authoritarianism, 150; in collectives, 58; consensus in, 122; in Corradini, 30–31, 32, 41; elite manipulation of, 120; in

democracy (*cont'd*)
  Engels, 63; in Evola, 198; and Fascism,
  8, 15, 107, 121, 171; in Futurism, 107;
  general will in, 121; in Gentile, 119–20,
  122, 171, 172; individual in, 41, 58, 97;
  in Italian Socialist party, 61; and liberalism, 41; masses in, 120; in Mussolini,
  100, 107; and nationalism, 36, 40, 41,
  58; in Panunzio, 72, 176; in Papini, 27;
  in Pellizzi, 171; representative, 120; in
  Rocco, 43, 58, 60; in Sighele, 40; and socialism, 41, 63; in Sorel, 64, 65; in syndicalism, 36, 107; totalitarian, 119–20; in
  Valli, 40; in Western thought, 120
De'Stefani, Alberto, 102
determinism, 54, 82, 95, 124
dictatorship, 155, 261. *See also* leader/
  leadership
Dopolavoro, 162
Dovere nazionale, Il, 59

Eastern Europe, 184
economy: in Actualism, 116, 139, 141; administrators in, 132; and Associazione
  nazionalista italiano, 34, 49; atomistic individuality in, 116; Bolshevik failures in,
  100, 102, 104; in Bombacci, 230; and
  capital resources, 44; and collectivity,
  118, 132; and community, 132; competitiveness in, 41, 46, 48, 50; corporativist,
  116, 117, 128, 173–74, 175, 233, 237;
  in Corradini, 29, 48, 49; in Corridoni,
  101; demand in, 44; development of, 26,
  43, 45, 100, 104, 175, 247; distribution
  of material benefits in, 20, 41, 44–45,
  50, 58; in Fascism, 12–13, 14, 21, 89,
  97, 101, 103, 105–6, 111, 113, 116,
  128, 163, 239, 256; in Fontanelli, 243;
  free enterprise in, 100, 116–17; free market, 104; in Gentile, 107; and human beings, 132; industrial, 19–20; intermediate agencies in, 118; international, 40,
  129, 163, 170, 236; in Italian Social Republic, 230–31; of Italy, 21–25, 100,
  104, 175; and law, 69; liberal policy in,
  105–6, 116, 123, 126, 131–32, 139,
  153, 238, 239; in List, 43–44, 45–46;
  market-based, 103, 104; in Marx, 70; in
  Marxism, 19–20; in Mussolini, 13, 100–
  101, 102, 104, 107, 129, 136–37, 178,
  191–92, 193, 228, 229, 245; national,
  135; in nationalism, 26, 59, 247; in Pa-

nunzio, 69, 72, 74, 75, 80, 103, 104,
  141, 143, 157, 176; in Pareto, 102, 103,
  126, 127; in Pellizzi, 170, 242, 243;
  planned, 238; plutocratic domination of,
  33–34; post–World War II, 13; private
  initiative in, 116, 117; private property
  in, 103; private vs. public in, 117; programmatic, 134–35; regulated, 134–35;
  representation in, 173, 174, 175; retrograde, 243; and revolution, 20, 56; in
  Rocco, 42, 43, 44, 45, 48, 51, 103, 153;
  in Schmitt, 182; in socialism, 50; socialization of, 228, 230, 231, 232, 244, 245;
  in Sorel, 70; Soviet, 100, 102, 243; in
  Spirito, 107, 109, 116–17, 123, 126,
  127, 130–36, 139, 236, 238, 239; and
  state, 100–101, 170; state control of,
  101, 106, 107, 108, 110, 117, 129, 132,
  138, 139, 140; and state corporativism,
  117; state interference in, 100; stockholders in, 132–33; in syndicalism, 101, 128;
  in Volpicelli, 107; worker governance of,
  232–34; and World War I, 5
education, 40, 49, 74, 119, 121, 122, 141,
  154, 156, 166, 167, 173, 241
Educazione fascista, 165, 177
elections, 59, 120–21, 146. *See also* democracy; representation
elite: in Actualism, 120; in Associazione
  nazionalista italiano, 49; and consensus,
  121; in Corradini, 32; in democracy,
  120; in Gentile, 123; government by,
  121; from Italian Socialist party, 32; leadership of, 32, 80, 121; from Marxism,
  32; and middle class, 32; and morality,
  149; in Mosca, 120; in Mussolini, 100;
  and nationalism, 32, 36, 38; in Panunzio, 66, 74, 80, 148–49, 176; in Pareto,
  120; in Pellizzi, 173; revolutionary, 121;
  rotation of, 32, 121; rule by, 123; in syndicalism, 32, 36; and threat, 121–22;
  and will, 149; workers as, 242. *See also*
  aristocracy
Emerson, Ralph Waldo, 30
emigration, 25, 27, 33, 40, 42
empire. *See* imperialism
empiricism, 71, 74, 75, 87, 92, 94, 95, 97,
  125. *See also* science
Enciclopedia italiana, 162
Engels, Friedrich, 46, 47–48, 52, 61, 63,
  67, 157
Enlightenment, 2, 8

enterprise, 133; free, 100, 116–17. *See also* economy
enterprise council, 231
entrepreneur, 35, 44, 60, 79, 131
epistemocracy, 27
epistemology: in Evola, 195; in Gentile, 94; in Mussolini, 212; in Spirito, 92, 93, 94. *See also* knowledge; thinking
Ethiopia, 25, 139, 170, 192
ethnicity, 188, 189. *See also* race
Europe, 23, 24, 42, 43
Evola, Julius, viii, 16, 133n, 158n, 195–207, 208–11, 212, 217–21, 222, 228, 255; *Fundamentals of Fascist Race Theory*, 211; *Heidnischer Imperialismus*, 200–201, 202; *Imperialismo pagano*, 196, 199, 200–201, 202; *Il mito del sangue*, 204; *Rivolta contra il mondo moderno*, 202–3, 204; *Sintesi di dottrina della razza*, 204–5, 211, 212, 217–18
expansionism, 41, 42, 46, 47–48, 163, 177, 178–79. *See also* colonialism; imperialism

Farinacci, Roberto, 168, 219, 220, 227–28, 258n
Fasci di combattimento, 10, 254
fascio interventionista, 77
Fascism: basis for, 2; and birthrate, 105; in Bombacci, 230; changing views of, vii—viii, 1–17; in contemporary thought, 259–61; as contradictory, 6, 7; culture of, 165–66; doctrinal coherence of, 111; as ecclesiastic, 141; economic growth under, 14; and employer organizations, 130; end of, 245, 246; as enemy of West, 2; evil of, 8, 15; as extremist, 3, 4, 198; and finance capitalists, 12; foreign policy of, 101, 163, 165, 177, 184, 256; and Great Depression, 137, 163; historical context of, 261–62; ideology of, 5, 9, 12, 14–15, 83–84, 149, 249; and industrial capitalism, 5–6, 7; and industrialists, 12; and infrastructure, 105; as inhumane, 256; institutions of, 111, 155, 163, 165; intermediate agencies of, 118; as irrational, 1–2, 3, 4, 6, 7, 9, 11, 16, 198, 249–50, 256; Italy controlled by, 99, 106, 155; and labor organizations, 130; and landholders, 12; and Matteotti murder, 98, 106; in Movimento socialista italiano, 261; and National Social-

ism, 2, 4, 179–80, 193, 195, 217, 220, 258, 259; and nation's general interests, 105; as progressive, 14, 15; and proletarian revolution, 1, 7; and proletariat, 14; and "Protection of Motherhood and Infancy" program, 105; rational programs of, 19; as regime, 98; restoration of, 224–30; and right-wing politics, 3, 4, 15, 16; rural population in, 12, 105; sources of support for, 21; spheres of influence in, 184; squadristi of, 166, 197; and state socialism, 170; support for, 106; themes of, 255–56; and thought vs. behavior, 248–49; as transitional regime, 106; and urban middle class, 12; and urban population, 105; and Victor Emmanuel III, 224, 225; and World War II, 224; *Ideas in*: Actualism, 86, 88, 97, 98, 99, 133; agriculture, 105; antihumanism, 198; anti-Semitism, 193, 194, 211, 212, 217, 220, 257–59, 261–62; civilization, 184; class, 89, 128; class struggle, 128; collectivity, 89, 97, 99; community, 255, 256; corporations, 128; corporativism, 97, 99, 239; democracy, 8, 15, 107, 121, 171; economic liberalism, 105–6, 113, 239; economy, 12–13, 14, 21, 89, 97, 100, 101, 103, 111, 113, 116, 128, 163, 256; education, 141; epistemarchy, 141–42; expansionism, 163, 177; general will, 121; imperialism, 184; individual, 89, 97, 256; industry, 108, 111; irredentism, 13, 261; Jews, 214, 216, 217, 220; land reclamation, 105; law, 111, 154–55; leadership, 142, 150; living space, 184; military, 13, 101, 105, 106; modernization, 108; morality, 4, 256; mysticism, 2, 205, 213; nation, 90, 255; nationalism, 35, 61, 99; nation-state, 89; parliament, 107; police, 101; pragmatism, 92; private property, 113; production, 12–14, 111, 128; psychology, 212; race, 185–90, 193–95, 200, 211, 211–12, 213, 214–17, 225–26, 257–59; science, 212; self-actualization, 255; self-realization, 256; single party rule, 142; state, 99, 100, 101, 255; syndicalism, 99, 170; syndicalism and nationalism unified, 61; technology, 12, 13; totalitarianism, 84, 97, 99, 107, 256; violence, 3, 8, 15, 17, 89, 141, 250–52, 253, 256; virtue, 141; war, 89; workers,

Fascism (cont'd)
105; In relation to: Bergson, 92; capitalism, 1, 7, 13, 18–19; Enlightenment, 2,
8; Evola, 196, 197, 198, 199, 200, 201,
202, 204, 210, 211, 219, 255; Futurism,
255; Gentile, 171, 172, 227; Gramsci, 5,
6; Hegel, 153; Lenin, 93; Marxism, 1, 5,
6–17, 19, 21; Mussolini, 1n, 137; Pantaleoni, 102, 103; Panunzio, 66, 83, 86,
154–55, 158–59; Pareto, 102–3; Pellizzi,
176, 242–43; Roman Catholic Church,
160; Schmitt, 183; Spirito, 91–92, 132,
238. See also Actualism
fascism, 1n, 4, 5–6, 8, 18n
Fascist Grand Council, 106
Fascist Labor Charter. See Carta del lavoro, La
Fascist Republican Party, 229
Fascist Social Republic. See Repubblica
sociale italiano
Ferraris, Dante, 59
finance capitalism, 12, 13, 18, 18n, 20
Finelettrica (electricity), 138
Finmare (shipbuilding), 138
Finmeccanica (mechanical industries), 138
Finsider (iron and steel), 138
Fontanelli, Luigi, 236, 240, 241, 244n,
259–60
France, 24, 28, 35, 42, 56, 63–64, 77,
191, 192
freedom, 76, 116, 122
free market, 45, 102
free trade, 44, 45, 101
French Revolution, 2, 8, 23
future, 66, 69, 70, 76
Futurism, 19, 83, 107, 227, 250, 251, 252,
253, 254, 255

General Confederation of Labor, Technology and the Arts, 232
Gentile, Giovanni: and Civiltà fascista,
165; and constitution, 107–8; contribution of, 17; Discorsi di religione, 235;
and Educazione fascista, 165, 177; and
Istituto nazionale di cultura fascista,
165–66; and Italy, 86; and "National
Fascist Institute of Culture," 165; preamble to Dottrina del fascismo, 119–20,
133, 152, 160, 241; and Roman Catholic Church, 133, 167, 168, 169, 188;
and World War I, 91; Ideas on: activity,
96; categories, 95; collectivity, 86, 87,

96, 110, 112, 122–23, 171; community,
114; consciousness, 94, 96, 259; corporativism, 113, 235, 236, 244; culture,
86, 236; democracy, 119–20, 122, 171,
172; economy, 107; education, 166, 167;
elite, 123; empiricism, 87; epistemology,
94; ethnicity, 189; experience, 159; history, 167, 189; humanism, 160, 235,
259; idealism, 87, 94, 96, 188; immanence, 159, 167; imperialism, 189; individual, 86, 87, 96, 97, 109, 112, 114,
152; industry, 86; intellectuals, 94; jurisprudence, 88; knowledge, 94, 159; law,
87, 88; leader, 87, 122–23, 149; liberalism, 97; materialism, 94, 189; morality,
88, 94, 96, 114, 159, 189, 242; nationalism, 37, 85, 86, 91; nationality, 189; nature, 94; object, 94, 159; objectivity, 94;
ontology, 94; personhood, 87; politics,
87; production, 242; race, 185n, 188,
189, 194, 226; religion, 159–60, 167;
representation, 87; self, 55, 87, 96–97,
109, 147, 152, 171; socialism, 235; spirituality, 86, 94, 96, 98, 176, 189; state,
86–87, 99, 152, 171, 176, 189; subject,
94, 159; syndicalism, 85, 86, 91; thinking, 94, 96, 115; totalitarianism, 87,
110, 247; transcendental self, 147; truth,
94; universality, 87; will, 86, 87, 146;
workers, 86, 98, 235, 235–36, 242; In relation to: Corradini, 85; Costamagna,
188, 189; Croce, 91; Evola, 133n, 196,
219–20; existentialism, 259; Fascism,
171, 172, 227; Hegel, 88; Kant, 87, 88,
94; Marx, 244; Mussolini, 54, 55, 88,
133, 241; neo-Hegelianism, 83; Olivetti,
235; Panunzio, 15, 82, 83, 85, 86, 87,
142, 150, 152, 159, 161, 162, 235; Pellizzi, 167, 172, 241, 243; Rocco, 85;
Rousseau, 147; Spirito, 90, 91, 92, 93,
94, 110, 111, 238, 239, 259. See also
Actualism
Gentile, Panfilo, 51–52
German Social Democratic party, 61–62
Germany, 137; and Austria, 193; expansionism of, 42; and industry, 19, 24; and
Italian socialism, 24; and Italy, 77, 139,
179–80, 183, 186, 191, 192–93, 195,
213–14, 222, 224, 228–29, 244, 258;
and Mussolini, 218, 221, 226; nationalism in, 56; oversight of production in,
244–45; in Panunzio, 78, 79; in Pellizzi,

176; race in, 185, 187, 218, 225; in Schmitt, 182; and Spain, 192; and Turkey, 35. *See also* National Socialism

Gini, Corrado, 105

Gioberti, Vincenzo, 26, 152, 161; *Del primato morale e civile degli italiani,* 23, 152

Giolitti, Giovanni, 10

Gobineau, Joseph Arthur de, 204

Gramsci, Antonio, 5, 6, 10–11

Gran consiglio (Grand Council of Fascism), 107, 138, 139, 162, 174, 223, 227

Grandi, Dino, 223

Great Britain, 24, 35, 42, 46, 47, 70, 77, 176, 191, 192, 223

Great Depression, 18, 129, 130, 137, 163, 231, 233

Green, J. H., 92

group, real vs. artificial, 72. *See also* community; society

Gumplowicz, Ludwig, 37, 67, 69, 79, 82, 90, 124, 212; *Die sociologische Staatsidee,* 67

Günther, Hans F. K., 204

Hegel, G.W.F.: and Fascism, 153; in Gentile, 88; individual in, 97, 133, 153; and Marx, 244; and Panunzio, 74, 86, 90, 141, 148, 151, 152, 162; and Rousseau, 147; self in, 97; state in, 133. *See also* neo-Hegelianism

heroes, 30, 32, 65, 66, 172, 210. *See also* aristocracy; elite; leaders; warrior-producer

history: in Actualism, 124, 125; in Corradini, 29, 48, 49; in Corridoni, 57; in Evola, 198, 200, 201, 202–3, 209–10; and Fascism, 261–62; in Gentile, 167, 189; of human beings, 39; leaders in, 30; in Marx, 62, 63, 69; in Olivetti, 36; in Panunzio, 69, 73, 78, 79, 82, 149, 151, 152, 154, 155; in Papini, 26–27; in Pellizzi, 172; in Rocco, 48, 49, 51; in Schmitt, 182; in Sorel, 65

Hitler, Adolf: anti-Semitism in, 215, 257n; and Evola, 199; and Mussolini, 192–93, 222n, 223, 224–25, 226, 228; and Panunzio, 158; race in, 158, 185, 214, 225. *See also* National Socialism

human beings: in Actualism, 124, 141; in Corradini, 29; and economy, 132; in

Evola, 205, 210; evolution of, 39; as group animals, 30; history of, 39; and immutable laws, 37; in Kant, 76; in Marx, 36; in Mussolini, 212–13; in nationalism, 30, 31; in Olivetti, 36; in Panunzio, 71, 75, 82, 141; and science, 53; and society, 124; society as immanent in, 141; in Sorel, 65, 82; in Spirito, 93, 124; in syndicalism, 30, 31

humanism, 160, 161, 168, 198, 209, 235, 259

Hume, David, 92

Hyperboreans, 201, 202, 203, 206, 207, 210

idealism, 54; absolute, 94; as antiindividual, 87; and Costamagna, 188; critical, 81, 90; in Evola, 195; in Gentile, 87, 94, 96, 188; in Missiroli, 55; in Mussolini, 55, 83n; in Panunzio, 74, 76, 81, 82, 90, 151, 152, 161, 162; in Pellizzi, 176; in Spirito, 92, 94, 238

Idea Nazionale, 37

imperialism: and Associazione nazionalista italiano, 34; in Corradini, 48–49; in Corridoni, 57; European, 24; in Evola, 205; and Fascism, 184; in Gentile, 189; and Italy, 183; in Mussolini, 184; and nationalism, 178; in Panunzio, 144; in Pellizzi, 176, 177, 179, 184; in Rocco, 48; in Schmitt, 180, 194–95. *See also* colonialism; expansionism

individual: in Actualism, 97, 113, 124, 128, 141; atomistic, 116, 124, 125–26; as autonomous, 114; civil rights of, 43; class identified with, 39, 55; and community, 116, 127, 128, 153, 154; community as core of, 114; community identified with, 79, 109, 122, 147; and corporativism, 117, 128; in Corradini, 153; in democracy, 41, 58, 97; in economy, 116; and education, 154; equality before law, 148; in Fascism, 89, 97, 256; freedom of, 116; in Gentile, 55, 86, 87, 96, 97, 109, 112, 114, 152; in Hegel, 97, 133, 153; in idealism, 87; and law, 87; in liberalism, 97, 113, 123, 124, 125–26, 127, 131–32; in List, 46; in Marinetti, 253; in Mazzini, 23; in Missiroli, 55; moral perfection of, 154; in Mussolini, 55, 90, 136, 137; in nationalism, 50, 98; nation identified with, 55, 149;

individual (*cont'd*)
in Panunzio, 72, 76, 77, 82, 83, 86, 90, 141, 146, 147, 149, 151, 152, 174; in Pareto, 126–27; in Pellizzi, 171; profit by, 136; as reality, 112; and right reason, 116; rights of, 43, 77, 148; in Rocco, 43, 44, 153; in Rousseau, 146, 147; sacrifice of, 153, 154; self-realization in, 55, 109, 141; socialization of, 154; and society, 126; as solitary, 114; in Sorel, 65; in Spirito, 109, 123, 127, 238, 239; and state, 127, 152, 153, 174; as state adversary, 127; state as core of, 114; state defense of, 112, 114, 148; state identified with, 55, 86, 98, 112, 113, 116, 128, 129, 131, 133, 134, 136, 149, 154, 238; in syndicalism, 39, 55, 58, 98; thinking of, 115; in totalitarianism, 97; in Western thought, 112; and worker bias, 132. *See also* self
industrial associations, 59, 108
industrialists, 12, 59, 99
industrialization, 45, 110, 243, 261
industrial revolution, 46, 47
industry: and Associazione nazionalista italiano, 34, 49, 50; in Bernstein, 61; and Bolshevism, 100; in Bombacci, 230; and class struggle, 128; competitiveness of, 41, 46, 48, 50; and corporativism, 59, 175, 233; in Corradini, 41, 49; in Corridoni, 56–57, 101; and democracy, 58; development of, 33–35, 43, 44, 46, 49, 50, 100, 175, 177–78; in economic liberalism, 239; and economy, 19–20; and expansionism, 177, 178–79; and fascism, 5; in Fascism, 108, 111; in Gentile, 86; in Germany, 24; Italian, 18–19, 20, 33–35, 50, 100, 175; in List, 45, 46; manager in, 232, 233, 238; in Marxism, 19–20; in Missiroli, 55; and modernity, 19; in Mussolini, 7, 55, 110, 140, 178, 229; in nationalism, 41; and national survival, 39–40; in Panunzio, 72, 76, 143; Papini on, 27; in Pareto, 103; in Pellizzi, 170, 172; raw material for, 27, 177, 178–79; in Rocco, 42, 43, 44, 45, 49, 50, 51; sacrifice of, 50; in socialism, 50; socialization of, 228; in Sorel, 64; and state, 54; state control of, 110, 138, 140; in syndicalism, 52, 56, 247; tariff protection for, 24, 40; and urbanization, 105. *See also* economy; technology

infrastructure, 44, 45, 46, 105
Institute of Management and Finance. *See* Istituto di gestione e finanziamento
institutions: corporativist, 113, 123, 169–70, 173, 174, 231, 232; Fascist, 111, 155, 163, 165; of integral corporativism, 240; in Italian Social Republic, 231, 232
intellectuals, 64–65, 94
internationalism, socialist, 37, 40
international relations: competition in, 40, 48, 55; and Fascism, 101, 163, 165, 177, 184, 256; and Italy, 21–22, 33, 37, 42, 42–43, 110, 165, 172; in Missiroli, 55; and Mussolini, 55, 110, 234; and nationalism, 56; in Valli, 39
irredentism, 13, 41, 261
Istituto di gestione e finanziamento (Institute of Management and Finance), 230, 231
Istituto di riconstruzione industriale (IRI), 137–38, 230–31
Istituto mobiliare italiano (IMI), 137, 138, 230
Istituto nazionale di cultura fascista (National Institute of Fascist Culture), 165–66, 169, 179, 241
Italian Nationalist Association. *See* Associazione nazionalista italiano (ANI)
Italian Radical party, 42
Italian Socialist party, 19, 24, 28, 32, 61
Italian Social Republic. *See* Repubblica sociale italiano
Italy: and Africa, 191, 223; as agrarian, 20–21, 56; and Austria-Hungary, 77; and Balkans, 184; capitalism in, 6; colonialism of, 25, 191–92; competitiveness of, 50; Corridoni on, 101; development of, 42, 57, 104; and Eastern Europe, 184; economic development of, 21–25, 100, 104, 175; emigration from, 25, 27, 33, 40, 42; and Ethiopia, 25, 139, 170, 192; exploitation of, 21–22; extended space for, 183; flawed national consciousness of, 40; foreign culture in, 42–43, 172; foreign domination of, 21–22, 33; foreign investment in, 42; foreign policy of, 165; and foreign relations, 37, 110; and France, 35, 77; in Gentile, 86; and Germany, 77, 139, 179–80, 183, 186, 191, 192–93, 195, 213–14, 222, 224, 228–29, 244, 258; and Great Britain, 77; and Great Depression, 129, 138; and

imperialism, 183; importance of, 20, 22, 24–25, 26, 32, 33, 35, 104, 166–67, 172, 175, 178; independence of, 172; industrialization of, 18–19, 20, 33–35, 50, 100, 175; liberal government of, 24; List on, 46; living space for, 183, 185; in Marinetti, 250–51; material resources of, 42; modernization of, 19; Mussolini's control of, 99, 106, 109, 155; nationalism in, 23, 24–25, 36; in Panunzio, 79, 104, 175; in Pellizzi, 166–67, 172, 174, 176; and plutocracies, 37; population of, 105; rebirth of, 22; regeneration of, 174, 176; resources of, 191; as retrograde, 14, 20, 35, 56, 57, 86, 97, 104; and Risorgimento, 23–24, 34; in Rocco, 42; and Russia, 21, 77; sealines of, 178; and Spain, 192; state control of, 138; technology in, 19; Vico on, 22; and war in Libya, 58; and war in Tripoli, 54, 55, 77; and war with Turkey, 35–36, 40; and World War I, 5, 77; and World War II, 176, 179, 183, 195, 222, 224

Japan, 139, 192
Jews: in Costamagna, 189–90; in Evola, 200–201, 207, 208, 218; in Fascism, 214, 216, 217, 220; in Italian-German meetings, 193; mass murder of, 216, 217, 226, 258; in Mussolini, 217; in National Socialism, 220. *See also* anti-Semitism; race
Jouhaux, Leon, 81

Kant, Immanuel, 92; in Gentile, 87, 88, 94; in Panunzio, 74, 75, 76, 77, 82, 83, 90, 141, 145; in Spirito, 94
knowledge: in Evola, 204, 208; in Gentile, 94, 159; in Spirito, 92, 94. *See also* epistemology; thinking

labor. *See* workers
Labor Charter of 1927. *See* Carta del lavoro, La
Labor Courts, 128, 130
Labriola, Arturo, 36, 66, 69
laissez-faire, 44
landholders, 12, 99
land reclamation, 105, 138
language, 115–16, 117
Lapouge, Georges Vacher de, 204
Lateran Accords, 160, 199

law: anti-Semitism in, 216; authority of, 77; basic syndical, 130; as collective will, 79; in community, 74; and corporativism, 113, 130, 175; and economy, 69; on employer organizations, 130; equality before, 148; extended space in, 180; in Fascism, 111, 154–55; force as origin of, 69; in Gentile, 87, 88; and hegemony, 182; and human condition, 71; and individual, 87, 148; international, 180, 181, 182, 183; in Italian Social Republic, 231; Monroe Doctrine in, 181; as moral, 87; in nationalism, 86; natural, 77, 124; in Panunzio, 69, 70, 71, 72, 73–76, 77, 79, 82, 83, 143, 145, 154–55; race in, 216; and society, 69, 70, 71; in Sorel, 70, 82, 83; and state, 75, 76, 112; as utilitarian, 75; violence and, 73–74; and worker organizations, 130
Lazzei, Gerolamo, 54
leader/leadership: and community, 122; in Corradini, 32; by dictator, 155, 261; by elite, 32, 80, 121; embodied in one person, 149, 171; in Evola, 201, 202; in Fascism, 142, 150; in Fontanelli, 243; in Gentile, 87, 122–23, 149; hierarchy of, 122; in history, 30; in Marx, 36; of masses, 32, 80, 148; in Mussolini, 107; Mussolini as, 88; in nationalism, 36; in Olivetti, 36; in Panunzio, 80, 148, 155; in Pellizzi, 170, 171, 172–73; and popular opinion, 123; and psychology of masses, 30; and racial homogeneity, 188; in Schmitt, 185; selection of, 120, 173; subordination to, 107; in syndicalism, 32, 36; in totalitarianism, 149–50; of workers, 36. *See also* aristocracy; elite; heroes
Le Bon, Gustave, 37
Lenin, V. I., 9; and Fascism, 93; Marxism in, 252; and New Economic Policy, 104; and Spirito, 93n; state in, 9, 157; *State and Revolution,* 157; violence in, 252
Leonardo, 25
Leopardi, Giacomo, 23, 26
Leyers, Hans, 244–45
liberalism: abandonment of, 58; in Actualism, 97, 126, 141; in Corradini, 49; in Corridoni, 101; and democracy, 41; disintegration of, 86; economic, 105–6, 116, 123, 126, 131–32, 139, 153, 238, 239; failures of, 41, 49–50; in Fascism,

liberalism (*cont'd*)
105–6, 113, 239; in Gentile, 97; individual in, 97, 113, 123, 124, 125–26, 127, 131–32; in Italian government, 24; in Italian Nationalist Association, 58; in Italian Socialist party, 61; in List, 44, 46; in Mussolini, 100, 136; in Panunzio, 86, 141, 176; in Pellizzi, 171; and positivism, 126, 127; in Rocco, 44, 49–50, 60, 153; and science, 123–24, 127; self in, 97; and socialism, 63; in Spirito, 109, 123, 126, 236, 238, 239
libertarianism, 64, 83, 90
Libya, 35, 58
List, Friedrich, 43–44, 45–46, 47, 48, 49
Locke, John, 92
Lombardo-Radice, Giuseppe, 54
Loria, Achille, 69
Ludwig, Emil, 193
Lupa, La, 35

Machiavelli, Niccolò, 21–22
Malaparte, Curzio, 92, 249; *L'Europa vivente,* 247
manager, 232, 233, 238, 239, 243
"Manifesto of Fascist Racism," 185, 194, 214–15. *See also* race
Maraviglia, Maurizio, 37
March on Rome, 21, 85, 90, 109, 130, 154
Marinetti, Filippo Tommaso, 227, 250–52, 253, 254–55; "Al di la del comunismo," 254; "Program Manifesto of the Futurist Political Party," 254
Marshall, Alfred, 67
Marx, Karl, 6; in Bernstein, 61; *Communist Manifesto,* 36; economy in, 70; in Evola, 200; expansionism in, 46–47; and Gentile, 244; Great Britain in, 70; and Gumplowicz, 67; and Hegel, 244; history in, 62, 63, 69; human beings in, 36; on industrial capitalism, 6–7; as Jew, 200; leaders in, 36; and List, 44, 46–47; in Panunzio, 67, 69, 72, 82, 157; production in, 46; productivity in, 46; progress in, 47; revolution in, 46; and Sorel, 65–66, 70; and Spirito, 93n; and syndicalism, 52; workers in, 70. *See also* socialism
Marxism: in Associazione nazionalista italiano, 50; in Bernstein, 61; capitalism in, 6; class in, 68–69; class conflict in, 27, 28, 63, 67; in Corradini, 27, 28, 29; in Corridoni, 56; economy in, 19–20; elite

from, 32; and Fascism, 1, 5, 6–17, 19, 21; industrial economy in, 19–20; international, 37; leadership of masses in, 30; in Lenin, 252; in Mussolini, 19, 21, 53, 54, 55, 102; nationalism vs. social revolution in, 24; in Panunzio, 67, 68–69, 90, 104, 156, 158; positivism in, 29, 62; and post–World War II economy, 13; proletariat in, 6, 10; revolution in, 6, 10, 20, 56; in Rocco, 37, 44–45; and science, 29; and science vs. myth, 69; and socialism, 24, 61; in Sorel, 17, 64, 65, 68–69; in Spirito, 91; and state, 157; in syndicalism, 56; syndicalist abandonment of, 37. *See also* socialism
masses, 29–30, 31, 32, 80, 120, 121, 148, 149
materialism: in Evola, 196, 198, 204, 205–6, 210; in Gentile, 94, 189; in Mussolini, 54, 55, 192; in Panunzio, 156; in Pellizzi, 243; in Spirito, 93, 94, 95; in syndicalism, 86
Matteotti, Giacomo, 98–99, 106, 109
Mazzini, Giuseppe, 23–24, 26, 152, 161
Mazzinianism, 63
Mexico, 47
Mezzetti, Nazareno, 60
Michels, Roberto, 17, 249
middle class: and Associazione nazionalista italiano, 34; in Bernstein, 61; in Corradini, 25; in Corridoni, 56–57; and elite, 32; and Fascism, 12; Gramsci on, 10; in industrial capitalism, 6, 7; in Mussolini, 225, 228; in nationalism, 36; in Olivetti, 37; in Panunzio, 72, 73, 76, 79; in Papini, 26; proletarianization of, 6; revolutionaries as, 56; in Sorel, 64, 65
military: and Associazione nazionalista italiano, 34; in Corradini, 49; in Corridoni, 101; in Fascism, 13, 101, 105, 106; and international survival, 40; in Mussolini, 193, 214, 226; in Panunzio, 66, 72, 156; and Rocco, 49; in Sorel, 65; support for Fascism, 106; in syndicalism, 55; in syndicalism vs. nationalism, 58; and World War II, 222, 224
Ministry of Corporations, 173
Ministry of Corporative Economy, 232
Missiroli, Mario, 55
modernity, 19, 33, 76, 79
Monicelli, Tommaso, 37
Monroe Doctrine, 180–81, 182

Montini, Giovanni Battista, 198

morality: in Actualism, 124, 141; and elite, 149; in Fascism, 4, 256; in Gentile, 88, 94, 96, 114, 159, 189, 242; identification in, 147; and individual, 154; and law, 87; and nation, 146, 148; in nationalism, 37; in Olivetti, 37; in Panunzio, 69, 71, 72, 76, 82, 141, 145, 146, 147, 151, 162, 253; in Pellizzi, 167, 176, 242, 243; and perfection, 147, 151, 154; in Rousseau, 147; in Sorel, 65, 82, 242; in Spirito, 94, 95, 96; and state, 118; in syndicalism, 37; and universality, 87; and will, 148, 149

Morocco, 35

Mosca, Gaetano, 27, 37, 67, 120

Movimento socialista italiano, 261

Mussolini, Benito, 2, 10; and Africa, 191; arrested, 223, 224; and Assembly of the National Council of Corporations, 240; astuteness of, 99; and Carta del lavoro, 140, 233, 234; and Central Corporative Committee, 163; and Concordat with papacy, 160, 198; conflicting interests surrounding, 99; *Dottrina del fascismo,* 119–20, 133, 150, 151, 152, 160, 241; and Fascist Social Republic, 219, 228; and foreign relations, 55, 110, 234; and Germany, 218, 221, 226; and Gran consiglio, 162; and Great Depression, 129, 233; and Hitler, 192–93, 222n, 223, 224–25, 226, 228; ideological success of, 12; and industrialists, 99; and landholders, 99; legacy of, 228, 229, 234; as Manchestrian, 102; and Matteotti murder, 98–99, 109; and *Il popolo d'Italia,* 81; power of, 99, 106, 109, 155, 174, 228, 234; and "Protection of Motherhood and Infancy" program, 105; restoration of, 224–25, 226, 228–30; and Roman Catholic Church, 160, 168–69, 198, 199, 218, 228; as ruler, 88; tactical compromises of, 99–100; and *Utopia,* 53, 55; and Victor Emmanuel III, 226, 228; and World War I, 53–54; and World War II, 13, 218; *Ideas on:* Actualism, 86, 98, 110, 137, 168–69; anti-Semitism, 193, 215; associations, 90; autarky, 135n; authority, 240; Bolshevism's failures, 100, 104; capitalism, 104, 140; collectivity, 136; colonialism, 139, 191–92; commune, 90; commu-nity, 137; corporations, 90; corporativism, 110, 111n, 131, 136, 140, 149n, 225, 233, 244; democracy, 100, 107; determinism, 54; discipline, 110; economy, 13, 100–101, 102, 104, 107, 129, 136–37, 138, 139, 178, 191–92, 193, 228, 229, 245; education, 241; elite, 100; families in, 90; historical materialism, 192; idealism, 55, 83n; imperialism, 184; individual, 55, 90, 136, 137; industry, 7, 55, 110, 140, 178, 229; international competition, 55; Jews, 217; leaders, 107; liberalism, 100, 136; living space, 183, 191; materialism, 54, 55, 192; middle class, 225, 228; military, 193, 214, 226; mysticism, 213; nation, 89, 90, 215; nationalism, 55; National Socialism, 211, 213–14; national socialism, 54, 55; national syndicalism, 81; neo-Hegelianism, 55; parliament, 107; party, 137; plutocracy, 110, 214, 225, 233; positivism, 53; production, 100, 108, 136; property, 137, 229; race, 193, 211, 213–15, 218; revolution, 54, 55, 100, 102, 225, 226, 229, 230, 234, 241; Rome, 254; science, 53, 212, 213; scientism, 83n; socialism, 53–54, 104, 241; socialization, 228, 232, 245; society, 229; spirituality, 55, 88n, 149n; state, 55, 100, 110, 136, 137, 157; syndicalism, 99, 109; totalitarianism, 98, 107, 110, 137; violence, 253–54; will, 53, 193; workers, 12, 108, 109, 136, 193, 225, 229, 233–34; *In relation to:* Baldazzi, 53; Blanqui, 53; Bombacci, 229; Evola, 197, 198, 199, 202, 211, 212, 217–18, 219; Fontanelli, 241; Futurism, 254; Gentile, 54, 55, 88, 133, 241; Gramsci, 6; Lazzei, 54; Lombardo-Radice, 54; Marxism, 19, 21, 53, 54, 55, 102; Missiroli, 55; Pantaleoni, 102; Panunzio, 77, 89; Pareto, 102; Pellizzi, 167, 170, 171, 172, 241; Piccoli, 54; Rocco, 42; Sorel, 54; Spirito, 91, 131, 135–36, 137, 239, 240n, 244n; Tasca, 54

mysticism, 2, 195, 202, 205, 213

myth, 65, 80, 82, 204, 208, 210

nation: collective mission of, 27; and community, 255; in Corradini, 27, 31–32, 32, 49; in Costamagna, 187; emerging,

nation (*cont'd*)
  60; as ethical organism, 148; expansionism of, 47–48; as *fascio nazionale,* 78; in Fascism, 90, 105, 255; general interests of, 105; individual identification with, 55, 149; and international relations, 31, 39; late-developing, 43, 44, 45; less developed, 45, 46, 56, 101; in List, 44, 45–46; and morality, 146; in Mussolini, 89, 90, 215; in Olivetti, 52, 80–81; in Panunzio, 78, 80, 89, 143, 146, 151, 157; in Pellizzi, 176, 177; plutocratic vs. proletariat, 33–34; and society, 144; in Sorel, 81; state as mediator of interests in, 53; in syndicalism, 31–32, 55; in syndicalism vs. nationalism, 58; unity of, 43, 51; Valli on, 39; workers' governance of, 242
National Council of Corporations, 173–74
National Fascist Institute of Culture, 165
National Institute of Fascist Culture, 165–66, 169, 179, 241
nationalism: in Actualism, 141; and Associazione nazionalista italiano, 34; class in, 36; and collectivism, 38, 41; colonialism in, 177; community in, 38, 39; contemporary relevance of, 260, 261; and corporative state, 59–60; in Corradini, 25–26, 27, 37, 39, 41, 108; in Corridoni, 58; in Costamagna, 189; in Croce, 26; democracy in, 36, 40, 41, 58; as developmental, 58; economic in, 26, 247; economy in, 59; elite in, 32, 36; elite manipulation of, 38; equity in, 31; in Europe, 23; in Evola, 197, 198; expansionism of, 41; in Fascism, 35, 61, 99; in France, 56; in Gentile, 37, 85, 86, 91; in Germany, 56; human beings in, 30; and imperialism, 178; individual in, 50, 98; industry in, 41, 59; and international relations, 37, 40, 56; in Italy, 23, 24–25, 36; in Jouhaux, 81; justice in, 31; law in, 86; and Lazzei, 54; leaders of, 36; and Lombardo-Radice, 54; masses in, 31; in Mazzini, 23–24; middle class in, 36; military in, 58; morality in, 37; in Mussolini, 54, 55; nation in, 58; in Olivetti, 37, 54, 58, 85; in Orano, 54, 58, 85; in Panunzio, 80, 83, 85, 90, 108, 141; in Papini, 26–27; parliament in, 32, 36, 41, 58; in Pellizzi, 176; positivism in, 36–37; production in, 80; productivity vs. domestic

distribution in, 41, 50; and psychology, 31, 212; revolution in, 32, 58; in Rocco, 37, 57, 108; and Roman Catholic Church, 40; sacrifice in, 50; self in, 98; society in, 38; in Sorel, 81; state in, 58, 86; and syndicalism, 28, 30, 31, 32, 33, 35, 36, 37, 38, 39, 39, 54, 55, 56, 57, 58, 59, 61, 80, 85, 86, 99, 103, 108, 109; in syndicalism, 37; technology in, 59; workers in, 39, 56; and World War I, 55
nationality: in Gentile, 189; in Olivetti, 53; in Panunzio, 78, 79, 144, 145; and World War I, 53
National Socialism: anti-Semitism in, 217, 257n, 259; in Costamagna, 189; in Evola, 158n, 199, 201, 205, 210, 219; and Fascism, 2, 4, 179–80, 193, 195, 217, 220, 258, 259; Jews in, 220; living space in, 184; in Mussolini, 211, 213–14; in Panunzio, 155, 156, 158; race in, 158, 185, 187, 188, 193, 194, 195, 201, 206n, 211, 213–14, 216. *See also* Germany; Hitler, Adolf
national socialism, 54, 55
national syndicalism, 32, 33, 35, 36, 56, 57, 58, 79, 80, 81, 83, 88, 89, 103, 108, 110, 230. *See also* nationalism; syndicalism
nation-state, 31, 89, 129, 181
nature, 94, 123, 124. *See also* science
neofascism, viii
neo-Hegelianism: in Gentile, 83; in Mussolini, 55; and national syndicalism, 83; in Panunzio, 75, 82, 145, 151, 161, 162; and Rousseau, 147; in Spirito, 91. *See also* Hegel, G.W.F.
New Economic Policy (NEP), 104
Niceforo, Alfredo, 62, 212
Nietzsche, Friedrich, 36
Nordic race, 200, 201, 202, 204, 207, 208
North Africa, 47
Nuovi studi di diritto, economica e politica, 109

object, 94, 159
objectivity, 92–93, 94, 124, 125, 203–4
Olivetti, A. O., 29–30, 35, 36, 37, 52–53, 54, 58, 80–81, 85, 193, 235, 249
ontology, 94, 195
ophelimity, 126, 127

Orano, Paolo, 29–30, 35, 36, 54, 58, 62, 85, 168; *Gli Ebrei in Italia,* 257–58
organizations. *See* associations/ organizations
owners, 232, 237, 238. *See also* property

Pact of Steel, 139
Pantaleoni, Maffeo, 102, 103
Panunzio, Sergio: and Associazione nazionalista italiano, 89; and Austria-Hungary, 78; and Carta del lavoro, 150; and *Dottrina del fascismo,* 150, 151; and *fascio interventionista,* 77; and Germany, 78, 79; and Italy, 79, 104, 175; and restoration of Fascism, 227; and World War I, 77–79, 80, 82–83, 89, 143, 145, 148, 154; and World War II, 176; *Ideas on:* Actualism, 83, 86, 88, 89, 141, 142, 150, 152, 159, 161–62; anarchism, 86; aristocracy, 66, 76, 88; authoritarianism, 73, 86, 176; authority, 70, 71, 73, 74–76, 75, 77; Bolshevism, 155, 156, 157; capitalism, 69–70; class, 68–69, 69, 72, 78, 156, 157; class conflict, 66, 67, 68, 72, 145; collectivity, 67, 68, 73, 90, 103, 141; community, 71–72, 74, 75, 76, 79, 151; consensus, 176; corporativism, 73, 76, 79, 141, 142, 143, 173, 174, 176; culture, 79; democracy, 72, 176; destiny, 74; dictatorship, 155; economy, 69, 72, 74, 75, 80, 103, 104, 141, 143, 157, 176; education, 74, 156; elite, 66, 74, 80, 148–49, 149, 176; empiricism, 71, 74, 75; entrepreneurs, 79; Fascism, 66, 83, 86, 154–55, 158–59; freedom, 76; future, 69, 70, 76; futurism, 83; general strike, 66, 73, 79; heroes, 66; history, 69, 73, 78, 79, 82, 149, 151, 152, 154, 155; human beings, 71, 75, 82; idealism, 74, 76, 81, 82, 90, 151, 152, 161, 162; immanence, 159; imperialism, 144; individual, 72, 76, 77, 82, 83, 86, 90, 141, 146, 147, 148, 149, 151, 152, 174; industrial unions, 76; industry, 72, 76, 143; institutions of corporativism, 173; justice, 75, 82; law, 69, 70, 71, 72, 73–76, 77, 79, 82, 83, 143, 145, 154–55; leaders, 80, 148, 155; liberalism, 86, 141, 176; libertarianism, 83, 90; masses, 80, 149; materialism, 156; middle class, 72, 73, 76, 79; militarism, 66; military, 72, 156; mission, 80; modernity, 76, 79;

morality, 69, 71, 72, 76, 82, 141, 145, 146, 147, 151, 162, 253; myths; 80; nation, 78, 80, 89, 143, 146, 151, 157; nationalism, 80, 83, 85, 90, 108, 141; nationality, 78, 79, 144, 145; national syndicalism, 79, 80, 83, 88, 89, 103, 108; order, 83; parliament, 72, 79, 141; patriotism, 66; philosophy, 74, 76, 77, 81, 143, 151; plutocracy, 176; politics, 141, 156; positivism, 62, 74, 81, 90, 145; pragmatism in, 81; private property, 103; production, 103; profit, 69; proletariat, 66, 72–73, 76, 80, 157; property, 77; race, 158, 226; religion, 156, 161; representation, 72, 79, 150, 176; revolution, 66, 67, 69, 70, 72–73, 74, 75, 76, 78, 79, 80, 86, 88, 104, 156, 157, 159, 253; scientism, 81; self, 152; self-government, 90; sentiment, 145; socialism, 66, 69, 70, 77, 83; social psychology, 68, 73; social sciences, 67, 68, 82, 143, 145; society, 68, 70, 71, 73, 75, 77, 79, 82, 141, 143–44, 145; sociology, 74–75, 145; solidarity, 83; sovereignty, 73, 143, 144; Soviet Union, 155, 156–58; spirituality, 82, 145, 151; state, 66, 72, 73, 75, 76, 79, 86, 88, 89, 90, 103, 104, 141, 143, 144, 145, 146, 148, 151, 152, 157, 174; state syndicalism, 90; syndicalism, 66, 72, 73, 74, 77, 78, 79, 80, 86, 89, 90, 103, 108, 143; syndicates, 76; totalitarianism, 155, 157; transcendence, 161; truth, 82; violence, 73–74, 77, 252–53; vitalism, 90; voluntary associations, 76; will, 73, 77, 146, 147, 149; workers, 66, 68, 69–70, 71, 72, 73, 76, 79, 80, 173, 176, 235; *In relation to:* Bergson, 90; Croce, 75, 82; Engels, 67, 157; Gentile, 82, 83, 85, 86, 87, 142, 150, 152, 159, 161, 162, 235; Gioberti, 152, 161; Gumplowicz, 67, 69, 82, 90; Hegel, 74, 86, 90, 141, 148, 151, 152, 162; Hitler, 158; Kant, 74, 75, 76, 77, 82, 83, 90, 141, 145; Marx, 67, 69, 72, 82, 157; Marxism, 67, 68–69, 90, 104, 156, 158; Mazzini, 152, 161; Mussolini, 77, 89; National Socialism, 155, 156, 158; neo-Hegelianism, 75, 82, 145, 151, 161, 162; Pellizzi, 241; Roman Catholic Church, 160, 161; Rosmini, 152, 161; Rousseau, 74, 77, 146–47, 148; Sorel, 68, 80, 82, 86, 90; Spaventa, 161, 162;

Panunzio, Sergio (*cont'd*)
Spirito, 91, 135, 142; Vico, 152, 161;
WORKS: *Il concetto della guerra giusta,*
82; *Il diritto e l'autorita,* 74–75, 76; *Una
nuova aristocrazia sociale: I sindacati,*
66; *La persistenza del diritto,* 70–71, 72;
Sindacalismo e Medio Evo, 76; "Socialismo, sindacalismo e sociologia," 67; "Il
socialismo e la guerra," 77; *Il socialismo
giuridico,* 70; *Lo stato di diritto,* 76;
"Stato e sindacati," 85, 86; "Lo stato fascista," 90; *Teoria generale dello stato fascista,* 151, 161
Papini, Giovanni, 25, 26–27
Pareto, Vilfredo, 17, 27, 32, 37, 67, 102–3,
120, 124, 126–27, 212
parliament: in Actualism, 141; competitive
politics in, 63; in Corradini, 30–31, 32,
49; factionalism in, 43; failures of, 41,
49–50; in Fascism, 107; in Mussolini,
107; in nationalism, 32, 36, 41, 58; in
Olivetti, 36; in Panunzio, 72, 79, 141; in
Pellizzi, 167; in Rocco, 43, 51; in Sorel,
64; in syndicalism, 31, 32, 36, 54
Partito fascista repubblicano, 227, 232
Partito nazionale fascista, 98, 162,
166, 174
party, 122, 137, 142, 155–56
Paul VI, 198
Pellizzi, Camillo: and *Civiltà Fascista,*
242; *Fascismo-aristocrazia,* 166; and
Germany, 176; and Great Britain, 176;
and Istituto nazionale di cultura fascista,
166, 169, 179, 241; and Italy, 166–67,
172, 174, 176; *Problemi e realtà del fascismo,* 166; and United States, 176; and
World War I, 172, 176; *Ideas on:* Actualism, 167, 168, 172, 176, 177, 243; aristocracy, 172, 173, 174, 176; authority,
170; Bolshevism, 243; civilization, 176,
177; class conflict, 167; corporativism,
165, 169, 170–71, 173, 242–43; democracy, 171; economy, 102, 170, 242; education, 173, 241; elite, 173; Fascism,
176, 242–43; heroes, 172; history, 172;
idealism, 176; imperialism, 176, 177,
179, 184; individual, 171; industrialization, 243; industry, 170, 172; leadership,
170, 171, 172–73; liberalism, 171; materialism, 102; morality, 102, 167, 176,
242; nation, 176, 177; nationalism, 176;
parliament, 167; production, 171, 242;

race, 186, 190, 226; revolution, 176,
177; Rome, 177; socialism, 167; spirituality, 176–77; state, 170, 172, 177; syndicalism, 173, 259–60; totalitarianism,
170, 171; transcendence, 177; workers,
171, 236; *In relation to:* Gentile, 167,
172, 241, 243; Mussolini, 167, 170,
171, 172, 241; Panunzio, 241; Roman
Catholic Church, 167, 168, 169;
Schmitt, 180, 185; Spirito, 167, 241; Volpicelli, 167
Piccoli, Valentino, 54
Pierandrei, F., 180, 186
plutocracy, 33–34, 37, 101, 110, 176, 178,
214, 225, 230, 233
politics, 3, 4, 30, 46, 87, 141, 156, 236
Popolo d'Italia, Il, 81
positivism: in Actualism, 123–25, 126; in
Ardigo, 62; in Corradini, 28–29; in
Evola, 203, 209, 210; and liberalism,
126, 127; in Marxism, 29, 62; in Mussolini, 53; in nationalism, 36–37; in Niceforo, 62; and Orano, 62; in Panunzio,
62, 74, 81, 90, 145; in Pareto, 124; of
Pareto, 17; and socialism, 62; in Spirito,
91, 92, 123–24; in syndicalism, 36–37
Pound, Ezra, 227
pragmatism, 81, 92–93
Preziosi, Giovanni, 194, 219, 220,
226, 228
Prezzolini, Giuseppe, 25
primordialism, 38, 39
production: in Associazione nazionalista
italiano, 50; collective control of, 103;
and confederation, 237; in Corradini,
32, 48, 48–49; domestic commodity, 45;
duality in, 236, 237, 240; in Fascism,
12–14, 111, 128; in Fontanelli, 240; in
Gentile, 242; German oversight of, 244–
45; during Great Depression, 129; in Jouhaux, 81; in Marx, 46; in Mussolini,
100, 108, 136; in nationalism, 80; in
Olivetti, 52; in Panunzio, 103; in Pellizzi, 171, 242; planned, 243; private organization of, 117; in Rocco, 48, 111;
single organization for, 237, 238; socialization of, 232; in Sorel, 242; in Spirito,
239; state control of, 172, 243; state interference in, 100; and syndicates, 129;
and totalitarianism, 171; workers in,
233–34, 240, 243
productivity, 41, 45, 46, 48

progress, 47–48
proletarianization, 6
proletariat: in Associazione nazionalista
italiano, 50; in Bernstein, 61; in Bombacci, 230; in Corradini, 27, 33; in Corridoni, 57, 101; dictatorship of, 157; and
Fascism, 14; Gramsci on, 10; in Marxism, 10; maturity of, 56, 57; in Panunzio, 66, 72–73, 76, 80, 157; in Papini,
26; and plutocracies, 33–34; and revolution, 1, 6, 11, 20, 33, 56; in Sorel, 65,
66, 68. See also workers
property: alienation of, 138; as historical
and social product, 118; holders of, 113;
in Mussolini, 229; ownership of, 118; in
Panunzio, 77, 103; private, 103, 137,
139, 229, 237; private vs. corporative,
132–33; social character of, 117, 132;
state control of, 237. See also owners
"Protection of Motherhood and Infancy"
program, 105
Provincial Councils of Corporative Economy, 130
psychology, 26, 27, 29–30, 32, 68, 73,
212, 230. See also social sciences;
sociology

race: in Actualism, 189, 190, 194, 195; in
Cantimori, 186; in Clauss, 207–8; in Costamagna, 187, 188, 189–90; in Evola,
158n, 200–201, 202–3, 204–6, 208–10,
212, 219, 221, 222, 225–26; in Fascism,
185–90, 193–95, 200, 211–12, 213,
214–17, 220, 225–26, 257–59; in Gentile, 185n, 188, 189, 194, 226; in Germany, 185, 187, 218, 225; in Gumplowicz, 212; in Hitler, 158, 185, 214, 215,
225; and homogeneity, 185–86, 187; in
law, 216; and leadership, 188; in Movimento socialista italiano, 261; in Mussolini, 193, 211, 213–15, 218; in National
Socialism, 158, 185, 187, 188, 193, 194,
195, 201, 206n, 211, 213–14, 216, 217;
in Niceforo, 212; in Olivetti, 193; in Panunzio, 158, 226; in Pareto, 212; in Pellizzi, 186, 190, 226; in Pierandrei, 186;
in Preziosi, 194, 226; in Rey, 186; in
Schmitt, 187; in Spirito, 226; in Volpicelli, 186. See also anti-Semitism; Jews
Radical party, 37
Raetzel, Friedrich, 67
Rahn, Rudolph, 245

Ratzenhofer, Gustav, 67
reality: in Evola, 195; objective, 94; in Spirito, 94, 95; state as antecedent and transcendental, 114; in Western thought, 112
Rechsstaat, 76, 77
Regno, Il, 25
religion, 125, 156, 159–60, 161, 167–68,
197. See also Roman Catholic Church
Renaissance, 123
representation, 55, 72, 79, 87, 120, 150,
173, 174, 175, 176. See also democracy;
elections
Repubblica sociale italiano, 219, 227, 228,
240; Council of Ministers of, 230, 231
revolution: anticapitalist, 18; in Associazione nazionalista italiano, 50; in Bombacci, 230; conditions for, 20, 56; in Corradini, 27, 32; in Corridoni, 56–57, 101;
in economy, 20, 56; elite in, 121; in Europe, 23; in Evola, 196, 197; international, 24, 157; left-wing vs. right-wing,
18; in Marx, 46; in Marxism, 20, 24,
56; in Mussolini, 100, 102, 225, 226,
229, 230, 234, 241; in nationalism, 32;
in nation-state, 31; in Panfilo Gentile,
51, 52; in Panunzio, 66, 67, 69, 70, 72–
73, 74, 75, 76, 78, 79, 80, 86, 88, 104,
156, 157, 159, 253; in Pellizzi, 176, 177;
and proletariat, 1, 6, 11, 20, 33, 56; in
socialism, 63–64; in Sorel, 64, 65, 81; in
Spirito, 134; in syndicalism, 32, 55; in
syndicalism vs. nationalism, 58; and
World War I, 53
Rey, L. Vannutelli, 180, 186
Ricci, Vittorio Rolando, 228
Rocca, Massimo, 35
Rocco, Alfredo: and Associazione nazionalista italiano, 43; and World War I, 49,
60; Ideas on: authoritarianism, 51; capitalism, 44; collectivism, 43; corporativism, 59–60; culture, 43; democracy, 43,
58, 60; economy, 42, 43, 44, 45, 48, 51,
103, 153; entrepreneurs, 44, 60; Europe,
43; history, 48, 49, 51; imperialism, 48;
individual, 43, 44, 153; industry, 42, 43,
44, 45, 49, 50, 51; liberalism, 44, 49–
50, 60, 153; military, 49; nationalism,
37, 57, 108; national syndicalism, 83;
parliament, 43, 51; production, 48, 111;
productivity, 45; redistribution, 50; socialism, 44–45; sovereignty, 51, 60;
state, 42, 51, 59–60, 103, 153; syndical-

Rocco, Alfredo (*cont'd*)
  ism, 57; workers, 51; *In relation to:* Corradini, 42, 48, 49, 57; Corridoni, 57;
  Gentile, 85; List, 43, 44, 45, 48; Marxism, 37, 44–45; Mussolini, 42; Olivetti,
  54; Orano, 54; Roman Catholic Church,
  58–59
Roman Catholic Church: and Actualism,
  160–61, 167–68; and corporativism, 59;
  in Costamagna, 187, 188; and *Dottrina
  del fascismo,* 160; and Evola, 198, 199,
  201; and Fascism, 160; and first nationalist congress, 38; and Gentile, 133, 167,
  168, 169, 188; and immanence, 167;
  and Italian Nationalist Association, 58–
  59; and Mussolini, 160, 168–69, 198,
  199, 218, 228; in nationalism, 40; in
  Orano, 168; and Panunzio, 160, 161;
  and Pellizzi, 167, 168, 169; and Rocco,
  58–59; sovereignty of, 199; in Spirito,
  91, 238; and state, 24, 59; and totalitarianism, 167–68; transcendence in, 167.
  See also religion
Rome, ancient, 177, 187, 198, 209, 254
Rosmini, Antonio, 152, 161
Rossoni, Edmondo, 249
Rousseau, J. J., 64, 74, 77, 119, 122,
  146–47, 148
RSI. *See* Repubblica sociale italiano
Rüstungs und Kriegsindustrie (RUK),
  244–45

sacrifice, 24, 50, 65, 149, 153, 154, 210
Schmitt, Carl, 179–88, 189; *Der Begriff
  des Politischen,* 179, 187; extended
  space in, 179, 180, 181, 182, 183, 185,
  190, 194–95; *Principii politici del Nazionalsocialismo,* 179–80; *Staat, Bewegung,
  Volk,* 186, 187; *Völkerrechtliche Gross-
  raumordnung mit Interventionsverbot
  für raumfremde Mächte,* 179
Schopenhauer, Arthur, 36
science: in Actualism, 123–25, 126; and
  corporativism, 134; in Corradini, 28–29;
  deterministic, 53; empirical, 125; in
  Evola, 203–4, 209, 212; in Fascism, 212;
  and human beings, 53; and liberalism,
  123–24, 127; and Marxism, 29, 69; in
  Mussolini, 53, 212, 213; objectivity in,
  125, 203–4; positivist, 28–29, 123–25,
  126; presuppositions of, 125; in Sorel,
  65; in Spirito, 123–24, 124, 126

scientism, 29, 74, 81, 83n, 91, 123, 198
Second Congress of Syndicalist and Corporativist Studies, 109, 111
self: absolute, 96; in Actualism, 96–97, 98,
  109; actualization of, 96–97, 98, 147,
  154, 240, 255; collective, 95, 96; commitment of, 147; communal, 97; empirical, 87, 96, 97; fulfillment of, 153; in
  Gentile, 55, 87, 96, 96–97, 109, 147,
  152, 171; in Hegel, 97; interaction with
  others, 98; in liberalism, 97; in nationalism, 98; in Panunzio, 152; profound,
  96–97; realization of, 55, 109, 112, 141,
  152, 256; in Spirito, 95, 152; state identified with, 97, 112; in syndicalism, 98;
  transcendental, 87, 95, 96–97, 147. *See
  also* individual
sentiment, 27, 29, 30, 54, 77, 82, 145, 147
Sighele, Scipio, 30, 35, 40
Sismondi, J. C., 148
Smith, Adam, 24
socialism: abandonment of, 58; in Associazione nazionalista italiano, 50; in Bombacci, 230; and capitalism, 50; class conflict in, 25; and corporativism, 134; in
  Corradini, 28; defeat of by *Fasci di combattimento,* 10; and democracy, 41, 63;
  determinism of, 54; disintegration of,
  80; distribution of material benefits in,
  50, 58; economy in, 50; in Evola, 198; in
  France, 63–64; German, 62; in Giovanni
  Gentile, 235; historic laws in, 63; industry in, 50; internationalism of, 40; and
  liberalism, 63; and Marxism, 24, 61; materialism of, 54; and Mussolini, 53–54,
  104, 241; in Olivetti, 36, 52, 80; in Panfilo Gentile, 51, 52; in Panunzio, 66, 69,
  70, 77, 83; in Pareto, 102; in Pellizzi,
  167; and positivism, 62; productivity in,
  50; reformist and revisionist, 61–64; revolution in, 63–64; in Rocco, 42, 44–45;
  and Sorel, 64–65; in Spirito, 134, 135,
  239; state, 170; in Turati, 63. *See also*
  Marx, Karl; Marxism
socialization, of economy, 228, 230, 231,
  232, 244, 245
social sciences, 67, 68, 82, 120, 122, 123,
  124, 143, 145. *See also* psychology;
  sociology
Societa finanziaria italiana (Sofondit),
  137, 138

society: in Actualism, 141; in Associazione
nazionalista italiano, 50; education by,
119; in Engels, 67; enterprise in, 117; in
Evola, 201; and Gumplowicz, 67, 68; historic laws in, 63; and human beings,
124, 141; as immanent, 141; and individual, 126, 154; intermediate agencies in,
118; and law, 69, 70, 71; in Marx, 67; in
Mussolini, 229; and nation, 144; in nationalism, 38; in Olivetti, 52; in Panunzio, 17, 68, 70, 73, 75, 77, 79, 82, 141,
143–44, 145; in Pareto, 127; and property, 117, 118, 132; in Sorel, 65; and
state, 144; in Turati, 63; will of, 171. See
also collective/collectivity; community
sociology, 27, 74–75, 145. See also psychology; social sciences
Soffici, Ardengo, 227
Sofondit. See Societa finanziaria italiana
(Sofondit)
soldier-producer, 34
Sombart, Werner, 67
Sorel, Georges, 17, 28, 37, 54, 64–66, 68,
70, 78, 81, 82, 86, 90, 242, 252–53; L'A-
venir socialiste des syndicats, 64; "The
Juridical Ideas of Marxism," 70; Reflections on Violence, 64
sovereignty, 51, 60, 73, 143, 144, 199
Soviet Union, 9, 21, 77, 100, 102, 138,
155, 156–58, 192, 243, 258. See also
Bolshevism
Spain, 192
Spaventa, Bertrando, 151, 161, 162; Principii di Etica, 87n
Spencer, Herbert, 30, 67
Spirito, Ugo: background of, 90–91; and
Carta del lavoro, 117, 237; at Ferrara
conference on corporativism, 133, 134,
135, 136, 140, 232, 236; and Great Depression, 130; and Nuovi studi di diritto,
economica e politica, 109; orthodoxy of,
135–36; Ideas on: activity, 92; Actualism, 92, 93, 94, 97, 99, 109, 111, 133,
236; autarky, 135n; Bolshevism, 134,
135, 239; capital, 131; capitalism, 238–
39; categories, 95; collective consciousness, 94; collectivity, 110; communism,
239; consciousness, 94, 95–96; corporations, 132–33; corporativism, 98, 111,
112–13, 116, 119, 129, 130, 131–36,
140, 141, 142, 237, 238, 239, 241; decision, 95; determinism, 95; economy,

107, 109, 116–17, 123, 126, 127, 130–
36, 139, 236, 238, 239; empiricism, 92,
94, 95; entrepreneurs, 131; epistemology, 92, 93, 94; Fascism, 91–92, 132,
238; free enterprise, 116–17; human beings, 124; human consciousness, 93; humanism, 259; idealism, 92, 94, 238; individual, 109, 123, 127, 238, 239;
intellectuals, 94; judgment, 95; knowledge, 92, 94; liberalism, 109, 123, 126,
236, 238, 239; materialism, 93, 94, 95;
morality, 94, 95, 96; nature, 94; object,
94; objectivity, 92–93, 94; ontology, 94;
ophelimity, 126, 127; politics, 236; positivism, 91, 92, 123–24; pragmatism, 92–
93; production, 239; race, 226; reality,
94, 95; revolution, 134; science, 124,
126; scientism, 91, 123; self, 95, 152; socialism, 134, 135, 239; spirituality, 94;
state, 109, 132, 135, 258; subject, 94;
subjectivity, 95; syndicalism, 109; thinking, 94, 95; totalitarianism, 110, 238,
239; truth, 92–93, 94; Western thought,
112; workers, 131, 236–37, 238; In relation to: Evola, 195–96; Fontanelli, 240;
Gentile, 90, 91, 92, 93, 94, 110, 111,
238, 239, 259; Kant, 94; Lenin, 93n; Malaparte, 92; Marx, 93n; Marxism, 91;
Mussolini, 91, 131, 135–36, 137, 239,
240n, 244n; neo-Hegelianism in, 91; Panunzio, 91, 135, 142; Pellizzi, 167, 241;
Roman Catholic Church, 91, 238;
WORKS: Capitalismo e corporativismo,
109; La critica dell'economia liberale,
109; I fondamenti dell'economia corporativa, 109; "The Individual and the
State in the Corporative Economy,"
130–31; Il pragmatismo nella filosofia
contemporanea, 92
spirituality: in Actualism, 168; in Costamagna, 187; in Evola, 196, 201, 204–5,
206, 207, 209, 210, 219; in Gentile, 86,
94, 96, 98, 176, 189; in List, 45; in Missiroli, 55; in Mussolini, 55, 88n, 149n;
national, 45; in Panunzio, 82, 145, 151;
in Pellizzi, 176–77; in Rocco, 57; in
Spirito, 94
squadristi, 166, 197
Stalin, Josef, 12, 93n, 157, 158
Starace, Achille, 166
state: in Actualism, 141; agencies of, 118;
as antecedent and transcendental reality,

state (*cont'd*)
114; and associations, 90, 118; and autarky, 170; authority of, 75; and Church,
24; as core of individual, 114; corporations as organ of, 133; corporative institutions of, 123; and corporativism, 35,
59–60, 110, 117, 170; in Corradini,
153; credit controlled by, 138; decentralized, 101; early support for, 24; economic control by, 101, 106, 107, 108,
110, 117, 129, 132, 138, 139, 140; and
economy, 100–101, 170; education by,
121; and entrepreneurs, 35; ethical, 99,
148; in Evola, 196, 197; as executive
will, 171; in Fascism, 99, 101, 255; in
Giovanni Gentile, 86–87, 99, 152, 171,
176, 189; in Hegel, 133; hierarchical,
171; and individual, 127, 152, 153, 174;
individual defended by, 112, 114, 148;
individual identification with, 55, 86,
98, 112, 113, 116, 128, 129, 131, 133,
134, 136, 154, 238; industrial control
by, 110, 138, 140; and industrialists' organizations, 108; and industry, 54; integralist, 60; intellectual environment of,
118; intermediate agencies in, 118; in
Italian Nationalist Association, 58; juridical, 148; and law, 75, 76, 112; in Lenin,
9, 157; Manchestrian, 101, 106, 107,
110, 137, 154; and Marxism, 157; as mediator, 53, 237; in Missiroli, 55; moral
environment of, 118; in Mussolini, 55,
100, 110, 136, 137, 157; in nationalism,
58, 86; and national syndicalism, 110;
nested associations of, 118; in Olivetti,
52–53; in Panfilo Gentile, 51–52; in Panunzio, 66, 72, 73, 75, 76, 79, 86, 88,
89, 90, 103, 104, 141, 143, 144, 145,
146, 148, 151, 152, 157, 174; in Pareto,
102; and Partito nazionale fascista, 98;
and party, 155; in Pellizzi, 170, 172,
177; production controlled by, 172, 243;
property controlled by, 237; in Rocco,
42, 51, 59–60, 103, 153; sacrifice to,
153; self identified with, 97, 112; socialist, 170; and society, 144; sovereignty of,
144; in Soviet Union, 9; in Spirito, 109,
132, 135, 238; and syndicalism, 51, 52,
54, 86, 90; and syndicalism vs. nationalism, 58; syndicalist-corporativist, 79; totalitarian, 99, 110, 134; and trans-class

interests, 53; in Western thought, 112;
and workers, 110, 117, 237; and workers' organizations, 108
Stato, Lo, 186
Sternhell, Zeev, 9, 17
STET (telephonic communications), 138
stock owner, 131, 239
subject, 94, 159
subjectivity, 95, 124
syndicalism: in Actualism, 85; and class,
32, 36, 55; collectivism in, 55; and community, 31, 32, 123; in Corradini, 28,
29, 31–32, 37, 57; and democracy, 36,
107; economy in, 101, 128; and elite,
32, 36; and Engels, 52; in Evola, 201; in
Fascism, 61, 99, 170; and first nationalist congress, 38; in Fontanelli, 259–60;
in Gentile, 85, 86, 91; human beings in,
30; individual in, 39, 55, 58, 98; industry in, 52, 56, 247; and Italian Nationalist Association, 57; in Labriola, 66; leaders in, 32, 36; and Marx, 52; Marxism
in, 37, 56; masses in, 31, 32; mass movements in, 29–30; materialism in, 86; military in, 55, 58; morality in, 37; and Mussolini, 99, 109; myth in, 29; nation in,
31–32, 55, 58; national, 32, 33, 35, 36,
56, 57, 58, 79, 80, 81, 83, 88, 103, 108,
110; and nationalism, 28, 30, 31, 32,
35, 37, 38, 39, 54, 55, 56, 57, 58, 59,
61, 80, 85, 86, 99, 103, 108, 109; and
nationalist loyalty, 37; in Olivetti, 35,
36, 37; in Panunzio, 66, 72, 73, 74, 77,
78, 79, 80, 86, 89, 90, 103, 108, 143;
parliament in, 31, 32, 36, 54; in Pellizzi,
173, 259–60; positivism in, 36–37; and
psychology, 31; representation in, 55;
and revolution, 32, 55, 58; in Rocco, 57;
self in, 98; in Sorel, 81; in Spirito, 109;
and state, 51, 52, 54, 58, 86, 90; violence in, 252; workers in, 32, 36, 39, 52,
56, 235; and World War I, 55, 56
syndicates: confederations of, 130; as consultative, 173, 175; in corporativism,
175; employer, 173; law on, 130; in Panunzio, 76; and production, 129; in totalitarian state, 134; workers', 173

Tarde, Gabriel, 37, 67
Tasca, Angelo, 2, 54
Tassoni, Alessandro, 22

technicians, 232, 239, 240, 243

technology, 12, 13, 19, 44, 49, 59, 238. *See also* industry

thinking, 94, 95, 96, 115–16. *See also* epistemology; knowledge

Third International, 10, 12

totalitarianism: corporations in, 134; and democracy, 119–20; in Evola, 198; in Fascism, 84, 97, 99, 107, 256; in Gentile, 87, 110, 247; individual in, 97; leadership in, 149–50; in Movimento socialista italiano, 261; in Mussolini, 98, 107, 110, 137; in Panunzio, 155, 157; in Pellizzi, 170, 171; and production, 171; and Roman Catholic Church, 167–68; Soviet, 157; in Spirito, 110, 238, 239; and state, 99, 110, 134; syndicates in, 134; and will, 146; and workers, 171

trade, 24, 33–34, 40

transcendence, 161, 177

Tricolore, 35

Tripoli, 41, 54, 55, 77

Tripolitania, 35

truth, 82, 92–93, 94, 205, 208, 213

Turati, Filippo, 63

Turkey, 35–36, 40

unions, 36, 76

United States, 47, 176, 223

urban population, 10, 12, 105

Ur-fascism, viii, 2

Utopia, 55

Valli, Luigi, 38, 39, 40

Viana, Mario, 35

Vico, Giambattista, 22, 152, 161

Victor Emmanuel III, King of Italy, 88, 106, 219, 223, 224, 225, 226, 228, 234

violence, 3, 8, 15, 17, 63, 73–74, 77, 89, 141, 250–54, 255, 256

Voce, La, 26

Volpicelli, Arnaldo, 107, 109, 119, 167, 179–80, 186

Ward, Lester, 67

warrior-producer, 78, 80, 81. *See also* heroes

Western thought, 112, 120. *See also* liberalism

will: in Actualism, 146; as Christian conscience, 146; common, 148, 150; democratic expression of, 150; and elite, 149; embodied in one person, 171; empirical, 146; general, 87, 119, 121, 122, 123, 146, 147, 148, 149; in Gentile, 86, 87, 146; and morality, 148, 149; in Mussolini, 53, 193; national, 86; objective, 148; in Olivetti, 36; in Panunzio, 73, 77, 146, 147, 149; in Rousseau, 122, 146; of society, 171; state as executive, 171; and totalitarianism, 146; transcendental, 119, 121, 123

Wolff, Karl, 245

Woltmann, Ludwig, 204

workers: as agents, 243; as aristocracy, 66, 242; associations of, 35, 76, 108, 130; and corporativism, 59, 134, 232, 238, 239; in Corradini, 31, 33; cultural character of, 236, 239; disputes of, 35; division of, 71; early support for, 24; and economy, 232–34; as elite, 242; emigration of, 25, 27, 33, 40, 42; in enterprise hierarchy, 133; and entrepreneurs, 35; exploitation of, 69; in Fascism, 105; in Fontanelli, 236, 240, 242, 243; general strike by, 66, 73, 79; in Gentile, 86, 98, 235, 235–36, 242; governance by, 229, 232–34, 242; hierarchy of organized, 134; individual bias of, 132; in Italian Socialist party, 61; in Italian Social Republic, 231, 232–33; law concerning, 130; leaders of, 36; and managers, 232, 233, 238; in Marx, 70; in Mussolini, 12, 108, 109, 136, 193, 225, 229, 233–34; in nationalism, 39, 56; in Olivetti, 37, 52, 235; and owners, 232; ownership by, 237; in Panunzio, 66, 68, 69–70, 71, 72, 73, 76, 79, 80, 173, 176, 235; in Pellizzi, 171, 236; and production, 240; in production, 233–34; production planned by, 243; public works employment of, 138; in Rocco, 51; self-actualization of, 240; self-development of, 241, 242; skill acquisition by, 240–41; skilled vs. unskilled, 240; and socialization of economy, 245; and social responsibility, 117; in Sorel, 64, 70, 81; in Spirito, 131, 236–37, 238; and state, 117; state control of, 110; state as mediator for, 237; as stockholders, 132–33; in syndicalism, 32, 36, 39, 52, 56, 235; and technology, 238; and totalitarianism, 171; triumph

workers (*cont'd*)
of, 63; upward mobility of, 240. *See also*
Carta del lavoro, La; proletariat
World War I, 19, 51, 57; and Corradini,
49; and economy, 5; end of, 86, 88; and
Gentile, 91; and Italy, 5, 77; and Mussolini, 53–54; and nationalism, 55; nationality in, 53; in Olivetti, 53; outbreak of,
54; in Panunzio, 77–79, 80, 82–83, 89,
143, 145, 148, 154; in Pellizzi, 172, 176;
and revolution, 53; in Rocco, 49, 60;
and syndicalism, 55, 56
World War II, 8, 139, 140; Gramsci on, 10,
11; and Great Britain, 223; and Italy,
176, 179, 183, 195, 222, 224; and Mussolini, 13, 218; in Panunzio, 176; and
United States, 223; and views of
Fascism, 1, 2, 4

Zetkin, Clara, 12

GPSR Authorized Representative: Easy Access System Europe - Mustamäe tee
50, 10621 Tallinn, Estonia, gpsr.requests@easproject.com